SOUTH AFRICA, *A Study in Conflict*

# SOUTH AFRICA,

## *A Study in Conflict*

*By* PIERRE L. VAN DEN BERGHE

UNIVERSITY OF CALIFORNIA PRESS

BERKELEY AND LOS ANGELES   1970

*University of California Press*
*Berkeley and Los Angeles, California*
*University of California Press, Ltd., London, England*

First Paper-bound Edition 1967
Second Printing, 1970

*Standard Book Number 520-01294-1*
*Library of Congress Catalog Card Number: 65-14053*
*Manufactured in the United States of America*

To two great South Africans:

Albert Luthuli and Alan Paton,

and to all others who seek to promote non-racial democracy in South Africa.

## PREFACE TO THE PAPER-BOUND BOOK

Some three years have elapsed since I last revised the text of this book. Considering the pace of change in Africa, this is a considerable period. However, if this book has erred in its predictions, it has been in the direction of expecting a faster pace of change in Southern Africa than has in fact taken place. In every fundamental respect, South Africa has not appreciably changed since this book first appeared. Hence, I have resisted the temptation to "update" it, except for the bibliography.

Chapter Ten is perhaps the only one which has been partially invalidated by recent events. The resilience of Portugal and of the white supremacist regime in Rhodesia has given the South African government time to develop a more effective repressive apparatus. South Africa still retains its *cordon sanitaire* of white controlled territories to the North; and the economic dependence of Lesotho and Botswana on South Africa is reducing the political independence of these former British High Commission Territories to an empty legalism. They are in Jack Halpern's phrase "South Africa's hostages." International pressures against South Africa have continued to mount but they have remained largely ineffective so far. Both the United States and Britain have cautiously inched away from South Africa while still reluctant to take direct action beyond an arms embargo rendered meaningless by the willingness of other NATO powers to sell the Republic modern weapons. The International Court's failure to pass judgment on South Africa's jurisdiction over South West Africa, while in no sense a vindication of South Africa, gave the Nationalist Government another tactical advantage.

Internally, the apartheid policies of the government did not change during the last years of Verwoerd's regime. The choice of Balthazar J. Vorster as Verwoerd's successor was consistent with the steady evolution of the Nationalist Party toward the right. Just as Verwoerd was further to the right than Strydom, Strydom than Malan, and Malan than Hertzog, so Vorster as an extremist among reactionaries was a logical choice to succeed the assassinated Verwoerd. The implementation of apartheid policies has, however, undergone rapid change in that the trend toward streamlining, rationalization and efficiency in the means of repression which was evident from 1961 continued. Military expenditures have climbed even higher; the secret police have become better trained; the public display of armed violence has been replaced by preventive arrests and invisible repression in the prisons and labor camps. All political groups left of the United Party have been increasingly suppressed and harassed. The United Party is still useful as a harmless pseudo-opposition which allows the government to parade as a parliamentary democracy.

The liberation of South Africa remains contingent on two main external factors. First, the territories north of the Limpopo must come under majority rule. Second, there must be effective outside support for the South African underground and an escalation of sanctions.

## Acknowledgments

T HIS work is the product of a five-year study of South Africa, including a twenty-two months stay in that country (February, 1960 to December, 1961). It is the third manuscript of book length to come out of my study. The first was an unpublished doctoral dissertation on race relations in South Africa; the second was a community study of a small sugar town in Natal; the present work, while greatly different from the previous two, grew out of them. Directly or indirectly, then, numerous people and organizations contributed to the present endeavour.

Among them, my wife Irmgard deserves a unique place for her unfailing moral support, patient clerical help, and sobering criticisms. The bulk of the material support which made our stay in South Africa possible came from a generous Ford Foundation grant and a Frank Knox Memorial Fellowship. In addition, I received assistance from the Harvard Laboratory of Social Relations, the Institute for Social Research at the University of Natal, Wesleyan University, and the State University of New York. To Gordon W. Allport and Talcott Parsons, my joint thesis directors at Harvard, I am grateful for providing me with intense intellectual stimulation, constructive criticism, and warm encouragement.

I should like to express my thankfulness for the many hundreds of South Africans whom I have formally interviewed or simply met during my stay in the country. Numerous local colleagues, acquaintances, and friends extended my wife and me their warm hospitality, and helped us in gaining a deeper insight into South Africa's problems. At the risk of making invidious distinctions, I should like to mention particularly Bill Bhengu, Ivar and Cynthia Chetty, S. P. Cilliers, Hamish and Elaine Dickie-Clark, Hans and Marie Holleman, Leo and Hilda Kuper, John and Ursula Laredo, Albert Luthuli, Ben Magubane, Jack and Len Mann, Joe Matthews, Philip Mayer, Ismael and Fatima Meer, Edna Miller, Jordan Ngubane, Anthony Ngubo, Alan Paton, Birbal Rambiritch, Margo Russell, Jack Simons, Johann and Pamela van den Berg, and R. G. T. Watson. During my stay in Paris in 1962, I greatly profited from my renewed association with Georges Balandier, Roger Bastide, and Jacques Maquet. To Ona Langer and Jean Coleman, I am grateful for typing the second and third drafts of the manuscript, and to Shirley Stout and David Frey for competently editing and criticizing the text.

Finally, I am indebted to my many predecessors in the field of South African scholarship. I found the works of Edgar H. Brookes, Gwendolen M. Carter, C. W. De Kiewiet, Ellen Hellmann, Muriel Horrell, Leo and Hilda Kuper, I. D. MacCrone, W. M. Macmillan, J. S. Marais, Leo Marquard, Philip Mayer, Sheila Patterson, B. G. M. Sundkler, Eric A. Walker, and Monica Wilson particularly useful. Authors of fiction such as Peter Abrahams, Sarah G. Millin, Ezekiel Mphahlele, and Alan Paton have also greatly contributed to my gaining a deeper understanding of their country. Indeed, the present work is, at best, a new interpretation and arrangement of known facts, and, at worst, a reformulation thereof in sociological jargon. Whatever I have contributed to the extension of factual knowledge about South Africa has been published mostly elsewhere. Errors of fact and interpretation which may have crept into my work, as well as the opinions expressed here, are entirely my responsibility.

*Buffalo, 1964*                                    P.L.v.d.B.

# Contents

# *Maps*

SOUTH AFRICA, *A Study in Conflict*

## CHAPTER ONE

## Introduction

THE present work constitutes an attempt to analyse South African society in its entirety, from a broad sociological perspective. This is by no means an easy task, for few countries exhibit as many complexities. South Africa is a highly pluralistic society wherein coexist several political systems, economies, and linguistic, religious, and "racial" groups which overlap only partly with one another. Every society is, of course, unique in some respects, but South Africa is, so to speak, more unique than others. Indeed, South Africa is not only internally compartmentalized into semiautonomous structures which complexly interact; it is also a society characterized by an extraordinarily high level of internal conflict, contradiction, and dysfunction. In some respects, notably in the system of production, South Africa has undergone rapid change, whereas, politically, and in its ascriptive system of stratification, the country has remained largely static. The very discrepancy between rapid change in some segments of the society accompanied by rigidity and inadaptability in others has greatly increased internal tensions and disequilibrium.

Conflict is certainly the most important characteristic of South African society, and, hence, the dominant theme of this book. At the most overt level, there is conflict over the distribution of social rewards between the four major groups which the

dominant Whites have defined in racial terms, as well as between the two main European ethnic groups (English and
Afrikaners). More abstractly, South Africa is ridden with almost
total lack of consensus on values, i.e., on what its people consider
desirable goals to achieve. At another level of analysis yet, South
African society is pervaded by contradictory imperatives and
principles regulating the main aspects of its social structure. The
Government and the White population which it represents
endeavour to maintain a rigidly ascriptive and particularistic
system of racial segregation and stratification based on a paternalistic, master-servant model of social relations. While such a
system was workable in an agrarian, isolated society such as
South Africa was in the nineteenth century, it is clearly incompatible with a complex industrial economy. Consequently, conflicts and contradictions, far from resolving themselves, have become increasingly acute over the years.

We shall postpone a discussion of some of the theoretical
problems raised by the present analysis until the last chapter,
but we may anticipate the inadequacy of a conventional functionalist approach, and the necessity, or, at least, the heuristic
value, of introducing Hegelian dialectical concepts in dealing
with South Africa.[1] The present work is clearly not a theoretical
treatise, and I shall endeavour to avoid burdening the text with
abstruse jargon. Yet, equally obviously, the empirical case under
study has important theoretical implications to which we shall
return at the end of the book.

What, then, is the major emphasis of this study, and at what
audience is it directed? I have endeavoured to steer a middle
course between purely empirical description and grand theory,
and to remain at the level that some sociologists have somewhat
pretentiously termed "total social system analysis." First and
foremost, the present work represents an attempt to analyse

---

1. Elsewhere, I have suggested that the two bodies of theory might be
fruitfully integrated. See my "Dialectic and Functionalism: Toward a
Theoretical Synthesis."

systematically a highly complex and unusual society which has not yet been subjected to this kind of treatment. Thus, I address myself both to my fellow sociologists and anthropologists who have an intrinsic interest in analysis of this nature, and to my fellow Africanists from other disciplines who, without specifically specializing in South Africa, want to gain a better understanding of it. The South African specialist will probably not find much here that is factually new to him, though, hopefully, some of the interpretations might cast a new light on familiar facts. This book is not primarily aimed at the "educated laymen" (in the broad sense of the word) who is looking for the one book that will give him most information on South Africa.[2] Although I have tried to write digestible prose, my analysis is already once-removed from the factual raw data (to which I do not claim to contribute significantly), and assumes some modicum of prior familiarity with South African conditions.

It is, of course, a truism that present conditions are a product of the past, and must be understood in terms of it. I shall deal quickly with the historical background in Chapter Two, but this work is by no means a history of South Africa. Past events and their significance will merely be referred to, rather than described at any length. Accepting the importance of history does not imply a denial of the reality of social structure, nor, conversely, does the structural approach imply an assumption that reality is either static or in equilibrium. A structural approach rather takes history for granted, and assumes that aside from diachronic determinism there also exists a synchronic determinism inherent in the structure of a society at any given time. The choice of emphasis is, or at least should be, heuristic and not dogmatic, and the two approaches should be complementary and not mutually exclusive.

In Chapters Three and Four we shall turn to a broad descrip-

2. Leo Marquard's *The Peoples and Policies of South Africa,* and, in fiction, Alan Paton's *Cry the Beloved Country,* are probably his best bets, in terms of maximizing factual information and reading pleasure.

tion of the social structure of South Africa. These chapters, like the preceding one, do not aim to give a complete picture of the society, but rather to sketch the skeleton of it and give the necessary background to the core of the work. Many existing books deal with special aspects of South Africa, and detailed descriptions would be redundant here.[3] The major aim of this study is to analyse the various sources of conflict and disequilibrium which are ever more ominously threatening the existing order of South African society. In studying strain and conflict, I hope to suggest answers to such questions as how South African society manages to hold together at all, how it has achieved a stage of "static disequilibrium," at least politically, how much more strain the system can take, and in what direction the system can be expected to change.

Three chapters will be devoted to the power conflict around which ethnic-group antagonisms have crystallized in South Africa. This power conflict has traditionally taken two forms: first, the struggle for Afrikaner versus English supremacy within the superordinate White group; and, secondly, the conflict between Whites and non-Whites, more particularly between Whites and Africans. This second form of power struggle constitutes the core of the so-called "race problem," and will entail an examination of the "Native policy" of successive governments, and of the various forms of reaction to that policy on the part of the oppressed groups.

In dealing with the South African economy, I shall try to show to what extent the political system is at odds with the principles of a supposedly "free" economy, and how economic forces inevitably erode the social structure which successive governments have endeavoured to preserve. Disequilibria resulting from value conflicts and centring on such institutions as the universities and churches will make the subject of Chapter Nine.

3. See bibliography, in particular the works of Brookes, Carter, De Kiewiet, Franklin, Hellmann, Horrell, Hunter, Leo and Hilda Kuper, Mac-Crone, Marais, Marquard, Patterson, Sundkler, Theal, and Walker.

In the same chapter the disruptive consequences of acculturation in a society like South Africa will be examined. An analysis of external pressures and their effect on the internal structure of the country will close the empirical part of the book, which I shall conclude by drawing theoretical implications from our case study.

The reader who is not intrinsically interested in South Africa may well ask why that country should be the subject of our study. Several factors make South Africa particularly crucial for sociological analysis. In a world of rapid "decolonization," the anachronism of its governmental policies and racial attitudes gives South Africa the value of a museum piece, of a living political dinosaur, all the more implausible in that the country also has a thriving and dynamic industrial economy. Furthermore, the extreme complexity of the country and the extraordinary virulence of its conflicts present a challenge to structural and functional analysis. From the practical point of view of improving race relations, Scuth Africa is an ideal negative case showing what must be avoided, and confirming in inverted fashion the principles of "racial therapy" developed elsewhere. Finally, the virtual certainty that South Africa will not escape the transformations taking place in the rest of the continent will provide social scientists with an opportunity to study rapid and drastic change.

It is perhaps appropriate to include some remarks here about methodology and the problem of objectivity. My interest in, and research on, South Africa date back to the summer of 1958 when I began to collect material for a study of race relations in that country.[4] This work was followed by a stay of nearly two years in South Africa, devoted partly to a community study,[5] and partly to a more general sociological study of the country as a

4. Pierre L. van den Berghe, *The Dynamics of Race Relations, An Ideal Type Case Study of South Africa.*
5. Van den Berghe, *Caneville, The Social Structure of a South African Town.*

whole. The present book is thus the product of a wide variety of methods of investigation. As primary sources for the documentation of social life and race relations in the seventeenth, eighteenth, and early nineteenth centuries, I have relied mostly on the memoirs and travelogues left by early travellers at the Cape. These documents are surprisingly rich in detailed descriptions of day-to-day life. The works of Percival, Damberger, Lichtenstein, Sparrman, Mentzel, Barrow, Vaillant, Chapman, Latrobe, Wright, Campbell, Kolben, Thunberg, and Patterson are particularly vivid.[6]

This historical research has, of course, been supplemented by secondary sources,[7] and by the visit of old farms, museums, churches, painting galleries, plantations, town houses, and public buildings in Cape Town, Stellenbosch, Paarl, Tulbagh, Swellendam, and other settlements of the old Cape Colony, and, for the

6. John Barrow, *An Account of Travels into the Interior of Southern Africa in the Years 1797 and 1798;* Jacques Boulenger, *Voyage de F. Vaillant dans l'Intérieur de l'Afrique, 1781–1785;* John Campbell, *Travels in South Africa;* James Chapman, *Travels in the Interior of South Africa;* F. Damberger, *Travels in the Interior of Africa from the Years 1781–1797;* Peter Kolben, *The Present State of the Cape of Good Hope;* C. I. Latrobe, *A Journal of a Visit to South Africa;* Henry Lichtenstein, *Travels in Southern Africa in the Years 1803, 1804, 1805 and 1806;* D. F. Mentzel, *A Description of the African Cape of Good Hope, 1787;* William Paterson, *A Narrative of Four Journeys into the Country of the Hottentots and Caffraria in the years 1777, 1778, 1779;* Robert Percival, *An Account of the Cape of Good Hope;* Charles P. Thunberg, *Travels in Europe Africa and Asia made between the Years 1770 and 1779;* William Wright, *Slavery at the Cape of Good Hope.*

7. J. A. I. Agar-Hamilton, *The Native Policy of the Voortrekkers, 1836–1858;* C. G. Botha, *Social Life in the Cape Colony in the 18th Century;* Henri Dehérain, *Le Cap de Bonne-Espérance au 17e Siècle;* C. W. De Kiewiet, *A History of Southern Africa;* Victor de Kock, *Those in Bondage;* Isobel E. Edwards, *Towards Emancipation: A Study in South African Slavery;* Alan F. Hattersley, *South Africa, 1652–1933;* H. C. V. Leibbrandt, *Précis of the Archives of the Cape of Good Hope;* J. S. Marais, *The Cape Coloured People, 1652–1937;* S. Daniel Neumark, *Economic Influences on the South African Frontier 1652–1846;* G. Theal, *South Africa;* and Eric A. Walker, *A History of Southern Africa.*

post-Great Trek era, the towns of Natal, the Eastern Cape, the Transvaal, and the Orange Free State.

For the contemporary period, aside from the extensive bibliography on many different aspects of South African society, including works of fiction, my knowledge of the country has been complemented by numerous other sources of information. The most important of them have been an intensive study of a small Natal community where I have used standard anthropological methods of field work; hundreds of formal and informal interviews with persons from all walks of life and from all major ethnic groups; close contact with numerous South African academics in both Afrikaans- and English-speaking universities, extensive travels and visits of schools, police stations, hospitals, mining companies, slums and "model" housing, urban "locations" and "Native Reserves"; direct observation of day-to-day racial interaction, including police behaviour during and after the 1960 emergency; more detailed questionnaire studies of racial attitudes, miscegenation, the Hindu caste system, and social distance; a close study of South African dailies and periodicals during my period of residence in the country; and attendance at political rallies, meetings, protest marches, and the like.

The problem of objectivity is, of course, especially crucial and difficult when one deals with a country like South Africa, where the central conflict impinges so directly on one's own values. To pretend Olympian detachment would be both foolish and dishonest on my part. It would be foolish because my writing would quickly reveal my position, and dishonest because I am anything but detached. Obviously, I am writing from the colourblind viewpoint of a universalistic ethos of equality of opportunity and legal rights, of freedom, and of self-determination. While I shall endeavour to present the facts as objectively as possible, I cannot help but find the policies of the government and the attitudes of most South African Whites distasteful in the extreme. It is for the reader to decide to what extent my

own values have coloured my interpretations. My only claims
are that my account is factually correct in every major respect
(though minor inaccuracies may have slipped in inadvertently),
and that most sociologists would have reached substantially the
same conclusions as I did.

To most White South Africans, and, indeed, to other White
supremacists, this book will necessarily, and, from their point of
view, rightly, appear biased. It may even seem slanted to many
Western scholars who, without being racists, still accept implicitly the ethnocentric myths of European colonialism concerning
Africa, such as those of the "civilizing mission of the West" and
African "primitivism." I have consciously tried to avoid any
invidious value judgments concerning the various cultures present
in South Africa, as well as the usual condescending vocabulary
of much Western scholarship dealing with Africa. E.g., such
terms as "primitivism," "native," "punitive expeditions," "disturbances," "tribe," "pacification," "exploration," "civilization,"
and "paganism" have all been discarded as far as possible because of their ethnocentric connotations. A similar problem arises
concerning the choice of words in speaking of South Africa's
indigenous black inhabitants. The country's Whites almost always refer to their black fellow citizens as "Bantu" or "Native."
Sometimes they also use the word "Kaffir" (an Arabic word meaning "heathen") which is now regarded as most insulting. The
terms "Bantu" and "Native," while not directly insulting, have a
derogatory connotation, and are resented by many Africans. The
word "Bantu" is also used by anthropologists to designate a
large group of peoples speaking related languages. Except in
quotations, official titles, and documents, or in the linguistic
context, I shall only use the term "African" in this work. The term
"South African," when used by Whites, refers almost invariably
to Whites only. The non-Whites are by implication denied common citizenship with the Whites. I shall always use the term
"South African" in the generic, and only meaningful sense,
except when otherwise indicated by quotation marks.

I have also avoided a presentation of South Africa as a White man's country with a colourful backdrop of "savages" who occasionally intrude into the foreground during "Kaffir Wars" and more recently during "disturbances." Since the seventeenth century, South Africa is a region torn in bitter strife between conquering Europeans and numerous indigenous groups, not to mention other immigrant communities and the people of mixed descent.

Finally, a fallacious impression which some readers might get from this book must be dispelled at the outset. Nowhere do I mean to suggest that White South Africans are peculiarly perverse, or that their colour attitudes and policies are unique. On the contrary, my argument is that South African racialism is a product of a historical tradition constantly reinforced by the social environment. In retrospect, the development of racism seems completely understandable, and, conversely, it becomes difficult to explain why not *all* Whites are prejudiced. Furthermore, racialism is by no means a South African monopoly, although its presence in the United States, Britain, Germany, the Soviet Union, and elsewhere does not justify it in South Africa.[8] Lastly, the policies of South African governments have paralleled rather closely those of other European powers in Africa during most of colonial history. Only during the last two decades have they grown increasingly at variance with the policies of all but

8. The ubiquity of racism in Western culture is well illustrated by this 1858 quotation from Abraham Lincoln:
I am not, nor ever have been, in favor of bringing about in any way the social and political equality of the white and black races; I am not nor ever have been in favor of making voters or jurors of Negroes, nor qualifying them to hold office . . . I will say in addition to this that there is a physical difference between the white and black races which I believe will ever forbid the two races living together on terms of social and political equality. And in as much as they cannot so live, while they do remain together there must be the position of superior and inferior, and as much as any other man I am in favor of having the superior position assigned to the white race.
Quoted in Wilson and Jane Cassels Record, eds., *Little Rock, USA*, p. 282.

the most archaic and obdurate of colonial powers, namely Portugal. It is thus essential that the reader keep South Africa in the broader perspective of Western imperialism, although it would take us too far afield to do so explicitly at any length here.

To conclude these considerations about the problem of objectivity in South Africa, I should like to quote at some length Danziger's perceptive remarks:

> In the South African case it would require an extraordinary intellectual feat to arrive at some synthetic perspective which combines the partial historical insights of Afrikaner nationalists, English liberals and African revolutionaries. Such a synthesis would simply constitute the philosophy of the bystander, the cognitive style of the socially uncommitted. But where the ubiquity of social conflict excludes the possibility of non-commitment the intellectual stance corresponding to it would simply become another version of *status quo* ideology.
>
> The fallacy of according greater truth value to the synthetic world view is based upon a failure to recognize the active role played by cognitive patterns in the historical process. Subjective views of the social process do not merely lead to meditation, they also lead to social action. Conservative or revolutionary ideology is not merely a matter of "intellectual position," but of practical policies and social movements which seek to impose a certain image on the world. Under these conditions social truth is created, not contemplatively interpreted, and he is nearest to the truth whose situationally transcendent ideas represent the interests of social forces which are favoured by the historical process.[9]

9. K. Danziger, "Ideology and Utopia in South Africa: A Methodological Contribution to the Sociology of Knowledge."

## CHAPTER TWO

## The Historical Background

Many people have remarked that the "race problem" of Africa is a White one, not a Black one. Indeed, racial prejudice and consciousness which greatly complicate and impede the present transition of African countries from subjection to independence are almost exclusively European imports. This is so much the case that there is a close relationship between the number of White settlers in any given territory, and the ease and speed of political transition. If the apologists of the "White man's burden" were correct, the reverse situation might have been expected: the more European colonists a country has, the "readier" it should be for self-government on a Western democratic model, and the sooner and the more easily it should achieve that avowed goal of most colonial powers. The events of the last twenty years, on the contrary, confirm the axiom that Africa has much more of a White immigrant problem than a "Native" one.

The "White problem" of South Africa begins in 1652 with the first permanent European settlement at the Cape of Good Hope. Previous sporadic intrusions by Portuguese sailors along the coast, starting in the late fifteenth century, have left no permanent trace. In 1652 the Dutch East India Company sent Van Riebeeck and a group of Company employees to the Cape in order to establish what De Kiewiet aptly called "a cabbage patch on the way to India,"[1] i.e., a refreshment station for Dutch vessels travelling between Holland and the East Indies. Five years later some colonists were emancipated from Company service and allowed to settle as free burghers. This event became the starting point of two important facts in South African history: first, of slavery, and, second, of "trekking."

Yielding to an increasing demand for cheap servile labour on the part of the Dutch settlers who quickly came to consider manual work below their dignity, the Company imported the first shipload of slaves in 1658. Through subsequent shipments, the number of slaves began to outnumber that of Whites by the first half of the eighteenth century, and the Western Cape became a firmly entrenched slave society until 1834, when slavery was abolished throughout the British Empire. These slaves came mostly from Madagascar, Mozambique, and the East Indies. In addition, the Cape was a convenient dumping ground for political exiles and prisoners from the Indies.

This early slavery situation gave rise to the first type of race relations which I have called "paternalistic,"[2] and to an ideological current which has mistakenly been termed "Cape liberalism." According to existing evidence, race or colour did not immediately become a primary criterion of stratification, but rather Christianity conferred by baptism, and the status of slave or free man.[3] Early cases of legal marriage between Dutchmen and baptised women of colour support that fact.

Within a generation or so, however, colour had become the primary index of status. The Calvinist faith of the Dutch settlers probably helped this process of increasing race consciousness. Indeed, one can plausibly extend Max Weber's argument concerning predestination to South Africa.[4] Weber argues that a

1. Cornelius W. De Kiewiet, *A History of South Africa*, p. 4.

2. Cf. Van den Berghe, "The Dynamics of Racial Prejudice: An Ideal-Type Dichotomy," and *The Dynamics of Race Relations: An Ideal-Type Case Study of South Africa.*

3. I. D. MacCrone, *Race Attitudes in South Africa*, pp. 40–41.

4. Max Weber, *The Protestant Ethic and the Spirit of Capitalism.*

belief in predestination leads to anxiety about one's salvation, and that one tries to resolve the uncertainty by seeking outward signs of God's grace. In the case of Calvin's Geneva that sign took the form of material prosperity, hence the link between Calvinism and capitalism. Accepting the urge to seek an outward sign of salvation, skin colour seemed the most obvious, indeed the almost inevitable choice in South Africa, all the more so that practically all dark-skinned people were in fact "heathens," and that darkness was traditionally associated with sin and evil in the Christian world view.[5] Hypothetical as this interpretation may seem, it is supported by the constant attempts on the part of fundamentalistic Afrikaners to seek Biblical justification for racial segregation and White superiority. Africans, so the argument runs, are the descendants of Ham, who was cursed by Noah, and are destined by God to be servants of servants, hewers of wood and drawers of water.

By the end of the seventeenth century, in any case, a rigid system of stratification based mostly on "race" was firmly established at the Cape. At this point, we must distinguish the settled districts of the Western Cape from the frontier districts of

---

5. For a similar interpretation, see Edward A. Tiryakian, "Apartheid and Religion"; and A. G. J. Cryns, *Race Relations and Race Attitudes in South Africa*, pp. 41–42. In addition to the religious factor in the origin of racialism in South Africa, Cryns mentions that the superior technology and social status of the Whites easily led to the notion of physical superiority. He argues, furthermore, that racial intolerance had survival value under rugged frontier conditions, and that racial barriers were erected by the Whites to preserve their dominant social position as non-Whites became acculturated. In other words, racialism became a second line of defense, when cultural and religious criteria of status no longer coincided with colour distinctions. Cf. Cryns, *op. cit.*, pp. 39–40. I agree with Cryns that all of these factors contributed to the development of White racialism in South Africa. The vulgar Marxist interpretation of colour prejudice as a conscious capitalist rationalization for the economic exploitation of the non-Whites is not only simplistic, but fails to account for the facts. While White vested interests do indeed make prejudice profitable, capitalism came much later than racialism in South Africa. Hence capitalism cannot satisfactorily account for the genesis of colour prejudice.

the "Trekboers" to which we shall turn later. The former extended in the eighteenth century as far as Swellendam in the east and Tulbagh in the north, and included, besides Cape Town itself, Stellenbosch and Paarl as sizeable towns. Only in that limited area, settled mostly by fairly prosperous wine, fruit, and wheat farmers living sedentarily on large autonomous farms, did the slavery system take root. The Whites were at the apex of society, and comprised transient sailors, a military garrison, employees of the Dutch East India Company, and free burghers established as artisans, shopkeepers, professionals, and farmers. They lived together with their slaves and with nominally free Hottentots (though the latter were more numerous in the frontier districts) in a relatively stable symbiosis based on rigidly ascriptive ties of masters and servants.

In spite of sporadic revolts of small groups of fugitive slaves repressed with great vigor, most contemporary and modern accounts agree that slavery at the Cape was a mild institution allowing for close affective bonds between masters and slaves.[6] The White farmer living on his autonomous estate constituted with his family and his retinue of slaves a large patriarchical unit in daily and intimate contact. Lichtenstein describes that paternalistic relationship existing in the first years of the nineteenth century in the following terms:

> He [i.e. an old slave] spoke with great warmth and gratitude of his master, Mr. Milde, who, he said, took such excellent care of him though he was not able to work any longer: praises which were echoed unanimously by all the slaves. Indeed, whoever had an opportunity of contemplating . . . the deportment of this excellent man toward his children, his household and dependents . . . must almost have fancied that he saw the days of the patriarchs revived. Nor are such instances rare. The truth is that instead of the odious representations which have been made by some persons of the behaviour of masters in this country towards their dependents

6. Dehérain, *op. cit.*, p. 212; Edwards, *op. cit.*, p. 16; Marais, *op. cit.*, pp. 162–172.

being descriptive of their general conduct, these have rather been taken from particular instances which ought to have been cited as exceptions.[7]

Many other documents of the period show the close affective and physical bonds that united masters and slaves. John Campbell, for example, writes in 1815:

> In general, the slaves are treated with tenderness in Cape Town. In the house where I lodged they are treated as if they were their own children, and most of them would be very unwilling to leave the family. Their children are put to school, and play about the room, where the family sit at their meals, with as much freedom, and receive as much attention as if they were their own children.[8]

A generation earlier, Sparrman related the following family scene:

> During the whole evening I had seen the slaves in such good humour, and so kindly and familiarly treated, that (with regard to their temporal matters at least) they really seemed to be better off than many servants in Europe.[9]

Slaves then, in particular domestic servants, closely shared the life of their masters. White and Black children played together and went in many cases to the same schools. The entire household often prayed together in the evening, although slaves were excluded from church worship; personal servants shared in every respect the intimacy of their masters' households, and lived in many cases under the same roof, as can be seen in the old town houses and farms of the Cape. A concomitant of this close emotional and special relationship was miscegenation which, throughout this period, was not only common but condoned in the form of concubinage between White men and women of colour. In 1787 Mentzel writes:

7. Lichtenstein, *op. cit.*, Vol. I, pp. 61–62.
8. Campbell, *op. cit.*, p. 5.
9. Andrew Sparrman, *A Voyage to the Cape of Good Hope*, p. 75.

Female slaves are always ready to offer their bodies for a
trifle, and toward evening one can see a string of soldiers and
sailors entering the slave lodge where they misspend their
time until the clock strikes 9. . . . The Company does nothing
to prevent this promiscuous intercourse, since, for one thing
it tends to multiply the slave population, and does away with
the necessity of importing fresh slaves. Three or four generations of this admixture . . . have produced a half-caste population—a mestizzo class—but a slight shade darker than some
Europeans. . . .

Boys who . . . have to remain at home during their impression-
able years between 16 and 21 more often than not commit
some folly, and get entangled with a handsome slave-girl
belonging to the household. These affairs are not regarded as
very serious. . . . The offence is venial in the public estimation.
It does not hurt the boy's prospects, his escapade is a source
of amusement, and he is dubbed a young fellow who has
shown the stuff he is made of. . . .

Female slaves sometimes live with Europeans as husband and
wife with the permission of their masters. . . . Her children
are the property of her master since children of female slaves
are themselves slaves.[10]

Percival describes the sexual hospitality of a Dutch family at
the Cape in 1804:

All children born of a slave woman, though got by a white
man, even by themselves, became slaves. It thus often happens, that the master has his own child a slave. . . . The Dutch
ladies have no reluctance to their slave girls having connection with their guests, in hopes of profiting by it, by their
being got with child. I myself know instances where they
have been ordered to wait on such a gentleman to his bed-
room.[11]

Sparrman mentions that his host, a Hanoverian farmer at the
Cape:

also gave me a list . . . of the constant order of precedence in
love, which ought to be observed among the fair sex in Africa:

10.  Mentzel, *op. cit.*, Vol. II, pp. 125, 109, 130.
11.  Percival, *op. cit.*, p. 291.

this was as follows. First the *Madagascar* women, who are the blackest and handsomest, next to these the *Malabars*, then the *Bugunese* or *Malays*, after these the Hottentots, and last and worst of all, the white Dutch women.[12]

The result of extensive miscegenation coupled with close symbiosis was the formation of the culturally homogeneous group of Afrikaans-speaking, Christian, Cape Coloureds.[13] Except for the Malays who retained their Muslim faith, this genetic and cultural melting pot of many different groups, from Hottentots and Indonesians to Malagasy, Africans, and Europeans, gave rise to a mixed population differing from the White settlers only through its skin colour and its depressed economic and social status. As we shall see later, the presence of the Coloureds, who are nearly half as numerous as the Whites, continues up to the present to exert a crucial influence on the entire social and political structure of the country.

Combined with these close physical ties between masters and slaves was a rigidly ascribed principle of inequality which made the White group dominant and all non-Whites, whether slaves or free men, subordinate. A complex etiquette of race relations continuously symbolized and reinforced this inequality. Numerous terms of address varying with status, age, and sex corresponded to the social roles of masters and servants. Sumptuary regulations, forbidding slaves, for example, to wear shoes or to smoke a pipe in the street, maintained social distance. Furthermore, the status of slave was difficult to escape. Out of a slave population increasing from over 2000 to nearly 15,000, only 893 slaves were emancipated between 1715 and 1792.[14] Under these circumstances, spacial segregation was unnecessary to the maintenance of White superiority. The racial hierarchy was unthreatened and maintained by other means. What little segregation existed was

12. Sparrman, *op. cit.*, p. 75.
13. In addition, of course, many people of mixed descent "passed" into the White group.
14. H. P. Cruse, *Die Opheffing van die Kleurling-Bevolking*, p. 253.

not a deliberate mechanism for keeping the non-Whites in subjection as became the case later.[15]

Such a paternalistic system of race relations with close personal bonds between masters and slaves living in constant contact on little autonomous land estates led to a fairly stable racial situation.[16] It also implied on the part of many slaves an acceptance of their subordinate status as inescapable, and even an internalization of a sense of their own inferiority. Similar situations have existed elsewhere, notably in the slave societies of the Americas such as in the southern United States and in northern Brazil.[17] To say that such systems were structurally stable and integrated implies by no means a value judgment as to their desirability. I do not intend to romanticize slavery, or to minimize its cruelty and debasement of the human personality. The cornerstone of such a system is the strict, permanent, unchallenged subordination of one group in relation to another, irrespective of individual merit. I fully concur, for example, with Bastide, who rightly points out that the existence of miscegenation in the form of concubinage, far from indicating an absence of racial prejudice, debases, on the contrary, the women of the subordinate group to the status of pleasure instruments for the males of the ruling group.[18] My contention is that there existed in the settled districts of the Western Cape in the eighteenth and early nineteenth centuries a stable, integrated society with a system of race relations quite different from that existing in South Africa today.

This old Western Cape society was, however, to leave legacies

15. For a theoretical treatment of segregation and etiquette as alternative mechanisms of distance see my article "Distance Mechanisms of Stratification."

16. A fuller description of what I mean by paternalistic systems of race relations can be found in my paper "The Dynamics of Racial Prejudice," and in my doctoral dissertation.

17. For a description of the Brazilian plantation system, see Gilberto Freyre, *The Masters and the Slaves.*

18. Roger Bastide, "Dusky Venus, Black Apollo." See also my paper "Racialism and Assimilation in Africa and the Americas."

in subsequent history, hence its importance for an understanding of modern conditions. Paternalism still lingers on as an ideal model of White-Black relationships for most White South Africans. Its milder form, which has been fallaciously termed "Cape liberalism," is in fact "Cape paternalism" with an injection of British nineteenth-century humanitarianism. In its extreme form, the official ideology of apartheid is also a brand of stern, rugged paternalism influenced by the frontier situation to which we shall turn shortly. The subsequent distinction between North and South that pervades the history of White politics in South Africa, and that is generally interpreted as a distinction between racialism and liberalism, could better be described as a relatively minor difference of opinion between two brands of paternalists. We shall return to that point later. The other legacy of the old Cape is, as we have mentioned above, the Cape Coloured group. This large, fully Westernized, brown appendage to the White group is one of major complicating factors in the structure of modern South Africa, and has no sizeable equivalent in the areas of the country invaded by the Whites in the nineteenth century.

Let us now turn to "trekking,"[19] the second major phenomenon in the social history of South Africa. Its origin, like that of slavery, can be found in the 1657 decision of the Dutch East India Company to free some of the settlers from its service. Indeed, only free burghers could travel at will. Naturally, this fact alone is completely inadequate to explain the slow dispersion and penetration of seminomadic Boers into the interior of the continent. The 1657 decision was merely a necessary condition thereto. It is, of course, impossible to assign an exact date to the beginning of trekking, but the nomadic move was certainly well under way by the first decades of the eighteenth century. The

19. The word "trek" means "travel" or "trip" in Afrikaans. It is also used as a verb. The derivatives "trekboer" and "voortrekker" mean respectively "frontier farmer" (or literally "travelling peasant") and "pioneers" (literally "forerunners"). The term "Great Trek" is reserved for the Boer migration of the 1830's and early 1840's.

trekking Boers were pastoralists, an occupation rendered profitable by the meat market of Cape Town. The relatively poor pastures were quickly exhausted and forced the Boers to move further inland with their cattle and sheep, every one to four years depending on local conditions. In addition to herding, cattle trading, with the Hottentots first, and later with the Bantu-speaking nations, was also attractive. Even more profitable was cattle raiding, through organized predatory commandos of mounted Boers against the aborigines. Neumark argues that cattle trading and raiding account for migration to an even greater extent than the need for new pastures.[20]

With an abundance of land which could be conquered relatively easily by the force of arms, and a scarcity of labour, it was almost a foregone conclusion that the Boers would become pastoralists, dependent on cattle and sheep both for subsistence and for trade. Livestock being self-transporting, other means of transport being virtually nonexisting, and Cape Town being the only sizeable trade centre, it followed that domestic animals were practically the only source of cash income at any distance from the Cape. Hence, cattle and sheep played a paramount economic role until the second half of the nineteenth century. Cattle raiding on the part of Boers, Hottentots, and Bantu Africans dominated the whole history of the South African frontier, because all three groups were pastoralists fighting over the control of the two main resources: livestock and land on which to feed it.

Another contributary factor to trekking was inheritance of land. Although Roman-Dutch law was not based on primogeniture, the incentive not to subdivide farms was great, and younger sons were often given their share of inheritance in cattle, sheep, and wagons to start life as pastoralists.

From the beginning, the established authorities at the Cape tried in vain to prevent trekking. First, the Company wanted to maintain a monopoly on cattle trade with the Hottentots. Second,

20. Neumark, *op. cit.*

the migratory Boers escaped the jurisdiction and control of the Company in the remote frontier districts. Third, the expanding frontier created a situation of perpetual chaos. The cattle raids and territorial encroachments of the Boers led to an endless series of frontier wars and counterraids by the aborigines. These are known in South African history as the "Hottentot Wars" of 1659 and 1673, the "Kaffir Wars" of 1779, 1789, 1799, 1812, 1818, 1835, 1846, and 1850, and the "Basuto Wars" of 1851, 1858, 1865, and 1880, not to mention almost countless smaller skirmishes, cattle raids, reprisals, and "punitive expeditions" which, in the case of the Boer commandos against the Bushmen, took the character of genocide. The Company and later the British government were reluctant to get involved in a situation which they were unable to control, and have always wanted to contain the Boer migration. The Company had no territorial ambitions at the Cape. It considered South Africa worthless, except as a steppingstone to the East.

Conditions on the frontier were obviously quite different from those in the settled districts of the Cape. The pastoralist Boers lived under much more rudimentary conditions than the sedentary farmers, and were on the average much poorer. Few could afford slaves, who were quite expensive, and most relied on Hottentot and, later, Bantu serfs, who cost nothing but a little food, and whose destitution forced them into the service of the Boers after the latter had deprived them of their land. Vaillant describes the living conditions of the frontier Boers in the 1780's as follows:

Les derniers, misérables et paresseux errent sur les frontières, promenant de pâturage en pâturage quelques bestiaux qui se nourissent comme ils peuvent. Quand leurs troupeaux les font séjourner quelque part, ils se construisent à la hâte quelque hutte grossière qu'ils couvrent de nattes, à la manière de ces Hottentots dont ils ne diffèrent que par les traits du visage et la couleur.[21]

21. Boulenger, *op. cit.*, p. 233.

A few years later, Barrow writes:

The boer, notwithstanding, has his enjoyments, he is absolute master of a domain of several miles in extent; and he lords it over a few miserable slaves or Hottentots without control.[22]

What little evidence exists on the type of race relations on the frontier indicates that the Hottentots were not as well treated, on the whole, as the slaves in the settled districts. Though the charges of cruelty made against the Boers in the Black Circuit of 1812 were shown to be exaggerated, the rugged and dangerous living conditions left little room for gentleness and humaneness.[23] Towards their own serfs, the Boers seem to have, in general, exhibited a stern paternalism which did not, in most cases, exclude a liberal dose of corporal punishment. At the same time, the common evening prayer in which the Hottentots and slaves participated is a cherished memory of the Afrikaner folklore. Towards men of colour outside the boundaries of White settlement, the attitude of the Boers was entirely hostile and predatory. Bushmen, who considered Boer cattle as fair game, were viewed as vermin, and shot at sight by organized Boer commandos. In 1774, for example, a Boer commando killed 503 Bushmen and captured 239. Between 1786 and 1795, 2503 Bushmen were killed and 669 taken as prisoners by the Boers. In the same period, the Bushmen killed 276 Whites and stole 19,161 heads of cattle and 84,094 sheep from the colonists.[24] Hottentots and Bantu likewise engaged in continuous warfare and cattle raiding with the Boers who either killed them, pushed them back, and annexed their territory, or stole their cattle and reduced the remnants of the aboriginal groups to a form of disguised slavery. The important point to note here is that the frontier model of White-Black relations within the Boer household was basically the same paternalism as in the settled districts, only much sterner

22. Barrow, *op. cit.*, pp. 72–73.
23. Agar-Hamilton, *op. cit.*, p. 109; Alan F. Hattersley, *op. cit.*, pp. 55–58.
24. Cf. Marais, *op. cit.*, pp. 15–20.

and much less humane. Africans or Hottentots who were not reduced to the status of slaves or serfs, the only status for a Black person which was acceptable to the Boers, were automatically treated as enemies. We shall later see how this outlook has been carried into the present.

Up to the Great Fish River, the Boers encountered little opposition to their migration. During the first half of the eighteenth century they gradually invaded a vast territory previously inhabited by Hottentots and Bushmen. The main flow of the migration followed the eastern coast of the continent where rainfall was the greatest. Smaller numbers of colonists, in particular "Bastards," i.e., people of mixed Boer and Hottentot descent, also went full north into the semi-desertic interior of the future Cape Colony and reached the Orange River.[25] This whole territory was inhabited only by small, thinly settled, nomadic bands of Hottentots and Bushmen who, not possessing any cohesive political organization, were no obstacle to the Boers with their guns, horses, and wagons. While it is incorrect to say that this part of Africa was empty, as does current government propaganda, the aboriginal population was certainly scarce and the area was a power vacuum.

In the second half of the eighteenth century, however, Boer and Bantu met on the Great Fish River. The large African nations were, like the Boers, pastoralists on the move, pushing one another southward in a great turmoil of wars and migrations. This time, the Boers encountered not a few isolated roving bands, unconnected with one another, but large cohesive nations numbering up to several hundred thousand members, and with a complex political and military organization. The firearms and horses of the Boers compensated for their numerical inferiority, but, nevertheless, the two migrant groups stopped one another around 1775, and the White frontier expanded only slowly until

25. For a history of the Bastard "states" on the Orange River see Marais, *op. cit.*, pp. 32–73, 217–245.

the 1830's. An uneasy deadlock resulted, punctuated by "Kaffir Wars," cattle raids, and vain attempts by the Cape authorities to "pacify" and to seal off the border. Whereas the Hottentots and Bushmen were either exterminated or absorbed into the Cape Coloured population through miscegenation and acculturation, the Africans were too numerous and too well integrated to share that fate. For the first time, on the Great Fish River, the two main antagonists in South Africa, Whites and Africans, were in presence. This equilibrium of forces was finally broken with the Great Trek of 1836, but, before turning to that important event, we must turn back to the first years of the nineteenth century.

After first capturing the Cape in 1795, and ceding it briefly again to the Batavian Republic in 1803, the British finally established themselves in 1806. With British rule, a new complicating factor appeared on the South African scene, namely Boer-Briton antagonism, with its complex repercussions on what White South Africans call the "Native problem." Until the last two or three decades, the struggle for supremacy between Boer and Briton even overshadowed the White-Black opposition. Most Afrikaner and African nationalists today are in basic agreement on at least one point, namely the interpretation of British policy in South Africa. That policy consisted broadly in consolidating the British position at the detriment of both Boers and Africans, and, if necessary, in using the latter against the former.

The new British government at the Cape strengthened its position before the Great Trek in three important ways: through English immigration, through its support of the activities of the London Missionary Society, and through a series of liberalizing measures ending with the abolition of slavery in 1834. By encouraging English immigration the government counterbalanced the influence of the Dutch colonists. In 1820, in particular, some 5000 English immigrants were settled in the frontier districts of the Eastern Cape to give Britain a better control of that crucial border area, and to interpose themselves between the Boers moving eastward and the Africans spreading southwestward. The Protestant clergymen of the London Missionary Society likewise enjoyed the support of the authorities. Here, too, Afrikaners and Africans agree in making them the first agents of British imperialism in the interior of South Africa.

While it would be a distortion of facts to consider the English missionaries simply as spies in disguise, it is clear that they were looked upon with favour by the British government, and that their humanitarian efforts to eradicate slavery and improve the abject condition of the Hottentots infuriated the Dutch colonists and coincided with government policy. Indeed, some of the missionaries were themselves aware of their political role. Thus John Philip stated in 1828:

> While the missionaries have been employed in locating the savages among whom they labour, teaching them industrious habits, creating a demand for British manufactures, and increasing their dependence on the colony, there is not a single instance of a tribe thus enjoying the labour of a missionary making war against the colonists, either to injure their persons, or to deprive them of their property. Missionary stations are the most efficient agents which can be employed to promote the internal strength of our colonies, and the cheapest and best military posts a government can employ.[26]

The Black Circuit of 1812 (in which judges investigated alleged atrocities committed by Boers against the natives), the 50th Ordinance of 1828 (abolishing the vagrancy laws that served as a pretext to reduce the Hottentots to serfdom), and the series of laws reforming and finally putting an end to slavery in 1834 are the product of British government policy influenced by the London Missionary Society. While these measures were also dictated by humanitarian considerations, they certainly had the effect of weakening the position of the Boers. In 1853 the granting of a qualified franchise to all regardless of colour in the Cape Colony was probably motivated in part by an attempt to attract

26. John Philip, *Researches in South Africa*, Vol. 22, p. 227.

the non-White elite into the British camp in order to offset the strength of the Dutch, as Cecil Rhodes later recognized.[27] Such has, in fact, been the effect of the limited non-White franchise at the Cape until its recent abolishment by the Afrikaner Nationalists. We shall return to that point later.

Let us turn now to that major turning point in South African history: the Great Trek. This event is important, not only for its objective consequences, but also because of its paramount place in Afrikaner mythology. Indeed, the Great Trek can be considered the starting point of Afrikaner nationalism, and its colourful epic has served more than any other single fact, except perhaps the Second Anglo-Boer War, to create Afrikanerdom.[28] The myth of the Great Trek goes as follows: Like the Chosen People who fled under Moses from Egyptian tyranny, our freedom-loving, God-fearing ancestors could no longer bear to live under British domination at the Cape. They courageously went into the wilderness, faced countless dangers, vanquished the Black heathens with the help of God, and settled into the Promised Land of the Transvaal and the Orange Free State. There they attempted, against the combined forces of evil (i.e., the African nations and British imperialism), to lead peaceful and free lives until they succumbed after a heroic fight against British aggression. But the Almighty was once more on the side of His Chosen People, who regained control of the country in 1948.

The myth of the Great Trek has, of course, some basis in fact. The frontier Boers certainly detested the British government and

27. Cf. Vindex, *Cecil Rhodes Political Life and Speeches, 1881–1899,* pp. 160–161. Rhodes' slogan of "equal rights to all civilized men" is alleged to have been an afterthought. Before, he had spoken of "equal rights to all *White* men."

28. F. A. van Jaarsveld, however, in his recent book *The Awakening of Afrikaner Nationalism, 1868–1881,* considers that the crucial catalysts for Afrikaner Nationalism were the British annexation of the Transvaal in 1877, and what, in the vocabulary of Afrikaner historiography, he calls the "First Transvaal War of Independence" (i.e., the First Anglo-Boer War of 1880–1881).

its reforms which put the "Kaffirs" and the "Hotnots" on the same foot as themselves. The Boers were "oppressed" by the British in that they were repeatedly frustrated in their continuing attempts to use the non-Whites as servile labour, and in that they were largely excluded from the Cape colonial administration. The emancipation of slaves little affected the Boers who went on the Trek since most of them did not own slaves, but the 50th Ordinance was undoubtedly a threat to the Boers' economic existence. The love of freedom emphasized in the mythology leaves, however, room for skepticism. First, the Boer concept of liberty never extended beyond the *Herrenvolk*. In their new republics, the trekkers promptly reintroduced a form of slavery disguised under the euphemism of the "apprenticeship system," and embodied in their constitution the principle that "the people will suffer no equality of Whites and Blacks either in state or in church."[29] Furthermore, one can plausibly argue that this love of liberty and this hatred of the British were more generally a love of anarchy and a hatred of all organized government. Indeed, as early as 1795, frontier Boers fought against the Dutch government at the Cape in what became known as the Graaff-Reinet Rebellion. In the Transvaal the several Boer republics which coexisted or succeeded one another were themselves only powerless and ephemeral shadows of government until the 1880's.

29. Constitution of the South African Republic of 1858. See also Piet Retief's 1837 statement on the aims of those who followed him in the Great Trek: "We are resolved wherever we go that we will uphold the just principles of liberty . . . and preserve proper relations between master and servant." (Quoted in William M. Macmillan, *The Cape Colour Question*, p. 245.) Piet Retief's sister Anna Steenkamp also complained about "the shameful and unjust proceedings with reference to the freeing of our slaves," but went on to give the main reason for the Great Trek: ". . . and yet it is not so much their freeing which drove us to such lengths, as their being placed on an equal footing with Christians, contrary to the laws of God, and the natural distinctions of race and colour, so that it was intolerable for any decent Christian to bow down beneath such a yoke; wherefore we rather withdraw in order to preserve our doctrines in purity." Quoted in Paton, *Hope for South Africa*, p. 27.

The myth most completely fails to check with reality where it makes no room for the economic causes of the Great Trek. For over half a century migrant Boers had exerted an increasing pressure on a nearly static frontier. The wasteful use of land on large farms of 6 to 10,000 acres must have created a dire need for new pastures. Cash agriculture was unprofitable for lack of near-by markets of any size. The only outlet was further migration into the interior. Since the road was closed by the African nations and the British military outposts along the eastern coast, the Boers circumvented that barrier by entering into the interior, turning around the mountains of Basutoland, and crossing the Drakensberg into Natal. In this vast outflanking movement they were ironically helped by the Zulu wars of extermination which had converted the southern part of Natal into a demographic, political, and economic near-vacuum a decade earlier.

Boers and Zulu met in a series of battles in Natal, culminating with the Zulu defeat at Blood River in 1838. This battle, which is still celebrated by the Afrikaners as a national holiday, temporarily broke Zulu power, and allowed the Boers to found their ephemeral Republic of Natal in 1838.[30] The Boers also fought against the British, who countered the Boer expansion by annexing Natal as a Crown colony in 1843. After failing to expel the British from Port Natal (Durban), most of the Trekkers recrossed the mountains into the high plateaux of the interior, and spread out into the vast territory that later became known as the Orange Free State and the South African (Transvaal) Republic.

A combination of factors made for at least three decades of near-anarchy in the score of successive Boer "Republics" that were governments only in name. A White population numbering at most 40,000 in the 1850's was scattered north of the Orange River over a territory of well over 100,000 square miles. Roads

30. The final elimination of the Zulu as a military might dates from the Zulu War of 1879.

and towns of any size were completely nonexistent. Furthermore, the Boers had to fight a succession of frontier wars against the African nations (mostly the Zulu, Ndebele, and Sotho) in order to conquer the land. These wars lasted until 1880, and the defeated Africans were either pushed back into the mountains of Basutoland and the arid regions of the Northern Transvaal, or reduced to serfdom on the Boer farms. In the case of the Sotho, the British intervened in their favour, or rather against the Boers, and saved the Sotho from total land expropriation by making Basutoland a British protectorate in 1868. This new British effort at containing the Trek gave rise, after Union in 1910, to a foreign enclave totally surrounded by and economically dependent on South Africa. Later, Swaziland and Bechuanaland joined Basutoland as British protectorates under the collective label of High Commission Territories. To this date, the three territories are a major bone of contention between South Africa and the United Kingdom.

Before returning to the Boer Republics and their defeat by the British, we must mention two important developments in Natal. In the late 1840's the British administrator Theophilus Shepstone established his famous system of Native Reserves that became the first large-scale scheme for the physical segregation of the races in South Africa, and the blueprint for subsequent "Native Administration" in the rural areas. Shepstone set aside dispersed land tracts for the exclusive occupation of Africans. This scattering served the dual purpose of making farm labour more easily accessible to White farmers, and of averting the threat of large concentrations of Africans. Subsequent legislation, such as the Native Land Act of 1913 and the Native Trust and Land Act of 1936, expanded and refined the Shepstone system. The arrival of East Indians constituted the second important event in Natal. In 1860 the first indentured Indian labourers were brought to Natal to furnish cheap and reliable workers for the expanding sugar-cane industry along the coast. The immigration of Indians introduced the last complicating element into an already varied population and led to what White South Africans call the "Indian (or "coolie") problem."[31]

The discovery of diamonds around Kimberley in 1867 was to change the face of the Boer Republics, and to foreshadow the even more important opening of the gold fields of the Witwatersrand around Johannesburg in 1886. In the first case, Britain annexed the diamond fields, then located on Boer territory, to the Cape Colony. The Orange Free State was in no position to contest the annexation by force, and an armed conflict between Boer and Briton was averted. In 1877, however, the British occupied the Transvaal, ostensibly to re-establish its bankrupt finances, to prevent the collapse of the Boer government, and to ward off a Zulu invasion. The 1877–1881 occupation was but one of Lord Carnarvon's several unsuccessful attempts to establish a British-controlled federation in South Africa.

The territory was then devoid of economic importance, and after a short fight and defeat at Majuba (in the First Anglo-Boer War), Britain withdrew in 1881.

The real nemesis of the Boer Republics was the discovery of gold around the future city of Johannesburg in 1886. A gold rush ensued, and, with it, the isolation of the Transvaal came to an end. By 1896 Johannesburg was linked by rail with Cape Town, Durban, and Lorenço Marques, and was fast becoming the nerve centre of the South African economy. The Transvaal had become economically attractive. The White miners and other White non-Boers, known as *Uitlanders* (foreigners), who settled in the boisterous boom town of Johannesburg threatened the political supremacy of the Boer settlers, who started dis-

---

31. The temporary introduction of Chinese labourers on the gold mines in 1904 left no permanent trace in South Africa, as practically all Chinese were repatriated upon expiration of their term of indenture. Today there are only about 2000 Chinese in South Africa. It is interesting to note how the sheer physical presence of a non-European group in South Africa is promptly perceived as a threat by the Whites, and defined as a "problem."

criminating against them by restricting the franchise. These *Uit-landers* soon became the pretext for British intervention. Under the instigation of Cecil Rhodes, motivated by his vision of a British Africa from the Cape to Cairo, a band of adventurers invaded the Transvaal from Bechuanaland in 1895—the Jameson Raid—and met with ignominious failure. But the British finally won the Anglo-Boer War of 1899–1902 after a long fight against Boer guerilla tactics. The British concentration camps, where Afrikaner women and children were interned and where some 27,000 of them died of disease, and the use of African troops (limited as it was) against the Boers have left a lasting legacy of anti-British hatred among many Afrikaners.

Although Britain won the war, it lost the peace and turned South Africa politically back to the Afrikaners, while English financial magnates retained control of the economy. After lengthy negotiations, the South Africa Act of 1909 made the country self-governing in 1910, within what later became known as the British Commonwealth. This settlement was extremely important for it determined the political structure of the country for half a century. Furthermore, it illustrates the practical implementation of British "liberalism" on the colour issue in South Africa. Although taking place when the Liberal Party was in power in Britain, the most salient feature of the postwar negotiations and settlement is that they were an all-White affair in which the majority of the country had no say.[32] Each of the four territories that were to constitute the Provinces of the Union of South Africa (Cape, Natal, Orange Free State, and Transvaal) was represented by an all-White delegation.

In most essentials, the 1909 agreement seemed to maintain the *status quo ante bellum.* Great Britain retained control of the High Commission Territories of Swaziland, Basutoland, and

32. Nearly half a century later, Britain turned another large slice of Africa over to a White-settlers' government when it launched the Central African Federation in 1953, in spite of bitter and nearly unanimous African opposition.

Bechuanaland, but a clause provided for their eventual transfer to the Union at an unspecified date. Two provisions known as the "entrenched clauses" required a two-thirds majority of both Houses of the South African Parliament for amendment. They concerned the official languages and the franchise. English and Dutch were declared as the only official tongues on a footing of equality.[33] None of the Bantu languages ever received any recognition as a national tongue.[34] The franchise clause retained the pre-Union situation in each of the four provinces, and, because of the light it throws on the practical meaning of English "liberalism," merits closer examination.

The Transvaal and Orange Free State delegations were, of course, adamantly opposed to any extension of the franchise to non-Whites in their provinces, and any attempt on part of the British to impose such an extension would have jeopardized the whole policy of compromise and co-operation between Boer and English on which the British government wanted to base the postwar settlement. What Britain wanted above all in South Africa was a friendly White-settler dominion with a secure preponderance of English economic interests. At the Cape the Dutch numerical superiority over the English had been accompanied, as we saw, by a qualified non-racial franchise in which a non-White minority of voters often sided with the English.[35] In 1892, however, as the number of non-White voters was steadily

33. Afrikaans officially replaced Dutch as a national language only in 1925.

34. Within the newly created "Bantustan" of the Transkei, however, Xhosa is to be recognized as an official language, but this does not apply to the country as a whole.

35. I oversimplified somewhat the position in the Cape, for a segment of the Afrikaners were in favour of the "moderate" line on the colour issue and of co-operation with Britain. The so-called "Cape liberalism" is not a purely English phenomenon and has had prominent Afrikaner proponents. This fact further confirms my interpretation of "Cape liberalism" as the offspring of old-style "Cape paternalism" and nineteenth-century British humanitarianism. The political division between North and South within Afrikanerdom can still be found in attenuated form today.

climbing, Rhodes raised the voting qualifications so as further to entrench political control in White hands, and conciliate White agitation against the "red-blanket Kaffirs."

Natal, a British Colony with few Afrikaners, was even less liberal than the Cape. It never had more than purely nominal and insignificant voting rights for non-Whites. This fact is easily understood when one considers that, in Natal, the English did not need any non-White vote to offset an already very weak White Afrikaner vote.[36] This interpretation is further confirmed by the fact that, on the franchise issue, the Natal delegation sided with the ex-Boer Republics, and not with the Cape as one might have expected. The end result was a retention of the existing franchise laws in each of the four provinces. The basic agreement on colour issues between most Afrikaners and English has been a constant fact of the South African political scene for over a century. With outstanding exceptions that no amount of cynicism can dismiss, the English, as a group, have only shown liberalism (carefully minimized at that) when it suited their interests as opposed to those of the Afrikaners.

The Union settlement was clearly intended by Britain to effect the reconciliation of the two White groups. The South Africa Act was rightly interpreted as a magnanimous gesture towards the defeated Boer Republics; but of this magnanimity, Britain reaped the rewards, and the non-White majority of South Africa bore the cost.[37]

36. Cecil Rhodes stated that the reason for the disfranchisement of Africans in Natal was that there was "no race question of English and Dutch there to divide them." Cf. Vindex, *op. cit.*, pp. 160–161.

37. This is also Nicholas Mansergh's thesis in his recent book *South Africa 1906–1961, The Price of Magnanimity.* Mansergh argues, however, that the British government could not have acted differently, because it has its hands tied by Article 8 of the Treaty of Vereeniging which put an end to the Boer War. In this article, Britain undertook not to extend the franchise of Africans in the former Orange and Transvaal Republics. (*Op. cit.*, p. 77.) Mansergh also pleads extenuating circumstances for Britain by arguing that her role must be evaluated by contemporary and not present standards. (*Op. cit.*, p. 64.) The dominant contemporary standards in both

The British hoped that the 1909 settlement would maintain a stable equilibrium between English and Afrikaners on the internal political scene. A large, mixed, "liberal" Cape and a small ultra-British Natal would, it was hoped, be counterbalanced by

---

Britain and South Africa were thoroughly dominated by a dual standard in dealing with Whites and with non-Whites. The contrasting treatment received, for example, by the Zulu and by the Boers after their defeat is evidence enough of this racism. So is the fact that the conscience of British liberals was uneasy about aggression against the Boers, but hardly at all about countless other colonial wars against Africans and Asians. This line of apology for Britain's role in the Union settlement is all the less convincing that such racialism and White supremacism dominated British policy in much of South, Central, and East Africa until the mid-fifties. Both Labour and Conservative governments had a clear responsibility in establishing the now defunct Central African Federation, which was a somewhat mitigated repetition of the Union settlement. Concerning the latter, Churchill was able to say in all seriousness as late as 1950: " . . . no act of reconciliation after a bitter struggle has ever produced so rich a harvest in goodwill." (Quoted by Mansergh, *op. cit.*, p. 99.) The attempt to justify Britain's dual standard by showing that racialism was deeply ingrained in British values is obviously circular. The only tenable line of apology for Britain is in terms of *Realpolitik*. In point of fact, the only significant forces in presence in South Africa at the turn of the century were the Afrikaners and the English. The African nations had been finally crushed by combined Boer and British forces twenty years earlier. To claim, however, that Africans were passively unaware of and uninterested in the settlement of Union is inaccurate. While mass political consciousness among Africans did not exist then as it does today, the South African Native Convention did pass an unequivocal resolution in 1909, registering "strong and emphatic protest" at the colour-bar to be imposed in the Union, and deploring that Britain's non-White subjects "have not been shown the same liberal and generous treatment" as shown towards the Boers. (Quoted in Mansergh, *op. cit.*, p. 94.) On the question of the Union settlement, see also G. B. Pyrah's recent book: *Imperial Policy and South Africa, 1902–1910*, wherein, like Mansergh, he accepts that the compromise was at the expense of non-Whites, but pleads extenuating circumstances for Britain. The British Liberal government, he argues, feared that forcing a liberal non-White franchise would unite White South Africans against the non-Europeans and promote racial strife. Hence, the Liberals adopted the lesser of two evils and hoped for the best, i.e., a gradual liberalization along Cape lines. Eric Walker also concurs that "The British Liberal Ministers brought no pressure to bear to ensure that the dominant Europeans should treat the vast non-European majority better than most of them had done hitherto." (*Op. cit.*, p. 533.)

a large, mixed, reactionary Transvaal and a small Afrikaner Orange Free State. In fact, however, the political dice were loaded on the reactionary Afrikaner side. Indeed, the limited non-White franchise in the Cape, sufficient to offset the extremist Afrikaner vote in that province, could not fulfill that role in the country as a whole. On the colour issue, the whole trend of South African politics since Union has been reactionary, with the major opposition party to the Nationalists gradually accepting backward change. On the issue of the relationship to Britain, a stable equilibrium was, however, maintained until 1948. Until then, enough "moderate" Afrikaners favoured close ties with Britain and joined forces with the South African English to counterbalance the extreme Afrikaner Nationalists. That equilibrium was only broken when Afrikanerdom rallied under the leadership of Malan in the "purified" Nationalist Party which was founded in the 1930's, gathered strength during the war years, and finally came to power in 1948.

In 1910, then, the major elements of the political structure of modern South Africa were already present and have remained fundamentally unchanged (except in a reactionary direction) up to this date. Economically, on the other hand, the country has expanded enormously, and secondary industry has taken an increasingly prominent place. With industrialization, the processes of urbanization and Westernization which had already begun in 1910 continued at a fast pace. Demographically the population has nearly tripled in the half century since Union. Rapid change in some parts of the social structure of the country, accompanied by political reaction, has led to an ever deepening state of disequilibrium and conflict which I shall analyse in this work. But before turning to that analysis, I must describe in the next two chapters the main intertwining, or, better, intercolliding, elements of the highly complex social structure of South Africa.

## CHAPTER THREE

## The Social Structure of Modern South Africa: Culture and Status

In our analysis of the structure of modern South Africa, we shall decompose that complex society into four major aspects and show their interrelations. We shall deal in turn with cultural divisions, with social stratification, with the political structure, and with the economy.

One of the salient characteristics of South Africa is its cultural pluralism. The country has become the meeting point of three broad cultural currents and many more specific cultures. The imported European culture of the conquerors, both in its Dutch and in its English variants, has, like in other parts of the colonial world, steadily gained ground at the expense of the indigenous cultures. Of the latter, the Hottentot culture has been entirely stamped out, and the Bushmen subsist only in small groups outside the boundaries of South Africa proper. The cultures of the Bantu-speaking peoples have, nevertheless, survived up to the present, however much they have been influenced by Western technology. The other imported cultural strain, the Asian one, came, as we shall see, in two waves: first from the Dutch East Indies, and since 1860 from India.

Let us turn first to Western European culture. Through a common confusion in South Africa, "race" and "culture," "White" and "Western" are identified. While it is true that Western culture was introduced into the continent by Whites, the latter ceased as early as the eighteenth century to be the only representatives of the European way of life. Today there exists at best a very imperfect correlation between skin colour and religious, linguistic, or other cultural characteristics. We must therefore treat the cultural complex as distinct from the racial makeup of the country, not only analytically but also empirically.

To all intents and purposes, European culture has only two main variants in South Africa: the Afrikaner and the English. The former is a derivative of Dutch culture. A group of French Huguenots landed at the Cape in 1688, but, within a generation, they were absorbed by the Dutch colonists. More recently other European groups entered the country, notably Jews of many nationalities, Germans, Frenchmen from Mauritius, Italians, and Greeks. Although there are a few pockets of French- and German-speaking people in South Africa, most immigrants have become assimilated into one of the two dominant European cultures.[1] Sizeable Jewish communities exist in Johannesburg, Cape Town, Durban, and other towns, but they are for the most part English-speaking, and, except for religion, well assimilated into the larger White society.

Aside from the Whites, the vast majority of the Coloureds and a small but growing minority of Africans and Indians are completely Westernized. One can safely say that nobody in South Africa has escaped Western influence, although the extent of that influence varies greatly from one person, from one group, and from one region to another. In the case of the Coloureds, the process of acculturation is completed, with one small and partial exception. Some 6 per cent of the Coloureds, known as "Cape Malays," have remained faithful to Islam (Table XIV),[2] but they speak Afrikaans as their mother tongue, and are deeply Westernized in most aspects unconnected with religious and dietary

1. In the former German colony of South West Africa, now under South African administration, the German influence is still strong, however.
2. The tables can be found in Appendix B.

practices. These Malays are the descendants of slaves and political exiles from the Dutch East Indies, and, through Islam, they have remained a cohesive and fairly closed group. During the period of slavery, they constituted an elite among slaves and were, for the most part, employed as skilled artisans. Even today their social status is higher, on the average, than that of the mass of the other Coloureds.

In 1955, 88.7 per cent of the Coloureds lived in the Cape, predominantly in Cape Town and vicinity. A glance at the distribution of Coloureds on a map of South Africa shows that the areas of greatest concentration coincide roughly with the settled districts of the Western Cape during the period of slavery. As we have already said earlier, the Coloureds are the product of a dual process of Westernization and miscegenation between Whites, Hottentots, and slaves.

Like most slave societies, the old Cape was particularly favourable to this cultural and physical amalgamation. Slavery is, paradoxically, a great cultural leveler insofar as it rapidly shatters the culture of origin of the slaves, and encourages miscegenation. African, Malagasy, and Asian slaves, who had already been forcibly torn away from their culture of origin, were then randomly distributed without regard for ethnic affiliation between isolated farms. The absence of a common culture, religion, or language between the slaves, and the impossibility of maintaining cultural ties between small, heterogeneous, and widely dispersed groups made for a quick adoption of the dominant European culture. The Muslims alone, through their strongly cohesive religion, managed to escape total acculturation, though even they adopted the language of their masters (while at the same time influencing what later became Afrikaans). The Hottentots were easily assimilated because of the fragility of their social organization, and they were quickly forced into serfdom by the Dutch. As to the Bushmen, they were exterminated or pushed back rather than assimilated. In 1951, 51 per cent of the Coloureds spoke Afrikaans only, 46.5 per cent spoke Afrikaans and

English, and a bare 2.5 per cent spoke English only. Eighty-nine per cent of the Coloureds spoke Afrikaans as their home language.[3]

The genetic counterpart of this process of acculturation was miscegenation, which took place simultaneously, and which was also favoured by slavery. The close symbiosis of masters and slaves, and the total subordination of the female slave to her male owners made for extensive intermixture. Other incentives accelerated the process. Through miscegenation the female slave could improve her condition and the status of her children. The White master, on his side, had, apart from sexual gratification, an economic interest in increasing and "improving" his human stock by producing highly priced mulatto slaves.

Had it not been for the development of a strong form of racial (as distinct from ethnic) prejudice, South Africa could have developed into the same type of harmonious society, racially mixed and culturally Western, as is found in Latin America. Indeed, from the cultural point of view, the Cape Coloureds belong to Afrikaner culture. They share with the *Herrenvolk* one of its three main identifying characteristics: the Afrikaans language. They meet only partially the second criterion, namely membership in one of the three Dutch Reformed Churches; just under 30 per cent of the Coloureds share the religion of the Afrikaners, but, still, the D.R.C.'s have more Coloured members than does any other denomination. Clearly, the main, not to say the sole, reason why Afrikanerdom rejects the Coloured is because of the latter's failure to fulfill the all-important criterion of superior status in South Africa, namely a "white" skin.

It is as fallacious to speak of a "Cape Coloured culture" as it is to speak of an "American Negro culture" distinct from the dominent White culture. Hottentot and Malay survivals in speech, for example, are found as much in the Afrikaans spoken by Whites as in that spoken by Cape Coloureds, and dialectical

3. Muriel Horrell, *A Survey of Race Relations in South Africa, 1958–1959*, p. 279; 1959–1960, p. 25.

or pronounciation differences are more a function of region and social class than of "colour." The racial prejudice of the Whites is solely responsible for the social existence of a distinct Cape Coloured group, a fact recognized by many "moderate" Afrikaners today, and indeed by some Hertzogites as early as the twenties. Except for the concern with colour of South African "Whites" (many of whom have themselves "Coloured blood"), Afrikanerdom would be nearly twice as large as it is today, and would outnumber the English-speaking Whites by well over two to one. For every six White Afrikaners there are approximately five Coloured Afrikaners and four English-speaking Whites. In the entire population there are four non-Whites to one White, if colour is the criterion; but, if mother tongue is taken as the criterion, there are only two non-Europeans to one European. Should religion be chosen as the index of Westernization, Christians outnumber non-Christians by over two to one.

Only a minority of Coloureds live outside the Cape Province. They are, for the most part, the product of more recent miscegenation between Whites and Africans, or, to a lesser extent, the descendants of the "Bastard" communities (such as the Griqua and Namaqua) who trekked to the North in the late eighteenth and early nineteenth century, and settled on the Orange River frontier. As the small number of non-Cape Coloureds indicates, the Northern part of the country, which never knew a slave plantation economy, was much less of a genetic melting pot than the Cape. Nevertheless, the Coloureds outside the Cape are also completely Westernized and their position *vis-à-vis* the Whites is very similar to that prevailing in the Cape. The Natal Coloureds and most of the urban Transvaal Coloureds speak English, as do most local Whites, rather than Afrikaans.

Western culture is also making steady progress among Indians and Africans, though the process of acculturation has been rather different in the two groups. Let us first examine the position among South Africans of Indian origin. Coming from five different linguistic groups (Hindi, Tamil, Telugu, Urdu, and Gujarati), the Indian immigrants quickly adopted English as a common tongue. Anglicization was further speeded up by the use of English as a medium of instruction in the racially segregated Indian schools. Today, all but elderly people and some of the women in the poorer or more conservative Indian groups speak fluent English. In 1951 only 21.5 per cent of the Indians spoke no European language, 62.8 per cent spoke English, 14.6 per cent were conversant in both English and Afrikaans, and 1 per cent spoke Afrikaans.[4] A growing minority of Indian families speak mostly English at home, and the younger generation is, as a rule, more fluent in that tongue than in any of the Indian languages.

Religiously, the vast majority of Indians have retained their faith in Islam (21.5 per cent in 1951) or Hinduism (67.2 per cent). Only some 6 per cent have been converted to Christianity (Table XIV). These figures understate, however, the indirect influence of Christianity on Hindus. While Islam has remained unaffected by Christianity, the latter has exerted a profound influence on South African Hinduism. Through its tolerance and complexity of ritual and theology which favour eclecticism, Hinduism syncretized some elements of Christianity, while at the same time becoming ritually and philosophically impoverished due to isolation from India. For many Hindus, their religious affiliation symbolizes mostly a vague cultural allegiance, and is accompanied by little religious practice (aside from domestic rites carried out mostly by women), and an almost total ignorance of the tenets of Hinduism. Christianity is tolerantly accepted as an alternative road to the same spiritual goals, Christ and Krishna are often identified, and Hindus exchange Christmas cards as much as Christians.

Among Indian Muslims the situation is quite different. They have remained a very cohesive group, and reject all other faiths as being in opposition to their own. Through its simplicity of

4. Horrell, *op. cit.*, 1958–1959, p. 279.

rituals and beliefs and its intolerance, Islam has retained its unifying strength and its dogmatic purity. It has also retarded the process of Westernization among Muslims (as compared to Hindus) in education and other secular aspects of life. One finds a much greater conservatism and traditionalism among Muslims than among Hindus, although, in such things as emancipation of women, Western influence is slowly introducing changes.

Some aspects of traditional Indian life have shown great resistance to change in South Africa. This is particularly true of cooking, family and kinship structure, and dress for adult women. Gradual change takes place nevertheless. To give only one example, neolocal residence with nuclear families tends to replace slowly the extended patrilocal household. Other important institutions of Indian life have survived only in vestigial form. The caste council (*panchayat*) has ceased to exist, and the caste system as a whole subsists, for all practical purposes, only in a tendency towards endogamy which is now anything but strict.[5]

In short, South African Indians are far from being completely Westernized as a group though they are certainly moving in that direction. Linguistically, the process is very far advanced, and many Indians can be regarded as English-speaking. Among the intellectual and professional elite, the younger generation is approaching complete acculturation to the West. But, for the masses, membership in two of the world religions has delayed cultural assimilation. The proud consciousness of belonging to a great civilization is also widespread among Indians, but I do not believe that this "cultural pride" has retarded Westernization. It has rather led to the self-conscious retention of certain outward symbols of Eastern culture, such as the wearing of saris by Hindu women, without impeding gradual acculturation in

5. For more detailed accounts of acculturation among Indians, see Hilda Kuper, *Indian People in Natal;* B. Rambiritch and P. van den Berghe, "Caste in a Natal Hindu Community"; and van den Berghe, *Caneville, The Social Structure of a South African Town.*

depth. Indeed, this "cultural pride" is most notably exhibited by intellectuals who are profoundly Westernized.

To trace the history and determine the extent of acculturation among Africans is difficult, for the process covers nearly 150 years, and encompasses many different African groups. Furthermore, the extent of Westernization covers a wide range from the almost totally Europeanized urban intellectual to the largely "tribal" peasant.[6] Unlike what happened among Indians, the first and the most important early agents of Westernization for the Africans have been the missionaries. Beginning in the first third of the nineteenth century, missionaries penetrated beyond the frontiers of White settlement, and entered into contact with the Bantu nations. Indigenous cults based on ancestor worship did not, like the Oriental religions, successfully compete with Christianity, and by the second half of the nineteenth century many Africans had become converted. Christianity also entailed exposure to the mission schools, and this early wave of conversions led, in some areas, to a sharp cleavage in rural African society between "school" and "red" people. This division is still found prominently in the Transkei.[7]

Today less than 40 per cent of the Africans are classified as "heathens," although nearly one-third of the Christians belong to a multitude of small African separatist sects, many of which have strong nativistic elements (Table XIV). These revivalistic movements are largely the result of disillusionment with the European-controlled denominations and their discriminatory practices.[8] In recent years, Christianity has become increasingly suspect to many educated Africans as a "White man's religion," and another disguised instrument of White oppression.

6. Among the best studies of African-European contact are the following: Monica Hunter, *Reaction to Conquest;* H. Kuper, *The Uniform of Colour;* Philip Mayer, *Townsmen or Tribesmen.*

7. Cf. Mayer, *op. cit.*

8. See Bengt G. M. Sundkler, *Bantu Prophets in South Africa.*

Linguistically, acculturation among Africans has been much slower than among Indians. This is due to a number of factors. First, the African languages were solidly rooted: three languages (Zulu, Xhosa, and Sotho) are spoken by over two million people each, and the first two are mutually understandable. Secondly, the mission schools (and now the government schools) used the child's mother tongue as the main medium of instruction, at least in the crucial first four years of school, beyond which the vast majority of pupils never went. Finally, many Europeans (mostly English ones) prefer to speak to their African employees in "kitchen Kaffir" (an impoverished pidgin), and resent English-speaking Africans, whom they consider "cheeky" and "spoiled." The rigid system of apartheid, by minimizing contact between White and Black, has also retarded linguistic assimilation. In spite of all these handicaps, at least half of the urban African men, a third of the urban women, and a smaller proportion of the rural Africans can express themselves in limited but fairly fluent English or Afrikaans. The 1951 census classified 29.2 per cent of the African population as able to speak a European language. Of those 7.3 per cent spoke English, 14.0 per cent Afrikaans, and 7.9 per cent both.[9] Most African men speak, in addition, several indigenous tongues, and Africans, as a group, are by far the most polyglottal group in South Africa. The completely fluent use of grammatical English is still limited to a small educated urban elite, however.

The schools for Africans which, historically, grew out of the missions, have played a leading role in assimilation. Of course, Africans have always been greatly discriminated against in education as in other aspects of South African life (Table XV and XVI). Since 1954, as a result of the counteracculturative endeavours of the government with its policy of "Bantu education," the situation has further deteriorated. Until the last few years, some 50 per cent of the African children never went to school, and those

9. Horrell, *op. cit.*, 1958–1959, p. 279.

who did rarely went beyond the lower primary standards. By now, the percentage has risen, but the quality of education (as measured, for example, by the rate of success in standardized examinations) has deteriorated. In 1958 only 3.2 per cent of all African schoolchildren were in secondary schools, compared with 22.7 per cent of White children.[10] About one African child out of four thousand finishes his secondary schooling. At the upper end of the educational pyramid, the racial discrepancy becomes greater yet. Of 33,242 students enrolled in South African universities in 1957, 29,775 (i.e., 90 per cent) were Whites (Table XVII). Approximately 1 White person per 100 was a student, compared to 1 per 400 among Indians, 1 per 2,500 among Coloureds, and 1 per 6,000 for Africans.[11] In 1953, on a *per capita* basis, the government spent sixteen times as much for White as for African school children.[12] All these handicaps notwithstanding, it was estimated that 35 per cent of the Africans over ten years of age were literate in 1958.[13] In the urban areas this figure exceeds 50 per cent, a proportion much higher than in any other part of sub-Saharan Africa with the possible exception of Western Nigeria. In spite of the fact that most of the lower primary school teaching has been done in the vernacular, the school programmes have been Western, and there is no question that the school has been a major agency of African acculturation. The tiny elite of university graduates is undoubtedly the most Westernized group of Africans.

Despite government attempts to revive the crumbling system of tribal authorities, the political structure of the "Bantu homelands" only preserves a superficial resemblance with the traditional system. The chiefs have, with some exceptions, become

10. *Ibid.*, 1959–1960, p. 214.

11. In spite of this racial discrepancy, South Africa has many more African university graduates, both absolutely and *per capita*, than most, if not all, countries of black Africa, a fact often cited by the government to "prove" how "progressive" its "Bantu education" policy is.

12. Horrell, *op. cit.*, 1959–1960, p. 210.

13. *Ibid.*, p. 240.

mere tools of the government, powerless and revocable at will, or, if they have shown any opposition, they have been promptly deposed and exiled. The most prominent of them, Chief Albert Luthuli, a Nobel Peace Prize Winner and the President of the banned African National Congress, was deposed, imprisoned, assaulted by thugs and by a prison warden, and subjected to countless other indignities. He now lives, under strict police restrictions, on his farm near Stanger, Natal, and is debarred from taking part in any political activities, from attending any gatherings, and from leaving the Stanger magisterial district except by special permission.[14] Many other less prominent chiefs have been summarily sacked for insubordination and now live in prison or exile, isolated from their people.

As under any colonial regime, powerful chiefs are "troublesome," and powerless ones are in constant danger of losing the respect of their people, of being regarded as tools of the colonial administration, and of becoming scapegoats for the people who resent the unpopular measures which the chiefs have to enforce. In either case, chiefs largely defeat the purpose for which the colonial regime intended them, namely as inexpensive go-betweens and as policy-enforcing officials. Only astute compromisers manage to walk the tightrope without becoming rebels or puppets, mostly the latter. While the empty forms of authority remain vested in chiefs, the latter have lost practically all of their former judiciary and military powers, and are disavowed by the majority of the urban population and many of the rural people.

Under the new Bantustan policy,[15] the powers and local autonomy of chiefs are being increased, to be sure; but as their tenure in office remains subject to their approval of apartheid policies, the increased powers of chiefs will probably result in further alienation from their people. Already, in the Transkei, many acts of terrorism (assassination, arson, cattle-maiming, etc.) against chiefs have taken place, and chiefs have been provided

14. See Chief Albert Luthuli's autobiography, *Let My People Go*.
15. For a treatment of it, see Chapter VI.

with "homeguards" for protection against their own subjects. "Native Law and Custom," which have been codified and administered by White officials in special courts, have in many cases been misunderstood by the government, or deliberately changed to suit White administration.

Economic forces have also played a powerful role in shattering the traditional rural structure and in exposing Africans to Western influences. As in other parts of the continent, the imposition of a capitation tax has, since the turn of the century, forced African men into the wage economy. The development of the "migratory labour system" in the mines and in other industries has been one of the most important factors of "detribalization." Operating in conjunction with the "pass system," the migratory labour system has disrupted the traditional family system by separating the men from their families for most of the year. The surplus of men in relation to women in the cities has its host of consequences, from prostitution and venereal diseases, to illegitimacy, broken marriages, and alcoholism. By throwing men of many different ethnic groups into the promiscuity of labour compounds,[16] ethnic ties and loyalties are undermined, and Africans slowly gain consciousness of belonging to a large proletariat rather than to ethnic or kinship units.

The migrant worker is exposed to modern political ideas of emancipation, comes into constant contact with the permanently urbanized African whose behaviour he often tries to emulate as more "civilized," and spreads Western influence into the rural areas when he returns home.[17] New economic needs are created

16. Some employers of African labour, notably some of the mining companies, have tried to segregate their workers by ethnic group, and others (e.g., the Natal sugar industry) have recruited their labour predominantly from a single ethnic area. The residential and educational segregation of Africans by linguistic groups, even in the urban areas, is a major aspect of the government's policy of apartheid. This is presumably done in an endeavour to divide the African population, to revive ethnic particularism, and to stem the growth of African nationalism.

17. As Philip Mayer has documented for the "red" Xhosa, some migrant workers are culturally conservative and resist Westernization, however.

which can only be satisfied by staying in a wage economy. Rural destitution and whatever few attractions city life may have for Africans make for a continuous urban influx. All attempts by the government to control and restrict this process of urbanization by mass arrests and deportations have been in vain. Large industrial centres like Durban, Cape Town, Port Elizabeth, and the Rand cities are cultural melting pots where the traditional way of life is gradually changed, and from where Western values and artifacts penetrate into the remotest parts of the interior.

The extent of Westernization among Africans is impossible to assess precisely, but a few generalizations can be advanced. There is no African group in South Africa that has not been profoundly affected by its contact with the West, in many cases for as long as a century or more. All African areas are closely dependent on the "White" part of the country, not only for their acquired needs for manufactured products, but also for their sheer subsistence. Few if any of the Native Reserves can feed themselves.[18] Two important (not to mention several smaller) pockets of cultural conservatism remain, however, in the Transkei and in Zululand, where a part of the peasant population has shown considerable resilience to Westernization. Most other Native Reserves are inhabited by a largely "detribalized" but only partly Westernized population. These peasants have become an impoverished rural proletariat, living well below the minimum level of requirements for health. The same applies to the third of the African population living as agricultural labourers and squatters on White-owned farms, except that the process of acculturation is somewhat more advanced there, and that, if their employer is humane, such Africans are better protected against starvation (though often at the cost of quasi-serfdom and debt peonage).

18. In 1953–1954, for example, approximately one-half of the food consumed by Africans on Reserves had to be purchased from outside at a cost of £25,000,000. Cf. F. P. Spooner, *South African Predicament*, p. 222.

The extent of acculturation among the some 32 per cent of urban Africans varies according to economic level, education, and length of urban residence. An increasing proportion of townsmen are born and raised in cities, and have few if any ties with the rural hinterland, but even these Africans are not completely westernized. While many of these townsmen are literate, speak a European language, are Christians, dress in Western clothes, and have adopted many tastes as well as the material culture of the Whites, they continue to speak their mother tongue, and to retain a number of African values and traditions, such as marriage by bride-wealth (*lobola*). Indeed, even the most highly educated Africans are deprived by the colour-bar from social contact with the Whites, and are forced to live in segregated Black areas. This forced segregation certainly hinders complete acculturation, in spite of a strong desire for cultural assimilation among many members of the African elite. Contrary to most Indians, most of the emerging African intelligentsia and clerical class exhibit a sentiment of "cultural shame" towards traditional rural life, which they consider primitive and backward. At the same time, economic, legal, and social barriers render full participation in the dominant Western society impossible.

In Chapter Nine I shall come back to the various reactions which the contact between different cultures have brought about, and to the conflicts engendered by this combination of Westernization and racial discrimination. Here I merely sketched in its broadest lines the "cultural map" of South Africa to show that, while culture overlaps with other aspects of the social structure, notably with "race," the overlap is far from complete. The phenomena of culture and culture contact must be clearly distinguished, both analytically and empirically, from the other elements of South African society.

In short, a number of cultures originating on three different continents met in South Africa. The net result of this extremely complex process of culture contact has been the gradual Westernization of all non-European groups. Of course, the influence has not been entirely one way. The South African variants of European culture bear some traces of Indian and African influences in the language, in cooking, etc., and traditional European values have been profoundly modified by the Whites in response to their privileged position. Colour prejudice and discrimination have hindered Westernization, and there have emerged counteracculturative movements such as the African separatist churches of the "Zionist" type, the prophetic movement of the Xhosas in 1857, and the Zulu Poll-Tax Rebellion of 1906. Though acculturation has taken place differently, and at varying rates depending on the period, the region, and the particular groups in presence, the overall trend in South Africa is towards a predominantly Western society, and a gradual cultural absorption of the remaining pockets of African traditionalism.[19]

We turn now to the second important aspect of the social structure of the country, namely social stratification and segmentation. It is not surprising that as heterogeneous a country as South Africa should have an extremely complex stratification, and that, in addition, it should be segmented in ways that cut across the social hierarchy. For broad descriptive purposes, the South African system of stratification can be described in terms of caste and class, as Warner, Dollard, Myrdal, and other authors dealing with the United States have done.[20] It is not my intention here to reopen the debate on the use of the term "caste" in a racial context, for the discussion is largely one of definition.[21] I shall therefore adopt a minimum definition of "caste" as an endogamous group, hierarchically ranked in relation to other groups, and wherein membership is determined by birth and for life.

19. In this respect, South Africa is qualitatively as well as quantitatively different from all the rest of the continent, where European cultural influence has been less profound, though obviously far from negligible.

20. See Gunnar Myrdal, *An American Dilemma;* John Dollard, *Caste and Class in a Southern Town;* Allison W. Davies, B. B. Gardner and M. R. Gardner, *Deep South.*

21. Oliver C. Cox is one of the prominent opponents of the use of the term "caste" in the racial context. See his *Caste, Class and Race.*

To avoid equivocation with Hindu caste, I shall speak, where necessary, of "colour-castes" or "racial castes."

In most general terms, South African society consists of four racial castes, and each of those is subdivided according to the usual criteria of a Western class system. Such a description is only approximative, however, insofar as many other lines of cleavage, some hierarchical, others not, further subdivide the population. Let us begin, nevertheless, with the most important criterion of status in South Africa, namely "race." Although race gives rise to an extremely rigid division into four easily recognized colour-castes, its social definition is oddly vague. There exist numerous legal definitions of "race," adopting differing combinations of physical appearance, ancestry, association with other people, and even "reputation"; (e.g., the testimony of witnesses can be accepted as evidence concerning one's racial membership). Unlike statutes in the southern United States which gave precise definitions of Negroes as any persons having more than a specified percentage of African "blood" (1/16th, 1/32d, etc.), no such precision exists in South Africa. This lack of formal precision about the most basic single principle on which society is organized is only one of the many paradoxes of South Africa.

In practice, however, there is relatively little confusion as to who belongs to which group, except in the Cape, where a long history of miscegenation allows many light-skinned Coloureds to "play White," and where many "Whites" have "a touch of the tar brush." A number of lighter-skinned Africans can also successfully pass for Coloured, but, in the large majority of cases, physical appearance is a reliable indicator of race. The four racial groups satisfy the minimum definition of "caste" given above. They are hierarchized, almost entirely endogamous, and mobility between groups is, with a few exceptions, impossible. Let us examine each of these three characteristics in turn.

The Whites or Europeans numbering 19.4 per cent of the total population are clearly at the top of the hierarchy (Tables I and II). Not only do they enjoy a much higher standard of living, education, and health than the vast majority of the non-Whites, but they virtually monopolize all the occupations above the level of semiskilled workers; they are, for all practical purposes, the only group to have political rights, and they enjoy countless other legal and customary privileges (Tables XV, XXII, XXIII, XXIV, XXVII, and XXVIII). By comparison, all three non-White races occupy a much lower status, and the differences between the three non-White groups are smaller than those separating Europeans and non-Europeans. The Coloureds (9.4 per cent of the total population) are nearest to the Whites insofar as they suffer under fewer vexations and legal disabilities than the other non-Whites, but, in terms of education and income, they stand perhaps a little lower, on the average, than the Indians, who constitute 3 per cent of the population. Indians and Coloureds occupy thus a nearly equal position in the hierarchy between the Europeans and the Africans, but nearer the latter than the former (Tables XXII, XXIII, and XXVIII). The Africans, more common-ly referred to by the Whites as "Natives" or "Bantu," number 68.2 per cent of the population and constitute the broad base of the racial pyramid (Tables I and II). Their standards of living, occupational status, and education are the lowest, and they are the target of most discrimination (Tables XXII, XXIII, and XXVIII). The three lowest colour-castes are often referred to col-lectively as "non-Whites" or "non-Europeans" to mark the gulf that separates them from the Whites, so that it might be more appropriate to speak of two colour-castes, the lower one sub-divided into three subcastes. For purposes of simplicity, how-ever, I shall speak of four castes.

Not only is the socio-economic gap between Whites and non-Whites wide and unbreachable, but, in some respects, the racial differential has increased until the mid-fifties, largely as a result of political restrictions. In spite of a tendency towards equal-ization of wages in developing economies, Africans then got a diminishing share of the National Income (less than 20 per cent), and were worse off in terms of purchasing power than before the

War (Tables XXII and XXIII). Educational statistics indicate that Africans are progressing proportionately faster than Whites (Table XV), but, since the passage of the Bantu Education Act, the quality of African schooling is steadily decreasing.

Endogamy, the second essential characteristic of caste, is likewise found in the four racial groups in South Africa.[22] Since 1949 marriage between Whites and all non-Whites is forbidden under the Prohibition of Mixed Marriages Act. There is thus complete compulsory endogamy between these two groups. Even miscegenation outside marriage is a criminal offense under the Immorality Act of 1927 as amended in 1950 and 1957. Marriages between Indians, Coloured, and Africans are legally permitted, but actually rare. The same was true of White-non-White marriages before they were forbidden. In 1946, for example, only 1 European out of 714 married outside his racial group. The corresponding figures for Coloureds, Indians, and Africans were 1 in 20, 1 in 31, and 1 in 67 respectively. Of the total number of registered marriages in 1946, only 1.38 per cent were racially exogamous.[23] Among the Europeans, there exists now, contrary to the tolerant attitude in the old Cape, a strong taboo against miscegenation, and even more so against intermarriage. In the other groups, the racial taboo is not as strong as among Whites, but other factors such as religion, language, and education level effectively hinder exogamy.

The four racial groups in South Africa also satisfy the minimum definition of caste, in that membership in them is ascribed at birth, and mobility is practically non-existent, except through surreptitious passing. The offspring of racially exogamous unions is defined at birth as Coloured, regardless of the parent groups. In fact, a number of light-skinned Coloureds manage to be accepted as Whites, and brown-skinned Africans as Coloureds. A number of first-generation Coloureds also become assimilated

22. For a more detailed study of mixed marriages and miscegenation see my article: "Miscegenation in South Africa."
23. *Ibid.*

in the African group. The extent of passing is, of course, impossible to determine accurately or even approximately, but, while passing has probably become increasingly rare during the last decade, the racial groups today are certainly anything but "pure" after three hundred years of miscegenation. Since the genetic situation remained relatively fluid until at least the first third of the nineteenth century, one can safety estimate that anywhere from one-tenth to one-quarter of the persons classified as "White" in the Cape Province are of mixed descent, and that almost every "old family" in White Cape society has genealogical connections with Coloured families. The passage of the Population Registration Act in 1950, however, intends to eliminate passing, and to make the four castes absolutely rigid. Indeed, the Act provides for the issue of identity cards where the race of the person will be indicated. Special boards are entrusted with the task of deciding once and for all the racial membership of marginal persons who contest their classification. While the task of these boards is still far from completed,[24] mobility between the colour-castes has become virtually impossible.

Besides the properties of the racial castes already mentioned, membership in a given "race" entails many other crucial consequences. We shall come back to various aspects of colour discrimination later, but, here, we must at least enumerate the main social correlates of skin colour in South Africa. To be White entails full humanity and citizenship plus a number of special privileges restricted to the master race. All Europeans over eighteen years of age (except convicted criminals) have the franchise at all levels of government. White workers are protected from non-White competition, insofar as they detain a virtual monopoly of skilled manual jobs, as well as of higher clerical, managerial, civil service, and professional posts, at rates of pay from *five* to *fifteen* times those of unskilled non-White jobs. They have the right to organize in trade unions, to go on strike, to

24. Some 21,000 borderline Coloureds have yet to be classified, according to a *Time* report of May 24, 1963.

bear arms, to own land in freehold in most of the country (except in the Native Reserves and in the few areas declared for occupation of Indians and Coloureds), to move freely in the entire country (except in certain African areas where they need permits), to change freely their place of residence, to buy and consume alcoholic beverages,[25] to stand for elective office, etc.

Technically, of course, the Europeans are subject to racial segregation, as are the non-Europeans, and a White person may not use facilities reserved for non-Whites, or live in non-White areas. In practice, such restrictions are only irksome to a small minority of liberal Whites who reject segregation in principle, and who resent the possession of racial privileges. For the vast majority of Europeans, these "restrictions" are, in fact, advantages, since the Whites monopolize the lion's share of existing facilities and resources, in terms of both quantity and quality. Whites own and occupy, for example, 87 per cent of the country's land. In many cases, a given amenity (e.g., park bench, swimming bath, golf course, cinema, etc.) is *only* available for Whites in a given community.

To be non-White means being deprived of most or all of the above advantages, and being treated as a helot and an unwelcome intruder in one's own country. Non-Whites are not only segregated, but almost invariably given inferior service and facilities, or no facilities at all, in practically every sphere of life, except in most shops (which have become sensitive to the threat of non-White economic boycotts). Racial segregation is the rule in restaurants, hotels, cinemas, hospitals, schools, waiting rooms, park benches, beaches, cemeteries, residential areas, ambulances, taxis, trains, buses, picnic areas, airports, entrances to public buildings, swimming baths, sport grounds, post offices, lifts, banks, toilets, bars, national parks, and many other places. Non-White servants accompanying their masters are, however, tolerated in many of these places, provided their servile condition is

25. Since 1962 this right has been extended to Africans.

unambiguous. Some of that segregation is "customary" (i.e., imposed by traditional White prejudices), while some is compulsory under law. To avoid any ambiguity as to whether segregated amenities must be equal in their physical plant, a special law, the Reservation of Separate Amenities Act, was passed in 1953, stating that facilities may not only be separate but also *unequal.*

All non-Whites (except foreign diplomats and the Japanese, who, for reasons of international trade, have recently been declared to be "White") are subject to the daily humiliations of segregation. No non-European may bear arms in the defence forces, stand as a candidate for Parliament, or live anywhere but in specially set-aside "Group Areas." Beyond these restrictions, there are differences between Africans, Indians, and Coloureds in the number and extent of disabilities and vexations. Africans are by far the most oppressed, and the Coloureds are the least underprivileged of the non-Whites, although their condition is rapidly deteriorating.

The Coloureds in the Cape Province still have a vestigial, though meaningless, franchise on a separate roll electing special White representatives to Parliament, whereas the Africans and the Indians have no franchise rights in the election of national, provincial, or municipal representatives.[26] The Coloureds still retain an increasingly precarious foothold in some skilled trades from which Africans and Indians are excluded. Unlike Africans who have to carry a "reference book" limiting their spacial mobility, and unlike Indians who are forbidden to enter or to stop in certain areas of the country (such as the Transkei and the Orange Free State), the Coloureds are relatively free to travel in South Africa. Coloureds have always had access to liquor, from which Africans, and to a lesser degree Indians, have been debarred by law until 1962. Where there is segregation between the non-White groups, as in schools, the amenities for Coloureds and

26. Since the establishment of the first Bantustan in the Transkei, Africans living in that area may elect a minority of the members of the Transkeian Assembly. See Chapter VI.

Indians are generally better than for Africans, though considerably inferior to the White facilities. Coloureds and Indians still have a limited right to strike which is completely denied to Africans. Similarly, Coloureds and Indians have a right to own land in freehold in certain small areas legally set aside for their occupation. Africans, on the other hand, with a few insignificant exceptions, may possess land nowhere in their own country. Land tenure in practically all Native Reserves is communal, not personal; in practice this means that the right to use and occupy land can be granted and revoked at the whim of government-appointed chiefs.

As can be seen from the above, the Africans bear the brunt of White oppression in South Africa. Well-to-do Indians and Coloureds can isolate themselves to a degree from much unpleasant contact with Whites, and from daily humiliation from the officialdom. Africans, on the other hand, are constantly exposed to police intimidation, imprisonment for purely technical offenses under the liquor or pass regulations, arbitrary deportation and countless other indignities.

Although "race" is by far the most important criterion of status in South Africa, it is not the sole relevant factor in the system of social stratification, for each racial group is internally subdivided. We shall take in turn the Whites, Coloureds, Indians, and Africans. The Whites are first segmented into three distinct subgroups along linguistic and religious lines, namely the Afrikaners, the "English-speaking South Africans," and the Jews, not to mention much smaller groups such as the Germans. These divisions are not directly hierarchical but they are related to social status and to political and economic power.

The Afrikaners (formerly known as the Dutch or the Boers) are the Whites who speak Afrikaans. The vast majority of them also belong to one of the Dutch Reformed Churches. Afrikaans-speaking Coloureds are, of course, excluded from the *Volk*. Afrikaners number approximately 57 per cent of the Whites, and, under a practically all-White franchise, they have played a predominant role in the politics of the country. Since 1948 they hold a virtual monopoly of political power through the Nationalist Party which represents the vast majority of them. In terms of education and economic status, however, they still lag behind the other Whites, on the average, although these differences tend to disappear. Among Johannesburg Whites in 1952, for example, only 1.5 per cent of the Afrikaners compared to 10 per cent of the English families earned more than £ 1000 a year.[27] In Durban in 1951 the mean *per capita* income was £ 299 a year for English-speaking Whites and £ 187 for Afrikaans-speaking Whites[28]

The Afrikaners are less urbanized than the English and the Jews, and their representation in big business, mining, and banking is still small compared with that of the English Whites. In 1949 it was estimated that Afrikaners were in control of 6 per cent of South African industry and 25 to 30 per cent of commerce. However, the number of Afrikaner-owned firms increased from 2428 to 9585 between 1939 and 1949, and Afrikaner gains have continued since.[29] Yet, in the mid-fifties, Afrikaner capital in all branches of mining controlled only 1 per cent of total production.[30] The "poor Whites," who continued to be numerous until the depression of the 1930's, were practically all Afrikaners, but through government subsidies and the so-called "civilized labour policy," "poor Whites" have disappeared as a class.[31] In spite of this, Afrikaners are more heavily represented than the English or the Jews in the lower White echelons of the occupational, income, and educational scale. In the medical and legal professions, however, the Afrikaners are rapidly increasing. The vast majority of civil service posts reserved for Whites are held by

27. Stanley Trapido, "Political Institutions and Afrikaner Social Structures in the Republic of South Africa."
28. Heinz Hartmann, *Enterprise and Politics in South Africa*, p. 64.
29. Sheila Patterson, *The Last Trek*, p. 163.
30. Leo Kuper *et al.*, *Durban, A Study in Racial Ecology*, p. 89.
31. Of course, improved economic conditions in the late 1930's and during the Second World War also contributed to the disappearance of "poor Whites."

Afrikaners, at all levels of administration. The 1957 civil service recruitment figures show that of 100 White entrants at the professional level, 81 were Afrikaners; at the clerical level, 89 per cent of the new recruits were Afrikaans-speaking.[32]

The term "English-speaking South African" is doubly ambiguous, insofar as it is not only a linguistic label, but also a racial and a religious one. English-speaking non-Whites are not included in this category, since, in the eyes of most Whites, they are not citizens of the country. This label sometimes also implies membership in, or allegiance to, one of the Christian denominations. While most Jews are linguistically assimilated to the English Whites, they generally consider themselves, and are considered by the Christians, as constituting a separate group. Altogether, some 39 per cent of the Whites speak English at home. The English and the Jews share many socio-economic characteristics, as opposed to the Afrikaners. Both groups are predominantly urban, the Jews almost exclusively so, detain a virtual monopoly of large commercial, mining, and financial concerns, and are practically excluded from political power and the civil service, except in the Natal Provincial Administration and in the large municipalities of the Transvaal and the Eastern Cape. Compared with the Afrikaners, the other two White groups are wealthier and more highly educated. This is even truer of the Jews than of the English. Politically, the majority of the English support the United Party, but in recent years the English upper class and many Jews have turned to the less conservative Progressive Party.

The three main White subgroups cannot be called "castes," as the divisions between them are not rigid. Intermarriages are fairly common; many persons of Afrikaner origin have become Anglicized; and conversely a few originally English families are Afrikanerized. The 1951 Census classifies 73 per cent of the Whites as bilingual, though only 2 per cent habitually speak both

32. Hartmann, *op. cit.*, p. 62.

European languages at home.[33] The main importance of the linguistic cleavage within the White caste is in the field of politics, as we shall see later.

The three White groups cannot be ranked hierarchically. While many Afrikaners have traditionally had a cultural inferiority complex *vis-à-vis* the English,[34] and while they are on the whole of a lower socio-economic status than the English and the Jews, the social class system cuts across linguistic and religious distinctions, and must be analysed independently. We shall presently turn to this task. In general, the White class system resembles that of the United States, Canada, or Australia, except for the virtual absence of a lower class. The class of impoverished farmers and unskilled labourers known as "poor Whites," which numbered up to one-sixth of the European population in the depression of the 1930's, has almost disappeared. White artisans enjoy a legally protected position and a relatively high standard of living, and lack any consciousness of belonging to a proletariat opposed to the White bourgeoisie, or having any common interests with the non-White proletariat. To speak of class alignments in the Marxian sense of relationship to the means of production does not correspond to social reality in South Africa. This absence of a White proletarian class consciousness accounts for the weakness of the South African labour movement. The latter has always been tainted by racialism in South Africa, and has always defined its function as that of protecting the White manual worker against non-White competition.

There is no clear-cut distinction between European artisans, smaller farmers, and petty civil servants or white-collar workers. Together they constitute what could be called a petty bourgeoisie or a lower middle class. Many White industrial workers come from a rural background, as a number of small farmers have been forced away from marginal land into the urban economy. This bottom stratum of White society has, in general, primary and

33. Horrell, *op. cit.*, 1958–1959, p. 279.
34. See for example: Patterson, *op. cit.*

some secondary or technical education, and an income of £40 to £80 a month; it lives in modest but comfortable houses, owns a small motorcar, and employs one or two non-White servants. Politically, members of that stratum are as conservative as other Whites, if not more so, and they distinguish themselves from the upper bourgeoisie mostly through lower income and education, and through taste and life-style differences which these imply. Rather than constituting a well-defined, corporate class in the Marxian sense, they are an amorphous stratum of individuals sharing roughly the same socio-economic status in the sense of Warner's "lower middle class."

The White upper bourgeoisie is similarly ill-defined. It consists of persons having at least secondary education, and occupying the higher echelons of the occupational scale. It includes as disparate groups as higher civil servants, managers, large farmers, small businessmen, and professionals. Its style of life is more luxurious than that of the petty bourgeoisie. Homes and motorcars are larger, newer, and more elegant, and the number of non-White servants often reaches three or four. Tastes in reading and entertainment become more "refined."

At the apex of White society, one finds small groups wielding considerable power. Like in many other "new" societies, there is no entrenched aristocracy in South Africa, but rather a number of distinct and conflicting elites or oligarchies competing for power. Of these, the most important are the big-business and the political groups. The relation between these two antagonistic groups will be examined later. The military is not a distinct power group in South Africa. The White intelligentsia is small, geographically scattered in the various universities and large urban centres, internally divided along political lines, largely excluded from direct participation in power, but nevertheless influential in certain spheres. Needless to say, these various White elites, while sharing a high socio-economic status, differ widely in their tastes and modes of life, and do not, in any sense, constitute a unitary upper class.

In short, we see that the White class system is relatively fluid and open. The fact that South Africa is a fairly "young" country may account, in part, for this fluidity, but the colour situation has also played an important role. South African Whites view themselves, first and foremost, as members of the dominant racial group. Internal class differences become secondary, and the gulf that separates Europeans from non-Europeans serves to minimize class consciousness and the perception of objective class differences within the dominant White caste. As a corollary of the rigid system of racial castes, there exists among Europeans what might be termed "*Herrenvolk* egalitarianism." Not only does colour-consciousness create bonds of solidarity between all Whites regardless of class, but it also prevents the establishment of class ties *across* racial barriers. Colour overshadows and weakens class and class consciousness.

The Coloured group is stratified along lines similar to the Whites, but at a much lower socio-economic level. The Muslim Malays are slightly better off than the other Coloureds, but, because of their greater conservatism, they are less well represented in the professions. Whereas the lower class is almost non-existent among the Whites, the vast majority of the Coloureds constitute an impoverished proletariat of agricultural workers, domestic servants, and unskilled or semiskilled factory workers. Above this lower class, one finds a much smaller but sizeable lower middle class of artisans and petty clerks, and a tiny upper middle class of small businessmen and professionals, mostly schoolteachers. In economic terms, this Coloured elite lives at about the same level as the White petty bourgeoisie, because Coloureds earn much less than equally qualified Whites doing the same work.

The Coloured stratification system is, however, qualitatively different from the White system in one important respect. Of the four racial groups, the Coloured group is the only one to be internally differentiated on the basis of physical traits. All other things being equal, the more closely a Coloured resembles a

White person in skin colour, hair texture, and facial features, the higher his status is. Coloureds are, on the average, at least as colour-conscious as the majority of the Europeans. In recent years socio-economic criteria have become more important than physical traits in determining status within the Coloured group, but appearance still plays an important role among older and uneducated people.[35] Educated Coloureds, for the most part, react strongly against status differences based on physical characteristics, and against the approval of concubinage with Whites among some members of the Coloured lower class as a method of "improving" the race. In practice, the two sets of status criteria are difficult to dissociate, because there is still a fairly high correlation between physical traits and various indices of socio-economic status within the Coloured group.

Racial consciousness among Coloureds has also entailed other consequences. As an intermediate caste, the Coloureds have traditionally been caught between their feelings of racial superiority *vis-à-vis* the Africans, and their constantly frustrated hope of acceptance by the Whites. This has led to ambivalent attitudes towards the Whites, to political passivity, and to a failure to identify with the Africans. The mass of the Coloured proletariat has, like the White manual workers, refused to identify with the African proletariat, which it views with feelings of superiority and hostility. We shall return to this marginal position of the Coloureds in the political context.

Of the four racial groups, the Indians are by far the most complexly stratified and segmented. They are first divided along religious and linguistic lines which are not hierarchical, but which are correlated with socio-economic status. The most profound rift is between Muslims and Hindus. Religious intermarriage is extremely rare, and social intercourse is limited largely to the fields of employment, education, and politics. The few Christians,

---

35. On this subject, see: W. van der Merve, "Stratification in a Cape Coloured Community," and van den Berghe, "Some Trends in Unpublished Social Science Research in South Africa."

who are almost all converts from Hinduism, interact rather freely with Hindus. Although there are some poor Muslims and a few rich Hindus, the Muslims are, on the average, considerably better off than the Hindus, and are overrepresented in the merchant class.

Each of the Indian religious groups is subdivided along linguistic lines. The Muslims are either Gujarati or Urdu, and the Hindus are divided among the Tamil, Hindi, Telugu, and Gujarati. The language groups are not as widely apart as the religious communities, but except between Tamil and Telugu, intermarriage is rare. The Gujarati, whether Muslim or Hindu, belong almost all to the merchant class, and constitute the conservative economic elite among Indians. Among Hindus there are profound cultural differences between the northern Indian groups (Hindi and Gujarati) and the southern groups (Tamil and Telugu). Each of the Hindu linguistic entities is itself subdivided into hierarchized *varnas* and castes, but these traditional cleavages are quickly losing in importance. *Varna* endogamy is still largely practiced, but the rules of caste endogamy are broken with increasing frequency. In other aspects of life such as religious practices, diet, commensality, and purification rituals, the Hindu caste system has practically ceased to operate.[36]

Yet another line of cleavage among Indians is the distinction between "indentured" and "passenger." The former are the descendants of indentured labourers who came to Natal to work in the sugar-cane plantations, whereas the latter paid their own sea voyage from India and established themselves mostly as merchants and clerks. Although the distinction is losing in importance, the passengers, who are in minority, consider themselves superior on the whole to people of indentured stock. Most passenger Indians were Gujarati, and to a lesser extent Hindi

36. For more detailed description of social stratification among Indians see H. Kuper, *Indian People in Natal;* van den Berghe, *Caneville;* van den Berghe and Edna Miller, "Some Factors Affecting Social Relations in a Natal North Coast Community"; Rambiritch and van den Berghe, *op. cit.*

and Urdu. A far greater proportion of Muslims than of Hindus is of passenger origin. The passenger-indentured division is thus correlated with religion and language groups, and is clearly hierarchical. Among the younger generation the distinction has, however, lost almost all of its meaning, as has the Hindu caste system. Religious barriers remain quite strong, but linguistic divisions progressively lose their rigidity, as English slowly supplants Indian languages in all spheres of life.

Western criteria of status, such as education, income, and occupation, on the other hand, are of growing importance, and stratify the Indian group along increasingly distinct class lines. Contrary to European belief, most Indians are poor, and are either small farmers, agricultural labourers, or unskilled and semiskilled industrial workers. Above this poor working class, one finds a lower middle class of medium farmers, clerks, small shopkeepers, and skilled workers. The Indian upper middle class is divided into two distinct groups: a conservative, traditional elite of large merchants, some of whom are quite wealthy, and a Western-oriented, politically active intelligentsia consisting mostly of teachers, physicians, and lawyers. The White image of the Indian is largely based on the small merchant class which is anything but typical of the Indian community.

The African "race" is both stratified into emerging social classes and segmented into ethnic groups, but the two types of division are in an antithetical relationship to one another. In short, one can say that ethnic affiliation recedes in importance as social classes emerge from the process of Westernization. This statement is too schematic, however, and covers a more complex reality. Since practically all Africans still speak a Bantu language as their mother tongue, and retain other African cultural characteristics, they almost all belong to a so-called "tribe" in a formal sense. For most town dwellers and many rural inhabitants, this ethnic affiliation has become vague, however, and has ceased to be an important social reality. Such people are integrated into the Western economic system; they have lost all political, and even sometimes kinship, ties with traditional society; they are Christians, at least nominally so, and they live altogether outside of the traditional environment. They continue to speak their mother tongue at home, and they may preserve a sense of affiliation to their original national group, but many factors make for the rapid disappearance of "tribalism."

All urban centres are ethnic melting pots where Africans learn not only European languages, but also Bantu tongues other than their own, and common "pidgin" dialects. The disintegration of the traditional family through the migratory labour system favours interethnic unions, in the form of both marriage and concubinage. More and more Africans are thus of mixed stock. As members of Christian denominations, as neighbours in the "locations," as fellow workers in the mines or factories, Africans of various linguistic groups constantly mix with one another. Moreover, Africans are becoming increasingly conscious that they are subject to a common system of political oppression and economic exploitation. Political consciousness militates against ethnic particularism and leads people to think in terms of "we Africans."

All of these factors notwithstanding, a substantial segment of the rural population remains integrated, through kinship and local political ties, in the traditional way of life. This is particularly true of the Transkei and Zululand, the two principal remaining pockets of cultural conservatism in South Africa. These people, known among the Whites as "raw Natives" or "red-blanket Kaffirs," enter periodically into the Western economy in order to provide minimum means of subsistence to their families in the impoverished Reserves, but remain often staunchly traditional and reject Christianity, Western education, and the other "White man's ways."[37] Even in these conservative rural areas, however, a segment of the population known as the "school" people have accepted missionary influence and are in the process of acculturation.

37. Philip Mayer documents this peasant conservatism in his *Townsmen or Tribesmen.*

Traditional Southern Bantu society is unstratified in Western class terms, though there are, of course, wide differences in status between commoners and chiefs, and between various clans. Ownership of cattle, polygyny, and a numerous descendance are important status symbols in traditional rural society, which has thus its own prestige system independent of the emerging class system of urbanized and Christianized Africans. Traditional Africans are on the margin of the class system which they do not accept, and in which they do not participate. At the same time they constitute a stratum at the bottom of the African community, insofar as status among Westernized urban people is largely a function of the degree of acculturation to the European way of life. The "raw" Africans are viewed by most educated urban Africans as backward, primitive, and ignorant pagans, or, at least, as naïve and unsophisticated countryfolk.

Among Africans at various stages of Westernization, class distinctions following Western lines are becoming increasingly sharp. Prestige is closely related with the extent to which a person has acquired European culture, and the urge towards Westernization is strong. This is not to say that urban or Christian Africans want to be "White," as many Coloureds do, but rather that they have accepted the values of Western culture. The principal criteria of status among urban Africans are education, Christianity, occupation, clothing, and moral "respectability." Wealth does not play the role that it does in the White community, because the scope for capital accumulation among Africans is stringently limited. An African may not acquire land, or open a business except in a few small areas, and discrimination debars him from practically all better-paid jobs, no matter how well qualified he is. The monotonous uniformity of municipal housing in the "Native locations" imposes a common mold and standard of living on Africans of all classes. Except in clothing and furniture, there is little scope for conspicuous consumption, and for material symbols of wealth.

The majority of Africans live on or below the minimum

standard for health, as domestic servants, mine workers, agricultural labourers, or unskilled workers in secondary and tertiary industry. Agriculture in the Native Reserves is almost invariably *sub*-subsistence, and must be supplemented by wage earnings. A small minority of petty white-collar workers live more or less precariously above the vital minimum as a *Lumpenbourgeoisie*, and an even smaller class of teachers, students, ministers, nurses, and other professionals constitutes the elite of the emerging African middle class. In 1959 there were 49 African lawyers, 67 librarians, 81 medical doctors, 73 chartered accountants, 176 laboratory assistants, and 61 analytical chemists in the entire country.[38] Even this elite lives at a material level inferior to that of all but destitute "poor Whites," in spite of the fact that many of its members have matriculated and hold university degrees. Literacy, knowledge of a European language, mostly English, membership in an established (i.e., non-"Zionist") church, and a certain standard of moral respectability are the minimum requirements for membership in the *Lumpenbourgeoisie*, and correspondingly higher requirements are necessary for membership in the tiny elite. It is largely from this last group that the political leadership of the liberatory movements is recruited.

Unlike among Indians, there is practically no African business class, partly for reasons just mentioned. The relative absence of an indigenous entrepreneur class is common to most African countries where commerce, finance, and industry have been monopolized by European and, secondarily, by Asian interests. But although the South African economy is considerably more developed than that of Ghana or Nigeria, the African entrepreneur class is even more embryonic than in these two countries. A survey of the South-Western townships of Johannesburg (the large ghetto for Africans some 12 to 20 miles from the metropolis) reveals that only some 1200 African traders serve a population of approximately 400,000. By far the greatest majority

38. Hartmann, *op. cit.*, p. 43.

of these traders are small businessmen with net assets of under £1000, such as 400 general dealers, 243 butchers, 176 fresh produce dealers, 136 eating-house keepers, 95 wood and coal dealers, etc. By far the greatest handicaps mentioned by a sample of forty-seven African merchants are lack of capital, and of police protection.[39] Rules of African hospitality (misleadingly termed "family parasitism" by Europeans), whereby a financially successful man is descended upon by numerous relatives who expect him to share his wealth, are of course another important hindrance to capital accumulation. This African system of familial social security, which had a definite function in a traditional rural milieu, thus becomes a liability in the urban environment, or at any rate in one that is dominated by a capitalist system of production.

In addition to this cultural limitation, and to crippling apartheid restrictions on the purchase of real estate, African traders are granted licences only in African areas, and draw their clientele almost exclusively from their own racial group, as the government intends that they should. Not only do their customers have limited purchasing power, but African merchants have to compete with larger European and Indian merchants, who generally undersell them through volume of trade. Lacking real estate as guarantees for loans, the raising of capital for Africans is extremely difficult, except in small sums and at usurious rates of interest. On the other hand, in order to retain customers, African traders have to extend credit beyond their financial capacity. This leads to a relatively high rate of bankruptcies, and the latter, in turn, reinforce the European stereotype that Africans constitute bad risks, and make it even more difficult to raise capital. In view of such staggering handicaps, it is a wonder that

39. Lawrence Reyburn, *African Traders*, pp. 2, 10–13. On the other hand, the government's policy of denying trade licences to persons of a race different from that of the population living in a specific "group area" has protected to some extent African traders from competition from European or Indian merchants.

any Africans at all have become successful businessmen, as indeed a few have.[40]

From the above description it can be seen that the stratification system of South Africa is far too complex to conform in detail to the American "class and caste" schema of Warner and others. The only principle which pervades the whole society is that of "race," leading to a rigid, fourfold classification imposed by the Whites, and rejected as illegitimate by the non-Whites. But each of the four colour-castes is internally subdivided and stratified according to criteria which differ from one group to the other. While there is a general tendency in all groups to develop social classes along Western lines, numerous other traditional factors continue to play an important role. Even when status is distributed according to Western class criteria, the standards of achievement are proportionally lower according to the position of the racial group in the colour-caste hierarchy. A middle-class African is, for example, not equal in status to a middle-class Coloured or White, because he belongs to a different "race" which is itself hierarchically ranked. Furthermore, the relative emphasis placed on the various criteria (such as wealth, education, and occupation) differs from one "race" to the other. Not only are the objective characteristics of class widely divergent from one racial group to another, but such class consciousness as exists is largely limited to one's racial caste. Because of the all-pervading racial barrier, each "race" constitutes at once a separate reference group in the status system and an autonomous subsystem of status with its own criteria. At the same time, the significance of "race" and the acceptance of racial criteria of status vary widely, being greatest among Whites and Coloureds, and minimal among Africans and Indians. Racial barriers are objective realities, but the vast majority of the non-Europeans are not accommodated to their lower status, and deny any legitimacy to the racial hierarchy which is ultimately maintained through the might of the White-controlled state.

40. For a more detailed treatment of the African urban middle class, see Leo Kuper, *An African Bourgeoisie*.

## CHAPTER FOUR

## *The Social Structure of Modern South Africa: Polity and Economy*

T HE political structure of South Africa reflects the country's social stratification. To date, the whole political history of South Africa has shown a progressive trend towards the complete monopolization of power in the hands of the Whites. By the 1880's the military might of the African nations had been broken; the indigenous political organization became modified to serve as a subordinate tool of White administration; and White hegemony was secure over the entire territory of present South Africa. Only since the Second World War has the growing challenge from the non-White liberatory movements begun to threaten seriously the existing system. The discussion of the power conflicts between the various ethnic and interest groups will be reserved for the next three chapters. Here we shall deal with the state apparatus as it exists since the founding of the Union of South Africa in 1910.

We have already seen that the South Africa Act of 1909 extended and entrenched the long-standing British policy of granting to the White settlers the power to manage the affairs of the country without any effective participation, or even consultation, of the majority of the population. Great Britain transferred, in effect, its prerogatives as a colonial power to the White-settler minority, giving rise to the dual nature of the South African government as "mother country" and a colonial power. The

Pretoria executive and the Cape Town Parliament constitute, in fact, a European power ruling over an internal colonial empire and a subject population.[1] The principle of White domination (or, to use the British euphemism, "civilized government") embodied in the South Africa Act was consistent with previous British policy, when the United Kingdom granted self-government to the White colonists of Natal and the Cape in the second half of the nineteenth century, and was only reversed in the late 1950's in former British Central and East Africa.

The Union (since 1961, Republic) of South Africa comprises four provinces (the Cape, Natal, the Orange Free State, and the Transvaal), and administers South West Africa since the end of the First World War, as a Mandate under the League of Nations. Since the Second World War, the international status of South West Africa is the object of a dispute between South Africa and the United Nations, but, for all practical purposes, that territory has been incorporated as a fifth province of the Republic. While the provinces enjoy a measure of autonomy in such matters as education and road construction, the provincial councils have limited powers. The sphere of autonomy of the municipalities is even more stringently restricted. While the national government is not as highly centralized as that of France, for example, one cannot speak of a federal structure. Most essential powers are vested in the central government.

As a compromise between the old Boer Republics and the old English colonies of Natal and the Cape, the three branches of central government have their seat in different towns: the executive capital is Pretoria, Parliament meets in Cape Town, and the supreme judicial authority is in Bloemfontein. The bicameral Parliament, consisting of a House of Assembly and a Senate, is modeled after the Westminster system. Until the proclamation of the Republic in 1961, and the withdrawal of South Africa from the Commonwealth, a Governor General represented the British

1. This dual nature of the South African state is lucidly analysed by Leo Marquard in *South Africa's Colonial Policy*.

Crown, but did not have any effective powers. That office has now been replaced by that of President. The Prime Minister and his cabinet are responsible to Parliament along British lines. Their maximum tenure is five years from the last parliamentary elections, but they can be voted out of office at any time by a majority vote of no confidence in Parliament.

This democratic façade is, however, devoid of reality, except, to a rapidly diminishing degree, for the Whites. Membership in Parliament is restricted to Whites under the South Africa Act of 1909, and the same rule applies to the provincial councils and practically all municipal councils, except in the Cape Province where a few Coloured representatives have held elective office, and in Stanger, Natal, where an Indian has been elected to the town council. Except in the Cape, the franchise is limited to Whites over the age of eighteen. In that province the Coloureds still have a vestigial voting right. Coloured men over twenty-one, fulfilling certain educational, property, and income requirements may elect on a separate roll four White representatives in Parliament. Except for subordinate posts, all positions in the civil service are held by Europeans, as well as all political and judiciary offices. A non-White is never in a position of authority over a White person. This applies even to the courts and administrative offices dealing exclusively with "Bantu affairs." Although the government has recently announced its intention to "Bantuize" the administration of the "Bantustans," and to promote Africans to higher positions, their authority will, however, still be limited to "their own people."

One of the cardinal principles of South African government is the removal of all non-Europeans from participation at all levels of the political process, and the relegation of "non-White affairs" to the sphere of arbitrary administration by the White authorities.[2] The non-Europeans are ruled entirely as subject peoples under laws passed by the White Parliament; these laws

2. Since 1962 the Bantustan policy represents a departure from this principle, as we shall see later.

give the executive branch of the government a wide and ever increasing range of arbitrary powers. Africans have been subjected to this colonial system ever since the European conquest in the nineteenth century. Since the establishment of Native Reserves in the 1840's, and the series of military defeats of the African nation-states in the 1860's and 1870's, White hegemony over the African population has been progressively increased and perfected. With the advent of the Nationalist government in 1948, rigid apartheid has been logically extended to the Coloureds and the Indians, who were already subject to many disabilities. Each of the subordinate races is now governed by distinct executive agencies: the Africans by the departments of Bantu Education and of Bantu Administration and Development, the Coloureds by the Department of Coloured Affairs, and the Indians by the Department of Asiatic Affairs. The various White municipal authorities also share, to a diminishing degree, in the administration of urban "Native locations," but the tendency is towards increasingly centralized control.

A parody of the African tribal system has been preserved in the rural Reserves, in that traditional institutions have been retained in modified form to suit the purposes of the White government. Local White administrators rule through the medium of appointed chiefs and headmen who are revocable and punishable at will, and who are deprived of most important powers. White functionaries administer justice in "Native Commissioner's Courts" according to a European conception of "Native Law and Custom."[3] In the urban areas White superintendents, assisted by the police, control the segregated "Native locations." Powerless "Native Advisory Boards," partly appointed, partly elected through a non-secret vote, are supposed to represent the wishes of the African population. Through this use of chiefs and headmen in rural areas, and advisory bodies in urban "locations," in industries, and in schools, the government maintains the fiction

3. This was codified in Natal, though not in the other provinces.

that Africans have a voice in their affairs and are regularly consulted. In fact, almost every aspect of the daily life of Africans, and increasingly of Coloureds and Indians, is regimented by a White administrative machinery which has at its disposal a wide range of arbitrary powers of perquisition, confiscation of property, imprisonment, expulsion from the country, and banishment to isolated areas, not to mention the extralegal but effective use of police intimidation and brutality.

Together, the departments of Bantu Education and of Bantu Administration and Development constitute a colonial state-within-the-state in that they rule over two-thirds of the population without any check from, or responsibility to, the Africans. Until 1961 three White representatives in the House of Assembly defended the interests of the Africans in Parliament, but even this last vestige of indirect participation in the political process has been abolished. Recent apartheid plans for "self-government" in the "Bantu homelands" show the government's desire to amend the existing system by creating different trappings, and giving Africans a somewhat greater degree of local autonomy, but without any effective transfer of control. A closer examination of the policy of apartheid and its antecedents will be reserved for Chapter Six.

A corollary of the principle of White supremacy is the maintenance of a monopoly of repressive force in the hands of the White group. Except under rarely granted permits, only the Whites may own and bear firearms. The sale, and even the loss through theft, of weapons and ammunition to Africans are severely punishable offences. Military service in peacetime is the exclusive prerogative of Europeans. During the two world wars, non-Whites enlisted in the South African Army, but they served in segregated, unarmed, non-combattant units. The police force has members of all racial groups, but only White policemen carry firearms. Non-White constables are always supervised by White officers, and are armed only with clubs, or occasionally with spears. African, Indian, and Coloured policemen are used mostly as auxiliaries to the White constables, in maintaining order and executing raids in their respective racial areas.

Since the abortive protest movement of 1960, the government is actively reorganizing its army and police, not so much to defend itself against possible (though unlikely) military intervention from other African states to the north, but primarily to suppress internal insurrections. Mobile commando and paratrooper units are created for the quick repression of revolts. The government even encourages the military training of the White civilian population against the non-Europeans. Pistol clubs where White women can be trained by the police to use firearms have been introduced in 1961, for example. By 1964 some 17,500 White civilians had been organized into four categories of police reserve to act as officially-sanctioned vigilantes in the event of internal uprising. The main role of the South African Police and Army is clearly the defence of White supremacy and privileges against the demands of the non-Whites.

Since the Nationalist Party victory at the polls in 1948, there has been a slow but steady deterioration of civil liberties for everybody, including the Whites, to the point where the democratic façade has become empty of meaning even for the privileged race. Successive dictatorial measures have slowly transformed South Africa into an increasingly arbitrary police state. Book and film censorship; indefinite imprisonment without trial; house searches and dawn arrests without warrant for political offences; banning of newspapers, of political parties, and of practically all forms of protest, including orderly meetings and passive resistance; declarations of states of emergencies; telephone tapping and other forms of police spying; political indoctrination in the schools; arbitrary refusal of passports; and political extradition have become the order of the day during the last few years of South African history.

In spite of a clear tendency towards totalitarianism, South Africa is not a Fascist state along the lines of Western European or Latin American right-wing dictatorships.[4] The government is oppressive and reactionary,[5] and attempts at all costs to maintain White supremacy, but the ideology of apartheid is more a brand of nineteenth-century colonial paternalism than a form of modern Fascism. In its endeavour to maintain a master-servant relationship between White and Black, and to return to the golden age of the pastoral Boer Republics, the Nationalist government is resorting increasingly to the repressive techniques of modern Fascism. These techniques are dictated, however, not by the ideology of apartheid, but by the nature of South African society. In order to maintain an antiquated colonial system characteristic of an agrarian society under urban and industrial conditions, and to crush the increasingly militant freedom movements among the non-Europeans, the government is forced to use the methods of modern totalitarianism, thereby creating a superficial resemblance between South Africa and Fascist police states. Nevertheless, South Africa distinguishes itself from Mussolini's Italy, Hitler's Germany, or Franco's Spain through a number of ideological and structural factors.

Ideologically, Fascism is based on the supremacy of the state, as represented by the party and the charismatic personality of the leader, over the individual. The ideology of Afrikanerdom and of the Nationalist Party is based on rugged frontier individualism, distrust of authority, and a sense of self-righteousness as God's Chosen People. The leader is fashioned after the image of the Biblical patriarch, and is more a traditional than a charismatic figure. The objective is not the creation of a new order, but the return to a romanticized pre-industrial past when the Afrikaners will again rule without the interference from British capitalism,

4. For an earlier statement of this argument see my article "Apartheid, Fascism and the Golden Age."

5. I am using these terms not as epithets, but in a precise sense. By "oppressive" I mean "ruling in the face of open opposition by the majority"; by "reactionary" I mean "endeavouring to re-establish past conditions."

overseas meddlers, and "cheeky Kaffirs." The ideal concept of government is one of "*Herrenvolk* egalitarianism" with only the minimum of central authority necessary to keep the Africans and the other non-Whites perpetually in the position of helots.

The racialism of Afrikaner ideology has often been compared with that of Nazism, and the rise of the Nazi-inspired Afrikaner organizations like the Ossewa-Brandwag[6] and the New Order has been pointed to in order to demonstrate the affinity between Afrikaner Nationalism and Fascism or Nazism.[7] Nazism and Afrikaner Nationalism are undoubtedly similar in their racialism and their exacerbated nationalism, but it does not follow that the movements are therefore identical. Racialism and Fascism are two distinct syndromes which were accidentally united in Nazism, but which are often dissociated. For example, Italian and Iberian Fascism are not racialist, and racialism is found prominently in the United States without any significant indication of Fascism. The English-speaking Whites in South Africa are as racialist as the Afrikaners, without either group showing ideological affinities to Fascism. The closest historical parallel to the South African political system is found in southern United States, and not in Nazi Germany.

It is also undeniable that Nazi-inspired Afrikaner movements arose in the 1930's, and that many prominent Afrikaner Nationalist politicians (including the present Minister of Justice Balthazar Vorster) openly sympathized with Nazi Germany. These facts do not allow one to jump to unwarranted conclusions, however. Afrikaner pro-German sympathies before and during the Second World War were much more the expression of anti-British than of pro-Nazi sentiments. This assertion is supported by similar shows of pro-German feelings among Afrikaners during the Boer War and the First World War, i.e., long before the rise of Nazism.

6. Literally, the "Ox-Wagon Sentinel."
7. For the history of the rise of Afrikaner Nationalist organizations, see Michael Roberts and A. E. G. Trollip, *The South African Opposition, 1939–1945.*

As to the neo-Nazi movements such as the Ossewa-Brandwag and the New Order, they failed to rally Afrikanerdom behind them. It was Malan's "purified" Nationalist Party which finally rallied Afrikanerdom after the Second World War, after having squashed the New Order and the Ossewa-Brandwag.

Besides ideological factors, important structural characteristics distinguish the South African state from modern Fascism. Fascism presupposes a strong military tradition and an influential caste of career officers, on which the charismatic leader can build up the backbone of his power. These conditions are nonexistent in South Africa, where the traditional Afrikaner form of military organization was the ill-disciplined, individualistic Boer commando, a temporary force raised *ad hoc* to fight the Africans, spontaneously formed and disbanded, and led by non-professionals chosen democratically by the Boer farmers among their own midst.[8]

Another characteristic of Fascist regimes is their attempt to gain wide popular support, or at least to create the illusion of such support, by means of political indoctrination, mass demonstrations, plebiscites, popular reforms, and other demagogic techniques. Fascist governments claim to express the will of the people, and try to unite the nation behind party slogans and policies. The latter often include revolutionary aspects that appeal to the masses, and in some cases, such as Peron's Argentina, it is even difficult to distinguish a rightist from a leftist dictatorship. Fascist regimes aim to destroy the existing order, and replace it with something different. None of the above characteristics are present in South Africa, where the government rules against the open opposition of some 90 per cent of the population, does relatively little to create the impression of wide support, deliberately divides the population into segregated groups

8. Even during both Anglo-Boer wars, the fighting forces of the Boer Republics were, with the exception of a few specialized units such as artillery troops, un-uniformed irregulars. Of the officers, only a handful were professional soldiers.

instead of uniting it behind a charismatic leader, and aims at maintaining the old colonial order. In domestic politics, if not in international forums, the South African regime shows its contempt for the aspirations of the non-Europeans masses by ignoring protests and denying legitimacy to popular leaders.

A certain amount of halfhearted and ineffective indoctrination of apartheid takes place in government-controlled schools, and through the medium of the state-controlled South African Broadcasting Corporation, and of official periodicals, such as *Bantu*. The Nationalists also claim, rather perfunctorily, that Africans support apartheid, except for a few misguided people swayed or terrorized by Communist or "Liberalist" agitators, outside meddlers, misguided clerics, and the English press. The authorities even quote puppet chiefs as "proof" of African support. Overseas, the State Information Office also engages in propaganda activities, but the latter are directed mostly at attracting tourists, by stressing how colourful the rhinos and the "Natives" are, and foreign capital, by pointing to the good investment climate, low wages, and other benefits favouring capitalists.[9] In recent years magazines like *South African Scope* also try to convince overseas readers that apartheid is a boon to the "Bantu," and that the Bantustans are but one step removed from independence; but the propaganda efforts of the South African government along the lines of political ideology are both clumsy and limited in scope.

All but the blindest of government officials are well aware of the overwhelming non-White opposition, and the government does not even resort to such old tricks as trumped-up plebiscites to salvage the fiction of popular support. Rather, the govern-

9. That propaganda contains patent lies; thus, *South African Scope* (April, 1964) states that, in December, 1963, there were "only 15,000 people out of work" in the country. A 1962 study of unemployment among the some 230,000 Indians living in Durban estimated those out of work and seeking work at over 15,100 in that population alone (i.e., in some 2 per cent of the total population). Cf. Margo Russell and I. K. Allan, *Unemployment Among Indians in Durban, 1962,* p. 5, Table 2.

ment's attitude is that non-White opinion is to be entirely ignored, and that, under no circumstances, should popular pressure be allowed to influence policy, as this would be interpreted as a sign of weakness. So entrenched is the tradition of ignoring non-White opinion that the government accepts with equanimity the statement of grievances, provided this is done with the proper subservience and through official channels. The subordination of non-Europeans is held to be of far greater consequence than their consent.

The Transkeian election of November, 1963, is interesting in this respect. For the first time the Xhosa of the Transkei were allowed to exercise the right of universal adult suffrage. The election was not a trumped-up plebiscite, since its results clearly indicated popular opposition to apartheid. The Transkeian constitution is such, however, that the "self-government" of the "Bantu-stan" consists of pro-apartheid chiefs, against whom the vast majority of the people voted. Thus the Transkeian election seems to be an extension of the grievance-stating machinery. A carefully controlled mechanism is set up whereby Africans are allowed to express discontent, but, after they have done so, their wishes are brushed aside, as being the product of agitation. Presumably, the government assumes that Africans will be satisfied to cast ballots, irrespective of whether they can thereby influence policy.

South Africa also distinguishes itself from Fascist regimes through the strength of its legal tradition and the survival of a measure of judiciary process. To be sure, the peculiarly South African heritage of judicial equity and autonomy, derived both from Roman-Dutch Law and English Common Law, is being gradually eroded and undermined through political appointments of judges, and the passage of legislation which conflicts with Western standards of justice. But the South African Nationalist regime never swept the legal system aside, as it had the power to do. There results the paradox that, in a state where the racialist legislation could hardly be any more far-reaching, a measure of fairness can still be expected in the courts. Policemen are sometimes still punished (although very mildly) for murder and brutality;[10] as late as 1961 political opponents were occasionally still tried for treason and acquitted;[11] and racial legislation can still be fought (with diminishing effectiveness) in court, as was the case during the long but unsuccessful legal battle to prevent the disenfranchisement of the Coloureds in the 1950's.

In short, while there exists an unquestionable trend towards dictatorship in South Africa, that evolution has been comparatively slow because of the inhibitory factors just mentioned. The last remnants of the rule of law are being eliminated, but the agony of conventional legal justice has been long-drawn. This is what the government means when it refers to its restraint in the use of force.

The government is reactionary, oppressive, and racialistic like few in the world, but it is not Fascist in its ideology or its structure. The totalitarian measures developed in recent years are not the result of a deliberate plan, for, in that case, they could have been made much more effective, and have been implemented much faster and more drastically. They are, rather, *ad hoc* measures passed in reaction to waves of popular protest, and intended to suppress the non-White liberatory movements. The White opposition and the English press have, so far, been left practically

10. E.g., in 1960 a police sergeant, N. J. J. Arlow, convicted of torturing and murdering African prisoners, was given a three-year gaol sentence, and was released in 1961 after serving fifteen months in prison.

11. In December, 1956, 156 opponents of apartheid were arrested on charges of treason. After a preparatory examination, 91 of them were brought to trial. The case lasted until March, 1961, when all were acquitted; the accused were tried mostly under English Common Law rather than under such draconian South African laws as the Public Safety Act or the Suppression of Communism Act. While the government failed to obtain convictions, it did succeed, however, in rendering many key persons almost as politically impotent as if they had been convicted. The case was, nevertheless, regarded as a fiasco for the prosecution and a victory for the defence. The 1963 and 1964 treason and sabotage trials are of a very different nature, since the accusations are now based on dictatorial pieces of legislation.

undisturbed, partly because they do not constitute a serious threat to the Afrikaner Nationalists, but also because they are White.[12] Similarly the parliamentary and electoral process has not been tampered with, except within the legally permissible rules of the game, in a similar way as previous governments have done. It is true that the White opposition has no chance of unseating the government by constitutional means, but the parliamentary façade could have been swept aside altogether.

Another line of evidence in favour of my thesis concerning the discrepancy between the means and the ends of apartheid can be found in an examination of legislation. Nationalist laws fall into two discernible categories. On the one hand, such acts as the Population Registration Act, the Prohibition of Mixed Marriages Act, the Group Areas Act, the Bantu Education Act, the Extension of University Education Act, and the Promotion of Bantu Self-Government Act all fall into an internally consistent, long premeditated, and undeviating pattern, namely the steadfast implementation of the ends of apartheid. On the other hand, laws like the Public Safety Act, the Suppression of Communism Act, the Criminal Law Amendment Act, the Riotous Assemblies Act, the Unlawful Organizations Act, the "Sabotage" Act of 1962, and the "No Trial" Act of 1963 share the character of improvised, *ad hoc,* repressive measures, hurriedly passed during, or just after, crises, to give the police powers to crush opposition. These purely instrumental laws do not fall into the coherent,

12. There have been numerous threats of censorship against the English daily press by Nationalist politicians, but these threats have not yet materialized. Under growing unrest and pressures, censorship of English dailies may well become a reality. On April 27, 1964, Verwoerd ominously declared that opposition newspapers approached "the border of treason" (*The Times,* London, April 28, 1964). So far, the English press has met these threats by "voluntary censorship." E.g., after the Sharpeville shootings of 1960, most papers refrained from publishing the photographs of the victims. Now that the African struggle for freedom has entered the violent stage, the government's tolerance of the White opposition has notably decreased, and it is an open question whether the self-censorship of the English press will keep pace with governmental demands for "White unity."

logical master plan of the apartheid laws proper. Rather, these laws, which fall more within the Fascist pattern, are hastily drafted, expedient responses to unforeseen contingencies. Interestingly, these laws are usually quite colour-blind in their provisions and apply indiscriminately to all, unlike the apartheid laws proper, which all contain specifically racial clauses.

The Afrikaner Nationalist government continues in the tradition of previous White South African governments. It is simply more thorough and more consistent in its attempt to restore the golden age of the Boer Republics and to entrench White supremacy. The South African state still preserves its dual character of a democracy for the *Herrenvolk* and a racialist colonial regime for the non-Whites. The increasing powers that the Afrikaner Nationalist government has arrogated itself have, so far, only been used against those Whites who have collaborated with Africans and Indians in the liberatory movements; the official opposition is willing to give sweeping powers to the government in order to keep control over Africans, and with the tacit understanding that the United Party will not itself become a victim of tyranny.

We must now turn to the last major aspect of the social structure of South Africa, namely the economy. The general trend of the economy has been towards increasing diversification and rapid industrial expansion. Whereas South Africa remained almost exclusively a pastoral and agricultural country until the latter part of the nineteenth century, it is today a relatively highly urbanized and industrialized nation. Of all the African countries, South Africa is by far the most economically developed: its Gross National Product accounts for 24 per cent of the total for the continent, while its population makes up about 6 per cent. With its per capita income of £152.5, South Africa stands out among African states, being twice to thrice as well off as Ghana, Gabon, the Ivory Coast, the former Central African Federation, and Senegal; five times as well off as the Congo (Léopoldville), Nigeria, Kenya, and the Sudan; and eight to ten times as well

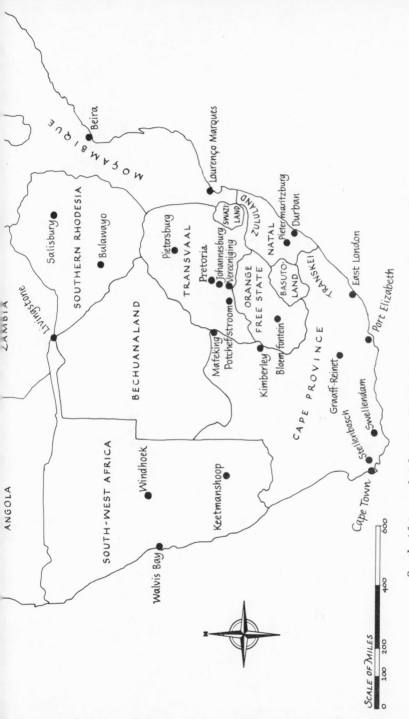

South Africa and Adjoining Territories. Provinces and Principal Cities.

off as most other African states south of the Sahara.[13] The three largest cities south of the Sahara are South African. Even by world standards, South Africa can be termed an industrial nation, since mining and manufacturing make up a third of the national income.

From its beginnings in 1652, as a refreshing station for Dutch vessels on the way to India, until the discovery of diamond fields in 1867, the South African economy was based mostly on cattle- and sheep-raising, and secondarily on cereal- and fruit-growing, and handicraft production. The vast territorial expansion of the Boers into the interior entailed few economic consequences, because the inaccessibility of markets forced the Boer farmers into the same type of pastoral subsistence economy as the Africans whom they displaced. The only marketable product of any importance was wool. Wool exports from South Africa increased rapidly after the Great Trek from 144,000 pounds in 1834, to 1,060,000 pounds in 1841, to 40,896,000 pounds in 1870.[14] This rapidly expanding trade did not, however, drastically affect the country's economic structure which remained based predominantly on subsistence and market farming.

The opening of the Kimberley diamond fields in the late 1860's marks the first major step in the diversification of South African production. Mining gradually overshadowed agriculture in relative importance, and remained the largest sector of the economy (in terms of contribution to national income) until the start of the Second World War. Surface deposits became quickly exhausted, and diamond diggings became deeper, thereby putting a premium on equipment and heavy capitalization. Large combines, such as De Beers, quickly dominated the mines, and ushered South Africa's entry into world capitalism. Spectacular as the diamond rush of the 1860's and 1870's had been, it was eclipsed in the late 1880's by the gold rush on the Witwatersrand. The

13. *Africa Report*, August, 1963, back cover.
14. De Kiewiet, *op. cit.*, p. 58; M. H. De Kock, *The Economic Development of South Africa*, pp. 36–42.

value of the Transvaal gold production increased from £1,869,000 in 1890 to £16,000,000 in 1898.[15] The White population of the Transvaal quadrupled between 1872 and 1890, while that of Natal, the Cape, and the Orange Free State only doubled during the same period.

Another immediate consequence of the opening of the gold and diamond fields was the rapid development of means of communication, mostly of railways. A Cape Town-Kimberley line was started in 1873, and by 1885 Kimberley was linked by rail with Cape Town, Port Elizabeth, and East London. In 1892 the Cape Town-Kimberley line was extended to the Rand; in 1895 another line linked Johannesburg with Lorenço Marques, and in 1896 the Durban-Johannesburg line was completed. In scarcely over twenty years the interior of South Africa had lost its isolation, and had become quickly accessible from all the major harbours.

The development of the mining industry also brought in its wake urban expansion. Until the 1860's Cape Town was the only town of any importance in South Africa. In 1871 Kimberley, with a population of approximately fifty thousand, had become the country's second largest town. The discovery of gold on the Rand quickly transformed the mushroom town of Johannesburg into the very heart of the South African economy, and contributed greatly to the expansion of Durban as the nearest South African harbour. By 1911 the population of Johannesburg already approached the quarter-million mark, overshadowing that of Cape Town by nearly one-half.

All these rapid economic transformations played a determining political role in bringing about the Second Anglo-Boer War and the downfall of the Boer Republics. By the beginning of the

15. M. H. De Kock, *op. cit.*, p. 52. Until 1961 the South African pound has been on par with the British pound sterling. Since the devaluation of the British pound in 1949, its value has fluctuated around $2.80. In 1961 South Africa adopted a decimal currency, the Rand, which is worth 10/ or $1.40. For purposes of simplicity, most values will be mentioned in pounds throughout this work.

twentieth century the old pastoral economy (and the social order that went with it) had been relegated to the second place. Mining, particularly gold mining, had become the mainstay of the economy; large urban concentrations had grown all over the country, linked by a rapid and reliable railway network; and Johannesburg had become an important centre of world finance. In short, South Africa had become the continent's first country to begin its industrial revolution.

Following the development of mining, South Africa entered the third and last major stage in its process of economic diversification, namely the growth of secondary and tertiary industry. Mining, with its consequent urbanization and rail transport system, created the necessary conditions for large-scale manufacturing. No precise date can be assigned for the beginning of this last phase of capitalist development, for manufacturing and service industries grew more gradually and less spectacularly than mining. World War One gave South African industrialization its first major impetus, but mining continued as the economy's most important single sector until the late 1930's. After the slowdown of the Great Depression, the economy started to recover in 1933. The Second World War and its prosperous aftermath established the preponderance of manufacturing over mining and the coming age of South Africa as a complex industrial country (Table XVIII). This is not to say that mining did not continue to expand and to be an important sector of the economy. Coal mining was developed in Natal, and, more recently, booming new gold fields were opened in the Orange Free State. Between 1911 and 1958 the value of mining production increased sevenfold from £36,000,000 to £256,800,000. In terms of percentage of national income, however, mining declined from 27.5 per cent to 12.9 per cent during the same period, whereas manufacturing increased from 6.8 per cent to 24.5 per cent (Table XVIII).

A few figures will illustrate the rapid rate of economic development in South Africa in the twentieth century. Between 1911 and 1955 the gross value of output in secondary industry increased seventy times. Between 1937 and 1951 alone, the increase was fivefold. Of course, inflationary prices account for a major portion of the growth, but even correcting on the basis of a price index, the value of the output did more than double in the 1937–1951 period.

This industrial expansion was accompanied by an increase in national income. Between 1912 and 1958 the national income increased over fifteen times, from £131,000,000 to £1,988,000,000; it has more than doubled between 1949 and 1958, and more than quintupled between 1938 and 1958 (Table XVIII). Correcting for the increase in prices and in population, the average *per capita* real income still shows a rise of some 40 per cent between 1938–1939 and 1952–1953. With an average annual percentage increase of 6.89 per cent in the value of manufacturing production between 1910 and 1940, South Africa's rate of industrial expansion was over three times faster than that of the United States (2.23 per cent) and Canada (2.06 per cent) and over seven times faster than that of Great Britain (0.87 per cent) during the same period.[16] South Africa's national income increased at an average annual rate of 3.81 per cent between 1910 and 1940, i.e., nearly twice the rates of Great Britain (2.12 per cent), the United States (2.02 per cent), and Canada (2.09 per cent).[17] In 1918–1919, 143,000 persons were employed in secondary industries, compared with 779,000 in 1950–1951.

An important demographic corollary of industrial development has been the rapid rate of urbanization. In 1904 only 23 per cent of the population were classified as urban, compared with 39 per cent in 1951. Absolute numbers showed a more than fourfold increase between the same two dates.[18] By 1960 nearly 47 per cent of the population, or 7.5 million people, lived in cities and nearly two-thirds of the urbanites were non-Whites (Table

16. J. C. du Plessis, *Economic Fluctuations in South Africa*, p. 36.
17. *Ibid.*
18. N. N. Franklin, *Economics in South Africa*, p. 241.

IV).[19] In 1911 South Africa had only two cities of over 100,000 inhabitants; in 1946 it had seven; and in 1957, eleven. In 1960 Johannesburg had passed the million mark, while Cape Town had over 700,000 inhabitants and Durban over 600,000. With urbanization, an ever growing proportion of the population is drawn from the traditional subsistence economy into the cash economy. Between 1946–1947 and 1952–1953, for example, wage earners increased at an average of 8.5 per cent a year, as compared with a population growth of 2.1 per cent a year.[20]

In short, South Africa has become, since World War Two, a complex industrial nation deriving over one-third of its national income from mining and manufacturing, and only a little over one-tenth from agriculture. Trade, finance, and transport together account for approximately one-fourth of the national income. As an industrialized country, South Africa occupies a unique position on the continent. No other African country has an economy that even remotely approaches the level of complexity of South Africa, and, were it not for political factors, South Africa could play an important role in the economic and technical development of the rest of the continent.

Several factors, however, give the South African economy a structure that is atypical of most industrial countries. The small portion of the national income contributed by agriculture is not only the result of the relatively high development of other sectors of the economy, but also of the *underdevelopment* of the rural areas. Some 53 per cent of the population are still living on the land, and contribute only a little over one-tenth to the country's wealth. Not only are the Native Reserves impoverished, eroded, overpopulated rural slums, incapable of feeding their population, and subsisting on the margin of the cash economy, but even the European farming areas have comparatively low yields because of low rainfall and poor soil quality. In this respect, South Africa

19. W. H. Hutt, *The Economics of the Colour Bar*, p. 181.
20. *The Manufacturer*, May, 1956.

is typical of the rest of the continent. There results an acute disequilibrium between the productive and the relatively unproductive sectors of the economy South Africa thus combines some of the characteristics of both industrial and developing countries. One may speak of two parallel economies: *sub*-subsistence agriculture on the one hand, and an industrial wage economy on the other.

The role played by gold mining is another factor making for the exceptional character of the South African economy. While the gold mines no longer play the paramount role that they once did, they still constitute the country's largest single industry.[21] Their importance resides not only in their contribution to the state budget, the national income, and to the South African balance of international trade, but also in the special character of gold. Because of the stability in the price of gold, gold mining constitutes a built-in antidepression mechanism. In a deflationary period, when the price of most goods and services tends to decline, the stable price of gold leads to an increased margin of profits for the mines. Conversely, in a period of prosperity, the gold mines constantly face the threat that increased wages would make production unprofitable. This is not to say that South Africa is immune to business-cycle fluctuations. The Great Depression of the early 1930's, for example, also affected South Africa. But, due to the fact that the gold industry operates in reverse to the

21. South African mining constitutes a tight oligopoly controlled by a largely English-speaking oligarchy. The main co-ordinating body for gold, uranium, and coal mining is the Transvaal and Orange Free State Chamber of Mines of which some ninety mining companies and thirteen financial corporations are members. Gold mining proper is controlled by seven major financial empires of which the Anglo-American Corporation is the largest. These giant corporations with interlocking directorates control an intricate pyramid of gold, coal, and other mining companies, banks, newspapers, manufacturing industries, and other subsidiary concerns. The pyramidal organization of these empires allows the major financial groups to control subsidiary companies in which they only own a small minority of the shares. Cf. *State of the Union Year-Book for South Africa*, 1959–1960, pp. 156–158.

rest of the economy, it plays an important stabilizing role, and tends to reduce the depth of the fluctuations.

Not only is gold an economic stabilizer; it also is the largest generator of wealth within the country, and it makes possible a much higher level of imports than would be possible without the export of bullion. In 1957, for example, the gold mines paid £17,000,000 in taxes, £73,000,000 in salaries and wages, and £105,000,000 for the purchase of supplies.[22] Only through gold exports does South Africa maintain a favourable balance of trade. From 1950 to 1958 the trade balance showed an export surplus of £459,100,000 if one includes the sale of gold. Without gold, the trade deficit would have been £1,091,300,000 during the same period (Table XX).

Another characteristic of the South African economy is the high degree of geographical concentration of its industry. The bulk of mining and manufacturing is centred in four areas. By far the largest industrial complex is the Witwatersrand. Johannesburg, Pretoria, and the satellite Rand cities such as Germiston, Springs, and Benoni constitute a large urban area of some two million inhabitants, and are the very heart of the country's economy. Following in order of importance as industrial centres are the three harbours of Cape Town, Durban, and Port Elizabeth. There are, in addition, other minor centres such as East London, Kimberley, and Bloemfontein, but large areas of the country such as the Great Karoo, the Northern Transvaal, and all of the Native Reserves are devoid of industry. Manufacturing clearly crystallized around the Rand mines and around the main peripheral harbours.

Like most other African countries, South Africa depends heavily on foreign investments. While British investors own by far the largest interests, the United States, Germany, and other Western countries also have sizeable assets in the Republic.

22. *Ibid.*, p. 157.

As of the end of 1956, for example, South Africa's total foreign liabilities were £1,396,400,000, while its foreign assets were only £411,100,000, leaving net liability of nearly £1,000,000,000.[23] A Nationalist industrial manager, Martinus Smuts Louw, estimated in 1958 that 88 per cent of South African banking, 71 per cent of short-term insurance, 60 per cent of the gold-mining industry, and 40 to 50 per cent of secondary industry were controlled by foreign owners.[24] The international implications of this situation are obvious. On the one hand, the value of South African shares on foreign stock exchanges is highly sensitive to internal unrest, but, on the other hand, Western investments have been one of the factors restraining the governments of the United States, Great Britain, and other Western countries from voting in favour of sanctions against the Republic at the United Nations. We shall return to this in Chapters Eight and Ten.

Finally, the unique socio-political structure of South Africa has a number of economic consequences, to which we shall return later, but which must at least be mentioned here. A number of politically inspired regulations restrict economic expansion and activity, notably in the field of labour migration. Political unrest and the repressive measures of the government undermine the confidence of overseas capital on which South Africa is still heavily dependent. Vast disparities in the distribution of income make for a low purchasing power of the masses, and, hence, for a small internal market for consumer goods. A number of factors contribute to the perpetuation of a vicious circle of low wages and low productivity. The divorce between economic power concentrated in the hands of a small English capitalist class and the political power of the Afrikaner Nationalists constitutes one of the aspects of the conflict between the two dominant White groups. The economic exploitation of the non-European masses and the repression of trade unions add to political oppression in creating an explosive situation. At the same time, the dynamic

23. *Ibid.*, pp. 304–305.
24. Cited in Hartmann, *op. cit.*, p. 30.

processes released by rapid urbanization and industrialization are in conflict with the reactionary objectives of the government, and generate ever deepening maladjustments in the structure of South Africa.

As a manufacturing and mining country, South Africa is more akin to the capitalistic countries of Western Europe in the nineteenth century than in the twentieth century. The weak position of the trade unions, heavy reliance on great masses of unskilled workers, low wages and low productivity, great wage discrepancies between various levels of employment, and high masculinity ratios in the urban areas are so many characteristics of the early stages of industrialization. Both the semicolonial nature of South Africa and the late date of industrial development (as compared with Europe and the United States) account for this state of affairs.

The intricate interrelations between the various parts of social structure will be treated in the following chapters. Before turning to that task, however, let us summarize the major characteristics of South African society. Few countries are as complex, heterogeneous, and ridden with conflict and disequilibrium as South Africa. Culturally, South Africa is the meeting ground of several African, European, and Asian peoples, but, due to European technical, economic, military, and political dominance, the general trend has been towards the gradual Westernization of the non-Europeans. This summary statement hides, of course, the extremely complex nature of the process of acculturation, but we shall return to that problem in Chapter Nine. Overlapping only in part with cultural differences, a rigid system of social stratification divides the South African population in a number of ways, foremost among which is "race." The ascriptive colour-caste hierarchy pervades practically every aspect of South African life, and contributes more than any other single factor to the country's uniqueness. Race consciousness is not the prerogative of South Africa, but in no other country, except in Hitler's Germany, has racism been erected into a paramount principle of statesmanship.

Politically, South Africa is an antiquated White-settlers' democracy, ruling as a colonial power over 80 per cent of the population. In its desperate attempt to maintain a pre-industrial, paternalistic relationship between Whites and non-Whites, the Afrikaner Nationalist government is turning increasingly, though halfheartedly and inefficiently, to the methods of modern Fascism, but, basically, the South African brand of tyranny is that of an obsolete, nineteenth-century, colonial state. The same dual character of the South African polity is reflected in the economy. The country is at once an underdeveloped colonial area and an industrial power. As a late-comer in the industrial race, South Africa presents most of the characteristics of European nineteenth-century capitalism.

## CHAPTER FIVE

## Socio-Political Conflicts: Afrikaners Versus English

T HE struggle for power in South Africa cannot be dissociated from the country's ethnic and racial groups around which the political process has always crystallized. South African politics have, since their origin, taken the form of a struggle for the hegemony of one group over the others. The main protagonists in this struggle have been the Africans, the English, and the Afrikaners.[1]

It is customary to distinguish "White politics," centring around the English-Afrikaner conflict, from "non-White politics," i.e., the non-European struggle against White supremacy. The distinction is useful, and we shall follow it here for purposes of analysis; White and non-White politics each operate in their own sphere, and follow different methods of achieving opposed objectives. Nevertheless, these two levels of the power struggle constantly react against one another in a dialectical fashion. To view the two as independent of one another, or to ignore one of them, would lead to a complete distortion of reality.

1. Among the most important works related to Chapters V, VI, and VII are the following: Leo Marquard, *The Peoples and the Policies of South Africa;* Gwendolen Carter, *The Politics of Inequality;* William Macmillan, *Bantu, Boer and Briton;* Sheila Patterson, *The Last Trek;* and I. D. MacCrone, *Race Attitudes in South Africa.*

Before turning to a more detailed analysis of socio-political conflicts in South Africa, we must first describe the major forces in presence and the evolution of their relationship to one another. In its simplest form, the South African power conflict could be schematized as a triangle of forces in which the Afrikaners, the English, and the Africans represent the three antagonistic poles. Africans have the power of numbers and, since the last two decades, the almost unanimous moral support of world public opinion. The English detain a greatly disproportionate share of economic power and of the daily press. Of 22 daily newspapers published in South Africa, only 5 are in Afrikaans. The 17 English daily newspapers, which support mostly the opposition United or the Progressive Party, accounted for a daily circulation of about 680,000 in 1959, compared to 168,000 for the Afrikaans dailies.[2] The Afrikaners, as the majority White group, and through the political settlement of Union in 1910, exert the dominant influence in the White parliamentary system and, hence, in the state apparatus (Tables X and XI).

This highly schematized outline hides, of course, a number of important complicating factors. The most important of them is that these three main groups do not directly compete with one another at the same level, since the Africans are excluded from the parliamentary process. The power struggle thus takes place at two levels. On the one hand, the two White groups compete within the constitutional framework for the control of Parliament and of the state apparatus, while, on the other hand, Africans and Europeans oppose one another on the extraparliamentary scene. The "Native policy" of the main European political parties has differed in details and in methods, but the vast majority of Whites, both Afrikaners and English, has always agreed on the perpetuation of White supremacy. Nearly all Africans, on their side, aim at the overthrow of the present system.

Another complicating factor is that White party alignments

---

2.  Thomas Karis, "South Africa," p. 513.

have not strictly followed the Afrikaner-English cleavage. Splinter parties have subdivided each of these two ethnic groups, and the Afrikaner vote has traditionally been split between an "extremist" Nationalist wing and a "moderate" group in favour of co-operation with the English.

Finally, the Coloureds and the Indians, although they are relatively poor, disfranchised, minority groups, have nevertheless influenced the political scene. Indians have played an important leadership role in the non-White liberatory movements (especially in the Congress Movement), and the Ghandian influence has contributed much to political ideology and resistance methods. The Coloureds, as a group, have generally played a passive role, but they have been an important pawn in the White political game. All of these complicating factors will be discussed further in the course of the following chapters.

Returning to the basic triangle of forces in the South African power struggle, the relations between the three groups have not remained static. It is therefore necessary to trace the broad lines in the evolution of that conflict. The first two protagonists, namely the Dutch colonists and the African nation-states, only came into contact on the eastern frontier of the Cape Colony in the second half of the eighteenth century, and the English only made their permanent appearance on the South African political scene during the first years of the nineteenth century.

The evolution in the power relations between the three groups can be divided into four main periods, keeping in mind that the dates are arbitrary. The first phase, beginning with the first "Kaffir War" of 1779 and ending with the Great Trek of 1836, is characterized by a policy of stabilization and defence of the frontier separating the White colonists from the Africans. The successive Cape governments wanted to contain the expansionist drive of the colonists, and to avoid military entanglements with the Africans. The second period from 1836 to approximately 1880 was dominated by the military conquest and subjection of the Africans living in the vast areas invaded by the Boers, and in the British-dominated Natal and Eastern Cape. Once White supremacy was well established, the power struggle between English and Afrikaners came into the forefront of politics, leading to the Boer War, the compromise of Union, and White party politics from 1910 to the Second World War. The latter and its immediate aftermath mark the beginning of the fourth phase of the political struggle. The scene is now dominated by the demands of the African population which has become conscious of being oppressed, and whose political organization increasingly threatens the White machinery of government. In the light of this acute White-Black clash, the English-Afrikaner conflict is receding into the background, and the appeal for "White unity" is heard more and more frequently.

One of the most characteristic (though not surprising) features of South African power conflicts is the almost insignificant role played by class struggles in the political process. Here too, "race" has claimed the paramount place, and class has been relegated to a secondary position. To be sure, some small parties, notably the Labour Party, have had a class basis, but they too were pervaded by racialism, and failed to cut across colour barriers. All the major political organizations, White and non-White, have drawn their membership from all social classes, have been based on racial or ethnic membership, and have emphasized colour or linguistic issues, while relegating the broader social and economic aspects of their platform to a secondary position. Even the non-White liberatory movements are racially based, as we shall see later, and have concentrated on political emancipation, while allowing wide divergences of opinion on social and economic issues to exist within their ranks. Any ordering of political organizations on a spectrum from right to left is therefore difficult, except on the colour issue.

We shall turn now to a more detailed analysis of White politics, starting with the English-Afrikaner conflict, and continuing in the next chapter with the study of "Native policy," i.e., the White endeavours to "solve the Native problem." In previous chapters, we have already related the first phases of the Anglo-Boer conflict: the Black Circuit of 1812; the 50th Ordinance of 1828; the abolition of slavery in 1834; the Great Trek; the annexation of Natal, Basutoland, and the Kimberley diamond fields; the occupation of the Transvaal; the First Anglo-Boer War of 1880; the Jameson Raid of 1895; and the Second Anglo-Boer War of 1899–1902. These events point to the persistent efforts of Britain to frustrate the expansionist and separatist moves of the Boers throughout the nineteenth century. Particularly since the days of Cecil Rhodes, one of the major figures in the scramble for Africa, the Boer Republics were regarded as a hindrance to northward expansion. Modern Afrikaner Nationalism is the direct product of, and counterreaction to, British nineteenth-century imperialism.

The South Africa Act of 1909 marked, as we saw, a decisive turning point in British policy. Great Britain hoped that the "Compromise of Union" would maintain an even balance of forces between Afrikaners and English, and would create a friendly self-governing White Dominion on the southern tip of Africa. From the foundation of Union in 1910, the conflict was thus no longer between the Boers and the British government, but between the two major groups of White settlers within South Africa.

The first two Prime Ministers, Louis Botha (1910–1919) and Jan Smuts (1919–1924), held to the spirit of the post-Boer-War compromise. Although they were both Boer generals who fought against Britain, they followed a policy of co-operation with the English, and resisted the extremist Afrikaner elements. At the outbreak of the First World War, an armed revolt of extremist Afrikaners who opposed South Africa's entry into the war on the British side was crushed. In 1922, when the White mine workers on the Rand struck in protest against the mines' policy of replacing White workers by cheaper non-White labourers in certain categories of skilled work, the Smuts government intervened on the side of English capital and repressed the White strikers.

The first Hertzog government (1924–1933) crowned the continuing rise of Afrikaner nationalism as a major political force, and marked a definite break with the policy of compromise. In 1924 Hertzog (likewise an old Boer-War general, who, in 1912, broke away from Botha and founded the Nationalist Party) formed a coalition Nationalist-Labour cabinet, in opposition to English big business, and to Smuts, whose repressive role in the Rand strikes had made unpopular. In 1926 Hertzog persuaded the Imperial Conference to specify in writing South Africa's dominion status, and, thereby, further secured his country's *de facto* independence. That period saw the passage of the first pieces of nationalist legislation (such as the Nationality and Flag Act of 1927), aiming at weakening the symbolic links with Great Britain. It also saw, in 1925, the substitution of Afrikaans for Dutch as one of the two official languages of South Africa.

In 1933 a *rapprochement* between Hertzog and Smuts led to the formation of a new coalition government with Hertzog as Prime Minister. The proximate consequence of this coalition between Hertzog's Nationalist Party and Smuts' South African Party (S.A.P.) was a drastic political realignment in 1934. As Hertzog had declared himself satisfied with the Statute of Westminster of 1931, his position had come closer to that of Smuts, but he had antagonized the militant republican wing of his party led by Malan. The latter split from Hertzog's party, and formed the "purified" Nationalist Party, while the Hertzog and Smuts groups fused into the United Party. Malan's "purified" Nationalists grew in strength, until they succeeded in gaining power by a narrow election victory over the United Party in 1948. By squashing other Afrikaner movements, such as the neo-Fascist Ossewa-Brandwag and New Order, Malan succeeded in rallying the great mass of the Afrikaner electorate under the banner of apartheid and nationalism, and assuring the political hegemony of Afrikanerdom.[3] But here we are anticipating the events.

3. The story of the rise of Afrikaner Nationalism is told in detail in: Roberts and Trollip, *op. cit.*

The newly formed United Party represented the older line of English-Afrikaner compromise, and of co-operation with Great Britain and the Commonwealth. The issue raised by participation in the Second World War led to a renewed split between Hertzog and Smuts. Hertzog favoured neutrality, while Smuts wanted South Africa to enter the war on the British side. In 1939 a parliamentary vote of 80 to 67 in favour of Smuts led to the formation of Smuts' United Party war cabinet. The Malan and Hertzog factions reunited into the *Herenigde Nasionale of Volksparty*, but on Malan's terms.

Contrary to the confident expectations of the United Party, the Nationalist Party, led by Malan, won 70 parliamentary seats to the United Party's 65, although the United Party polled over 120,000 more votes (Table XI). However, Malan was not yet strong enough to rule alone; he was forced to enter into coalition with N. C. Havenga's Afrikaner Party which had won nine seats in the 1948 election, thereby giving the new government a narrow parliamentary majority of 79 to 74 for the opposition United Party, Labour Party, and "Natives' Representatives." Malan thus became Prime Minister (and Havenga, Deputy Prime Minister) of an all-Afrikaner cabinet. Three years later Malan was strong enough to rule alone, and the Afrikaner Party merged with the Nationalists. By rallying the mass of the Afrikaner electorate, the Nationalist Party eliminated the necessity of compromise with the English, gained control of the entire country, and opened the way for more extremist policies.

At first, the control of the Nationalist Party was precarious, but the new government lost no time in consolidating its position, and manipulating the parliamentary and elective machinery to the point where the Nationalists became practically unseatable by constitutional means. Through the loading of rural constituencies, the elimination of the Cape Coloureds from the common roll, the abolition of "Native Representatives," the reduction of the voting age from twenty-one to eighteen, the disproportionate representation of South West Africa, the enlargement of the Senate, and the intensive indoctrination of their supporters, the Nationalists steadily grew in power. They increased their majorities at the elections of 1953, 1958, and 1961, and they now control over two-thirds of the seats in the House of Assembly (105 out of 156), although they have the support of, at most 55 per cent of the electorate. The opposition parties would have to secure a substantial majority of popular votes to gain a bare majority in Parliament.

As the position of the Nationalists became more secure, and that of the opposition United Party more impotent, government policies grew increasingly reactionary. The extremist Transvaal and Orange Free State elements within the Nationalist Party wielded an ever growing influence, as against the slightly more "moderate" Cape elements. Malan's successor Strydom was considerably more extremist than his predecessor, and Verwoerd, who became Prime Minister in 1958, gradually eliminated remaining "moderates" from positions of influence in the government.[4] The ultra-nationalist secret organization, known as the *Broederbond,* has increased its occult power in the government. The *Broederbond* is a relatively small, elitist body consisting of perhaps two or three thousand prominent members of the Dutch Reformed Churches, the professions, business, and the universities; it is led by an executive committee known as "The Twelve Apostles," and aims at the promotion of all the interests of Afrikanerdom by all conceivable means. Today practically all the leading members of the government belong to the *Broederbond,* and "The Twelve Apostles" constitute, in fact, a secret executive committee of the Nationalist Party, and, hence, of the government.

4. Interestingly, Verwoerd was no more Strydom's choice as his successor than Strydom had been Malan's. Both Strydom and Malan have expressed preference for less extremist men as their respective successors, namely Havenga and C. R. Swart. This clearly indicates the growth of reaction within the Nationalist Party. Cf. Marquard, *The Peoples and Policies of South Africa,* pp. 164–165.

Afrikaner Nationalists gradually secured for themselves the leading positions in all branches of the civil service (notably in the police, the railways, education, and "Native Administration"), infiltrated diplomacy and the judiciary by political appointments, increased the importance of the Afrikaans language at the detriment of English in government and the schools, eliminated the last symbols of Commonwealth ties in the design of coins and stamps, extended the scope of government-controlled industries (such as ISCOR, the main South African iron and steel enterprise), encouraged the expansion of Afrikaner business, attacked the autonomy of the English-speaking universities, curtailed the activities of the Catholic Church and the English Protestant missions, heavily subsidized White farming which is predominantly in Afrikaner hands, and encouraged the Afrikaans press while threatening the English papers with censorship.

The final triumph of Afrikanerdom came in 1961 when the government declared South Africa to be a Republic after winning a bare 52 per cent majority of the all-White electorate in a referendum on the question. South Africa was subsequently forced to withdraw from the Commonwealth, thereby severing its last symbolic ties with Britain. The good old days of the Boer Republics had returned, and the bitter humiliation of defeat in the Boer War was wiped out. God had favoured His Chosen People and given them unlimited control over the Promised Land.

On first sight, it is surprising that the White English opposition has done practically nothing to combat the ascendency of Afrikaner Nationalism, except through futile protests in the English press, and in political speeches and meetings. The United Party, as the main official opposition group in Parliament, has supported the government on a number of issues, including many pieces of dictatorial legislation that vastly extended the power of the Nationalists. In the course of years the United Party, an ultra-conservative group, even followed the reactionary lead of the Nationalists, and gradually adjusted its policies to those of the government in the hope of attracting the electorate. To be sure, a number of individual English churchmen, intellectuals, and political leaders, belonging to as disparate organizations as the Catholic and Anglican churches, the English-speaking universities, and the Liberal and Communist parties, have taken a courageous stand against the government, and have fought it through action as well as words. But the English, as a group, remained politically passive, and never constituted a really effective opposition to the Nationalists.

On closer examination, however, the political apathy of the English is comprehensible. In the first place, the traditional English respect for parliamentary legalism has militated against resort to extraconstitutional action. Even though most intelligent English politicians realize that the government cannot be unseated, nor even hindered, by parliamentary means, they do not consider the adoption of other tactics. Short of violence, and within the framework of legality, it is clear that the English possess sufficient economic power to exert considerable and efficacious pressure on the government, for example by means of industrial shutdowns.

The real crux of the answer, however, lies in the "Native problem." The English share all the privileges of the other Whites, and they do not want to change the existing system of White oppression. The dictatorial measures of the government do not effect the daily life of the English, as they are intended to suppress the non-White opposition. The government is prepared to tolerate the parliamentary White opposition because such opposition does not constitute a threat. At the same time, many English political and industrial leaders probably think that the Nationalists do a better job of keeping the Africans down than they themselves would. In order to maintain White supremacy and privileges, the mass of the English is willing to pay the price of increasing dictatorship, of gradual Afrikanerization, and of a measure of economic interference.

The economic cost of apartheid is one of the most common

complaints in the English press, but, while this cost is undoubtedly heavy for the country as a whole, the most powerful financial and industrial group in the country, namely the Chambers of Mines and the related Anglo-American Corporation, has, on the whole, to gain through the maintenance of the *status quo*. Indeed, all the mines, as well as other English-controlled undertakings such as the sugar industry, have become entirely dependent on cheap, migratory African labour, and, except for taxation, find little in government policy that affects them adversely.

The more intelligent English leaders are becoming aware of the ever increasing tension generated by Nationalist policies, but they also realize that any change of government is likely to entail very much greater political and economic upheavals than they are prepared to accept. Even those who advocate cautious, gradual reforms begin to understand that what they propose can only be implemented through extralegal action (violent or otherwise), and that such action would lead to a complete change in the social structure of South Africa. Rather than to unleash a rapid sequence of long-delayed change, the English prefer to acquiesce and even to collaborate behind the scenes with a government they despise. "White unity" and "*swart gevaar*"[5] are but two aspects of the same reality. As racial tension between Whites and Africans mounted, and as non-White political consciousness increased, the Afrikaner-English conflict receded in importance. From that point of view, the Nationalists are correct when they claim to have contributed to White unity. They have achieved the union of practically all Europeans in a retrenched camp against the "sea of colour."

A number of non-political factors that are often not sufficiently emphasized complicate and add to the bitterness of the Afrikaner-English conflict.[6] One of the most important of these is the

5. Literally "black danger," in Afrikaans.
6. The best treatment of these factors is to be found in Patterson's perceptive book, *The Last Trek*.

cultural factor. English, as a world language with an abundant literature, has an enormous advantage over Afrikaans, a derivative of Dutch (itself a language of limited distribution), spoken nowhere else, and which only in the last century attained the status of a standardized written tongue. The Afrikaners' fight to develop their tongue into a medium of scientific, artistic, technical, and commercial expression that could compete with English has been a very uneven one, and English still retains an undeniable superiority in many fields, notably in business and in university education. The English are conscious of that superiority and some of them still look down on Afrikaans as a "kitchen Dutch," hardly worthy of being called a language.

Many Afrikaners, on the other hand, exhibit ambivalent feelings towards their culture. While they deeply resent the "superior" English attitude, they also suffer under a cultural inferiority complex *vis-à-vis* the English. In the past many Afrikaners have therefore sought to become Anglicized, and to educate their children in English in order to secure certain professional, intellectual, and commercial advantages. This fact was viewed with alarm by Afrikaner politicians who feared loss of cultural identity, and the Nationalist government introduced compulsory mother-tongue instruction in the schools to stop that trend.

Class differences further poison Afrikaner-English relations. While at present Afrikaners and English are represented at all levels of the White class hierarchy, the English still enjoy, on the average, a higher socio-economic status. In spite of the upward mobility of many Afrikaners, that group is still overrepresented in the lower income and educational brackets. This is in great part due to the rural background of many Afrikaners. During the 1920's and 1930's many Afrikaner farmers migrated to the cities without any industrial skills, and constituted the vast bulk of the "poor Whites." The government intervened energetically by means of farm subsidies, and the "civilized labour policy" whereby unskilled Whites where absorbed in public service at "civilized" (i.e., White) pay rates. While, today, the Afrikaner "poor White" class has practically disappeared, big business is still largely English, and the Afrikaners are still overrepresented in farming and in manual occupations. In 1946, for example, 85.54 per cent of White farmers were Afrikaans-speaking; only 10.2 per cent of all engineers and industrial chemists in South Africa were Afrikaners.[7] A more recent estimate puts the Afrikaners' share of the country's professional personnel at 30 per cent.[8] In spite of the diminishing class difference between the two White groups, the class prejudices of many English against the Afrikaners continue to make for ill feelings. A number of English Whites condescendingly look on the Afrikaners as uncouth, uneducated, homely, simple, jovial, and hospitable countryfolk who speak a primitive but colourful dialect. Conversely, Afrikaners resent the English as snobbish, haughty, distant, and cool.

Finally, certain demographic factors make for mutual distrust. The English, as the minority White group, feel all the more "swamped" by the Afrikaners as the latter are slowly increasing their majority through a higher birth rate. The younger age of the Afrikaner population is symptomatic of a higher birth rate. The English Whites in 1936 were outnumbered 115.5 to 100 in the age group of persons 20 years and over, 180.2 to 100 in the 7 to 20 age group, and 215.0 to 100 in the group of children under 7.[9] In recent years, however, the Afrikaner birth rate has sharply declined. The Afrikaners, on their side, fear that urbanization and other factors already mentioned could lead to gradual absorption by the English, and loss of cultural identity.

7. Cf. Trapido, *op. cit.*
8. Hartmann, *op. cit.*, p. 62.
9. Trapido, *op. cit.*

## CHAPTER SIX

*Socio-Political Conflicts: "Native Policy"*

W E must now examine "Native policy," i.e., the theory and means advocated and implemented by the successive White governments to rule over the Africans and perpetuate European supremacy. From the following analysis, the essential agreement of all major European parties on the colour issue will become clear. In fact, the term "Native policy" is too restrictive for we shall also examine government policies towards the Coloureds and the Indians. The more inclusive term "race policy" is, therefore, more appropriate, although the numerical importance of the Africans has given them a choice place in the successive programmes of repression.

The following basic aims and principles of "race policy" have been shared by all South African governments since Union:

1. The maintenance of paternalistic White domination.

2. Racial segregation and discrimination, wherever there was any threat of equality or competition between Whites and non-Whites.

3. The perpetual subjugation of non-Europeans, and particularly Africans, as a politically powerless and economically exploitable group.

The Nationalist policy of apartheid is only the last phase in a long process of continuous strengthening of the system of White oppression. Apartheid differs from the race policy of earlier governments mostly in that its ideology is more explicit, its rationalization more elaborate, and its implementation more thorough and systematic. Before describing the implementation of race policy previous to and since the Nationalist regime, it is important to understand the philosophy which underlines that policy. The model of race relations which all South African governments have tried to maintain is one of old-style colonial paternalism. South African Whites have looked at themselves, like other settler minorities, as a superior group endowed with greater intelligence, initiative, and inventiveness. They have considered their language, religion, technology, and culture in general as unquestionably better than those of the "primitive savages" whom they conquered. Conversely, they have looked down on the Africans as backward, immature, stupid, irresponsible, uninhibited grown-up children incapable of managing their own affairs. As carriers of a "higher civilization," the Whites cast themselves into the role of the stern but just master who has to look after the welfare of his childish and backward servants.

The "White-man's-burden" attitude is a useful rationalization of European domination, because the benevolent aspect of paternalism appears to reconcile despotism with justice. The fact that this benevolent aspect was rarely implemented in practice is irrelevant here. The ideology of paternalism allows the White group to believe in all sincerity that its domination is not only just, but beneficial to the people it oppresses and exploits. Paternalism has transformed the reality of the "Black man's burden" into the myth of the "White man's burden." The master-servant relationship is considered by the majority of Whites as the ideal and only conceivable relationship between Europeans and non-Europeans, and the successive governments have basically aimed at extending and preserving that model at the national level.

In South Africa, European ethnocentrism was combined with White racialism. Not only did the Whites consider themselves *culturally* superior, but also endowed with greater *innate* capacities than the Africans. Thus, the differences between Whites and

Blacks were assumed to be permanent and immutable, or at best changeable only over extremely long periods of time.

Racial segregation and discrimination are at once logical developments from the policy of paternalism, and indices of its failure. The purpose of segregation is not to prevent contact between Whites and non-Whites. South African Whites do not object to prolonged and intimate contact with non-Europeans, so long as the latter are in a servile capacity. Segregation aims clearly at preventing *egalitarian* contact between the "races." Domestic servants, for example, may accompany their White masters in a number of areas, such as beaches, that are reserved "for Europeans only." Racial separation has grown increasingly rigid over the years, as more and more non-Whites have risen in socio-economic status to a position where they could associate on equal terms with the Whites. Similarly, discrimination based on colour, whether legal or customary, is an attempt to prevent competition on the basis of merit between White and Black, and constitutes an avowal that the Whites need the protection of an artificial colour-bar in order to maintain their dominant position. Racial segregation and discrimination have been rationalized by the various governments as the best means to prevent racial conflict. In fact, they are attempts to perpetuate racial inequality, in a situation where the paternalistic master-servant relationship has ceased to be the only form of contact between the racial groups.[1]

Because of his intellectual and political stature, we may take Jan Smuts as the mouthpiece of pre-Nationalist White thinking on the "race problem" without opening ourselves to the criticism of selecting statements from rabid, pathological racists. Smuts, who rightly traces his intellectual ancestry back to Rhodes, calls his brand of paternalism "trusteeship." He writes: "Cecil Rhodes used repeatedly to say that the proper relation between Whites and Blacks in this country was the relation between guardian

1. On this point see also my article: "Distance Mechanisms of Social Stratification."

and ward. This is the basis of trusteeship."[2] Smuts never questioned the principle of European domination: "We are for the leadership of the European race in South Africa, and no one will dispute it, and no one will endanger it except ourselves if we do not do our duty."[3] In 1945 Smuts said in Parliament: "There are certain things about which all South Africans are agreed, all parties and all sections, except those who are quite mad. The first is that it is a fixed policy to maintain white supremacy in South Africa."[4] While Smuts was intelligent enough to realize that his endeavours to enforce segregation had had "disappointing results" and were doomed to failure,[5] he was nevertheless a fervent segregationist: "Generally our Natives, for good and sufficient reasons which I quite approve of, have been put apart in the urban areas, they have been segregated and given their own locations or townships to live in."[6]

On the role of the White trustee towards his Black wards, Smuts' thinking shows a curious and revealing contradiction. On the one hand, he emphasizes the benevolent as opposed to the dominatory aspect of paternalism and logically concludes from his assumption of White cultural superiority that "the lot, the advancement, the upliftment of the backward peoples is the sacred trust of civilization."[7] Not only are these pronouncements incompatible with Smuts' repressive measures when he was in office, but he even contradicts himself verbally when he states elsewhere: "In this lecture I have emphasized the importance of preserving native institutions, of keeping intact as far as possible the native system of organization and social discipline."[8] In other

2. J. C. Smuts, *The Basis of Trusteeship in African Native Policy*, p. 7.

3. Quoted in *Treatment of Indians in South Africa*, p. 2.

4. Quoted in Oliver Walker, *Kaffirs are Lively*, Title page.

5. Smuts, *op. cit.*, p. 9.

6. *Ibid.*, p. 15.

7. *Ibid.*, p. 7.

8. Quoted in Walter A. Cotton, *Racial Segregation in South Africa*, p. 45.

words, while the "backward Natives" must be "uplifted," it also serves the purposes of White supremacy to keep the Africans as they are.

In his eulogistic biography of his father, Smuts' son quotes the former Prime Minister's views on the "Native problem":

> This type [i.e., the African] has some wonderful characteristics. It has largely remained a child type, with a child psychology and outlook. A child-like human cannot be a bad human. . . . Perhaps, as a direct result of this temperament the African is the only happy human I have come across. No other race is so easily satisfied, so good-tempered, so carefree. . . . The African easily forgets past troubles and does not anticipate future troubles. This happy-go-lucky disposition is a great asset, but it also has its drawbacks. There is no inward incentive to improvement, there is no persistent effort in construction, and there is complete absorption in the present, its joys and sorrows. . . . No indigenous religion has been evolved, no literature, no art. . . . They can stand any amount of physical hardships and sufferings. . . . [Racial] separation is imperative, not only in the interests of a native culture, and to prevent the native traditions and institutions from being swamped by the more powerful organization of the Whites, but also for other important purposes, such as public health, racial purity and public good order. The mixing up of two such alien elements as white and black leads to unhappy social results—racial miscegenation, moral deterioration of both, racial antipathy and clashes, and to many other forms of social evil. . . . It is however, evident that the proper place of the educated minority of the natives is with the rest of their people, of whom they are the natural leaders, and from where they should not in any way be dissociated. Far more difficult questions arise in the industrial plane. It is not practicable to separate black and white in industry.[9]

A final quotation from Smuts' son gives a picture of the statesman's attitude towards Africans:

> It was the little piccanins, however, he preferred, with their

9. J. C. Smuts, *Jan Christian Smuts*, pp. 307, 308, 311.

shiny, shaven heads and big, dark eyes, and with their wide, white flashing smile. Their behaviour suggested to him the elemental wild animal of nature of which he was so fond. Their eyes, in fact, held a doe-like look which strengthened this feeling. These wild, colourful people, he was fond of photographing with his cine whenever he had the opportunity.[10]

Smuts represents, in its most sophisticated form, the typical, "moderate," pre-apartheid brand of White South African paternalism. Similar statements could be quoted from many other prominent people. Only recently a tiny minority of White intellectuals has emancipated itself from this paternalistic ideology. In the past and even today, dedicated and sincere Whites have been or are with few exceptions benevolent paternalists who implicitly equate the terms "civilized" and "White." This statement applies to practically all White missionaries, humanitarians, reformers, and "Cape liberals."

From the ideological point of view, the advent of apartheid meant the triumph of the stern frontier paternalism of the Boer Republics over the more benevolent and sophisticated paternalism of the Cape. In every essential respect, however, the race policies of the Afrikaner Nationalists represent a logical evolution from, rather than a rupture with, the traditional White South African *Weltanschauung*. As conditions of rapid urban, industrial, and social change increasingly endangered White supremacy and the paternalistic model of White-Black relations, White governments grew more and more repressive. They failed to adjust to changing conditions, and they clung to the old pre-industrial, colonial pattern.

The term "apartheid" (literally "separation") is an Afrikaans neologism first coined in 1929. It only entered into common usage in 1948, however, when it became an election slogan and, after

10. *Ibid.*, p. 313. This was written in 1952. Even today this "benevolent" attitude of regarding Africans as part of the fauna, as a colorful backdrop along with the baboons of the Kruger National Park, is still widespread.

the Nationalist victory, the official designation of government policy. Since then, an abundant literature has developed around apartheid.[11] As presented by its intellectual apologists, notably by the members of the South African Bureau of Racial Affairs (SABRA), the argument in favour of apartheid runs as follows: We, Afrikaners and White South Africans in general, have no homeland other than South Africa. The country is ours, and we have no desire or intention to leave it. We have just as much right to be here as the "Bantu," and we have arrived in South Africa at about the same time as they. We want to preserve our superior "White civilization" and maintain our racial identity, but we are surrounded by an overwhelming majority of non-Whites who threaten to swamp us culturally and racially.

Integration, the argument continues, is unthinkable, because, no matter how slow and gradual, it must end in black domination, miscegenation, and swamping of "White civilization." Any White South African in his right mind can only look at these prospects with horror and disgust. Therefore, the only salvation of the White race in South Africa is through apartheid. The races must be physically segregated from one another to avoid conflict and competition. Each racial group must have its own areas where it must develop along its own lines and according to its own traditional way of life. The Bantu must remain Bantu, and not try to become "imitation Europeans." For a long time to come, the "Bantu homelands" (i.e., the old Native Reserves) must remain under the control of Whites, because the Bantu are still unable to govern themselves, but eventually these areas may become independent. In the "White" part of the country (i.e.,

11. Among other works, see S. Pienaar and A. Sampson, *South Africa, Two Views of Separate Development*; N. J. Rhoodie and H. J. Venter, *Apartheid: A Socio-Historical Exposition of the Origin and Development of the Apartheid Idea*; P. V. Pistorius, *No Further Trek*; B. B. Keet, *The Ethics of Apartheid*; E. P. Dvorin, *Racial Separation in South Africa*; P. L. van den Berghe, "Apartheid, Fascism and the Golden Age," as well as the many publications of the S. A. Bureau of Racial Affairs and the S. A. Institute of Race Relations.

about 87 per cent of South Africa), the Whites must retain complete control, and the non-Whites can only be tolerated there as a migrant labour force for the Whites. Small areas with limited local self-government must be allocated to the Indians and the Coloureds along the same lines as the "Bantu homelands."

The phrase "ideal apartheid" has been used by a number of people, but it is somewhat misleading in that it has two widely different meanings. Government officials often oppose "ideal" to "practical" apartheid; by the former they mean total geographical segregation by race, a goal which they deem desirable but unrealistic in the near future. As used by non-Nationalists, "ideal apartheid" means the "positive" or "benevolent" aspects of the doctrine, as contrasted to the repressive ones. The following statement by M. D. C. De Wet Nel, the Minister of Bantu Administration and Development, expresses this second meaning of "ideal" apartheid:

> The Government's policy is actuated by a sincere desire to establish conditions which would make possible the ideal of harmonious co-existence of all the groups. It is the well-considered conviction of the Government that any form of racial intermingling and integration is the breeding ground for inter-racial jealousy, strife and ultimately hatred.[12]

The extent to which the "positive" aspect of apartheid is translated into actual practice is open to interpretation. There is no question that the government looks upon subservient Africans with benevolence, and that paternalism is an important aspect of apartheid, as we shall presently see. At the same time, other statements by prominent Nationalists also indicate that White domination is the government's uppermost consideration, and that "idealistic" statements have a propaganda function.

The proponents of "positive" apartheid claim that "parallel development" will eliminate White domination, and establish an equitable geographical partition, but Strydom, the second post-

12. *Bantu,* 11, June, 1964, p. 247.

war Nationalist Prime Minister, stated categorically: "Our policy
is that the Europeans must stand their ground and must remain
boss in South Africa."[13] Verwoerd now speaks of "independent
Bantustans," but in 1951 he said in Parliament: "Now a Senator
wants to know whether the series of self-governing Native areas
would be sovereign. The answer is obvious. . . . It stands to reason that White South Africa must remain their guardian. . . . We
cannot mean that we intend by that to cut large slices out of
South Africa and turn them into independent States."[14] Some
observers have seen a sign of "liberalization" of apartheid in the
Bantustan policy, but Verwoerd himself has convincingly refuted
this theory when, on January 25, 1963, he reasserted: "We want
to make South Africa White . . . . Keeping it White can only mean
one thing, namely White domination, not leadership, not guidance, but control, supremacy."[15]

In 1959 Eiselen, the Secretary for Bantu Administration and
Development, declared: "The utmost degree of autonomy which
the Union Parliament is likely to be prepared to concede to these
areas [the Bantu homelands] will stop short of actual surrender
of sovereignty by the European trustee. There is, therefore, no
prospect of a federal system with eventual equality among members. . . . The maintenance of White political supremacy of the
country as a whole is a *sine qua non* for racial peace and economic prosperity in South Africa."[16]

Apartheid supposedly aims at getting rid of the racial hierarchy by granting equal opportunities to each racial group in its
own area, but Schoeman stated as Minister of Labour: " . . . pick
and shovel work is the natural work of the Native . . . the Native
has a special aptitude for repetitive work."[17] He further defined

13. Quoted in *Africa Today*, 11, March, 1964, p. 2, from speech in the
House of Assembly, January 25, 1963.
14. Quoted in *Treatment of Indians in South Africa*, p. 5.
15. Quoted in *Report of the United Nations Commission on the Racial
Situation in South Africa*, p. 153.
16. Quoted in Horrell, *op. cit.*, 1958–1959, p. 50.
17. Quoted in Ralph Horwitz, *Expand or Explode*, pp. 33–34.

"Native Reserves" of South Africa.

apartheid as meaning " . . . that Non-Europeans will never have the same political rights as Europeans; that there will never be social equality; and that the Europeans will always be *baas* in South Africa." A Nationalist candidate in the 1948 elections made his party's view concerning Indians equally clear: "The dregs of India came here half a century ago to work on the sugar plantations. . . . The coolie is not an inmate of this country, but a usurper and exploiter. Millions of people have recently been shifted in Europe to solve racial problems. Why can we not shift 250,000 coolies?"[18]

Segregation is, of course, the cornerstone of apartheid. In theory, apartheid aims at complete geographical separation whereby each racial group will develop "along its own lines," but Malan recognized as early as 1950 that this was impossible: "if one could attain total territorial apartheid, if it were practicable, everybody would admit that it would be an ideal state of affairs. . . . It is not practicable and it does not pay any party to endeavour to achieve the impossible."[19] Verwoerd defines apartheid even more explicitly: "Apartheid is a process of continually increasing separation in all spheres of living, and this takes place even when there is no territorial separation."[20] In other words, when physical segregation is impossible then racial discrimination must step in to maintain White supremacy. In the "European" areas, the non-Whites must remain helots at the service of the master race.

It is useful at this point to refine somewhat the analysis of segregation as practiced or advocated by the Nationalists. Depending on the actual physical distance between racial groups, one may speak of "micro-segregation," "meso-segregation," and "macro-segregation." The blueprint calls for maximization of segregation, but government policy is prepared to accept a lesser degree of physical separation when it is expedient. In the direct

---

18. Quoted in Michael Scott, *A Time to Speak*, pp. 146, 236.
19. Quoted in *Report of the United Nations Commission*, p. 140.
20. Quoted in Ellen Hellmann, *In Defence of a Shared Society*, p. 4.

work situation, i.e., in factories, farms, shops and the like, *micro-segregation* is acceptable to the Nationalists. In practical terms, this means that White and non-White workers associate on the job, but use separate dressing rooms, toilets, dining halls, elevators, waiting rooms, post-office counters, etc.

As soon as these non-Whites who work with Europeans leave the immediate job situation, the blueprint calls for *meso-segregation*. They board completely segregated means of transport to go to widely separated residential areas where they have virtually no contact with Whites, except for policemen, and "location" superintendents, but where they are within commuting distance of the White world for work purposes. Increasingly, the government attempts to suppress *micro-segregation* off the job, as, for example, in the case of domestic servants living on the premises of their employers (albeit in special servants' quarters). Apartheid calls for *meso-segregation* off the job, as this is the greatest physical distance compatible with any sort of economic activity at all. *Meso-segregation* is, of course, costly and wasteful in terms of transport costs, man-hours, fatigue, and frustration, but yet economically feasible, as the last fifteen years have shown. As the voteless non-White masses have had to bear the main cost of this *meso-segregation*, the Whites have only voiced minor protest at the inconvenience of not having servants live on the premises.

Finally, for those Africans not actually in the employment of Whites, apartheid calls for *macro-segregation*, i.e., round-the-clock separation in totally distinct regions, namely the Native Reserves, now in the process of restyling under the name of Bantustans. *Macro-segregation* thus becomes synonymous with the government's notion of total territorial partition, accompanied, of course, by White political paramountcy, even in the African areas. The three degrees of segregation can thus be considered as a scale wherein, according to Nationalist ideology, the greater degree is preferable to the lesser ones, unless practical economic contingencies make the introduction of a lesser degree of physical distance imperative.

Paternalism is also a prominent feature of apartheid applied to Africans, as a glance at government-sponsored publications, such as *Bantu* and the *Bantu Education Journal*, quickly reveals. High-ranking White officials of the Department of Bantu Administration and Development, for example, are described as "fathers of the Bantu."[21] African chiefs pledge their undying servility and gratitude to their Great White Fathers, and the latter condescendingly receive tribal honours, assure their "children" of their sympathy, and dispense government favours.[22]

In connection with White control over the "Bantu homelands," the words "trustee" and "guardian" appeared in quotations earlier. The Minister of Native Affairs expressed the same idea in 1948 when speaking about the field of labour: "The Nationalist Party is opposed to the organization of Natives into trade unions, and advocates a system whereby the State, as guardians, will take care of their interests."[23] In 1959 Verwoerd said: "We are giving the Bantu as our wards every opportunity in their areas to move along a road of development by which they can progress in accordance with their ability."[24] Malan best summed up this paternalistic attitude: "I regard the Bantu not as strangers and not as a menace to the white people, but as our children for whose welfare we are responsible, and as an asset to the country."[25]

In recent years even the apologists of apartheid are becoming sensitive to accusations of racialism directed at them, and deny that Afrikaner Nationalists adhere to a doctrine of White superiority. Such denials are, however, contradicted not only by the

21. *Bantu*, 8, January, 1961, p. 34.
22. *Ibid.*, pp. 7–14.
23. Quoted in Horrell, *Non-European Policies in the Union*, p. 19.
24. Horrell, *A Survey of Race Relations in South Africa*, 1958–1959, p. 50.
25. Quoted in Dvorin, *op. cit.*, p. 95.

practice of apartheid, but also by the very pronouncements of its apologists. For example, Professor L. J. Du Plessis states: "We wish to separate ourselves from the Bantu not because we regard them as being inferior, but because they . . . threaten to overwhelm us by the numerical superiority, and are culturally different and *less developed than we are.*"[26] A publication sponsored by the South African State Information Office speaks of culture contacts in the following terms: " . . . cultural transference mainly proceeded from the *higher European* to the *lower Bantu culture.*"[27] The same brochure later declares: "The Bantu require careful and sympathetic handling and guidance. . . . The repeal of such laws specially affecting the Bantu could only result in chaos through placing *races at different stages of development on the same level* . . . as the Bantu become *sufficiently advanced* to manage their own affairs in their own area, the administration of such affairs should be gradually transferred to them."[28] Rhoodie and Venter complain that opponents of apartheid misleadingly "try to create the impression that the Afrikaner regards the Bantu as an inferior being," and emphatically assert that "this attitude . . . is most decidedly not a premise of apartheid to-day";[29] yet earlier they defended the rise of apartheid among Afrikaners in terms that deserve being quoted at some length, because they illustrate the inextricable confusion of cultural and racial factors that dominates the thinking even of Nationalist academics:

> The three foundation stones of apartheid are Western culture, Christian morality and a specific racial identity. In the case of the Afrikaner there is a powerful connecting link between these three elements. His own particular bio-genetic character is, for example, associated with a particular sociocultural way-of-life and to give up either through amalgamation *with a more primitive culture or race* must necessarily

26. Quoted by Rhoodie and Venter, *op. cit.,* p. 37. Italics are mine.
27. Anonymous, *The Pattern of Race Policy in South Africa,* p. 7. Italics are mine.
28. *Ibid.,* p. 28; italics are mine.
29. Rhoodie and Venter, *op. cit.*

result in the destruction of the other. To the Afrikaner cultural assimilation is synonymous with racial assimilation—there can be no *laissez-faire* middle path. He believes that his socio-cultural and racial identity is something which must be entrenched—thence his comprehensive apartheid programme. The first entrenchment concerns the daily contact between White and Black. Practices such as miscegenation and mixed residential areas are regarded as dangerous in the extreme and must therefore be eliminated by means of racial separation.

Sustained cultural assimilation generally results in social and eventually biological assimilation. It is for this reason that apartheid is not limited only to the prohibition of miscegenation, but also regulates cultural and social contacts in such a way that the above-mentioned chain reaction cannot be set in motion.[30]

In a 1954 reply to a letter by an American clergyman, the former Prime Minister D. F. Malan emphasized both his belief in White superiority and his confusion of colour and culture:

The deep-rooted colour consciousness of the White South Africans . . . arises from the fundamental difference between the two groups, White and Black. The difference in colour is merely the physical manifestation of the contrast between two irreconcilable ways of life, between barbarism and civilization, between heathenism and Christianity, and finally between overwhelming numerical odds on the one hand and insignificant numbers on the other. Such it was in the early beginnings and such it largely remains. The racial differences are as pronounced to-day as they were 300 years ago. Small wonder that the instinct of self-preservation is so inherent in the White South African. He has retained his identity all these years. He is not willing to surrender it now.[31]

In one important respect, the Nationalist brand of paternalism is different from that of Smuts and other more "moderate" racialists. The Nationalists have resolved the contradiction between

---

30. *Ibid.;* first italics are mine.
31. Quoted in L. Kuper, *Passive Resistance in South Africa,* p. 218.

the "civilizing" mission of the Whites and the idealization of "Native institutions." For the Nationalists, paternalism has been used to try to impede Westernization and "retribalize" Africans. "White civilization" is, of course, superior to the "primitive" tribal culture, but it does not follow that the Whites must try to "uplift the Bantu" to their own level. On the contrary, the "Bantu way of life" must be preserved and revived, because it is best adapted to the primitive mentality of the Bantu. Addressing a group of Africans, Malan said: "What you want is a rehabilitation of your own national life, not competition and intermixture and equality with the white man in his particular part of the country."[32] In 1959 the Minister of Bantu Education said in the Assembly: " . . . it is the basic principle of Bantu education in general that our aim is to keep the Bantu child a Bantu child. The Bantu must be so educated that they do not want to become imitators of the Whites, but that they will want to remain essentially Bantu."[33] Recently, De Wet Nél developed the same theme of the evils of Westernization for the "Bantu":

> Not only is the culture of the Whites slavishly imitated, without any consideration of its merits or demerits, but the Bantu is exposed to evils of a different kind, evils which were formerly unknown to him. He becomes acquainted with crime and confusion and subjected to ethical, moral and spiritual decay.
> Since these phenomena are alien to the traditional Bantu way of life, he tends to degenerate, and if the process continues unabated it can result in a rootless, urbanised and semi-Westernised Bantu society that is a danger to itself.[34]

It would be out of place here to refute the racist assumptions on which apartheid is based, or to take a stand on the ethical merits of that policy, or to discuss its practicability. Suffice it to say that the "ideal" form of apartheid as equitable partition is

32. Dvorin, *op. cit.*, p. 95.
33. Quoted in Horrell, *A Survey of Race Relations in South Africa,* 1958–1959, pp. 254–255.
34. *Bantu,* 11, June, 1964, p. 253.

a convenient rationalization, which, accepted at face value, allows well-meaning paternalists to call themselves Nationalists, and serves as the ineffective basis of international apologetics, but that the government has never seriously envisaged its implementation. The implementation of "ideal" apartheid would entail the political and economic disruption of the entire country. "Practical" apartheid, on the other hand is simply a more systematic and internally consistent policy of White oppression. We shall now describe in its broad lines the practical application of colour policy from 1910 to the present.[35]

The segregation of rural Africans in Native Reserves was already an accomplished fact long before the time of Union. The establishment of the Native Reserves system goes back, as we saw, to the work of Theophilus Shepstone in the 1840's in Natal, and to the "Native policy" of the Boer Republics. That system was consolidated and expanded under the Native Land Act of 1913. In urban areas the diamond and gold mines led the way in racial segregation and discrimination by establishing special compounds for their African workers. The Mines and Works Act of 1911 was the first piece of legislation making for a compulsory colour-bar in employment. This Act excluded non-Europeans from skilled jobs in the extractive industries. Residential segregation of Africans in cities, which had hitherto been enforced by the mines and by municipal regulations, was made uniform by the passage of the Native Urban Areas Act of 1923. By the time Hertzog came to power in 1924, the basic pattern of racial discrimination in employment and of physical separation of Africans in urban and rural areas had thus been legislatively established.

Hertzog's rule from 1924 to 1939 was characterized by inten-

35. Among the many publications on this subject see Ellen Hellmann, *Handbook of Race Relations in South Africa;* Muriel Horrell's yearly *Survey of Race Relations in South Africa;* Gwendolen M. Carter, *The Politics of Inequality;* Eugene P. Dvorin, *Racial Separation in South Africa;* Leo Marquard, *The Peoples and Policies of South Africa;* and the numerous pamphlets of the South African Institute of Race Relations.

sified racialism, and it foreshadowed the post-1948 apartheid programme. As a result of pressure from the White trade unions, and of the White labour revolt on the Rand in 1922, the Mines and Works Act was amended and made more stringent in 1926. Non-Whites were subjected to further disabilities in the field of labour through the Industrial Conciliation Act of 1924, amended in 1937, the Native Service Contract Act of 1932, and the Masters and Servants Amendment Act of 1926. These acts denied the right to strike to Africans, and made a breach of contract on the part of servants a criminal offence. In 1927 the Immorality Act prohibited extramarital sexual intercourse between Europeans and Africans. Residential segregation of Africans was further entrenched by the Native Urban Areas Amendment Act of 1930, and the Native Trust and Land Act of 1936. The Native Administration Act of 1928 prohibited the sale of alcoholic beverages to Africans (except for "Kaffir beer"); and the Arms and Ammuniton Act of 1937 practically restricted the ownership of firearms to Europeans.

As regards the franchise, the Hertzog regime steadily reduced the importance of the non-European vote in the Cape. The Women Enfranchisement Act of 1930 extended voting rights to White women only, and thereby reduced by half the relative weight of the non-White vote; the Franchise Laws Amendment Act of 1931 waived the property, income, and education qualifications for White voters but not for non-Whites; finally, the Native Representation Act of 1936 eliminated Africans from the common electoral roll in the Cape, and instituted a system whereby qualified Africans, on a separate voting list, elected three White representatives in Parliament. This act, together with its companion piece, the Native Trust and Land Act, was considered by Hertzog as the permanent solution to the "Native problem."

In one important respect, however, the Hertzog colour policies differed from present-day apartheid. The legislation mentioned above affected almost exclusively the Africans, and left the Coloureds almost untouched. Although Hertzog was opposed to miscegenation, he saw in the Coloured group a "natural ally" of the Whites against the "Black menace," and favoured a policy of economic, cultural, and political assimilation for the Coloureds. For obvious demographic reasons, this "softer" line towards the Coloureds still appeals to the more intelligent "moderate" Nationalists today.

Far from marking a more liberal turn in racial policies, the second Smuts regime (1939–1948) further perfected Hertzog's colour policies. Indeed, Smuts was directly associated with them as the second most prominent member of the Hertzog cabinet from 1933 to 1939. As Prime Minister he continued to entrench "White leadership." The Native Urban Areas Consolidation Act of 1945 systematized further the provisions of the Native Urban Areas Act of 1923 and 1930. The Apprenticeship Act of 1944 further secured skilled manual jobs for the Europeans. Smuts' great contribution to the edifice of White supremacy, however, was his anti-Indian legislation. The Indians had already been subject to countless discriminatory measures, such as the Transvaal Law of 1885 (which confined them to small urban ghettos), exorbitant taxation in Natal, and complete exclusion from the Orange Free State. The Trading and Occupation of Land Restriction Act of 1943 (better known as the "Pegging Act"), and the Asiatic Land Tenure and Indian Representation Act of 1946 (the "Ghetto Act"), prevented Indians from acquiring any new real estate property. These acts were passed largely as the result of White agitation against "Asiatic invasion" in certain "White" residential areas of Durban during the war years. The "Ghetto Act" also granted Indians a nominal separate representation by Whites in Parliament. The conditions of this representation were such a parody of democracy that the Indians boycotted the scheme, and never elected any White M.P. to the Union Parliament.

When the Nationalists won the 1948 election, they only had to extend and systematize an already imposing structure. The Prohibition of Mixed Marriages Act of 1949 forbids any marriage between a White and a non-White. The Immorality Act of 1927 was made more and more stringent in its 1950 and 1957 amendments to the point where "immoral or indecent acts" between a White and a non-White of opposite sexes are punishable with whipping and up to seven years of prison. The process of disfranchisement of the non-Whites was pursued to its logical conclusion. After a five-year constitutional fight, starting with the Separate Representation of Voters Act of 1951 and the High Court of Parliament Act of 1952, the Cape Coloureds were finally eliminated from the common roll in 1956. In 1960 the last token representation of Africans by White M.P.'s was abolished.

A number of laws extended the scope of compulsory physical separation between the four main racial groups. The most important of them is the Group Areas Act of 1950, amended in 1952, 1955, and 1957, which provides for the establishment of segregated residential areas for each "race," and for the mass removal and expropriation of members of the "wrong" skin colour in any given area. This act affects mostly the Coloureds and the Indians, as the Africans were already rigidly segregated when the Nationalists came to power. The main consequence, if not object, of this law is to threaten the livelihood of the Indian merchant community. In theory, the Group Areas Act also applies to Europeans, but, in practice, its implementation results in the mass expropriation and uprooting of non-Whites. In a 1960 court case brought up by a group of Indian plaintiffs against the government, the Minister of the Interior openly admitted that "it could be reasonably inferred from the many provisions of the Group Areas Act that it permits a substantial measure of partial and unequal treatment between the races." The principle of separate and *unequal* treatment is also explicitly entrenched in the Reservation of Separate Amenities Act of 1953. This law was passed after non-Whites won a court case on the plea that the facilities reserved for them were not equal to those available for Whites. While the court ruled in favour of the "separate but equal" principle, the 1953 Act circumvented the court decision by specifying that segregated amenities could also be unequal.[36]

The Bantu Authorities Act of 1951 provides the blue print for the Nationalist "new deal" in "Native Administration." In theory, the government envisages the creation of "independent Bantustans" in the old Native Reserves, but, in practice, Bantu Authorities are a more efficacious version of the old system of appointed chiefs and advisory bodies, with somewhat increased local autonomy. The Native Building Workers Act of 1951 and the Native Labour (Settlement of Disputes) Act of 1953 put the African workers under further occupational handicaps. The Native Administration Amendment Act of 1956 and the Natives (Urban Areas) Amendment Act of the same year extend arbitrary powers of imprisonment and exile over Africans. So as to prevent the passing of Coloureds for Whites, the Population Registration Act of 1950, amended in 1956, provides for the issue of racial identity cards. Special White boards are to decide on the "race" of marginal persons who wish to contest their classification.

In the field of education, the Nationalists passed two important laws. The euphemistically named Extension of University Education Act of 1959 forbids all non-Europeans to attend the English-speaking universities, and provides for the creation of separate "university-colleges," not only for each of the four racial groups, but even for each of three main African linguistic groups. The universities of Cape Town, the Witwatersrand, and Natal were the only educational institutions of higher learning where both Whites and non-Whites could enroll (except for the University of South Africa, a correspondence school); this act thus makes for complete racial segregation at all levels of education.[37]

36. Unlike in the United States, for example, the role of the South African judiciary is largely confined to enforcement and interpretation of legislation, and the courts have only limited powers to pass judgment on the constitutionality of laws.

37. Non-White students enrolled at English universities before the act was passed may complete their studies, however. The medical school of the University of Natal may continue to enroll non-Europeans, but that school has always been segregated *de facto*.

Previous to the Bantu Education Act of 1953, most African primary and secondary schools were controlled by various Protestant and Catholic missionary groups. This act removes African education from mission control, and vests it completely in the hands of the central government. The latter has full powers to appoint and dismiss teachers, and controls the curriculum which avowedly intends to prevent the Westernization of Africans and to "keep the Bantu child a Bantu child." Mother-tongue instruction in Bantu languages is emphasized at the detriment of European tongues; manual labour is stressed to prepare the child for his subservient role in South African society; and Whites may use African schoolchildren for farm labour.[38]

The most eloquent statement about the aims of "Bantu Education" has been made by H. F. Verwoerd in his capacity as Minister of Native Affairs:

> I believe that racial relations will be improved when Bantu Education is handled in the manner proposed by us. Racial relations cannot improve if the result of Native Education is the creation of a frustrated people who as a result of the education they receive, have expectations in life which circumstances in South Africa do not allow to be fulfilled . . . when it creates people who are trained in professions not open to them . . . . Good racial relations cannot exist when the education is given under the supervision of people who . . . believe in a policy of equality.[39]

Finally, a number of laws give the government wide powers of perquisition, confiscation of property, banning of organizations, exile, extradition, arrest, and detention without trial. The most important of them are the Suppression of Communism Act of 1950, amended in 1954, the Criminal Law Amendment Act of

38. See Horrell, *A Survey of Race Relations in South Africa*, 1958–1959, pp. 254, 260–261. On the Nationalist educational policy, see also L. Kuper's true-to-life satire *The College Brew,* and I. B. Tabata, *Education for Barbarism.*

39. Quoted by S. Uys. "Dr. H. F. Verwoerd, Prime Minister of South Africa."

1952, the Public Safety Act of 1953, the Riotous Assemblies Act of 1956 and the Unlawful Organizations Act of 1960. These acts, which followed waves of non-White protest, forbid practically any form of opposition, by peaceful means or otherwise, and enable the government to repress the non-White liberatory movements. Communism is made illegal and is defined as "any doctrine or scheme which aims at bringing about any political, industrial, social or economic change within the Union by the promotion of disturbance or disorder, by unlawful acts or omissions or the threat of such acts or omissions."[40]

Two recent laws overshadow all previous ones, however. The first, the 1962 General Law Amendment Act, popularly known as the "Sabotage Act," further extends the already wide limits of arbitrary government powers. It provides for a minimum sentence of five years of prison and a maximum sentence of death for "sabotage," and places the burden of proof on the accused. The concept of "sabotage" includes any attempt to promote disturbance, to disrupt any industry, to hamper the maintenance of law and order, to encourage any social or economic change, and to promote hostility between different sections of the population. Illegal possession of explosives or illegal entry into any building is considered sufficient evidence of an intention to carry out acts of sabotage. The act also extends previous government powers to ban newspapers, organizations, and gatherings, and to imprison any person for any length of time without due process of law, and without having to declare a state of emergency.

On May 1, 1963, an even more draconian General Law Amendment Act was passed, once more with the support of the United Party. The act provides for repeated detention of persons for ninety days at a time, for questioning; refusal to allow anybody, including legal counsel, to see detained persons; total prohibition on the courts to interfere with this form of detention; indefinite imprisonment without trial for persons having com-

40. Quoted in *Report of the United Nations Commission on the Racial Situation in the Union of South Africa,* p. 93.

pleted ordinary gaol sentences; powers to hold letters, telegrams, and parcels sent by post; death penalty, applicable also to juveniles, for receiving training in the use of violence outside South Africa, or for achieving the objects of a banned organization; and fifteen years of prison for entering a "protected" area without consent. In defending his party's support of this act a United Party M.P. said: "We have no choice. Long ago we fought to prevent trouble developing. When it did develop, we could not refuse the government powers to cope with it."[41] The act has appropriately been nicknamed the "No Trial" Act.

The above survey of legislation is by no means exhaustive. Only the most important acts have been mentioned. Even a complete list of racial laws would not give a comprehensive picture of the mechanisms of White domination, and of the sources of interracial conflicts. The government, and the White group which it represents, resort to at least five other major forms of discrimination besides legislation. These extra- or para-legal types of racial discrimination contribute even more to tension than legislation as such, and must therefore be mentioned at some length.

The first of them consists of the innumerable police and municipal regulations, ministerial orders, and government gazette proclamations which regiment almost every aspect of the lives of non-Europeans. These regulations and orders are based on legislation, of course, but the scope for arbitrary action in laws governing "non-European affairs" is so wide that the various branches of the executive practically constitute autonomous legislative bodies responsible only to the Prime Minister. By far the most important of these regulations is the vast and intricate system of "pass laws" and "influx control." The pass laws constitute the cornerstone of government control over the African masses, and are the most detested aspect of discrimination. More than any other set of measures, they harass the daily life of

41. *Africa Digest*, 10, June, 1963, p. 195.

Africans. Pass laws go back to the nineteenth century, and have grown over the years to reach their present scope under the Nationalists.

Under the system of pass regulations, any adult male African must carry at all times a "reference book" containing his employment history, as well as a number of documents such as tax receipts and various sorts of permits. In short, an adult African may not reside anywhere without permission, may not move outside his allotted place of residence without approval of the authorities, is subject to a curfew at night, may not live in any "White" area without being gainfully employed, may not own land in freehold (aside from some insignificant exceptions), and may be expelled from his residence and deported to any place, when the administration deems his presence to be "undesirable" or "redundant." In a number of cases, persons have literally no right to live *anywhere* in their own country, and are susceptible to be arrested for illicit residence no matter where they are.

The objects of the pass laws are to restrict African migration to the cities, to prevent the rise of a stable African urban middle class, and to keep the masses under the continuous control of the police. In all these objectives, the pass regulations have only met with limited success. Urban migration continues at a fast rate in spite of all influx control measures, the African middle class and intelligentsia are steadily growing, and the population is harassed and frustrated, rather than controlled, by the police. The main effects of the pass laws have been to disrupt countless African families, by separating for long periods the wage earner from his dependents; to promote violence, anger, prostitution, and juvenile delinquency; and to waste labour potential by maintaining the mass of the workers in the position of an unskilled, floating proletariat.

The second form of discrimination falling outside the strict scope of legislation is partial and unequal treatment of non-Whites in the courts. It remains true that, up until recently, the

South African judiciary has shown a greater measure of equity than other branches of the government, and has imposed an effective brake on the dictatorial tendencies of the executive. Nevertheless, judges, who are all Whites, share for the most part the prejudices of their group. Not only have they been forced to implement discriminatory laws, but, even where the law makes no racial distinction, the private prejudices of judges have introduced a strong factor of partiality. Whites committing offences against non-Whites are almost invariably punished much more lightly than in the reverse case, and a dual standard of justice is evident in many cases.

Another curious way in which the dual standard operates is in the more lenient punishment of Africans committing crimes against Africans, than of Whites against Whites. This seeming bias in favour of Africans does, in fact, mean that law-abiding Africans have no adequate protection against criminals. In most cases where non-Whites have been victims, the police does not investigate the crime with nearly the same zeal as when a White is involved. If a case of African against African comes to court, which is more the exception than the rule, many judges tend to regard the offence as less serious than similar offences of a White against a White, because of the lower status of the victim, and because they often assume that violence is "natural" among Africans, and, hence, involves less responsibility.

A few examples among many will illustrate the dual standard of South African "justice." Awarding £16 damages to an African who had been shot and seriously wounded by a European, a South African judge declared: "I am of the opinion that in awarding damages for pain and suffering one must take into account the standing of the person injured. . . . For example I would award a larger sum for damages in the case of injury to a European woman than I would to a Native male. Similarly in the present case, if it had been a European of some standing I would have awarded greater damages than I now propose to do."[42] Another judge justified his decision in a rape case involving an African woman in the following words: "We know generally that Natives do not consider rape as seriously as Europeans do."[43] A White murderer who had beaten an African to death was found guilty of culpable homicide and fined £10 or one month in gaol.[44] Police Sergeant Arlow, who had previously been convicted for brutally beating prisoners, was sentenced to three years of prison for torturing to death an African, and was freed for good behaviour after serving fifteen months of his term.[45] A White who had shot and wounded an African guitar player in the face because he had "an aversion for Native singing and music," was fined £10.[46] On the other hand, ten African members of a mob who were found guilty of lynching nine policemen in Cato Manor, Durban, were condemned to death, even though the share of individual responsibility for the death of any of the victims was impossible to ascertain in most cases.[47]

A third type of extralegal discrimination consists in the various forms of economic exploitation to which non-Whites, and particularly Africans, are subject. Contrary to the general belief that the Whites carry the financial burden for non-European facilities, the official government policy is that each racial group must pay its own way. In fact, the position is reversed, and one may speak of a "Black man's burden." Through artificially low wages resulting from "job reservation," the repression of non-White trade unions, restrictions on labour mobility, and other measures, the non-White worker subsidizes White industry, and contributes heavily to the high living standards of the Europeans. In addition, Africans must pay a number of

42. Quoted in Walker, *op. cit.*, p. 167.
43. *Ibid.*, p. 169.
44. *Ibid.*, p. 169.
45. Johannesburg *Sunday Times*, September 3, 1961.
46. *The Natal Mercury*, January 7, 1961.
47. *Ibid.*, December 16, 1960.

special taxes, such as the yearly capitation tax, school, hospital and tribal levies, and municipal taxes on "Kaffir beer," to which other groups are not subject. Proportionally to their income, the Africans are much more heavily taxed than the Whites. According to a press statement released by the Minister of Native Affairs in 1956, the amount spent by the government on services for Africans is about the same as that contributed by that group in taxation.[48]

The fourth source of racial tension and extralegal control of the non-Whites by the government comes from the intimidatory role of the police and army. In the last few years the police and Defence Force are being reorganized and reinforced, in part to crush any internal disorders. Since 1960 the size of the Permanent Defence Force has increased from 9,019 to 15,288 men, exclusive of some 10,000 army reservists on active duty at any given time. Purchases of modern weapons, including airplanes, from Britain, France, Belgium, and Italy have sharply risen. The government intends to spend about £700,000,000 in military equipment over the next ten years.[49] By 1960 there were, in addition to the Defence Force, 175 Rifle Commandos in existence with a total strength of 80,000 men. These reserve Commando units are described in the following terms:

> An annual quota of ammunition is issued to encourage rifle shooting practice. Additional ammunition and rifles are sold to Commando members at reduced prices. The standard of marksmanship is one of the highest in the world. The main function of this organization, during a conflict will be internal security duties.[50]

48. *African Taxation,* pp. 18–19. This pamphlet by the Institute of Race Relations analyses carefully the relation between African taxation and services, and comes to the conclusion that the South African tax structure is based on pigmentation and is regressive.

49. *African Digest,* 10, No. 6, June, 1963, p. 198. Anonymous, *Report of the Special Committee on the Policies of Apartheid of the Government of the Republic of South Africa,* p. 121.

50. Anonymous, *State of the Union Year-Book,* 1959–1960, p. 49.

The internal role of the military establishment was also stressed in 1961 by J. J. Fouche, the Minister of Defence:

Because our armed forces have to be prepared to combat internal subversion as well as outside aggression, the best weapons have to be supplied for this purpose.[51]

As of early 1963, in addition to the Commando units, the South African security forces included some 25,000 well-equiped soldiers, and 28,385 members of the police. The military budget nearly trebled between 1961 and 1964 (from £40,000,000 to £104,000,000), making it the largest of any African state.[52] (Nigeria, for example, with over three times the population of South Africa, had an army of 8,000 men in 1963, and an annual military budget of about £10,000,000.) Also of interest is the meteoric development of a South African arms industry in anticipation of an international arms embargo. In 1961 approximately £180,000 were spent to develop weapon production; in 1962 the figure had increased tenfold, and by 1963 fortyfold. The 1964 appropriation for that purpose is nearly £12,000,000.[53]

While the stage of large-scale terrorism has not yet been reached, the police is deliberately used as an instrument of intimidation and harassment of the African population. Under the cover of enforcing the pass and liquor regulations, the police constantly raids African locations at night, and carries out systematic house searches and mass arrests. In 1957, 1,021,190 Africans were convicted of crimes; in 1958 the number had reached 1,122,081. About 60 per cent of these cases covered violations of the pass and liquor regulations to which only Africans are

51. Anonymous, *Report of the Special Committee on the Policies of Apartheid of the Government of the Republic of South Africa*, p. 125.

52. *Africa Report*, 9, January, 1964, p. 18; and *Africa Today*, 11, March, 1964, p. 6. Interestingly, the 1964 military budget is approximately as large as the sum proposed by the Tomlinson Commission for the development of the "Bantu homelands" over a ten-year period.

53. *Africa Today, ibid.*

subject.[54] On the basis of official crime statistics, I would conservatively estimate that one African adult man out of three is arrested and convicted of an offence each year. Over the years few urban African men have escaped imprisonment for purely technical offences against discriminatory laws. The police arrests an average of 3000 Africans *a day*. In addition to these "routine" arrests, mass waves of political arrests are becoming increasingly frequent. To mention a few instances, over 2000 African women were incarcerated in Johannesburg alone between October 21 and October 28, 1958, during an anti-pass campaign; in May, 1960, during the post-Sharpeville emergency, the Minister of Justice admitted that 1907 political prisoners were detained without trial under the provisions of the Public Safety Act, and that another 18,011 persons had been arrested under other laws and regulations. More recently, during the year 1962, a total of 5293 persons were detained on alleged security crimes.[55]

These police raids are almost invariably accompanied, at best, by gross discourtesy and manhandling, and frequently by beating, shooting, theft, and destruction of property. Constant patrols with armoured cars and vans circulate in the African areas. Low-flying aircraft are used to spot any concentrations of people, and, at night, some "locations" are swept by powerful projectors. During times of "emergency," police raids are further intensified. Objects such as walking sticks, umbrellas, bicycle chains, kitchen knives, screwdrivers, hammers, and sickles, are confiscated as "weapons" without giving receipts. Conditions in non-White prisons have been well documented. Overcrowding with up to 120 inmates in one cell, lack of adequate sanitary facilities, and unhygienic diet lead to epidem-

54. Horrell, *A Survey of Race Relations in South Africa*, 1958–1959, p. 303; 1959–1960, p. 266.

55. *Ibid.*, 1958–1959, p. 122; 1959–1960, pp. 79, 84; *New York Times*, June 21, 1963.

ics among African prisoners.[56] During the 1960 emergency, for example, a score of African infants carried by women prisoners are alleged to have died of dysentery in gaol. Vexation, humiliation, assault, torture, and murder of prisoners are common occurrences.[57] The testimony of Michael Scott, an Anglican priest, is also revealing:

> The cells of the Non-European section of the gaol were so crowded that at night the floor space was entirely covered with the forms of prisoners lying alternatively head to foot with room only for a pail of drinking water and a latrine bucket. . . . Many of the warders took an obscene delight in the searches that were made at each parade for tobacco or anything else that could be concealed on the person. The Non-European prisoners were made to strip naked in view of all of us and perform the most grotesque antics so that the warder could satisfy himself that nothing was concealed between the legs or toes or anywhere else on the prisoner's body. Worst of all were the days when corporal punishment was inflicted. . . . Those due for this barbaric treatment were made to undress and stand naked besides their heap of clothes in the yard. . . . The warders who were to inflict the punishment would pass the time of waiting by practicing their strokes in view of the waiting prisoners, with a cane about four feet in length. Then one by one the prisoners would enter the shed to be tied to a triangular frame and undergo their sentence. Sometimes there were screams, sometimes there were not; but always when the victim emerged from the shed, he would be hardly able to stand.[58]

The use of firearms by the police is a common method to disperse crowds. Until recently, when the police became better trained to curb open displays of violence, tear gas, blank cartridges, fire hoses, and the like were seldom used against African

56. Horrell, *A Survey of Race Relations in South Africa,* 1958–1959, p. 303.

57. Anthony Sampson, *Drum, A Venture into the New Africa,* pp. 185–197.

58. Scott, *op. cit.,* pp. 142–143.

gatherings. Baton charges are one of the milder techniques resorted to by the police. The Sharpeville shooting on March 21, 1960, was only the bloodiest in recent years, but there have been many other similar incidents on a smaller scale.[59] During the 1952 passive resistance campaign, for example, the police killed 32 Africans and wounded at least 159 in four shooting incidents within less than a month.[60] At Sharpeville the police shot indiscriminately with automatic weapons into an unarmed African crowd of peaceful demonstrators including women and children. Sixty-seven persons were killed and 186 wounded, according to official figures. Of the victims, 155 were shot from the back while fleeing.[61] Between March 21 and April 9, 1960, official sources admitted killing 83 non-White civilians and injuring 365.[62]

The South African police is not only brutal, but corruption is common in its ranks. The police "protects," and takes a "cut" from almost every illicit activity (notably until 1962, the liquor traffic) in the African areas. On the other hand, it offers law-abiding non-White citizens almost no protection against thugs and racketeers operating in the "locations." Under these conditions, it is no wonder that the Africans regard the police purely as an instrument of White oppression, and as a public enemy. Imprisonment is so frequent that it has lost any stigma, and has even acquired an aura of manly accomplishment. The distinction between real common-law crimes and purely technical offences has become blurred.

In short, in a country where the law-making and law-enforcing process has become a major means of political oppression, it is difficult for Africans to dissociate authority from its

59. A summary of recent disturbances can be found in Horrell, *A Survey of Race Relations in South Africa*, 1958–1959, pp. 122–147; 1959–1960, pp. 39–89.

60. Leo Kuper, *Passive Resistance in South Africa*.

61. For a detailed description of the Sharpeville events with photographic documentation, see Ambrose Reeves, *Shooting at Sharpeville*.

62. *A Survey of Race Relations in South Africa*, 1959–1960, p. 68.

abuse, or "law and order" from the *status quo*. Denying any legitimacy to the state, the average African has basically the same negative attitude to law and law-enforcement as the psychopath or the criminal. Where civil disobedience against unjust laws, and, more recently, acts of sabotage have the aura of heroism, common-law crimes such as theft and murder become redefined as permissible when their victims are Whites. In fact, the political underground becomes infiltrated with common thugs, and there results a growing demoralization and *anomie* in the society at large, not unlike what took place in the European countries under German military occupation during the Second World War. The average African can, of course, distinguish a *tso-tsi* (young criminal) from a political organizer, but many have lost any respect for law as such, and regard breach of law as a courageous and honourable activity. Perfectly "respectable" Africans, such as mission-educated university students, openly brag about their terms in gaol, their ability to deceive the police, their cleverness at faking documents, and the frequency with which they break laws. Some would not even hesitate, for example, to receive or buy goods which they know to have been stolen from White-owned stores.

The fifth and last type of extralegal discrimination would deserve a book by itself, and we can only deal with it very cursorily here. It concerns the private behaviour and attitudes of Whites towards non-Whites, or, in other words, the day-to-day race relations.[63] White colour prejudice is, of course, at the root of the racial conflict in South Africa. Legislation and the whole state apparatus reflect accurately the attitudes of the dominant White group. At the same time, however, official segregation and discrimination reinforce the already existing prejudices, and make for further increases in private discrimination.

63. I have dealt at greater length with this topic in *Caneville* and in "Race Attitudes in Durban, South Africa," see also MacCrone, *op. cit.;* H. Kuper, *The Uniform of Colour;* Thomas F. Pettigrew, "Social Distance Attitudes of South African Students"; and Paton, *Cry the Beloved Country.*

Private and public racialisms are thus the two mutually reinforcing elements in a vicious circle of ever deepening racial conflict.

As Smuts rightly remarked, practically all White South Africans, "except those who are quite mad," share the firm conviction of belonging to a *Herrenvolk*. Although the White stereotypes of the various non-European groups are quite different, and although private White attitudes and behaviour range from benevolent paternalism to virulent hatred, all Whites, except for a few liberal and leftist intellectuals, believe themselves to be an innately superior group, born to dominate the non-Europeans. This superiority complex leads to countless forms of private discrimination which greatly contribute to racial tension. At the most superficial level of etiquette, the Whites insist on the maintenance of master-servant relations. Non-Europeans are expected to show subservience and self-deprecation, and to extend to the Whites the titles of "Sir," "Madam," "Master," or "*baas*."[64] The Europeans, as a rule, refuse to extend the use of titles and other forms of elementary courtesy to non-Whites, and call the latter by first names (real or fictitious), or by the terms "boy" and "girl." Some even use racial epithets such as "Kaffir," "Hotnot" and "coolie."[65]

In its extreme form, White racialism expresses itself through institutionalized brutality in the police and prison system. But quite a number of civilian White farmers and hooligans beat and maltreat non-Europeans and go mostly unpunished. In rural areas, the use of the *sjambok*[66] and other forms of physical abuse were current practices until recently, and have not yet disappeared. The common belief that lynching does not exist in South Africa is a myth. Aside from many legalized police lynchings, a number of non-Whites have been murdered by

64. Literally "boss."
65. These insulting terms refer respectively to Africans, Coloureds and Indians.
66. A whip made of hippopotamus or oxen nerve.

Whites under conditions that can only be described as lynch-ings.[67] Such behaviour occasionally finds support on the floor of Parliament. A Nationalist M. P. declared in the House of Assembly in 1946: "If Mr. Hofmeyr ever succeeds in bringing Indians and coloured persons into the House as members of Parliament, I should be given a machine gun, and they will be brought down as fast as they come in."[68] The most that can be said concerning lynching in South Africa is that the phenom-enon has not become as institutionalized as in the southern United States.

Most Europeans avoid any contact with non-Whites which does not conform to the stereotyped master-servant pattern. The maintenance of the master-servant relationship is the *raison d'être* of segregation, as we have already seen. Few Whites object to interracial contact, no matter how intimate, so long as the non-Whites "stay in their place." Where there is no legal pro-vision for segregation, the "customary" colour-bar sets in to prevent egalitarian contact. Where such contact is unavoidable, the Whites expect and receive preferential treatment, such as being served first in shops. In other words, the potentially equal relationship of co-customer is made unequal by racial dis-crimination.

In general, "customary" discrimination and segregation (which the Whites often term "voluntary") have preceded and exceeded, by far, legal apartheid. Such has been the case for interracial marriage and commensality; discrimination in salaries; the occupational colour-bar; service in shops; and segregation in churches, sports, private clubs, and many other places.[69] The presence of the "customary" colour-bar has led many English-speaking Whites to criticize apartheid laws as "unnecessary." Indeed, for most practical purposes, many of the apartheid laws

67. Oliver Walker cites several cases in his book, *Kaffirs are Lively*, pp. 164, 169, 216.
68. Quoted by Walker, *op. cit.*, p. 106.
69. See for example my study of Caneville.

simply rigidified the *status quo,* and were intended to eliminate a few aberrant exceptions to customary apartheid, or to prevent organized campaigns by multiracial organizations from breaking down "voluntary" segregation. Even today, when the scope of apartheid legislation has become very wide indeed, the private colour-bar extends much further yet, and seems to anticipate future laws, as it has in the past. The pressure of White public opinion makes almost impossible all forms of egalitarian inter-racial contact, even those which are still legal (such as private gatherings), and subjects the White "delinquent" to severe ostracism. At the same time, the existence of apartheid laws provides the prejudiced Whites who claim to oppose the racial policy of the government with a convenient excuse for private discrimination.

The combined forces of White public opinion and the law thus constantly reward and reinforce colour prejudice, and punish non-discrimination to the point of making it practically impossible. The few liberal Whites are not only compelled to comply with apartheid laws if they want to stay out of gaol; they are also viewed as "quite mad," or, worse, traitors to their "race," if they transgress the colour *mores* of the White group. Many non-Europeans also regard the behaviour of White liberals as suspicious because it is unusual, and question the motives of such Europeans. At the same time, because his behaviour is not allowed to be consistent with his principles, the liberal White suffers under a constant burden of guilt.

In one respect, some observers might argue, government policy towards Africans has shown some signs of "liberalization."[70] The Bantustan policy, as formulated in the Promotion of Bantu Self-Government Act of 1959, represents the degree of "positive" apartheid that the government is prepared to offer Africans. Verwoerd's plan consists of consolidating the existing

70. Gwendolen Carter, for example, holds the view that the Bantustan plans "counterbalance the negative, restrictive *apartheid* provisions." Cf. Carter, *Independence for Africa,* p. 62.

scattered Native Reserves into eight more or less compact areas that are to become the "homelands" of the respective African ethnic groups. The total area of the Bantustans will be substantially the same as the old Native Reserves, i.e., some 13 per cent of the country. With provisions for economic development, including urbanization and industrialization of the "border areas" between the Bantustans and the "White" areas, the government hopes that an increasing proportion of the Africans will be settled in these "homelands," and, conversely, that the "White" areas will gradually rid themselves of "transient" Africans. This grand design for territorial apartheid was already developed in its broad lines a decade ago. Its practicability in sheer economic terms, quite apart from moral and political considerations, has been questioned by every non-Nationalist economist. It is hardly conceivable that areas incapable of providing for the sheer *survival* of some four million people could ever support three or four times that population, barring, of course, staggering capital investments in non-economic ventures. But we are more concerned here with the political implications of the Bantustans than with their economic feasibility.

Since 1961 two seemingly "liberal" developments have taken place in Verwoerd's Bantustan policy. In clear contradiction to earlier statements by himself and by other Nationalist politicians, Verwoerd has used the word "independence" in connection with the Bantustans. Second, in the blueprint now being implemented in the Transkei (the first of the Bantustans), greater powers are ostensibly given to Africans. What do these "new" developments imply in practice? My argument is that the word "independent" is devoid of meaning in this context, and that the new Bantustan scheme represents a cautious substitution of a Lugardian type of indirect rule for the old system of direct rule. The Transkei and the other African areas are not intended by the government to become sovereign states, but rather to remain South African "protectorates" under the control of Pretoria, and without any representation in the central government.

To speak of "eventual independence" without any suggestion of a timetable as Verwoerd does, is clearly devoid of meaning in the Africa of the 1960's. Furthermore, recent statements by Verwoerd[71] and by the Minister for Bantu Administration and Development, M. D. C. De Wet Nel, confirm our hypothesis, and eloquently refute the theory that apartheid is in the process of liberalization. In Febuary, 1963 De Wet Nel denied once more any intention to make the "Bantu homelands" sovereign: "The Republic of South Africa, of which the Transkei and also the other Bantu homelands form an integral part, under international law form a sovereign unitary state."[72]

If these statements are not accepted as compelling evidence of the government's intentions, then actual implementation of Transkeian "self-government" should dispel any doubts. The scheme was first devised and then implemented while the Pondo peasantry in the Transkei was in open revolt against the government. Starting in 1960 the Transkei has been subjected to emergency regulations, and militarily occupied, and meetings of more than ten Africans have had to be approved by the Bantu Affairs Commissioner. Such were the conditions under which the November, 1963 elections took place. Numerous uprisings, armed clashes with the police, political assassinations of government-appointed chiefs, burning of huts, killing of cattle, and other acts of terrorism and sabotage against the authorities have taken place. To suppose that the South African government contemplates relinquishing control over a major centre of revolt from which underground activities could easily spread to the rest of the country would be an insult to Verwoerd's intelligence. Furthermore, the Bantustan programme, in full conformity with the principles of apartheid, excludes the possibility of a federal

71. January 25, 1963 statement quoted on page 118.
72. Speech by De Wet Nel in House of Assembly on second reading of the Transkei Constitution Bill.

union of equal units represented in a central parliament, and reserves for the South African government all control over foreign affairs, defence, internal security, immigration, customs, transport, post and telegraphs, and currency.

While the new Transkei constitution extends the scope of local autonomy, "self-government" is firmly vested, not in popularly elected representation, but in government-appointed and revokable chiefs. The Transkeian Legislative Assembly consists of 109 members, of whom only 45 are elected. Thus, the present "self-governing" Transkei has as prime minister Chief Kaiser Matanzima, an avowed supporter of "separate development," who received only about one-fourth of the popular vote in the November 1963 elections, but who commands a secure majority of the Assembly.[73] His main opponent, Victor Poto, although himself a chief, leads the Democratic Party, which has a multiracial platform and opposes apartheid. Even though Poto received a clear popular mandate in November, 1963, his party is reduced to impotence in the Assembly, as he only controls 33 of the 45 elective seats, and 16 of the 64 appointed chiefs. In May, 1964, the Assembly chairman, N. J. Busakwe, a Poto supporter, was deposed by the majority of appointed members, thereby reducing the opponents of apartheid to even more complete impotence.[74]

Not content with this degree of control, and in the event the chiefs themselves would become unpliable, Pretoria reserves itself a blanket veto right on all legislation passed by the Transkeian Assembly; jurisdiction over serious court cases involving

73. The propaganda pamphlet *South African Scope* (November–December, 1963) cynically describes Matanzima as having "defeated the advocate of multiracialism, Chief Victor Poto, in the race for the Chief Ministership of the new state."

74. *The Times*, London, December 2, 7, and 9, 1963; May 7 and 8, 1964. Another chief who opposes the Bantustans, Sabata Dalindyebo of the Tembu, told his people: "The freedom you are getting in the Transkei is a fowl-run." Cf. *Report of the Special Committee on the Policies of Apartheid*, p. 52.

such crimes as treason, murder, sabotage, rape, theft, and witch-craft; the collection and allocation of taxes; and the supply and control of technical personnel and advisors. Furthermore, the Transkeian Assembly is not empowered to amend the constitution under which it operates.

In some respects, the new Transkeian Assembly is even less democratic than the old Transkei General Council or *Bunga*, most members of which were elected, even though their functions were purely advisory. Nevertheless, to much of the United Party White opposition, and to some Afrikaner Nationalists, Verwoerd's concept of Bantustans looks dangerously "liberal." Ironically, then, Verwoerd is now being outflanked on the right within his own party and by the English United Party opposition which, for political purposes, pretends to accept Verwoerd's "independence" promise at face value.[75]

Obviously, the Bantustan policy does not in any way meet non-White demands. This is true, not because the government "concessions" do not go nearly far enough to placate African Nationalists; but, rather, because the Bantustan policy, far from meeting African demands part of the way, does in fact run counter to them in two basic respects. In the first place, African nationalism is adamantly opposed to any extension of the powers of traditional chiefs, and favours democratic government with universal adult suffrage. Secondly, most politically conscious Africans are against any territorial partition along ethnic lines,

---

75. E.g., in January, 1962, S. F. Waterson (a United Party Member of Parliament) said in the House of Assembly in reference to the Bantustans: "We are being asked to pay globular sums for the privilege of giving away large parts of the heritage of the people of this country." He further emphasized that the notion of Bantustans meant the abandonment of any idea of White leadership in South Africa, the creation of a series of Black independent states which might be hostile and would control South Africa's labour supply, and the fostering of political demands on the part of the non-White majority left in "White" South Africa. Cf. *Natal Mercury,* January 27, 1962.

and will not settle for anything less than control over the entire country.[76]

Yet the extreme rightist opposition is possibly correct in seeing in the Bantustans an opening of Pandora's box for White domination. In as explosive a situation as that of South Africa, any slight change might be interpreted, however wrongly, as a weakening of the government's grip, and could easily precipitate much more drastic change. Some traditional chiefs, e.g., Victor Poto, the leader of the opposition in the Transkeian Assembly, have already shown signs of pressing for more autonomy, and oppose apartheid. Some of them might gain support among conservative peasants by appealing to ethnic particularism, or simply by showing opposition to the government and belatedly staging a "revolt of the puppets." If, on the other hand, chiefs continue to play a subservient role, peasant unrest is likely to increase; it would then be exploited to the utmost by militant African nationalism, and would probably be led and organized by terrorist organizations.

Another possibility is that the government's policy of creating uniracial Bantustans might backfire and be seized upon by African leaders to adopt an ideology of Black racialism. This could have a wide demagogic appeal, and would be relatively safe, as it could be done without ostensibly opposing apartheid. Interestingly, Poto, in his opposition to Matanzima, is adopting what outwardly looks like a pro-White stand, and Matanzima, in his support of the Bantustan concept, could easily adopt a position similar to that of the Pan-African Congress.

There is one important element of novelty in the Transkeian scheme which may prove difficult for the government to control. Nearly 900,000 Africans have been allowed to cast a ballot, and to form political parties represented in a legislative body. The extremely circumscribed scope given to the expression of African

76. Some, like Jordan Ngubane, have advocated "culturally autonomous provinces" in a federal republic.

political aspirations may not be as important as the catharsis involved in political action.

Let us summarize the policies of the successive South African governments towards the three main non-White groups, and, by the same token, the White attitudes which these policies have reflected. The traditional White policy and attitude towards Africans have been paternalistic. Africans are considered a backward, simple, childish people who must be ruled by their White guardians, and whose place in South African society is that of servants and manual labourers. So far as possible, the "good old tribal way of life" must be maintained because it is well adapted to the "primitive Native mentality," and because the "raw tribal Kaffir" knows his place and respects his White *baas*. Where the Whites need Black labour, the Africans must be segregated from, and prevented from competing with, the Whites. The urban Africans must be kept as a migrant proletariat, to prevent their taking root in the "European" part of the country. All Africans, whether urban or rural, must remain perpetually a rootless, powerless, unorganized helotry without any civic rights in South Africa. A White-controlled form of local self-government under government-appointed chiefs must be maintained and developed in the "Bantu homelands."

The rise of political consciousness among Africans, resulting from urbanization, industrialization, education, and outside influences, has led to a change in White attitudes and politics. Besides the stereotype of the childish, happy, irresponsible, subservient, stupid, tribal African, there arose the spectre of the threatening urban African who no longer respects his White master, and has the audacity of demanding certain rights. All available means of repression must be used to crush this "detribalized scum." The rise of the politically conscious African led to a hardening of anti-Black prejudices away from the old, benevolently paternalistic model, towards a virulently competitive form of racial hatred. Simultaneously, government policy became more and more oppressive and dictatorial. This is not to deny that the *ideology* of apartheid does have a benevolent dimension within the master-servant framework. However, as the urban and industrial structure of modern South Africa rendered increasingly hopeless any attempts to impose an obsolete model of race relations based on nineteenth-century, rural conditions, and as the growing militancy of African nationalism could not be counteracted, the government increasingly resorted to the totalitarian measures.

The traditional White attitude towards Coloureds has also been paternalistic. The stereotyped Coloured, as viewed by the Whites, is a gay, musical, careless, irresponsible, humourous drunkard. As he has White "blood," he is considered superior to, and more intelligent than, the African. Before 1948 the Coloureds were treated as a bastardly offshoot of the *Herrenvolk,* deserving of sympathy. Previous governments, including the Hertzog Nationalists, always kept alive the Coloureds' hope of political and economic assimilation to the Whites, while opposing miscegenation; and the status of the Coloureds was markedly superior to that of the Africans and the Indians. Until 1948 the Coloureds were treated as *Lumpenweisse.* With the advent of apartheid, however, every prospect of assimilation to the Whites has evaporated, and the position of the Coloureds has steadily deteriorated. The Coloureds are segregated and treated as one of the three non-White groups, without any direct participation in the country's government.

With the creation of a Department of Coloured Affairs, there emerges a "new deal" towards that group. "Separate development" is to proceed as vigorously for the Coloureds as for the other racial groups, and, with the introduction of the Coloured Persons Representative Council Bill, a set of special "self-governing" institutions are going to be created. A Coloured Legislative Council of thirty elected and sixteen nominated members is to come into being, with limited powers in such matters as local government, education, community welfare, and pensions. Election is to take place every five years by universal suffrage of all

Coloureds over twenty-one.[77] This form of "self-government" is to replace the vestigial Coloured representation in Parliament. Thus, the Coloured policy parallels the "new deal" for Africans, except for the lack of any sizeable "Coloured homelands." The Coloureds can look forward to many little ghettos instead of a few large Bantustans, or, to use our earlier distinction, to a system of *meso*-segregation, as opposed to the "ideal" of *macro*-segregation for Africans.

South African Indians have been the object of the most virulent form of racialism. Like Jews in other countries, with whom they have often been compared, Indians are in the position of scapegoats. Most Whites view Indians as dishonest, sly competitors whose intelligence, greed, and high birth rate make all the more dangerous. While official policy statements concerning Africans and Coloureds have generally had the appearance of benevolence, and while these two groups have always been granted a place, albeit an inferior one, in South Africa, all governments have deliberately tried to rid the country of its Indian population, by means of exorbitant taxation,[78] "repatriation" schemes, and, now, expropriation under the Group Areas Act.

A Nationalist Party programme states: "The Party holds the view that Indians are a foreign and outlandish element which is unassimilable. They can never become part of the country and must therefore be treated as an immigrant community."[79] Before the Nationalists, Smuts and the United Party also accurately reflected the attitudes of the English-speaking Whites in being virulently anti-Indian. After the failure of all attempts to "repatriate" Indians who have been settled in South Africa for a century, the government in 1961 "recognized the existence" of the Asian community. This declaration will allow Indians to "develop

77. *South African Scope*, March, 1964, p. 1.
78. Before World War One, Indians over fourteen years of age who were not indentured labourers had been subject for a time to a special annual tax of £3, i.e., the equivalent of five to six months' wages for an indentured workers.
79. Quoted in *Thought*, p. 7.

along their own lines" as voteless subjects in their own "group areas."

This point of view was expressed by W. A. Maree, the Minister of Indian Affairs, in a 1962 policy statement: "The government has realized that the Indians are a permanent part of the population of this country . . . the task of my Department is in the first place to guide the Indian people toward development so that they can have control over their own affairs to an ever-increasing extent."[80] A National Indian Council of twenty-one appointed members first met in March, 1964. Its functions are purely advisory. Thus, the Indian version of "self-government" does not even include the fiction of elective representation, as in the case of the Coloured and Africans. Apartheid for Indians involves maximum discrimination under *meso*-segregation.

Government policy towards the Coloureds and the Indians explodes whatever rationalizations the Nationalists have devised to defend apartheid. Apartheid, we are told, aims at the development of distinct ethnic groups, conscious of their cultural identity and eager to retain it. This development is to take the political form of ethnic nationalism, in that each of these ethnic groups is to constitute a "self-governing" nation-state, a "Bantustan." Verwoerd's "new deal" for the Africans has some superficial similarities with the above principles, and these have led some analysts to interpret apartheid as a move away from White domination and towards the political recognition of ethnic pluralism.

In my estimation, the Nationalist policy towards the Indians and Coloureds utterly refutes this interpretation. The Coloureds, as we have seen, are not an ethnic group in any sense of the word. If ethnicity were the criterion for separate development, then the "Coloureds" would become identified with either Afrikaans- or English-speaking South Africans. As to the Indians, apart from the fact that many of them are strongly Anglicized,

80. Quoted in *South African Scope*, April, 1964, p. 4.

they belong to five main traditional language groups, and to two main religions. In the case of both Indians and Coloureds, the criterion of group definition is obviously not ethnicity, but whatever nebulous concept the dominant group has of "race." The fiction of apartheid as envisaging territorial partition between ethnic groups is also exploded by the government's Coloured and Indian policy. The "national homelands" of these two groups have even less reality than in the case of the impoverished Native Reserves; they consist of hundreds of little ghettos termed "group areas." Any interpretation of apartheid other than that of a system of oppression and segregation based on race clearly conflicts with objective evidence.

## CHAPTER SEVEN

## Socio-Political Conflicts: The Non-White Opposition and the Internal Power Balance

U NTIL now, our analysis of racial conflicts has been confined mostly to the White side of the colour line. We have dealt with the English-Afrikaner conflict and with the racial attitudes and policies of the Europeans towards the non-Whites. This emphasis is justified insofar as the Whites have created the "racial problem" in South Africa, and as the non-Europeans have mostly reacted against White racialism. To view the non-Europeans purely as passive objects of discrimination, however, would lead to a gross distortion of reality.

Although the modern liberatory movements are a development of the twentieth century, the African masses never accepted the consequences of military defeat. Early in the nineteenth century, Gaika, a great African chief, was quoted as saying with bitter irony: "When I look at the large extent of fine country that has been taken from me, I am compelled to say that, though protected I am rather oppressed by my protectors."[1] The first expression of anti-White opposition that followed military defeat took the form of nativistic or messianistic movements. As in most other parts of the colonial world, the introduction of Christian

1. Walker, *op. cit.*, p. 40.

messianistic concepts, combined with the frustration and social disorganization following European conquest, led to the rise of native messiahs and prophets who promised to rid the land of the invaders, and to re-establish the golden age of the past. The most famous of these early movements was the disastrous cattle-killing of the Xhosas in the 1850's. Early, pre-industrial, ethnic nationalism also took the form of armed revolts without a messianistic basis, such as the Zulu Poll-Tax Rebellion of 1906.

Both of these pre-industrial forms of anti-White opposition, nativism and messianism, survive to this day. The 1960 revolt of the Pondo peasantry is the most recent example of non-religious, ethnic nativism. The rebellion flared up locally and spontaneously without much outside contact, and without any well-defined aims or political ideology in the modernist sense. Characterized by assassination, arson, and cattle killing directed against government-appointed chiefs, the Pondo revolt is a clear example of nativistic rejection of all that is European, including such "progressive" measures as soil conservation, and cattle culling and dipping. It is not only a rebellion against the government and Bantu authorities, but an expression of ethnic nationalism and peasant conservatism against European culture.

Messianism has likewise survived to the present in the form of many hundreds of small "Zionist" African sects. The 1951 census lists nearly 1.6 million people, i.e., one-third of the African Christians, as members of "Native Separatist Churches."[2] While these churches clearly express their members' frustration and dissatisfaction with the discriminatory "White man's" Christianity, they no longer have a political character, and the government tolerates them as a harmless derivative for anti-European feelings. In the past there have been violent clashes between the

2. These statistics include not only the syncretistic "Zionist" sects, but also the more orthodox "Ethiopian" sects under African leadership. On the subject of messianism, see B. G. M. Sundkler, *Bantu Prophets in South Africa.* Sundkler clearly emphasizes that the rise and success of the independent African churches must be explained by discriminatory practices in the White-controlled "orthodox" Protestant denominations.

government and "Zionist" sects, notably in 1920, when some three hundred members of the "Israelite" church were killed by the army after refusing to vacate their "sacred" hill.

The possibility that messianism can become an important political force for African emancipation seems remote, however. Most of the sects number only a few hundred members or less, and even the larger groups (such as the Shembe church among the Zulu) are generally restricted to one linguistic group. Like other forms of ethnically based movements, messianism is doomed to failure as an instrument of liberation, and can only have a diminishing appeal in an industrial and urban society which is becoming increasingly Westernized and secularized. Not only do the reactionary aims of nativistic and revivalistic movements make them ill-adapted to modern conditions, and unlikely to attract the crucial urban masses, but such groups totally lack the revolutionary discipline and techniques necessary to overthrow a well-equipped colonial government. Such movements may at most play a secondary and auxiliary role in the African liberatory struggle, largely because their thunder has been stolen away by the secularized and modernist political movements.

Education, industrialization, and urbanization brought about profound political changes starting at the beginning of the twentieth century. The missions spread not only Christianity among Africans, but also Western values of equality, individualism, and democracy, and the rudiments of European education. Mission education and life on the rural mission stations were the first steps away from traditional life for many Africans. The process of education and "detribalization," which the missionaries initiated over a century ago, was further accelerated with the rise of industrial centres. In the mines, great masses of African peasants were gradually transformed into a mobile urban proletariat. Cities became ethnic melting pots where workers became emancipated from traditional ties, learned the rudiments of European languages, developed common pidgin tongues, and were exposed to modern political concepts.

Urbanization lies at the root of the development of non-White political consciousness and of modern emancipatory movements led by a Western-educated intelligentsia.[3] Several circumstances have given the evolution of non-White political opposition a special South African character, however. As in most other European-dominated countries, these movements have been strongly influenced by the West in both their ideology and their organization, and bear relatively few traces of indigenous political traditions. But, in South Africa, the lengthy stay of Mahatma Gandhi has left a deep mark on non-European politics, which has survived to this day in the Congress Alliance, the main non-White opposition group. Most of the older non-White leaders, and many of the younger ones, adhere to the ideal of non-violence, and are schooled in the techniques of passive resistance, self-discipline, and self-denial. South Africa became the first testing-ground of *Satyagraha*, and, through the Mahatma's experiences, has indirectly influenced the evolution of India. More than any other single figure, Gandhi may be called the grandfather of South African non-White politics.

The non-White movements in South Africa also differ from those found elsewhere on the continent, in that their primary objective is not to gain political freedom from a distant colonial power, but to reach a *modus vivendi* on terms of equality with a sizeable, permanent White minority. In short, the non-Europeans seek freedom through equality rather than through independence. Non-White leaders are nearly unanimous in rejecting in principle any scheme for racial partition, and most of them envisage various forms of a multiracial country within present frontiers.

3. The principal recent works on the non-White opposition movements in South Africa are Edward Feit, *South Africa, The Dynamics of the African National Congress;* Mary Benson, *The African Patriots;* Leo Kuper, *Passive Resistance in South Africa;* Albert Luthuli, *Let My People Go;* and Jordan K. Ngubane, *An African Explains Apartheid.* The autobiographical works of Mahatma Gandhi are invaluable for the early period. Some of the main opposition periodicals in English include *Contact, The New African, Fighting Talk,* and *New Age.*

The secondary role played by trade unionism is a third characteristic of the South African freedom movements. Non-White trade unionism has been hampered by repressive action on the part of both industry and government, which both aim to keep the non-European workers cheap, docile, unorganized, and powerless. Furthermore, White trade-union leaders who, in the past, had the most experience, and could have played a leading role in organizing the African masses, have for the most part been racists, and have often defended the interests of White skilled workers against non-European competition.

For a decade, from 1919 to 1929, the Industrial and Commercial Workers Union (ICU) under the militant leadership of Kadalie was active and moderately successful in organizing strikes and fighting court cases. The ICU was definitely an African working-class movement, but it lacked any clear political ideology or platform, its goals being mostly economic. When it called for a boycott of municipal beer halls in 1929, the police repressed and destroyed the union and banished its leaders, spelling the doom of the greatest and most militant of the African trade unions. A consequence of the underdevelopment of non-White trade unionism since the 1920's, has been that the freedom movements have, until recently, lacked mass support, and have been relatively small groups led by moderate liberals drawn mostly from the African and Indian intelligentsia.

Fourthly, the non-White political movements have themselves not escaped the surrounding climate of South African racialism. Not only has a Black counterracialism developed in reaction against White racism, leading to the split of the Pan-Africanists from the African National Congress in 1959, but the main freedom movement, the Congress Alliance, is itself segregated into racial branches. Although the Congress Alliance preaches racial equality, mutual antagonism and mistrust between the followers and even some leaders of its component racial branches hinder co-operation. The only truly non-racial political groups, the Communist Party and the Liberal Party, have remained small and relatively ineffectual. We shall return to this problem of racialism in the freedom movements later.

The relative political passivity of the Coloureds constitutes the fifth special characteristic of non-White South African politics. The privileged position of the Coloureds among the non-Whites largely accounts for this fact. Until 1956 the Coloureds enjoyed a limited franchise in the Cape Province, which set them apart from the other non-Whites. Similarly, in the sphere of employment, many Coloureds occupied artisanal positions on terms of near equality with Whites. To these structural factors must be added the subjective factor of prejudice. Along with the rest of White South African culture, many, if not most, Coloureds have adopted European attitudes on colour, and consider themselves racially superior to the Africans, against whom they hold at least as strong prejudices as the Whites do.

In short, the Coloureds, as a group, have internalized the colour prejudices of the Whites. They have hoped to become "White," and so long as the government kept alive the prospect of eventual assimilation, the Coloureds have been apprehensive of jeopardizing their privileged position by joining forces with the Africans. Furthermore, prejudice against Africans has prevented such a *rapprochement*, while the internalized feeling of racial inferiority *vis-à-vis* the Whites, and the adoption of racial criteria of status within the Coloured community have deeply undermined the self-respect of that group, and further enhanced its colour-consciousness. The heritage of slavery has also left its marks on the Coloureds, and symptoms such as alcoholism and illegitimacy show the Coloureds to be the most socially disorganized racial group in South Africa. The Coloureds show the classical symptoms of social marginality, and their position is closely analogous to that of Negroes in the United States.

In the last few years, however, rapid changes are taking place in Coloured attitudes. As the discriminatory measures of the Nationalist government made increasingly clear that the assimilation dream would never be realized, and that the Coloureds' status would deteriorate to the African level, militant anti-White feelings developed among the Coloureds. Since 1960 or 1961 a substantial segment of the leading Coloured intelligentsia has joined the mainstream of non-White opposition, and strongly reacts against Coloured racialism.

The arrival of Mahatma Gandhi in South Africa in 1893 marks the beginning of the modern era in non-White opposition politics.[4] In 1894 he founded the Natal Indian Congress, the first branch of what later became broadly known as the Congress Movement or Alliance. The years 1907–1913 saw the world's first campaign of Gandhian passive resistance, when thousands of participants courted arrest, and went on strike in protest against discriminatory laws affecting the Indian community. This early era of resistance came to a close with the foundation of the African National Congress in 1912, the Gandhi Strike of 1913, and the Mahatma's departure from South Africa in 1914.

Another great wave of unrest swept through the country in the early twenties. In 1920 some 40,000 African mine workers went on strike on the Witwatersrand, and in 1922 a strike of White workers directed against the rise of African labourers to skilled jobs degenerated into an armed insurrection and an anti-African pogrom. Since the Second World War protest movements and unrest have succeeded one another at relatively short intervals. In 1946 some 60,000 African miners went on strike on the Rand, while the Indian Congress leaders launched the second passive resistance campaign against the so-called "Ghetto Act." Durban was the scene of bloody anti-Indian riots in 1949, when young Zulu men looted and destroyed Indian properties, and killed or wounded hundreds of Indians. At first, police inactivity allowed the riots to spread, and later indiscriminate police gunfire greatly added to the casualty figures. In all, 142 persons were

4. On Gandhi's role in South Africa see his *Autobiography or the Story of My Experiences with Truth,* and his *Satyagraha in South Africa.*

killed and 1087 injured. A mass passive resistance campaign occurred in 1952,[5] and was followed by the 1956 Johannnesburg African bus boycott, and the 1958 manifestations by African women against the pass system.

The year 1960 saw the most widespread wave of protest to date. The anti-pass campaign organized by the Pan-African Congress and later joined into by the African National Congress led to the police massacre of Sharpeville on the Rand, to the Pan-African-led protest marches and "stay-at-home" in Cape Town, and to many other African anti-apartheid manifestations in Durban, Johannesburg, Port Elizabeth, East London, Bloemfontein, and Pietermaritzburg. Shortly thereafter, a large-scale peasant revolt against "Bantu Authorities" flared up in Pondoland. The government declared a state of emergency, mobilized army reserve units, intensified its repressive measures, banned the African National Congress and the Pan-African Congress, and made thousands of political arrests without trial.

In December, 1961, the outbreak of acts of sabotage opened a new phase of the liberatory struggle, which the drastic penalties of the "Sabotage Act" of 1962 are unlikely to bring to an end. Between October and mid-December, 1962, there were forty-five reported sabotage attempts, of which thirty-three were successful.[6] On the Witwatersrand alone, there were six cases of railway sabotage between September, 1962, and April, 1963, involving damage of £21,000, and twenty-three cases of sabotage not on railway property since December, 1961.[7]

By 1962 at least three distinct underground organizations were active. One, Poqo, ("We Stand Alone") is allegedly connected with the Pan-African Congress, while the other two (the Spear of the Nation and the National Liberation Committee) seem to be offshoots of the African National Congress. At any

5. This campaign was studied in detail by Leo Kuper in his book *Passive Resistance in South Africa*.

6. *Africa Today*, April, 1963, vol. 10, No. 4, p. 3.

7. *Johannesburg Star*, May 18, 1963.

rate, members of the African National Congress have, on occasions, claimed credit for acts of sabotage conducted by the Spear of the Nation.[8] Balthazar Vorster (formerly a Nazi sympathizer, now Minister of Justice) declared in Parliament that, during 1962, 3246 persons had been arrested as suspected members of Poqo. Between January, 1963 and June, 1964, 431 persons have been convicted of sabotage under the "Sabotage Act," and 78 Africans were found guilty of political murder.[9] During 1963, 3355 people have been arrested, detained, or banned under security laws, 1186 of them without charges.[10]

In the early months of 1964 there were two important sabotage trials. On April 15, 1964, eleven accused were found guilty of belonging to the National Liberation Committee (also known as the Yui Chi Chan Club). The aims of the organization were described by the judge in the following terms: "By means of a combination of political agitation and guerilla warfare, supplemented by widespread sabotage, strikes and demonstrations, they aimed at the overthrow of the Government."[11] Another trial, the "Rivonia" case, involving such prominent African National Congress members as Walter Sisulu and Nelson Mandela, revealed the existence of a sabotage plan called "Operation Mayibuye" developed by the Spear of the Nation (which also goes under the African name of *Umkonto we Sizwe*).[12] Mandela, while stating that *Umkonto we Sizwe* was unconnected with the African National Congress, gave two reasons for the establishment of the new underground organization dedicated to sabotage against property, but not to terrorism against persons:

1. We believed that, as a result of Government policy, violence by the African people had become inevitable and that unless a responsible leadership was given to control the

8. *Africa Digest,* 10, June, 1963, pp. 196–197.
9. *Africa Today,* 11, June, 1964, p. 16.
10. *Africa Digest,* 11, April, 1964, p. 145.
11. *The Times,* London, April 16, 1964.
12. *Ibid.,* April 21, 22, 23, 24, 1964.

feelings of our people there would be an outbreak of terrorism which would cause bitterness between the various races of the country.

2. We felt that without sabotage there would be no way open to the African people to succeed in their struggle against the principle of white supremacy. All other means of opposing this principle were closed by legislation.[13]

This brief summary of protest actions does not exhaust the topic. Since the Second World War hardly a week has gone by without some racial disturbance or anti-apartheid manifestation, whether spontaneous or organized, violent or non-violent. In the course of the last years, the forms of protest action have become fairly standardized. The first type of action is the organized call by the liberatory movements for mass meetings, protest marches, boycotts, strikes, or civil disobedience. Meetings and marches, although peaceful in their aims and methods, have often led to violence, because of police harassment and provocation. The frequent use of firearms by the police in order to disperse peaceful crowds of unarmed civilians has recently led the Congress leadership to turn away from crowd action as an opposition tactic.

Boycotts against municipal transport, beer halls, private shops, and Afrikaner-made products have only had a limited economic effect. They have generally been successful to the extent that they have had very specific aims, such as getting more courteous treatment in certain shops, or rescinding a price increase in bus transport. Nevertheless, such nearly unanimous actions as the Johannesburg bus boycott of 1956 did have an important role in developing political consciousness among the African masses. The boycott also has the advantage of being almost impossible for the government to combat. Civil disobedience, courting of arrest for breaking apartheid regulations, and pass-burning have, like the boycotts, little direct effectiveness. The main limitation of civil disobedience is that it must rely on highly disciplined and courageous activists trained in the techniques of passive

13. *The Times,* London, April 21, 1964.

resistance, and, hence, cannot easily become a true mass movement. Furthermore, such campaigns can also easily be discredited by isolated acts of hooliganism, as was the case in 1952 when an impressive passive resistance campaign was finally called off for that reason. Heavy penalties on acts of passive resistance, combined with its limited practical effectiveness, have prompted the non-White leadership to seek new opposition tactics.

Although strikes are illegal for Africans, work stoppages are common occurrences in South Africa. In 1958, for example, 7128 Africans were involved in 64 strikes. In 9 cases, the strike resulted in higher wages or better conditions, but, in 23 instances, the strikers were prosecuted, 453 persons being convicted.[14] Most strikes are local, and of an economic nature. Government and industry generally co-operate closely in repressing strikes. Chronic unemployment enables employers to sack and replace workers at short notice.[15] Only well-planned general strikes on a national level can exert any significant political pressure on the government. However, repressive measures, police intimidation, and the fact that the mass of Africans live at, or below, the bare subsistence level, militate against the success of general strikes. Furthermore, the use of intimidation by some strike organizers has opened the Congress Movement to ideological criticism. The most wide-spread "stay-at-home" movement to date occurred in March–April, 1960, but it was still far from complete, and the April, 1961, call for a general strike was a nearly complete failure.

Next to politically organized action, the second major type of non-White protest is the local and spontaneous manifestation generally arising from trivial and secondary causes, such as anger over working conditions, petty vexations, and provocations by the authorities; low quality of food or beer provided in govern-

14. Horrell, *A Survey of Race Relations in South Africa*, 1958–1959, p. 223.
15. This is often done on a racial basis (e.g., Indian workers being replaced by Africans), thereby contributing to racial tension between non-White groups.

ment schools or municipal beer halls; and the unpopularity of particular officials. These spontaneous manifestations are much more frequent than organized ones, and often result in violence, rioting, and arson. The pattern is fairly standardized. A group of Africans lay down tools, go on a hunger strike, send a protest delegation to the local authorities, or simply begin to assemble and discuss their grievances. The authorities pay no attention to the protest, curtly tell the people to go through the "official channels" (i.e., the powerless advisory boards and chiefs), or, even more frequently, call the police to disperse the mob and arrest the leaders. The crowd gets increasingly irritated, and begins to sing and shout political slogans; the police becomes more and more brutal and provocative; the crowd starts to stone the police, and to set government buildings on fire, and the police shoots in "self-defence."[16] Such sporadic and spontaneous protests are, of course, quickly repressed and rarely achieve their aims.

Finally, the non-Whites, and particularly the Africans, resort to a third type of opposition, namely the "invisible" and individual expression of anti-White and anti-apartheid hostility. This type is by far the most common and may well be the most efficacious, although most Whites are unaware of its existence. Individual output restriction by "going slow"; minor industrial sabotage by pretending incomprehension of orders or unfamiliarity with equipment; deliberate waste of raw materials; telling lies or otherwise deceiving White supervisors and officials; making fools of Whites and undermining their authority through ridicule; ingenious intrigues; countless methods of circumventing regulations; falsifying documents and sabotaging the administrative machinery from within are so many variants of this "invisible" opposition. The effect of these subtle tactics is impossible to assess accurately, but it must be appreciable. To cite only one

16. Albert Luthuli gives a perceptive analysis of the role of the police and of the pattern of rioting in South Africa. See his *Let My People Go*, pp. 125–128.

instance, the enforcement of pass regulations, liquor laws, and influx control is well beyond the capacity of the police, and the faking of documents has become a profitable business. In 1962 liquor restrictions for Africans were finally abolished, not as a "liberalizing" measure, but as a consequence of police inability to enforce regulations which, unlike the pass laws, did not contribute much to the maintenance of the political *status quo*.[17]

One of the remarkable features of the South African political scene, attributable in great part to the Gandhian influence, is that, up to 1961, non-White opposition tactics have been predominantly non-violent, except as a result of severe police provocation. Furthermore, the open expression of non-European hostility has been almost exclusively directed at the government and its agents, and has not generalized to the White population as a whole. This is not to say that there does not exist a large degree of anti-White feelings among the non-Whites, but rather that non-White aggression has been specifically directed at the state and the administration. The 1949 anti-Indian riots are, of course, the outstanding exception to the rule. In that case, Africans clearly displaced their hostility on a relatively safe scapegoat. There have also been numerous incidents of violence between Africans, but these have generally involved either rival criminal gangs or traditionally based factions or ethnic groups. Such fights have little if any significance in the general political context.

The extreme policies of the last decade have, however, brought about a change towards radicalism among the leadership and the rank and file of the African opposition. Black racialism, as represented by the Pan-African Movement and some prominent members of the African National Congress, has rapidly developed as a reaction against White racialism. In addition,

17. Police Brigadier R. J. van den Bergh welcomed in November, 1962 the lifting of liquor restrictions for Africans on the ground that it relieved the police for other duties. Cf. Anonymous, *Report of the Special Committee on the Policies of Apartheid*, p. 89.

many of the younger and more radical African leaders privately (if not openly) advocate violent guerilla tactics as the only ones likely to bring about a political change.

Several factors account for the lack of success of the non-White opposition. Indeed, not only have the liberatory movements failed to gain any concessions from the government, but each wave of protest has been accompanied by more police repression, and followed by increasingly dictatorial legislation. In the first place, the government has hindered the operation of the non-White movements. Police intimidation scares the masses away from active political participation; opposition organizations are banned, and forced to work underground; and the leadership is constantly disrupted by arrest and imprisonment. However, it would be erroneous to attribute the failure of the non-White movements only, or even principally, to government action. Although the state uses force unhesitatingly, its power apparatus (including the secret police) has been relatively inefficient by modern totalitarian standards, at least until 1960, when noticeable improvements began to take place.

Economic factors have powerfully hindered non-White political action. The non-European organizations have lacked the financial resources of the White parties, and, unlike the latter, have never had any support from industry. On the contrary, industrialists have co-operated with the government in keeping the non-White workers down. A population at, or near, the starvation level cannot easily be expected to participate in a general strike, when practically no material compensation for wage losses is available.

Racialism among the non-Whites has militated against the formation of a truly united non-European front. The Congress Alliance claims to represent such a front, but is itself divided into racial branches for reasons that we shall examine presently. The Pan-African Congress is militantly anti-Indian, anti-European and anti-Coloured, in spite of declarations to the contrary. Because of their political passivity and racial feelings, the

Coloureds are regarded with mistrust and hostility by the mass of Africans. Although Indians and Africans have closely co-operated at the leadership level of the Congress Alliance, anti-Indian prejudice is strong among many Africans, who, like the Whites, have used the Indians as scapegoats, and have viewed Indian merchants as exploiters. Conversely, most Indians remember the 1949 pogrom, and as a small, defenceless minority, they are justifiably afraid of Black nationalism. Within the African group itself, the remnants of ethnic antagonisms are still a serious obstacle to political unity, particularly in the more rural areas.

Finally, a number of secondary factors have also hindered a non-White political action. Among these are the low education level of most Africans, peasant conservatism, the vested interests of the customary chiefs, the urban and intellectual character of the non-White leadership which has often lacked contact with the rural masses, and personal rivalries or ideological differences within the various organizations.

To conclude this chapter we must assess the present power balance in terms of organized political groups, summarize the main developments of the last few years, and attempt a prognosis. On the White side of the political fence, three parties are represented in Parliament, and reflect almost the entire range of White political thinking. Two of these parties, the Nationalist Party (N.P.) and the United Party (U.P.), account for the vast majority of both seats and supporters, and the third, the Progressive Party (P.P.), is a small splinter group with one parliamentary seat after the 1961 general elections. A fourth party, the National Union (N.U.) splintered from the Nationalist Party, campaigned in alliance with the U.P. for the 1961 elections, won a single parliamentary seat, and merged with the U.P. soon afterwards.

The main difference between the U.P. and the N.P. is not one of right *versus* left, but one of ethnic composition. Although the N.P. has a handful of English members, it is, for all practical purposes, an Afrikaner party, and it has now rallied the vast majority of the Afrikaner vote. The U.P. attempts to keep alive the fiction of representing both White groups by placing Afrikaners in many of its command posts, but, since World War Two, it has lost more and more of its Afrikaner supporters, and has become increasingly an English party. Every successive election has confirmed the linguistic cleavage between the two major parties. The Nationalists gradually entrenched themselves by uniting the White Afrikaner majority, and the U.P. is left with the White English minority. In addition, the Nationalists have manipulated the electoral system and gerrymandered the constituencies so as to put the U.P. under maximum disadvantage. This was easily achieved because of the heavy concentration of the U.P. vote in large urban centres, in the Province of Natal, and in the Eastern Cape.

With 49 parliamentary seats against the Nationalists' 105, the U.P. has practically no chance of gaining power by constitutional means. On matters of policy, the main difference between the two parties was that the Nationalists have advocated and recently achieved a republican form of government, while the U.P. was in favour of close ties with the British monarchy and the Commonwealth. The proclamation of the Republic and the withdrawal of South Africa from the Commonwealth in 1961 have been accepted, however reluctantly, as a *fait accompli* by the U.P., and leave that Party with even less of a distinctive platform than it had before.

On the colour issue, the two major parties are in almost complete agreement as to the basic aims, and differ only in questions of practical details. At most, one can say that the racial policy of the N.P. is reactionary, and that of the U.P. ultraconservative. While the U.P. accepts much of the Nationalist colour legislation, and "security" measures, it favours a more subtle, flexible, and empirical implementation of apartheid, and is prepared to grant a nominal parliamentary representation to Coloureds and Africans along Hertzogian lines. In addition, the U.P. recognizes that the African urban middle class cannot be wished away in the Reserves, and that economic imperatives make government plans of macro-segregation impracticable. The U.P. colour slogan is "White leadership with justice." In a nutshell, the U.P. colour thinking can be summarized as follows: We Whites can maintain the upper hand better and longer if we are less rigid and dogmatic about segregation, and if we introduce some palliatives to eliminate some of the superficial symptoms of racial friction. In the economic sphere, "integration" (i.e., the exploitation of African labour) is inevitable, and any attempt at rigid territorial apartheid is both costly and impracticable.

In 1959 eleven of the more "liberal" U.P. Members of Parliament split from that party, and formed the Progressive Party (P.P.). The P.P. also looks to the past for its colour policy. It essentially advocates a return to the "Cape liberalism" of the nineteenth century. Its franchise proposals make voting rights dependent on educational and property qualifications regardless of race. The qualifications are such, however, that the Whites would retain a secure majority of the votes for at least twenty or thirty years. In addition to such a "colour-blind," single-roll franchise, the P.P. opposes racial segregation by law, and has pledged itself to the abrogation of much apartheid legislation, but it has taken an equivocal stand on "voluntary" and "social" segregation.

The P.P. has even less chance than the U.P. of coming to power, or even of exerting a noticeable influence in Parliament. Its policies are far too liberal to attract more than a small minority of the White voters. In the 1961 elections (the first one contested by the U.P. dissidents) only one of the eleven P.P. members retained a seat in Parliament.[18] On the other hand,

18. When the eleven dissident M.P.'s splintered from the United Party to form the Progressive Party, they retained the seats which they had won as members of the U.P. The 1961 elections were, then, the first test of P.P. strength among the Whites. The P.P. contested twenty-three seats, won one, lost another two to the U.P. by a narrow margin, and polled 8.5 per

P.P. policies are far too conservative to appeal to more than a handful of non-Whites, or even to serve as a bridge between White and non-White politics. In view of the increasing polarization of opinion, the chances of the P.P., negligible as they are, can only diminish steadily.

The ephemeral National Union (N.U.), founded in 1960, was to the N.P. what the P.P. is to U.P. A small group of "liberal" Afrikaners whom republican sentiments made reluctant to join either the U.P. or the P.P. formed a new group. The N.U. agreed with the N.P. on the issue of republicanism and Afrikaner nationalism, but advocated a slightly less reactionary colour policy, much along U.P. lines. The N.U. had so little hope of attracting more U.P. or N.P. supporters, much less of ever coming to power, that it soon amalgamated with the U.P.

The White political scene has reached a deadlock which ensures continued power to the Nationalists (barring extra-constitutional changes), and which makes any change within the parliamentary system extremely unlikely. The very structure of White politics is responsible for the present deadlock. None of the European parties significantly cuts across the White ethnic line, and this ethnic cleavage has become more and more rigid over the years. In other words, the traditional alliance between the English and the "moderate" Afrikaners, which was the keystone of South African White politics until the 1940's, has been broken. A new equilibrium has been reached: insofar as the N.P. has succeeded in uniting the vast majority of the

---

cent of the votes, indicating that perhaps one-fourth to one-third of the English-speaking Whites, and 2 or 3 per cent of the total population, support P.P. policies. Nevertheless, the apparent "non-racialism" of the P.P. franchise proposal makes some appeal among English-speaking intellectuals, and even among some of the more conservative overseas critics of apartheid. For example, Gwendolen Carter dismisses the demands of the Congress Alliance for universal adult franchise in the following terms: "In the existing primitive state of the great majority of Africans, this demand is obviously unwarranted." Cf. Carter, "Can Apartheid Succeed in South Africa?" p. 300.

Afrikaners who constitute nearly two-thirds of the electorate, neither the U.P. nor the P.P., which are almost exclusively English parties, can hope to gain a parliamentary majority. Aside from this factor of ethnic cleavage, the mechanics of the electoral system further stack the cards against the U.P. and the P.P., through the loading of rural constituencies and other devices.

The second factor making for the deadlock is the colour prejudice of the Whites. All White parties stand for European domination, whether that domination is called "apartheid," "White leadership with justice," or "equal rights to all civilized men." No party can have any hope of support from the all-White electorate unless it guarantees the protection of White privileges. Faced with a choice between a more and a less conservative party on the colour issue, the vast majority of each White language group logically vote for the party that offers the best promise of "keeping the Natives down," namely the N.P. for the Afrikaners and the U.P. for the English. All attempts by the U.P. to attract more Afrikaners by trying to show that it is just as repressive as the N.P. have failed, because the U.P. has become an English party, and because, objectively, it is not quite as "good" as the N.P. in maintaining White supremacy.

There remains, of course, one other theoretical possibility of constitutional change in South Africa, namely a significant split within the Nationalist Party. Such a possibility appears remote at present, as shown in 1961 by the small appeal of the N.U. among Afrikaners. It is true that the N.P. is still internally divided between an "extremist" wing, drawing its support mostly from the Transvaal and the Orange Free State, and a "moderate" wing, represented mostly in the Cape. But the whole evolution of Afrikaner Nationalism in the last thirty years has shown a trend towards reactionary extremism. As the Nationalist government became more firmly entrenched, its policies became more repressive, and today the "extremists" are in a stronger position than ever. The influence of "moderate" Nationalist intellectuals and clergymen has become negligible, and the *Broederbond* gradually purged such organizations as SABRA[19] of "liberal" dissidents. Within the cabinet and in other leading political posts, the *Broederbond* replaces more and more moderates with extremists, and pressure has been brought upon liberal clergymen of the Dutch Reformed Churches to toe the party line. The rank and file of the N.P. is behind the Verwoerd extremists, and there is little, if any, chance of a significant split. If anything, Verwoerd himself may become seriously outflanked on the right by rural Afrikaner opinion.

Besides parties, other organized interest groups exert influence on White politics, mainly industry, the churches, and the universities. Here, too, these interest groups are divided along the English-Afrikaner line. Most businessmen and industrialists are English, and support either the U.P. or the P.P. They generally oppose the government verbally and ideologically, while cooperating with it as suits their interests. Their main argument against apartheid is not one of principle, but rather that apartheid is costly and impractical. Organized capital is, therefore, not a source of serious opposition to the Nationalists, although economic forces undermine apartheid from within, as we shall see later.

The churches are clearly split along White linguistic lines. The three Dutch Reformed Churches, to which the vast majority of Afrikaners belong, support the government; and the Catholic and other Protestant churches oppose apartheid in principle, but often practice segregation within their own congregations. For all practical purposes, only the Catholic and Anglican churches, or, better, a few prominent clergymen within these denominations, have openly attacked the government and actively fought against apartheid. The English-speaking universities, particularly those of Cape Town and the Witwatersrand, have been active

19. The South African Bureau of Racial Affairs is a supposedly independent intellectual group entrusted with the task of developing the ideology of apartheid. The Stellenbosch branch of SABRA included, however, a number of "moderates" in leading positions until 1961.

centres of opposition, and have tried to resist encroachments against academic freedom, but they too have not been free of the stigma of racial discrimination; the Afrikaans universities support the government, of course. In short, few of the White-controlled organizations have used their influence against the government, nor can they be expected to exert a determining pressure in the future. Industry is largely dominated by considerations of self-interest. The liberal high clergy is hampered by the conservatism of its White rank and file. The labour unions, universities, and other interest groups have themselves been pervaded by racialism, and have rarely gone beyond verbal protests expressed through petitions or resolutions.

Two other political parties, the Communist and the Liberal parties, exist in South Africa, but, because of their very special characteristics, they have not been included in the above discussion. Although the Liberal Party had a "Native Representative" seat in Parliament until 1961, both parties are now extra-parliamentary. The Communist and Liberal parties are the only fully non-racial political bodies in South Africa, and they constitute the only bridges between White and non-White politics. The Communist Party (C.P.) is an illegal organization and operates entirely underground. Little is known about it except that it is numerically very small, but relatively influential through its increasing infiltration of the Congress Movement.

The Liberal Party (L.P.) was founded in 1953 and is still legal, although constantly harassed by the police. It only counts a few thousand members, most of whom are non-Whites. Many of its leading members are Europeans, however, and many White intellectuals belong to it. At the time of its foundation, the L.P. was almost as conservative as the P.P. now is, but since then it has moved rapidly to the left. Through its policy of universal adult franchise, and its total rejection of racial discrimination in any form, the L.P. now stands ideologically very close to the Congress Movement, with which it has generally had fairly close and amicable contacts. The L.P. has nevertheless failed to gain wide support among the non-Whites because its conservative origins have given it the image of a party led by White paternalists, and because its intellectual, non-racial outlook lacks any mass, emotional appeal. To many African intellectuals who have adopted one form or another of socialism, the L.P. is too conservative on such economic issues as land reform and nationalization of basic industries. Mphahlele probably expresses the point of view of the majority of the African National Congress intelligentsia towards the L.P.:

> A second front has been opened in Africa to try to kill Socialist ideas of any kind at the root. It consists of white African liberals, particularly those in Central and Southern Africa. They have set out to give African nationalism a big build-up. . . . Some South African liberals sing praises to African chauvinism. . . . The trouble with liberals in South Africa, of course, is that they spend two-thirds of their energy trying to avert a revolution and one-third to verbal protest against repressive legislation. Their attraction for a certain class of the non-White elite fits in with their anti-socialist sentiments.[20]

We turn now to an examination of the major bodies in non-White politics. By far the most important one is the Congress Alliance with its five constituent organizations: the African National Congress (ANC), the South African Indian Congress (SAIC), the Congress of Democrats (COD), the Coloured People's Organization (CPO), and the South African Congress of Trade Unions (SACTU). The first four of these branches restrict their membership by race, while SACTU is interracial. The ANC is by far the largest branch, and counted some 70,000 members when it was banned by the government in 1960. Although many of its leaders have been arrested or placed under other restrictions, the ANC continues to operate underground. The SAIC, which is the oldest branch of Congress, is much smaller numerically, but its leadership has exerted considerable

20. Ezekiel Mphahlele, *The African Image*, p. 87.

influence on the ANC. Both the ANC and the SAIC can claim the support of the mass of the African and Indian population. The COD is the small White branch counting only some two hundred members, mostly Communists and left-wing socialists. However, the influence of the COD on Congress as a whole is greater than its numerical strength indicates. The CPO is the weakest branch of Congress and is practically a paper organization. In terms of total membership, the Congress Alliance is thus over-whelmingly an African body, while its leadership is about equally shared between Whites, Indians, and Africans.

The programme of Congress embodied in the 1955 Freedom Charter includes universal adult franchise, the total abolition of all forms of racial discrimination, and some vaguely defined socialist measures such as land redistribution and nationalization of some industries. Politically, the Congress programme is almost identical with that of the Liberal Party, but economically it goes further to the left. Within Congress there exist, however, wide ideological divergences. The COD consists almost entirely of extreme leftists of various descriptions. In the SAIC leftist leaders have also gained much influence recently, but the older leaders adhere mostly to a mild, Gandhian, humanitarian social-ism. Within the ANC at least three main currents are represented: the "bourgeois-liberal" old guard, represented by Professor Z. K. Matthews, the late Dr. A. B. Xuma, and Nobel Peace Prize Winner Albert Luthuli; the younger Communists and left-wing socialists, such as Nelson Mandela, Raymond Mahlaba, Joe Slovo, Joe Modise, Walter Sisulu, and Joe Matthews, who have recently risen into many key positions and seek to displace the more conservative old guard;[21] and the younger Black racialists, who advocate an all-African state. Many of the latter have joined the dissident Pan-African Congress (PAC), but racialist thinking is still represented in the ANC. On questions of method, the Congress Alliance is still officially committed to a policy of non-

21. Some are now in exile, while others have been convicted in the "Rivonia" sabotage case.

violence, but more and more of the leftist leaders privately advocate the resort to violence, or redefine non-violence as allowing sabotage, so long as loss of life or injury to persons is avoided.

The racial division in the structure of Congress in undoubtedly a severe ideological liability. Why, then, is the Congress internally segregated along colour lines in spite of considerable internal opposition to such segregation? The proponents of racial segregation justify their stand on historical and tactical grounds. The ANC and the SAIC, they say, grew as separate organizations, and each has its own history and traditions. This is, of course, no argument against merging into one non-racial body. The advocates of segregation in Congress also claim that, as each racial group is affected by different laws, it is tactically expedient to fight apartheid through racially distinct organizations. This argument is a disguised bow to the racial mistrust which the mass of Africans, Indians, and Coloureds nourish toward each other.

The real reason for continued segregation is to be found, paradoxically, in Communist influence. At present, each racial branch of Congress has equal representation in the policy-making central committee of the Alliance, regardless of its membership figures. The minute, Communist-dominated COD thereby exercises a completely disproportionate influence on Congress as a whole, and more particularly on SACTU and the ANC. The same applies, to a lesser extent, to SAIC, which is also small in relation to the ANC, and strongly Communist-infiltrated. Through racial segregation, the Africans have thus been placed in a disadvantageous position in Congress, and a Marxist minority has succeeded in wielding disproportionate power within the Alliance, while keeping the more conservative old guard as popular figureheads.

Next to the Congress Alliance, the Pan-African Congress (PAC) is probably the largest non-White political body. The PAC, an all-African organization, split from the ANC in 1959, and was banned by the government in 1960. Except in the Cape, where it was notably successful in 1960, the PAC is poorly organized. Its programme and its ideology are vague, and rest on two main elements: anti-Communism and Black racialism. PAC leaders split from the ANC because they claimed that Congress was dominated by White and Indian Communists. The PAC demands "all power to Africans" while denying any charge of racialism, and claims to favour private enterprise, and to oppose violence. Economically the PAC is more conservative than the ANC and closer to the Liberal Party, but through its racial extremism it distinguishes itself from all other non-White organizations. In a climate of virulent White racialism and anti-African discrimination, the Black counterracialism of the PAC inevitably has a strong emotional appeal, and the popular support for the PAC is probably growing.

Other smaller non-White political bodies include the Non-European Unity Movement (NEUM), and the Natal Indian Organization (NIO). The NEUM grew out of the fairly conservative All-African Convention founded in 1935. It has become a small intellectual clique of leftist students, mostly Trotskyites. It lacks both a clear programme and any mass support, and has the character of a debating society, spending most of its energies on disputes over minor points of Marxist theory and attacks against the Congress Alliance. The NIO is a conservative body representing the interests of the Indian merchant class, and favouring a cautious policy of compromise with the government.

As we have seen throughout this chapter, political conflicts in South Africa have centred around racial and ethnic divisions, much more than around social class. The foundation of Union in 1910 marked a decisive point in the country's political evolution. With Union, the country continued on the road of White domination, and engaged itself in a vicious circle of repression and extreme racialism. From then on, a return to sanity became increasingly unlikely and difficult. The great mistake of the Union compromise was to believe that peace and stability in South Africa depended on the reconciliation of Boer and Briton. In that avowed aim, the Union settlement did succeed in maintaining for thirty-eight years a relatively stable co-operation between the English and "moderate" Afrikaners. By uniting Afrikanerdom, however, the Nationalist Party broke the balance of forces, and secured for itself a monopoly of power.

When the Union compromise was broken in 1948, the struggle between Afrikaners and English had receded into the background, however, and the main issue had become one of White *versus* Black. With education, urbanization, and Westernization, the non-Whites became politically conscious and organized. Non-White opposition was met, not with reforms and concessions, but with ever more repression. The two World Wars accelerated this process of deepening racial conflict and hatred, until, at present, little if any possibility of a peaceful solution remains. What is surprising is not that the gulf is now seemingly unbreachable, but rather that it should have taken so long to widen. Indeed, the African leadership has consistently shown a great degree of restraint and patience. The 1949 Programme of Action, and 1955 Freedom Charter mark the first truly militant and outspoken platforms of liberation, and the first unequivocal departures from the more conciliatory approach of the older leadership in the ANC and the All-African Convention represented by such leaders as Dr. Xuma and Professor Jabavu. By now, however, Whites and non-Whites have grown so far apart that reconciliation seems impossible, and practically all channels of communication have been broken. Official channels such as the Native Advisory Boards are media of sycophancy rather than of communication, while potentially intermediary groups such as the Progressive or Liberal parties soon tip into one of the opposing camps. The L.P. has been forced out of Parliament, and has almost become the right wing of non-White politics, whereas the P.P. has chosen to remain in the White camp.

White and non-White politics nevertheless react to one another in complex ways, and cannot be viewed separately.

Not only does the government devise improved methods of repression in answer to new tactics of resistance; the very antagonism between Europeans and non-Europeans profoundly affects political developments *within* each of the two camps. White oppression has increased non-White solidarity and consciousness, and is favouring the extreme Communist and Black racialist elements within the liberatory movements. The Coloured leadership is recently turning away from its political fence-sitting, and begins to co-operate with African leaders. Conversely, the growing "Black menace" has united the Whites into a desperate back-to-the-wall stand, and has contributed to the consolidation of Nationalist power. Indeed, the U.P. and the majority of the English are willing to pay the price of Afrikaner Nationalist dictatorship to preserve White privileges. The ever deepening racial conflict is favouring political polarization and extremism.

For reasons examined earlier, the possibility of a change of government within the parliamentary framework is remote. The Nationalists are too firmly entrenched to let themselves be unseated by the opposition. Should the Nationalists have any prospect of losing an election, they would not allow the election to take place, or they would fake the results. The Nationalist Party itself is less likely to split than it has ever been, and it has gone much too far on the road of repression to run the risk of making concessions. Even if Nationalist leaders were prepared to negotiate with the non-White opposition, they know that only increasing ruthlessness can keep them in power. From the White side of the political arena, a complete deadlock has been reached.

The non-Europeans, on the other hand, are legally denied any participation in the process of national government, and any constitutional method of remedying their grievances. The liberatory movements, most particularly the Congress Alliance and the Liberal Party, have utilized every conceivable non-violent method of opposition, from passive resistance and civil disobedience, to petitions, protest meetings, marches, boycotts, and strikes. While these methods have undoubtedly played an important role in mass morale and political education, they have consistently failed to achieve any but the most limited of practical aims. On the contrary, each new resistance technique or campaign has been countered with increasing police action and draconian laws forbidding all forms of protest.

Under these circumstances violence and revolution seem inevitable, although the prospect of a successful upheaval is remote without outside intervention. The discussion of international pressures against South Africa must be reserved for a later chapter. It is clear, however, that the government cannot resist much longer the combination of mounting internal and external pressures, and that political change in South Africa cannot be peaceful. Indeed, all the symptoms of a pre-revolutionary situation are clearly present. The opposing forces of Afrikaner and African Nationalism have become increasingly polarized ideologically, and both have shown an increasing readiness to use violence to achieve their aims. Lack of communication between the antagonists is complete; so are their unwillingness to compromise or negotiate, their disagreement about the "rules of the game," and their reciprocal denial of legitimacy.

## CHAPTER EIGHT

# The Economic System and Its Dysfunctions

I N Chapter IV we have sketched the broad lines of the economic structure of South Africa. We shall now concentrate on the imbalances and contradictions relating to the system of production. For analytical purposes, we shall deal in turn with three types of factors:

1. The imbalances inherent to an economy in transition from "underdevelopment" to industrialization.

2. The economic dysfunctions arising from private and official discrimination and prejudice.

3. The tensions arising from the particular relationship between economic and political power.

The political dualism of South Africa as a "mother country" and a colony is also reflected in the country's economic structure. Side by side with destitute, stagnating, subsistence agriculture and herding, there coexists a prosperous, expanding money or market sector. The resulting imbalances are, to a large degree, typical of all "developing" countries going through the process of industrialization, and are thus found throughout Africa.[1] The

---

1. For discussions of economic dualism in Asia see J. S. Furnivall, *Netherlands India, A Study of Plural Economy;* and J. H. Boeke, *Economics and Economic Policy in Dual Societies.* In spite of the recent critique of the concept of dual economy made by Bohannan and Dalton, I find that notion not only useful but inescapable. I agree, of course, with Bohannan and Dalton that the subsistence economy is by no means simple nor homogene-

scarcity of technical skills necessary to industry leads to high wages for specialized labour. Conversely, depressed rural conditions make for abundant and, hence, cheap unskilled labour. There results a wide wage discrepancy between levels of manual labour, and, more generally, a highly unequal income distribution. In 1953–1954, Spooner has estimated that the mean family income for South African Whites was £1616 a year, compared to £308 for Coloureds and Indians, and £119 for Africans (Table XXIII). Whites thus enjoyed a standard of living which was about five times higher than that of Coloureds and Indians, and thirteen times higher than that of Africans. The figures for Africans included families living in towns, in the Native Reserves, and on White farms. In cities, the mean African family income was £213 a year, compared to £120 for Africans living on White-owned farms, and £97 for Reserve Africans. The latter figure includes an estimated £30 as the value of subsistence agricultural production.[2]

Moreover, indications are that, if one controls for increases in the cost of living, racial inequalities in the distribution of income have increased until the 1950's. Spooner estimates that, between 1938–1939 and 1953–1954, Whites enjoyed a 46 per cent increase in purchasing power, compared to an increase of 11 per cent for Coloureds and Indians, and a *decrease* of 6.5 per cent for Africans (Table XXIII). Out of a 1953–1954 Geographical National Income of £1,559,000,000, nearly three-fourths accrued to Whites who constituted one-fifth of the population. This racial disparity in earnings has somewhat decreased in the late 1950's. While, in 1954, the *per capita* income of Whites was 12.7 times higher than that of Africans, by 1960 the ratio had fallen to 9.0 (Table XXII). It is therefore clear that the Whites were practically the sole beneficiaries of economic prosperity

---

ous, and that the borderline between subsistence and market or money economy is not clear-cut. See Paul Bohannan and George Dalton, *Markets in Africa*, p. 25.

2. Spooner, *op. cit.*, pp. 172–174.

until 1954, and that the relative standard of living of Africans remained stationary for fifteen years. At last, since the late 1950's, rises in non-White wages are slowly reversing that trend, so that non-Whites may now look forward to being slightly better off *vis-à-vis* Europeans than they were after the Great Depression, some thirty years ago.

"Cheap" labour in itself entails a whole set of factors retarding economic development: lack of incentive to mechanize, a small internal market for consumer goods resulting from low purchasing power, and the vicious circle of low-wages-low-productivity. Cheap labour is generally improductive, first because it is often malnourished, fatigued, or debilitated by disease; but more importantly, because its very cheapness makes unprofitable the major means of increasing productivity, namely mechanization. In a nutshell, unskilled labour is cheap because it is abundant, it remains cheap because it is improductive, and it is improductive because it is cheap.

All the above factors are too common and too well-known to require further elaboration. However, several specifically African conditions aggravate the imbalances and tensions inherent to an economy in rapid transition. Unlike in Europe and in Asia, the economic transition in much of Africa was not simply from a rural to an urban way of life, but from a rural *subsistence* to an urban *money* economy. Whereas, elsewhere, the use of currency preceded by far industrialization and cushioned somewhat the latter's impact, it was unknown in many traditional African societies which thus had to make a double jump. To be sure, cash agriculture and herding have existed for some three centuries in South Africa, but wherever they appeared, they were practically monopolized by the White settlers.

The presence of the Whites complicates and aggravates transition problems. Indeed, overlapping with the agriculture-industry dichotomy, one finds in South Africa a "White" *versus* an "African" economy. These terms are somewhat misleading because Africans also constitute a majority of the working force in the White economy. Yet the racial factor occupies a prominent place in the country's economic system, as well as in all other aspects of South African society. For all practical purposes, the Whites control all sectors of the money economy, whether in industry, mining, commerce, or agriculture.[3] Although White cash agriculture is only engaged in by some 13 per cent of the Europeans, and although it is relatively unproductive compared with the other sectors of the White economy, it accounts for an overwhelming proportion of the total agricultural production. The some 400,000 Whites living on farms occupy some 87 per cent of the land, and produce at least twenty to thirty times as much as the 3.7 million Africans living on subsistence farming and herding in the Native Reserves.[4] On a *per capita* basis, each rural White holds an average of 375 acres of land, compared with 6 acres per rural African.[5] In addition to the enormous racial discrepancy in the size of land holdings, White farmers benefit from much easier credit (and, hence, higher capitalization), and from much heavier government subsidies than African farmers receive. In the 1960–1961 fiscal year, for example, the state spent £17,090,000 in subsidizing White agriculture, and in

3. The only sizeable exception to that statement is the relatively small sector of retail trade which is Indian-controlled.

4. An accurate estimate of the cash value of African agricultural production is very difficult to make, but that value is undoubtedly low. An estimate for 1953–1954 puts African farm income at £38,000,000, i.e., 2.4 per cent of the national income. Of the 11.8 million heads of cattle living in South Africa in 1956, 6.9 million were owned by Whites, and 4.9 million by Africans. These figures do not take stock quality into account, however. The overwhelming majority of meat- and milk-producing cattle is European-owned. Between 1930 and 1956 the number of European-owned heads of cattle increased by 32.7 per cent, while the figure for African-owned stock *declined* by 7.5 per cent. This reflects an increasing discrepancy in living standards of White as opposed to African farmers, as well as a growing deteriorating of pastures in the Native Reserves. Cf. *State of the Union Year-Book for South Africa*, 1959–1960, p. 222; and Spooner, *op. cit.*, p. 270.

5. Luthuli, *op. cit.*, p. 57.

1960 the Land and Agriculture Bank loaned European farmers another £17,463,896. By comparison, the total expenditure on "Native Administration" was only £16,616,000, of which only a small fraction was devoted to African agriculture.[6] In the first twelve years of Nationalist rule (1948–1960), the government spent only £35,400,000 on the purchase and development of African land, a yearly average of less than £3,000,000.[7]

As the Reserves fall far short of feeding their own population, the phrase "subsistence agriculture" has become a misnomer and a euphemism. In order to earn the necessary cash to feed their families in the Reserves, practically all able-bodied African men are forced to enter the White economy, either as quasi-servile[8] labourers on the White farms, or as lowly paid urban or rural proletarians. As a result, Africans are obliged to spend their low wages on high-priced food grown by themselves on land which the Whites have appropriated mostly by force. In order to insure a high standard of living for White farmers, the government maintains the price of staple foods at an artificially high level. Large-scale land encroachment by the Europeans, combined with African population increase, has thus transformed the traditional African subsistence agriculture into *sub*-subsistence starvation. Thereby, new economic forces were set in motion: first, a continuous and abundant supply of cheap labour for the European economy, and secondly, a progressive deterioration of the remaining African land through the familiar sequence of overpopulation, overgrazing, and erosion.

These facts have been confirmed by careful surveys. A 1949

6. Trapido, *op. cit.; Year Book and Guide to Southern Africa*, 1962, p. 38.

7. Hartmann, *op. cit.*, p. 27.

8. I am using the term "quasi-servile" advisedly, as many of these agricultural workers receive no cash wages. Under the system known as "labour tenancy" an African works a specified number of days per year for the White farm owner in exchange for grazing, residential, and tillage rights. Other African farm labourers work for wages in both cash and kind. Cf. Marquard, *The Peoples and Policies of South Africa*, p. 55.

inquiry into the rural economy of the Ciskei (one of the Native Reserves of the Eastern Cape where rainfall and soil conditions are relatively favourable) revealed that only 6.8 per cent of the farmers' average income were derived from agriculture.[9] Soil deterioration is reflected in steadily falling crops in the Native Reserves. In the 1923–1927 period, 620 million pounds of maize and 148 million pounds of "Kaffir corn" were produced; in 1935–1939, the corresponding figures were 478 and 122, a decline of about 20 per cent in a little over a decade. By 1949 average yields in maize in African areas were as low as thirty pounds an acre.[10] South African Whites have, of course, conveniently blamed the "wasteful," "irrational," and "backward" agricultural techniques of Africans for the destitute condition of the Reserves, and for soil erosion. Available evidence, on the contrary, indicates that the introduction of Western methods of land exploitation are largely responsible for much of the damage. D.F. Kokot, a member of a committee of seven scientists appointed in 1948 to study erosion in South Africa, states unequivocally:

> *The indisputable and alarming fact is that there has been serious deterioration of the vegetation and hydrological conditions. And everywhere there has been almost terrifying erosion of the soil.* The majority of the Committee were quite convinced that all the damage could be explained in terms of the impact of man, with his plough and his domestic animals, upon a land that was from the very start extremely vulnerable. . . . Throughout the Union of South Africa soil erosion is triumphantly on the march.[11]

In short, Africans have not only lost most of their land to the Whites; they have also been forced out of their remaining Reserves, not fundamentally because of the "lure of the city," or opportunities for higher wages, but rather because migration was an imperative necessity for sheer physical survival. The

9. P. de Briey, "The Productivity of African Labour."

10. *Ibid.*

11. D. F. Kokot, "Desert Encroachment in South Africa." Italics are the author's.

"push" factor away from the Reserves was certainly much more basic than the "pull" factor towards the cities. Left to themselves, these economic forces would already have had highly disruptive social consequences. But, as we shall see presently, government policies and private employment practices have further worsened the position of the Africans. Before we touch on these, however, we must emphasize another characteristic, common to many African countries, which makes the transition to industrialization particularly disruptive.

In the classical pattern of European urbanization and industrialization, the transition has been predominantly *diachronic* and *unidirectional*. Peasants have gradually moved to the cities, adapted to the urban environment, and settled there permanently. In Africa, on the other hand, there has typically been a long-range tendency towards increasing urbanization, but, simultaneously, there took place a constant, two-way, cyclical migration of workers to and from urban centres. Not only have African societies undergone a steady transformation over time, but large numbers of people are "commuting" at any given time between two widely different types of social environment. Through the large-scale use of migrant labour by much of White industry, the social change brought about by economic forces has been much more traumatic and disruptive of traditional peasant society than would have been the case with gradual, one-way migration. First, the African migrant worker is separated from his family for long periods; and, second, cyclical two-way migration necessarily involves a much greater proportion of the population in a shorter time space. We shall return to the causes and consequences of the African migratory labour system presently.

Let us review our argument so far. Industrialization inherently entails a number of disruptive consequences. South Africa shares these special conditions with the rest of colonial or formerly colonial Africa, but in a particularly extreme form. Indeed, the process of industrialization is far more advanced in

South Africa than in all the rest of the continent, and, hence, it has left practically nobody unaffected. Furthermore, local Africans have been dispossessed of their land to a greater degree than in any other part of the continent. The factors mentioned so far differentiate South Africa from all other countries only in degree. We must now turn to more specific conditions that make for uniquely South African sources of conflict and dysfunction.

As might be expected, the South African syndrome of racial prejudice and discrimination, in both its private and its governmental forms, makes a significant contribution to economic dysfunction. The bearing that racial legislation, executive action, and discrimination in private employment have on the system of production must, therefore, be examined in some detail. The measures and practices which we shall mention are all interrelated, but for purposes of analysis we shall have to deal with them singly.

At least one-third of South Africa's Black labour force consists of migratory workers who come from the Native Reserves, the British High Commission Territories, and the neighbouring countries, mostly Rhodesia, Nyasaland, and Mozambique, to complete a term of contract, usually of six-months duration. Almost all of the 500,000 African miners, as well as many of the workers in large-scale cash agriculture (such as most of the 100,000 people employed in the Natal sugar industry) and in secondary industry, are housed in military-type barracks where they are completely cut off from their families; on completion of their contract they return to the Reserves, usually for several months. In the case of the diamond mines, the African workers (but not the White workers) are locked inside the mine compound for the entire contract period.

In some rural areas, work conditions for Africans can only be described as involuntary servitude. The state co-operates with the White farmers in supplying the latter with Africans, who are locked up in prison out-stations, or in huts erected by the farmer. These Africans have generally been arrested for technical offences, such as pass violations, and given the option of prosecution or a three- or six-months term on a White farm at wages of two shillings a day. Workers are often locked up at night in overcrowded huts, with insufficient water, "filthy blankets or sacks that were infested with lice," and "extremely inadequate" food. They are, furthermore, beaten by African "boss-boys."[12] The Bethal district of the Transvaal is particularly notorious for the treatment of African farm labourers who work up to fourteen hours a day and are frequently beaten with *sjamboks*.[13]

We have already mentioned the social and political effects of the migratory labour system, namely the disruption of the African family, the promotion of concubinage and illegitimacy due to the large excess of men over women in urban areas, the breakdown of customary authority, the escape from traditional kinship obligations, profound and disruptive transformations in the bride-wealth system (known as *lobola*), the lowering of ethnic consciousness, and the promotion of proletarian consciousness along racial lines. All these processes add enormously to tension in South Africa; but the migratory labour system also has dysfunctions of a directly economic nature. The workers spend close to half of their economically active lifetime in the Reserves, where their productivity is almost nil. This results in a gigantic waste of labour force potential. In addition, the economy has to bear the cost of moving annually millions of workers over distances of up to a thousand miles. With high turnover rates, industry finds it unprofitable to invest in the training of its African workers, since most of them never return to the same employer. This is a further factor reducing productivity.

In short, one can probably say that the migratory labour system makes a greater contribution to economic waste, social disruption, and political tension in South Africa than any other

12. Horrell, *A Survey of Race Relations in South Africa*, 1958–1959, pp. 308–320.
13. Scott, *op. cit.*, p. 177. See also Luthuli, *op. cit.*, p. 218, for a description of work conditions in prison out-stations on White-owned farms.

single factor. Why, then, has such a system perpetuated itself for about a century, and why do large segments of industry and government continue to join forces in preserving it, regardless of cost? The answer is fairly simple. The system arose spontaneously from the development of the diamond and gold mines in the nineteenth century. Single men, attracted by the opportunity of earning cash wages, were drawn to the mines, and the latter found it convenient for purposes of discipline and theft-control to house their workers in barracks. To insure a steady supply of labour, the mines soon set up a complex machinery of recruitment in the African Reserves. Discriminatory taxation and labour legislation also played a significant role in the institutionalization of the system. Every adult male African is forced to pay a poll (i.e., capitation) tax in money, and, thereby, to enter the wage economy. Laws prohibiting strikes by Africans and making breach of contract a criminal offence have likewise kept migrant labour cheap, docile, and reliable.

To be sure, most industrialists have realized for some years the wastefulness of the migratory labour system, and some have made efforts to stabilize the labour force. But a powerful combination of forces prevents the rationalization of employment practices. First, the initial capital investment in providing even rudimentary housing for entire families is much higher than that required for single men's barracks. Whatever long-range benefits might result from such a shift, most industries are either unable to carry the cost of family housing or reluctant to do so.

Secondly, the Chamber of Mines, which represents the gold industry and constitutes the most powerful economic group in the country, has a strong vested interest in the migratory system. The low gold content of the ore and the fixity in the price of gold would render exploitation unprofitable if wages were substantially raised, and migrant labour has proven the cheapest and most docile. The extractive industries, along with employers of domestic and agricultural workers, pay the lowest African wages, and it is in mining that the wage discrepancy between Whites and

Africans is the widest. While the average yearly wage of a White miner in 1962 was £1281, the corresponding figure for African workers was £77.[14] This ratio of 16.6 to 1 is about four times higher than in secondary industries which employ non-migrant labour to a considerable degree (Table XXIV). While the migratory system makes for underutilization and low productivity of labour, it also contributes to the depression of African wages and to the subsidization of White wages. Any drastic change in employment practices would be a serious threat to gold mining as a private enterprise.

Thirdly, the government, for political reasons, throws its entire coercive force behind the migratory system with implicit support from the mining concerns. In its endeavour to enforce apartheid, the South African government wants to prevent Africans who live in the Reserves from settling permanently in the White parts of the country, and tries to send back to the Reserves the Africans already settled in the White areas. Officially, and with a few minor exceptions, an African may only stay in White areas on sufferance, and so long as he is employed by a White. A cumbersome state machinery of pass offices, labour bureaux, Native courts, and police endeavours to enforce this policy of mass removal, euphemistically known as influx control. In practice, the policy involves constant police raids in the African "locations," 300,000 to 400,000 arrests and convictions each year, forced expropriation of landowners and removal of squatters, "re-settlement" in already overpopulated Reserves, and forced labour for nominal wages in rural prison out-stations. Petty White officials of the Department of Bantu Administration and Development have almost unlimited power to "endorse" any African out of any area. The latest piece of legislation designed to tighten further the control of migrant workers is the 1964 Bantu Laws Amendment Bill, which has led the Anglican Bishop of Pretoria, Edward Knapp-Fisher, to denounce the "inhumanity"

14. *Africa Today*, 11, March, 1964, p. 1.

of the law, and the Anglican Bishop of Kimberley, Philip Wheeldon, to declare that the bill "amounts to slave labour."[15] This bill extends influx control regulations to the White rural areas; forbids Africans from seeking work outside Reserves except through state labour bureaux; and deprives the last few thousand Africans previously exempted from arbitrary deportation of their right of permanent residence in urban areas. It also empowers the Minister of Bantu Administration and Development to detain unemployed Africans under twenty-one in "youth camps" and to detain unemployed adult Africans in "labour depots." Thus, the principle that Africans are transient labourers in urban areas has been carried to its ultimate conclusion.

The Nationalist government is, of course, realistic enough to know that White industry could not exist without Black labour, and, hence, that total territorial apartheid is impossible. But the only form of African influx into the White areas which the government accepts as desirable, or at least unavoidable, consists of migrant labourers who leave their families behind in the Reserves, return periodically to the latter, and do not establish any permanent roots in the cities. The long-range plan involves the forced removal of all other Africans from White areas as "redundant Natives."[16] In other words, the government favours and maintains the migratory labour system for political reasons which are quite extraneous to economics, and it does so with the tacit support and co-operation of the Chamber of Mines, and a number of other concerns which maintain or patronize recruiting agents throughout South Africa.

In spite of large-scale resort to force, the government has proven unable to check the permanent settlement of increasing numbers of Africans in towns. A 1957 estimate indicates that some 38 per cent of the Africans lived in the Reserves, 34 per

15. *The Times,* London, April 2, 1964.
16. For details on the implementation of influx control and the pass laws, see Horrell's yearly *Survey of Race Relations in South Africa.*

cent in White rural areas, and 28 per cent in cities.[17] In 1951 the respective figures were 43 per cent, 30 per cent, and 27 per cent; and in 1911, 44 per cent, 43 per cent, and 13 per cent (Table VI). The 1960 census shows that the urbanization rate for Africans continues to be much faster than for the Whites, who are now outnumbered in all the large cities. Between 1951 and 1960 the number of Africans in urban areas increased by 45 per cent, or some 1,081,000 people. In Johannesburg alone, the African population rose by 32 per cent during that period while the European population declined by 13 per cent.[18]

If government policies have not stopped existing trends, one can reasonably assume that they have at least exerted a retardative and interfering effect on normal mobility. More precisely, the state has fostered a type of labour mobility, namely the migratory labour system, which is economically wasteful in advanced industrial societies, as well as socially disruptive; at the same time it has hindered the "free" supply of labour in answer to the industrial demand. To the extent that the Africans are not free to move within the country, and to offer their services on a free labour market, wages are kept artificially low, and the expansion of secondary industry is hindered. Africans are not the only group to be restrained in their movements; Indians are likewise subject to stringent restrictions, and are totally excluded from residence in the Orange Free State. (Technically, Whites are also forbidden to enter most African "locations" and Reserves without permits, but these regulations are seldom enforced, except against political organizers and social scientists. *Bona fide* tourists, for example, are never interfered with when they visit Native Reserves.)

One of the most basic requirements for a complex capitalist economy is a freely mobile labour force which is responsive to labour demand. In South Africa such conditions exist only for

17. Horrell, *A Survey of Race Relations in South Africa*, 1958–1959, p. 103.

18. *Africa Digest*, 11, February, 1964, p. 111.

the Whites, and, to a limited extent, for the Coloureds. The least that can be said about the effect of government labour policy is that the vast machinery of influx control as well as the lost productivity resulting from mass deportations and arrests have involved a cost which is not less enormous for being impossible to assess, and have been contrary to any principle of economic rationality in a capitalist system of production. The state, the mining magnates, and the White farmers have, for different reasons, shared a common interest in maintaining such an anachronistic and repressive labour system.

Other forms of racial discrimination have contributed their share of economic dysfunctions. One of them is "job reservation," i.e., the set of laws and government regulations connected with the occupational colour-bar. Non-Whites have been excluded from all skilled work in the mines since the passage of the Mines and Works Act of 1911; since then, the legal colour-bar has been extended to an ever increasing number of occupations and industries. Even where the law does not debar non-Whites from certain jobs, the private prejudices of employers and White workers have the same effect. Non-Whites are also excluded *de facto* from many occupations through their being denied admission to the White trade schools, high schools, and universities, where they could acquire the necessary skills. In practice, then, except for a small Coloured artisan class in the Cape, and a tiny non-White elite of professionals and semiprofessionals (mostly nurses and teachers working in segregated hospitals and schools), it is virtually impossible for a non-White to be anything but a domestic servant, a subsistence farmer or farm worker, or an unskilled or, at best, semiskilled industrial labourer.

The economic consequences of such discrimination are obvious. Recruitment for jobs is largely on the basis of the ascriptive criterion of race, rather than of competence. More accurately, rational criteria of selection are operative only within rigid racial categories. The potential talent of 80 per cent of the population to fill skilled positions is wasted, while incompetent Europeans, whose sole qualification is skin colour, occupy responsible jobs because there are not enough qualified Whites to fill all such positions. The civil service (in particular the railways, the police, and the post office) has become a field of protected employment for otherwise unemployable Whites (mostly Afrikaners) of substandard education and intelligence. Industry also suffers from the scarcity of qualified Whites to fill important jobs. A 1960 South African government survey disclosed labour shortages ranging from 12 to 18 per cent in such key occupations as engineers, physicists, and chemists. A 1956 statement by the Minister of Labour alleged that there was a 9 per cent shortage of artisans and a 16.2 per cent shortage of apprentices.[19] Whites, in effect, have chosen to monopolize all skilled occupations in a complex industrial economy which supports a population that is five times larger than the pool of workers eligible to do practically all but the most menial jobs. The results, obviously, are vast underutilization of non-White skills, and a corresponding over-employment of Whites. Both of these take an enormous toll in industrial and administrative efficiency.

We have already referred to the great wage differences between skilled and unskilled labour. Legally, most minimum wage determinations are based on job categories rather than directly on race; but as race coincides almost entirely with occupation, the wage discrimination is, in fact, racial. Depending on the industries, White manual workers earn between five and fifteen times as much as non-White workers. Even when, through fictitious relabeling of jobs, Whites and non-Whites perform essentially similar tasks (as happens surreptitiously in many secondary industries), the Europeans are paid three or four times as much as the non-Europeans. In government service, equally qualified Whites and non-Whites performing similar jobs (e.g., policemen, teachers, nurses, etc.) are paid widely different salaries. The principle of unequal pay for equal work has even been adopted

19. Hartmann, *op. cit.*, pp. 39–40.

by most religious denominations in the payment of teachers' and clergymen's stipends.

Aside from the occupational colour-bar, several other factors contribute to the perpetuation of this wage differential. While Whites are free to strike and to unionize, the Africans are not; breach of contract is a criminal offence for Africans but not for Europeans; pass regulations force Africans into the least remunerative jobs; severe educational restrictions on the non-Whites keep the average skill-level low; private discrimination by employers has led to an interpretation of minimum wage regulations as *maximum* wages for non-Whites, while White workers have successfully organized for continuously rising wages.

The wage gap is usually defended by Whites as being based on a productivity differential. To be sure, White workers *are* more productive, on the average, than non-White labourers, largely because they are more skilled, healthier, better nourished, and in more mechanized jobs.[20] But the factors examined above depress non-European wages far below the productivity level, while the reverse is true for Europeans. In fact, cheap non-White labour subsidizes the high European living standard, not only of the entrepreneur, but also of White manual workers. While the existing wage gap results, thus, partly from the country's economic structure, racial factors have further increased it.

Another variant of White justification for paying Africans low wages, is that Africans are "target" workers, i.e., that they enter the money economy temporarily in order to buy specific items, to pay their poll tax, etc., and that, once they have accumulated the necessary sum, they return to the subsistence economy.[21] Hence, the argument continues, there is an inverse relationship between wages and the supply of labour, and the only way to keep labour plentiful is to pay low wages. Of course, "target labour"

20. For a treatment of factors limiting the productivity of African workers see: P. de Briey, *op. cit.*

21. For a discussion of "target labour," see Bohannan and Dalton, *op. cit.*

is well known to students of African economics, but the phenomenon is extremely limited in South Africa. Indeed, the existence of "target labour" presupposes a subsistence economy. In South Africa two-thirds of the Africans live outside of the Reserves, and the latter are *below* subsistence. The main "target" which most African workers have in South Africa is to ward off starvation, and this forces them to work for wages most of the time.

Besides the objective economic dysfunctions of a widely unequal income distribution (in terms of productivity, purchasing power, size of the internal market, and rate of savings, capitalization, and industrial expansion), the subjective consequences of racial disparities in wealth certainly add to tension. With no prospect of job improvement, non-Whites have little incentive to work better; on the other hand, the privileged, protected, European worker likewise has little incentive to improve his performance, because he is assured of remunerative employment. Non-White proletarians become totally alienated from their jobs, or indeed from the whole system of production, and respond to discrimination with output restriction, passive resistance, minor sabotage, and boycotts of shops and products. The frequent White argument that the "Natives" should be happy because they earn more than do "their brothers" elsewhere on the continent is not only racialistic but also entirely besides the point. Obviously, the African compares his position to that of local Whites, and not to that of foreigners who happen to have the same skin colour.

Racial stereotypes may also have an indirect economic effect, though there is little solid evidence for it. For example, the White view of the non-White worker as "unreliable" and "irresponsible" can easily become a self-fulfilling prophecy. A worker who has been reprimanded for showing initiative, and who is treated as a simpleton, is likely either to lose all interest in his job and perform his tasks unthinkingly and apathetically, or to exhibit his spite by deliberate irresponsibility, coupled with punctilious obedience to the letter of stupid orders. This method can be an

effective means of passive resistance and could have an appreciable effect on production.[22] Fulfillment of role-expectation provides the non-White worker with a relatively safe and satisfying
way of expressing hostility towards Europeans.

Returning to more objective sources of economic dysfunctions, several further aspects of government policy have an
adverse effect on the economy. The most obvious, but not the
most important, of these is the financial cost of racial segregation
in all public amenities. In some cases, the duplication of facilities
is, of course, a complete waste of money. However, the direct
cost of segregation to the government or to the White taxpayers
is minimal, for, in most cases, an amenity is segregated in the
sense that it is available only to Whites. An effort, or even a
serious pretence, to establish "separate but equal" facilities has
hardly ever been made. If a given amenity is available at all to
non-Whites, it is generally of such an inferior quality as to represent a saving over what it would cost to offer all citizens
adequate facilities. Furthermore, each racial group is expected
to finance its own segregated amenities such as schools, hospitals,
churches, beer halls, etc. In practice, then, the non-Whites, and
particularly the Africans who are the most destitute, bear the
main cost of segregation, and are forced to pay (under strongly
regressive taxation) for a system they abhor. This situation is
accepted as "natural" by most Whites. The argument that the
White electorate is going to stop supporting apartheid because
of its financial cost is consequently devoid of substance.

A number of government projects are, nevertheless, quite
costly and senseless, insofar as they run counter the most elementary principles of economic rationality, although their political
motivation is both transparent and "rational" in terms of the
government's premises. For example, the government spends con-

22. Whatever evidence I have on this point is of a fragmentary and
impressionistic nature, but I have heard of, or personally experienced, several
instances of this type of behaviour. In addition, I have observed dramatic
changes in performance among Africans, in response to courteous treatment.

siderable sums in promoting European immigration to South Africa, while at the same time deporting thousands of "foreign Natives," forbidding Indian immigration, and encouraging the "repatriation" of South-African-born Indians to India. South Africa is said to need more people (i.e., Whites) and to be a land of unlimited opportunities, while the government also complains about the presence of "redundant Natives" and the danger of "Asiatic invasion."

The geographical situation of African urban townships likewise bears no relation to economic realities, and it is determined almost purely by political and military factors, irrespective of cost. These African "locations" are often built ten to twenty miles from the White cities, in part to maximize physical segregation as an end in itself, and in part for reasons of security and repression in case of revolt. That hundreds of thousands of Africans have to pay up to 20 per cent of their already insufficient wages for transport, and waste up to three or four hours a day in commuting to their place of employment where they arrive tired and incapable of efficient work, is of little concern to the government, although many industrialists complain of lowered productivity and increasing tardiness and absenteeism among their African workers. The indirect cost of this form of segregation to the economy as a whole is certainly quite high.

Of a similar anti-economic nature are government plans to "rehabilitate" the Native Reserves, and to establish "border industries," townships and "university colleges" in or next to the Reserves. These schemes are part of the apartheid master plan whereby most Africans will live in prosperous, self-sufficient, autonomous Bantustans. In the White areas, there would remain only the necessary minimum of Black labour. So far, the amount spent on this totally impracticable plan does not remotely approximate the £104,000,000 recommended in 1956 by the Tomlinson Commission, even though such an estimate was then considered grossly insufficient by most economic experts. It is clear, however, that whatever money has been spent has largely been spent on schemes which bore little relationship to economic contingencies.

What could be the purpose of establishing "Bantu university colleges" in the middle of the bush, except to isolate the students from "dangerous" currents of thought in the cities, and keep them out of the political struggle? What economic reason could one advance for artificially developing towns in the middle of destitute Reserves with no economic infrastructure, or even transportation system to support them? The "border industries" scheme is similarly questionable. In order to "decentralize" industry, the government is encouraging the building of factories on the border of the Native Reserves. The true reason for the scheme ties in again with the general apartheid blueprint; but the pseudo-economic rationalization for the plan is that industry will benefit through the proximity of the labour supply. In other words, the location of industry will be determined by proximity to the most mobile of its prerequisites, namely labour. Such considerations as transport of raw materials over a non-existent road or rail network, proximity to harbours, availability of a reliable water supply, location of the consumer market, etc. are regarded as secondary, provided that the scheme fits into the political master plan.

We still have to examine another repercussion of racist policies on the South African economy, namely the internal consequences of the external reactions to political events in South Africa. These reactions affect adversely the economy in two different ways. First, evidence of racial unrest in South Africa or in neighbouring countries leads to a loss of confidence in the country's stability, and hence to a flight of foreign capital through panic sales of South African stocks. In 1960 there was a net outflow of £97,000,000 of private capital, mostly foreign-owned, from South Africa (Table XIX). As the internal buying capacity to compensate for heavy sales on foreign stock exchanges is limited, prices of South African stocks are very sensitive to political events. After the manifestations and police shooting of

March–April, 1960, for example, the value of South African shares declined by nearly £600,000,000 between February and April, 1960, some stocks going down by as much as 50 per cent. Foreign reserves were also adversely affected, and went down from £157,000,000 to £85,000,000 by December, 1960.[23] Since then, the repressive measures introduced by the government and the relative absence of major outbreaks of violence have again convinced overseas investors that South Africa is a good risk, and the stock market has recovered, but any new wave of revolt would have an immediate economic effect. Political instability in the rest of the continent further heightens South Africa's vulnerability in this respect.

Of another nature are the economic repercussions of foreign indignation at apartheid. A number of countries have imposed economic sanctions against South Africa or have threatened to do so. While these sanctions have so far had little noticeable effect on the economy, because none of the countries involved has been a major trade partner of South Africa, they are likely to increase in gravity. A more detailed discussion of this point will be reserved for Chapter Ten.

There is, however, another side to the importance of foreign investments. The Western countries, and most particularly the United Kingdom, have been reluctant to adopt economic sanctions against South Africa at the United Nations, at least in part because of their sizeable trade with, and investments in, the Republic. It is certainly no accident that the countries that have the most important financial and trade interests in South Africa have also been the most restrained in their condemnation of apartheid.[24] Possibly, the restraining aspects of foreign trade and investments overbalance their disruptive effects through flight of capital in periods of crisis.

We are left now with the task of analysing the third class of dysfunctional factors involving the economy, namely the tensions

23. Hartmann, *op. cit.*, p. 19.
24. See Chapter X.

arising from the particular relationship between economic and political power. In a nutshell, we find, once again, the basic triangle of forces contending for supremacy in South Africa: the Afrikaners, who detain the monopoly of political power; the English, who dominate the economic scene; and the African masses, who threaten to overthrow the existing system.

The dichotomy between the holders of political and economic power is a recent development arising from the Nationalist election victory of 1948. Under most previous governments, the dominant note has been one of reconciliation between the English and the Afrikaners, and of close co-operation between the state and large-scale finance and industry. To be sure, the 1924 Nationalist-Labour government under Hertzog led to a temporary estrangement between big business and the state, and was a prelude to the present situation; but the Hertzog-Smuts coalition of 1933 re-established the general community of interests between business and political elites.

The present clash between business and government does not result so much from ideological disagreements between the Nationalist Party and the official opposition, as appears on the surface from a reading of the daily press. This conflict is rather the incidental consequence of class distribution between the Afrikaners and the English. Economic issues occupy a distinctly secondary position on the platforms of all the major White political parties, except insofar as the United Party attacks apartheid as detrimental to business, economically unsound, and impractical. Party affiliation is determined almost entirely by ethnic membership, but the latter overlaps in considerable degree with class distinctions: the majority of the White farmers and manual workers are Afrikaners, while the bulk of big business and finance is English-controlled. The Labour Party's attempt to organize White opinion along class rather than linguistic lines has failed, partly because the racialism and the privileged position of the White working class prevented the Party from taking a leftist position. The Labour Party thus became a White trade-union lobby to protect European workers against non-White competition. This anomalous position of the Labour Party made its 1924 coalition with the old Nationalist Party a logical development. Even the small Communist Party had an all-White membership in the early 1920's; during the 1922 Rand strike, it favoured the European workers as the "vanguard of the proletariat" whose slogan was: "Workers of the world fight and unite for a White South Africa."[25]

The Nationalist Party is certainly not anti-business *per se*. Indeed, some of its prominent members occupy important business positions, and the government makes every effort to promote Afrikaner economic interests. At the same time, there is a strong undercurrent of anti-capitalism in Afrikaner Nationalist ideology. To view that undercurrent as a sign of economic radicalism, however, would be a complete distortion of facts. Big business and finance have been historically linked with the English and the *Uitlanders* in South Africa. Consequently, Afrikaner anti-capitalism is a secondary derivative of anti-English attitudes, and, even more generally, of the romantic idealization of rural life and distrust for corrupting cosmopolitanism which are still part of the Afrikaner ethos. By the same token, the opposition United and Progressive parties are not anti-labour organizations. They are English parties drawing their membership and support from the English working class, as well as from the middle and upper class. This is true in spite of the fact that these two parties, along with the English daily press which propagandizes their platforms, are financed and controlled by the English business elite.

However, although the paramount salience of racial issues has largely driven class and economic issues within the White group out of the political arena, the power conflict between the two White elites, namely the Nationalist politicians and the English capitalists, is nonetheless quite real. Two views on the

25. Thomas Karis, *op. cit.*

relationship between these two groups must be rejected at the outset, one as too naive, and the other as too simple. The naive view consists in accepting verbal statements and press propaganda at face value, and in assuming from them that the two groups are irrevocably opposed to one another, and engaged in a bitter fight for supremacy. The simplistic, Marxist view, on the other hand, sees the two groups as disagreeing overtly while quietly co-operating behind the scenes. The true relationship between the two elites must be analysed in terms of co-operation-in-conflict. To understand this complex and delicately balanced relationship, we must once more introduce the third side of the triangle, namely the Africans.

The English business elite is bitterly opposed to the Nationalist government, not only at the overt level, but also in a deep emotional way. It shares for the most part a conviction in the superiority of English over Afrikaner culture, and typically looks on the latter with disdain. The "Nats" are considered as uncouth political *parvenus*.[26] The English business class perceives the Nationalist government as threatening in several ways. In the strictly political sense, big businessmen notice with alarm the gradual erosion of the civil liberties and privileges which they have so far enjoyed as members of the dominant White group. Culturally, they fear the eclipse of the English language and way of life, and witness with dislike the gradual Afrikanerization of the country. Economically, they view government policies as interfering with free enterprise, and with almost every rational principle of industrial development, as well as endangering export markets through increasing isolationism and unpopularity abroad. Finally, they attack Nationalist racial policies for a variety of reasons that we must examine more closely.

Most English businessmen do not oppose apartheid because

26. For a more detailed discussion of the relationship between the English business elite and the Nationalist government at the local level, see my study of Caneville.

they are liberals. While a minority of them support the cautious programme of gradual change advocated by the Progressive Party, the majority still adhere to the racialist, segregationist platform of the United Party. Some have even recently begun to attack the Nationalists on the right, by accusing Verwoerd of wanting to create hostile "Native" states in the midst of "White" South Africa. The English elite and the English press, which it controls, attack apartheid as impractical, costly, harmful to their own economic interests, and politically dangerous. Ethical objections to apartheid, if mentioned at all, appear as an afterthought thrown in for good measure.

The English capitalist and managerial class would probably be willing to pay a certain economic cost for apartheid if it were convinced that Nationalist racial policies could maintain or at least prolong the *status quo*. But, for the most part, that class perceives that tensions are mounting, and is convinced that the inflexible repressiveness of the Nationalist regime constantly aggravates the situation, and is likely to precipitate a revolutionary upheaval. At the same time, the English elite, through its own conservatism and racism, fails to comprehend that mounting conflicts have resulted, at least as much, from external developments in the rest of Africa, and from the internal dynamics of South African society, as from aggravating Nationalist policies. It therefore believes, for the most part, that the minor palliatives and the somewhat more flexible and empirical methods of White domination advocated by the United Party would be sufficient to alleviate tension and perpetuate the economic *status quo*. A less conservative segment of the English managerial and business group, whose most prominent spokesman is Harry Oppenheimer, supports the Progressive Party.

The Nationalists, on the other hand, are hostile to English capitalism as epitomizing to them the force which, in conjunction with aggressive British imperialism, has oppressed and frustrated Afrikanerdom throughout South African history. While only pathological English-haters like Albert Hertzog openly express virulent anti-English sentiments in public, such feelings occupy a prominent place in the thinking of leading Afrikaner Nationalists, most of whom belong to the militant *Broederbond*. At the more overt level, the business-controlled English press is the main target of Nationalist innuendo in speeches and in Afrikaans newspapers. The English press is constantly castigated for "unfairly" attacking the government and subverting the non-Whites. The Nationalists also view the United Party approach to race as leading to gradual integration, and selling the "White man's heritage" for the sake of the selfish short-range interests of the English business class.

These, then, are the main areas and sources of conflict between the economic and political power groups. While this conflict is real and not simply verbal, the presence of the third force, the Africans, also makes for a wide area of agreement and cooperation between the two conservative elites, both of which have a vested interest in the *status quo*. The two dominant White elites have thus developed over the years an uneasy *modus vivendi* based on compromise, behind-the-scene negotiations, and tacit agreement on basic aims.

English capital is undoubtedly in a weaker bargaining position than the government in this process of co-operation-in-conflict. The fundamental, tacit rule of the game between Nationalist and English leaders is that, given agreement on the issue of White domination, the English opposition (both in its political and business form) will not resort to any "dangerous" action (such as in industrial shutdown), and will keep exclusively to ineffective parliamentary action, negotiation, and restrained verbal attacks in the press. In return for English "self-restraint," i.e., self-condemnation to political impotence, the government tacitly promises to interfere with business as little as is consistent with the gradual implementation of apartheid, and not to use the wide dictatorial powers at its disposal to muzzle the English press and ban the United Party.

The English leaders, both politicians and businessmen, have little alternative but to "play the game," unfavourable as the rules are. Politically, an "opening to the left" entails the prospect of losing the conservative English vote, as shown by the failure of the dissident Progressive Party to win more than one seat in the 1961 parliamentary elections. Moreover, any deviation from opposition methods that the government considers "fair" would bring immediate retaliatory action under the existing arbitrary legislation. Finally, such economic protest action as an industrial shutdown has no likelihood of being used, because the English industrialists fear that it could trigger off a revolution, and that the only realistic alternative to White Afrikaner Nationalism is Black African Nationalism. Conversely, the government knows that, faced with the threat of African Nationalism, the English opposition will support the existing system.

In other words, the existence of militant and growing African Nationalism not only condemns English economic interests to political impotence, but even insures the government of active English support in periods of crisis. During the 1960 State of Emergency, for example, the United Party supported most repressive measures of the government, and it has fairly consistently continued to do so since that time; when the Congress Alliance called for a three-day "stay-at-home" strike in protest against apartheid in May 1961, almost all industrial concerns adopted a "business-as-usual" policy, and many of them threatened would-be strikers with dismissal. This happened in spite of the fact that the demonstration was timed to coincide with the official proclamation of South Africa as a Republic outside the Commonwealth, a move which the overwhelming majority of the English electorate bitterly opposed. A few of the more "progressive" English industrialists have established informal contact with leaders of both the Pan-African Congress and the African National Congress, and would probably show enough flexibility to throw their weight quickly on the side of any future, non-leftist, African government. However, it is highly improbable that such a shift will occur before a successful African revolution.

Let us analyse now the role of African Nationalism in its relation to the system of production. As a result of political oppression and economic exploitation, practically all Africans share a common interest in drastic social change. A few marginal groups such as African policemen and chiefs do, of course, have a vested interest in apartheid, but their role is negligible. In Marxist terms, the African group is characterized by the almost total absence of a bourgeoisie, even of a petty bourgeoisie, and consists almost entirely of a large peasantry, a large urban proletariat, a small white-collar class, and an even smaller intelligentsia. None of these four classes has much to lose in the *status quo,* and all four are alienated from both the state and the system of production. The nearest thing to a "bourgeois" outlook among Africans is found in the white-collar class of petty clerks, civil servants and the like, who have some job security and live above the starvation level. The urban proletariat stands to gain political power, and hopes to improve its economic position. The fact that revolution is not likely to result in rapidly improving standards for the African masses is irrelevant here. Indeed, the expectation rather than the prospect of such an improvement creates revolutionary attitudes.

The intelligentsia probably stands to gain most through change. Its skills and its dominant role in the liberatory movements destine it to occupy command positions in any future Black government. Before the emergence of mass political consciousness, and as long as the educated African elite was offered any hope of assimilation to the dominant group, the intelligentsia remained relatively conservative, and saw the future in terms of compromise, reforms, and gradual concessions. This was true of the African National Congress and the All-African Convention until the post World War Two years, when the Youth League of the ANC was founded, and the militant

1949 ANC Programme of Action was proclaimed. The 1955 Freedom Charter represents a further step towards increasingly militant demands. Now, with a mass following and no prospects of reform, the intelligentsia is necessarily turning to radicalism, either in the Black racialist or in the leftist direction.

Even the African peasantry, usually a conservative group, has little to lose by change. Roughly half of the peasants live as quasi-serfs on White farms, while the other half vegetate on insufficient Reserve land, which they merely occupy, but do not own in freehold. While, in the more isolated areas, the peasantry is still very traditional in such things as cultivation methods, and resists technological innovations, most African farmers would probably support land redistribution and a change from "communal" to individual land tenure.

A word must be said about the Coloureds and the Indians. Neither group is likely to play a leading role in future political development, not only because of demographic and historical factors already mentioned, but also because each group contains a sizeable and influential bourgeoisie (the Indian business class and the Coloured petty bourgeoisie) with *some* vested interest in the economic *status quo*. Both groups are probably going to be pushed increasingly on the African side, because of White rejection and a desire to propitiate the growing Black Nationalism; at the same time, they are likely to remain in the sidelines of the African movements, except, perhaps, at the leadership level.

To review briefly the complex interlocking of economic and political forces in South Africa, and the resulting dysfunctions for the society as a whole, we identified three broad sources of tension. The first source is inherent in the internal dynamics of an economy in transition from underdevelopment to industrialization. Special conditions make that transition particularly traumatic in Africa, and even more so in South Africa. Apart from the strains intrinsic in economic development, a second class of aggravating factors is related to the peculiarly South African complex of race. Both government colour policies and private discrimination introduce into the system of production elements of tension and malfunction, which are extraneous to economic processes. Finally, the particular distribution of economic and political power along ethnic lines led us back to the basic three-cornered struggle which we had already encountered when we dealt with South Africa from the political angle.

Before concluding this chapter, let us try to reach a higher level of synthesis in relating the South African economy to the rest of the society. The South African process of industrialization, looked at from a strictly economic point of view, offers nothing startling to the analyst. A straightforward description of economic changes does not reveal anything basic that most other countries in a comparable stage of development have not experienced, except for the very special role of gold mining. A classical theoretical model of dynamic equilibrium would serve adequately to describe the adjustments and transformations that have taken place within the system of production. As in other industrializing countries, changes in the mode of production have set in motion a complex set of trends in other parts of the social system: urbanization, spacial or horizontal mobility, a rise in material and educational standards, secularization, the breakdown of traditional peasant cultures, a tendency towards greater cultural homogeneity, the shift from extended to nuclear family structures, the politization and "proletarianization" of the urban masses, social mobility on the basis of achievement, and the decay of rigidly ascriptive criteria of stratification.

We have hardly touched on these trends in South Africa because their detailed description would have offered nothing new. In its economic dynamics of change, South African society has behaved very typically, in a way which a conventional equilibrium model would satisfactorily approximate. The great empirical contribution of our case study comes in, however, where South Africa has deviated from the "expected" pattern. Far from adjusting to the trends set in motion by economic changes, the political system has reacted in a maladjusting direction. South Africa thus presents the spectacle of an equilibrium system that has "run amok," and where the polity, by introducing reactionary change, attempts to reverse the social, political, and cultural tendencies brought about by industrialization.

The trend towards social mobility and the breakdown of traditional status barriers was countered by racial legislation to transform the colour groups into rigid, ascriptive castes. The tendency towards Westernization and the decay of African cultures was met with counteracculturative measures to revive traditional institutions. Rigid segregation in education attempts, among other things, to hinder the acquisition by non-Whites of universalistic values, including "dangerous" notions of freedom and equality. Far from extending the franchise and other civic rights, the state gradually deprived the non-Whites of the few rights they possessed in the nineteenth century. Examples of political reaction could be multiplied to the point of boredom. The result of such policies has, of course, been a cumulative maladjustment between a modern, expanding economic system on the one hand, and a political dinosaur coupled with a racial caste system inherited from an agrarian society on the other hand. How long this basic vicious circle of ever deepening tension can subsist is an open question. That South Africa has survived so long in such an acute state of disequilibrium is indeed highly problematical for sociological theory.

To close this chapter we must answer an obvious question that seems to invalidate our analysis. If the South African economy is so ridden with conflict and malfunction, why does it, far from collapsing, even continue to expand? One may, of course, point to the fact that, during the late-fifties, the rate of expansion has slowed down, but that phenomenon is typical of all economies once they have reached a certain degree of industrial maturity. Industrial expansion from a low-production base line is necessarily more rapid than when production has reached a high level. One may also cogently argue that the rate of expansion would have been much more rapid of it had not been for the "irrational" factors introduced by the government, but this *ex post facto* statement is unprovable, and, hence, can at best reach the level of plausibility without answering the question. The latter must be faced squarely.

Geographical and geological factors place South Africa in a privileged position. Among these are the presence of two of the best natural harbours (Durban and Cape Town) in Africa, a mild Mediterranean climate in the southern hemisphere permitting the cultivation of fruits for out-of-season export in the European market, and the availability of minerals, mostly gold, diamonds, and coal. Among the minerals, gold has played the most important role, as we already saw. The whole industrial complex of the Witwatersrand developed around gold mining, and indirectly Durban greatly benefited from Rand industry, as it constitutes the major sea outlet for Johannesburg. Furthermore, the special position of gold as a fixed-price commodity in constant demand has had a strong stabilizing influence on the South African economy. However, environmental factors do not provide a satisfactory answer to the problem of continuing prosperity. One can also plausibly point to unfavourable and limiting influences such as low rainfall in most of the country, lack of any internal waterways, low hydroelectric potential, and large semi-desertic areas such as the Karoo.

The real crux of the problem must be sought within the social system. First, the abundance of cheap labour and high custom barriers have enabled South African industry to expand in spite of inefficiency, and of inability to compete in many fields with foreign products. The same applied earlier to agriculture and animal husbandry. Even though Boer methods of cultivation were highly wasteful, there was abundant land into which to expand after the aborigines had been pushed back. In other words, the supply of human and natural resources has been plentiful enough to allow for both expansion and inefficiency, and has not yet put a premium on the more intensive exploitation methods used in more advanced and densely populated industrial countries.

Secondly, the relatively high level of skills and training of the population, both White and non-White, has put South Africa at an advantage, compared with other African countries where technical skills are still scarce, and where technical competence still creates an important bottleneck in the process of industrial expansion. In fact, South Africa, through its occupational colour-bar, underutilizes the available skills of its non-White population.

Thirdly, the process of uneasy compromise and negotiation between the government and industrial leaders has generally had the effect of mitigating the economically deleterious aspects of apartheid policies. The government has been stopped, or at least slowed down, by budgetary considerations, in the implementation of some of its schemes. As to business firms, they have tried to delay or circumvent compliance with inhibitive government regulations (for example, by reclassifying and renaming job categories so as to enable cheaper non-White labour to occupy them). When forced to comply, they have obviously attempted to minimize cost and disruption. Whereas the moral considerations and the socially disruptive effects of apartheid have rarely if ever hindered its implementation, economic cost has undoubtedly played an important delaying and mitigating role. There is no question that a rigid application of apartheid (in the sense of macro-segregation) would quickly bring the entire economy to a standstill.

To accept the fact of industrial expansion as evidence invalidating our analysis is, however, erroneous. The fact that the economy has expanded does not mean that it is not inefficient, ridden with dysfunctions, and generative of mounting conflicts. The very process of expansion, as we saw, inherently contains many disruptive forces. The apparent contradiction just raised is thus easily resolved. We still face, however, a much more fundamental question already suggested by our analysis of social and political conflicts, namely: How can societies in a state of acute disequilibrium continue to exist for long periods without showing any tendency towards adaptive change?[27] While we must reserve the treatment of theoretical problems for the final chapter, we may at least anticipate an answer. Clearly, the functionalist model of society as characterized by a high degree of integration, normative consensus, and equilibrium must be regarded as one-sided, and revised to incorporate the concepts of conflict, malintegration, and disequilibrium. Although there are probably limits to the amount of tension and internal contradictions which a society can take without disintegrating, the South African case suggests that these limits are quite wide.

27. Of course, South Africa has shown some adaptability at the technological and instrumental level, e.g., in improving its production methods, its repressive techniques, etc., but it has failed to alter essential elements of its social structure to any significant degree.

## CHAPTER NINE

## Value Conflicts

O NE of the main interests of South Africa for the development of sociological theory is the absence of consensus about values in that society. It should not be surprising that the many sources of conflict and contradiction arising from the South African social structure should also be reflected in lack of agreement about what is socially desirable. Yet several "structure-function" theorists, notably Talcott Parsons, postulate value consensus as a necessary condition to the existence of a society.[1] Unless most members of a society broadly agree on and internalize a common set of values, the most important and basic condition for social integration is lacking, according to many functionalist analysts.

We shall return in the final chapter to the problem raised by the consensus assumption. Meanwhile, let us provisionally accept, in minimum form, the functionalist postulates that a certain amount of integration is essential to the existence of a society, and that value consensus is an important source of integration in most social systems. We may even go one step further and accept that absence of consensus is at once a symptom and a cause of malintegration. However, the postulate that value consensus is a functional prerequisite of any society is patently

1. Cf. Talcott Parsons, *The Social System,* pp. 36–37, 326, 350–351; *Structure and Process in Modern Societies,* pp. 172–176.

contradicted by the existence of numerous culturally pluralistic societies wherein several groups have radically different values. One can, of course, stretch the concept of consensus to the point of meaninglessness, or deny that such social systems constitute societies; but either of these ways of evading the difficulty is unsatisfactory. Societies can be integrated on bases other than value consensus, e.g., through economic interdependence and political coercion, as is the case in South Africa.

What are the main sources of value conflict and dissension in South Africa? Basically they are reducible to two. First, since South Africa is a culturally pluralistic society, each culture represented in that country has its own idiosyncratic value system. In this respect South Africa is far from unique. Indeed, almost all of the world has experienced, at one time or another, the co-existence of widely different cultural traditions within broader social structures. Secondly, the value system of the dominant White group contains within itself crucial contradictions. Here, also, South Africa is not unique, but it certainly represents an extreme case. Both of these sources of value conflict will now be examined in greater detail.[2]

The different value orientations represented in the various ethnic groups, while not always conflicting, have nevertheless entailed tensions, misunderstandings, and mutually unfavourable stereotypes. A complete account of this source of value conflicts would involve a depth study of the value systems of all the cultural groups represented in South Africa. This is obviously beyond the scope of this study. We shall therefore confine

2. While solid quantitative data on value differences between various groups in South Africa are still scanty, the few studies in this area have shown important group differences. Cf. S. Biesheuvel, "Further Studies on the Measurement of Attitudes Towards Western Ethical Concepts"; Leonard Bloom et al., "An Interdisciplinary Study of Social, Moral and Political Attitudes"; K. Danziger, "Value Differences among South African Students"; J. M. Gillespie and G. W. Allport, Youth's Outlook on the Future; J. W. Mann, "Race-Linked Values in South Africa"; Pierre L. van den Berghe, "Race Attitudes in Durban, South Africa."

ourselves to a few salient aspects of the problem. Different notions of property, and more particularly of land ownership, have often led to conflict in European-African contacts. In South Africa, as elsewhere, the Europeans have introduced the alien notion that land could be individually owned and sold like any other commodity. On the other hand, the indigenous African groups shared a totally different conception of land, generally described as "communal tenure." In traditional African culture, land is a natural resource; land occupation by a certain group gives that group the right to exploit the land, but no individual may lay a property claim on any part of it. Within the group, land may be redistributed for use, according to the needs of the extended families which compose the larger group. As in many other parts of Africa, such widely different notions of property have led to misunderstandings and violent conflicts, especially in the period following the Great Trek, when land-cession "treaties" were signed between the Boers and the African nations.

Incompatible attitudes concerning cattle still play an important role in cultural clashes. The Europeans view cattle as consumption goods, whereas the traditional African outlook is to consider cattle primarily as capital goods. Heads of cattle are accumulated mainly for prestige reasons, and because cattle is the main medium of exchange in payment of the bride-wealth (*lobola*). The consumption of meat, milk, and hides is only a secondary by-product of livestock ownership. As cattle is convertible into women (and, hence, even more importantly into children), the entire network of matrimonial exchanges, and, indeed, the whole kinship structure, and much of the legal system revolve around it. In terms of the role of cattle in traditional rural African society, it becomes perfectly rational to maximize the size of one's herd, irrespective of meat quality and milk production, and beyond the point of what Europeans consider economically sensible. To say that Africans are indifferent to stock quality is, however, completely untrue. One should rather say that the African sense of quality in cattle is more aesthetic than economic.

When the government, therefore, attempts to limit the size of herds, and to improve stock quality at the expense of quantity, it meets with stubborn (and understandable) opposition. Cattle culling not only means a destruction of capital (in much the same way as burning of banknotes would to a European), but also undermines the entire social structure of traditional African society. Not only do the Whites attempt to impose their view of cattle as the only valid and rational one, but they also disregard the fact that they have themselves contributed greatly to the economic vicious circle of overgrazing and erosion, by depriving Africans of most of their land. As a Zulu told a White official who inveighed against overgrazing, "It is not that we have too many cattle for our land, we have too little land for our cattle."[3]

A similar ethnocentrism and cultural misunderstanding characterize the entire government-imposed programme of "land betterment" which is so bitterly opposed by many rural Africans. There is increasing evidence that traditional African techniques of agriculture and animal husbandry were well adapted to soil and climatic conditions, and much less wasteful of natural resources than many of the European techniques of intensive exploitation. Yet, after having been confined to overpopulated Native Reserves which cannot possibly support their population, Africans are accused of being backward, conservative, and wasteful of land resources, and are expected to turn into intensive cash farmers without the capital necessary for such development, and without any consideration for the socially disruptive implications of technological innovations. For example, the introduction of the oxen-drawn plow has revolutionized the sexual division of labour in many African societies, where agriculture has traditionally been the task of women, and animal husbandry that of men.

3. Quoted in Max Gluckman, *Analysis of a Social Situation in Modern Zululand*, p. 67.

In short, Europeans have uncritically assumed that economic rationality and materialism are universally valid concepts, and have more or less forcibly imposed these values on African populations in total disregard of indigenous values. In many cases, new techniques were introduced without any proof that they were adaptable to the African environment, and that they would, in the long run, be more productive than traditional methods. On the whole, it appears that Europeans are responsible for a much more wasteful exploitation of African resources than the Africans themselves. One needs only to think of wanton destruction of game; large-scale deforestation; and soil exhaustion through intensive planting of such crops as cotton, and through large-scale sheep grazing; not to mention the colossal waste of human resources, first through the slave trade (which cost Africa at least fifty million lives), and then through various forms of compulsory labour conscription and "contracting" on mines, plantations, railway and road construction projects, etc. These considerations apply not only to South Africa, but to the continent as a whole.

Other incompatible values have led to friction and conflict between Whites and non-Whites in South Africa. A classical example is the European (or, more generally, industrial) notion of time as a valuable and rigorously measurable commodity. While insistence on punctuality and speed is obviously functional in an urban, industrial society, it is much less important in a rural context, and, hence, alien to traditional African values. Also related to industrialization, and alien to African culture, is the "Protestant Ethic" concerning work and the accumulation of material goods as morally desirable ends in themselves. The absence of such values in indigenous cultures has led to the European stereotypes of the African as "lazy," "indolent," "improvident," "irresponsible," etc.[4] In terms of practical policy, the

4. These stereotypes have a long history. See MacCrone, *op. cit.*, pp. 46–49. In 1653, one year after founding the Dutch settlement at the Cape, Van Riebeeck describes the Hottentots as "these stupid, lumpish, and lazy,

Western outlook on work has led to the introduction of such measures as "poll taxes," and more or less compulsory "recruitment" schemes to force Africans into the wage economy and "teach the Natives habits of industriousness."

These measures have been bitterly opposed by Africans, not so much at first because they were discriminatory and reduced them to industrial wage slavery, but rather because they were utterly senseless in terms of traditional values. Failing any incentive to accumulate wealth for its own sake (and, for that matter, any opportunity to do so to any significant extent), and viewing work as a necessary evil to sustain life, rather than as a rewarding and morally laudable end in itself, the traditional rural African has little motivation to participate in the wage economy, other than the sheer necessity of survival.[5] This lack of motivation is interpreted by the Whites as "laziness," and used as a rationalization for low wages. Since rural Africans do not want to earn as much as possible, but rather earn enough in a few months of work to be able to live from the savings for the rest of the year, many Whites argue, a rise in wages leads to a

---

stinking people." Quoted in H. Sonnabend and C. Sofer, *South Africa's Stepchildren*, p. 17. In 1831 Peter Kolben devotes an entire section of his *The Present State of the Cape of Good Hope* to "A Review of the Vices and Virtues of the Hottentots," in which he describes them as lazy and improvident. Cf. *op. cit.*, Vol. I, pp. 324–339. However, indignant as the Dutch were about the "laziness" of slaves and Hottentots, they were themselves unwilling to do any manual labour, which they regarded as degrading. Jan van Riebeeck already complains that the Whites "preferred like Seigneurs to spank about with the cane in the hand and leave everything to their slaves." Quoted in Victor de Kock, *Those in Bondage*, p. 65.

5. For an eighteenth-century account of value conflict, see Sparrman, *op. cit.*, pp. 232–233. He writes: "The extreme indolence of the [Hottentot] lad . . . excited in me just at that time the greatest indignation, as well as the utmost contempt for the Hottentot nation . . . the lad, from his habits as well as nature, could very easily make shift with a moderate quantity of food . . . . The principal reason of this disposition that prevails with most Hottentots is, perhaps, that their wants are extremely few; and consequently, being without care or employment of any kind, they are inactive and idle."

decrease in the labour supply. Therefore, wages must be kept low. That this rationalization is based on less than a half-truth does not concern us here. Even when the African becomes Westernized enough to accept the "Protestant Ethic" on work, productivity, and wealth accumulation, he finds himself caught in an exploitative and grossly discriminatory system of production from which there is no escape, and which makes his newly acquired values a source of frustration and bitterness rather than an incentive to work. We shall return to that point later, as it belongs more to the second major source of value conflict.

African and Indian values regarding marriage, sex, and the family are also a common source of European stereotypes and misunderstandings. For example, the more permissive standards of premarital sexuality found in many African cultures, and the payment of fines in cases of adultery, lead to the European stereotypes of Africans as being "lascivious," "oversexed," and as prostituting their wives.[6] The custom of *lobola* is viewed by most Europeans as a degrading trade in women, whereas, in fact, the payment of *lobola* gives status and security to the wife in traditional African society. The African and Indian desire for a large number of children is interpreted as improvidence, irresponsibility, and animal-like behaviour. ("They multiply like rabbits.") In fact, traditional African techniques of birth control and prohibitions favouring the spacing of pregnancies (such as the postpartum sex taboo) have fallen into disuse largely because of disruptive Western influences.

Polygyny is also completely misunderstood, and accepted as evidence of African lasciviousness. Clear deviations from traditional standards of morality and behaviour, such as high rates

6. Thus, as early as 1831, Peter Kolben writes: "The Negro-Women at the *Cape* are very lascivious Creatures. As they are excus'd there from Working, and indulg'd in an idle Life, for about Six Weeks before and Six Weeks after Travail, they are the most intemperate Wretches upon Earth in the Article, and greedily swallow, and enflame themselves with, all the Provocatives they can come at, till they are got with Child." *Op. cit.*, Vol. II, p. 340.

of illegitimacy, delinquency, prostitution, alcoholism, and divorce in urban centres, are interpreted, not as the consequences of social disorganization brought about by industrialization and racial discrimination, but as reflecting the "aggressive," "violent," or "immoral" nature of Africans, for which the only cure is police repression.

Of course, misinterpretation of behaviour based on misunderstanding of underlying values is mutual. Many Africans and Indians regard White bathing costumes and heterosexual dancing as immoral, to cite only two examples. However, as many Africans and Indians have become largely Westernized, and have themselves internalized European values, the stereotypes and distorted views are stronger on the White side of the colour fence. This is particularly true of those Europeans who claim to "know the Native" because they have spent much time in close physical contact with Africans (e.g., farmers, administrators, plantation and mine supervisors). In fact, as these whites have only had highly segmental and utilitarian relations with Africans, and as these relations have been defined by a rigorous strait jacket of master-servant etiquette, such Europeans generally exhibit in strongest form all the prevalent stereotypes about Africans.

In summary, South Africa, as a culturally pluralistic society, represents a wide variety of value systems. The racial situation, by discouraging contact between members of different ethnic groups, and indeed by making completely uninhibited relationships across the colour line virtually impossible, perpetuates cultural misunderstandings and reinforces stereotypes. If the consequences of value pluralism were to stop at misunderstandings, stereotypes, and invidious comparisons, such pluralism would simply lead to interpersonal frustration, annoyance, and tension, more than to an intensification of group conflict. Through its dominant position, however, the White group has been able to impose its value system, and to transpose value-judgments in the realm of discriminatory and coercive policies.

We have already given several examples of the practical

implementation of European values, such as the capitation or poll tax, land-betterment schemes, and cattle culling. But we must examine more closely the mechanisms through which values have been translated into policy. The simplest and most direct one is ethnocentrism. Europeans have naturally assumed that their values had absolute validity and universal applicability, and that any other outlook was either immoral or irrational. They have consequently imposed their values on the non-Europeans, and framed policy accordingly. However, European ethnocentrism in South Africa has not entailed its logical corollary, namely a policy of cultural assimilation, as has been practiced, for example, by the Portuguese and Spaniards in America. Had the White South Africans adopted assimilation as the consequence of their belief in their own cultural superiority, a short phase of acute cultural and social disorganization would have resulted (as in the period following the Spanish conquest of America), but the end result would have been considerable cultural homogeneity.[7]

White South Africans were, however, quick to perceive that cultural assimilation would be accompanied by social integration and "bastardization" of the *Herrenvolk*. Within a generation of the first Dutch settlement at the Cape in the seventeenth century, the baptism of slaves began to be resisted, and White South Africa launched on a deliberate anti-assimilationist policy. In this respect, as in many others, the Nationalist programme of apartheid represents a mere continuation and accentuation of a long-standing trend. The Nationalists not only endeavour to prevent Africans from becoming "imitation Englishmen," and to "keep the Bantu essentially Bantu"; they even want to reverse the process of "detribalization," to revive moribund traditional institutions, and to "re-Bantuize" the urban Africans.

The official position of the Dutch Reformed Churches

7. For a treatment of important differences in the colonization of Africa and the Americas, see my article "Racialism and Assimilation in Africa and the Americas."

(D.R.C.'s) is identical with that of the government. Though the D.R.C.'s engage in missionary activities and do not oppose the Christianization of Africans, they strongly assert the principle of "separate development," and defend it on Biblical grounds.[8] A 1952 statement, for example, reads:

> The Conference [of Dutch Reformed Churches] holds that our Church's acceptance of a policy which regards the separate development of the various races each according to its own nature, is in accordance with the teachings of Scripture. The fundamental principles of Diversity in Unity, of the recognition of the Divine Purpose, and of the urge for national self-expression must be borne in mind.[9]

How has this White-imposed nativism been implemented in practice? Clearly, traditional African societies have not been kept intact, even in the remotest rural areas. For one thing, no amount of government regulation could stop the process of acculturation. Secondly, while anti-assimilation was unambiguously aimed at the perpetuation of White political and economic supremacy, certain important aspects of traditional society obviously had to be modified in order to entrench White domination. Notably the entire African political system was completely subjugated to the White authorities, and reduced to a shadow

8. For a long time the Dutch Reformed Churches have been much less active than English and foreign missionary societies, except, for historical reasons, among the Cape Coloured. Consequently, as of the 1951 population census, only 3.9 per cent of the Africans belonged to the three principal D.R.C.'s, compared to 12.2 per cent who were Methodists; 6.8 per cent, Anglicans; 5.4 per cent, Roman Catholics; and 4.9 per cent, Lutherans (Table XIV). Even many of the Coloured have turned away from the D.R.C.'s. Although 89 per cent of the Coloureds speak Afrikaans as their home language, only 29.5 per cent belong to the D.R.C.'s. The respective percentages for Whites are 57 and 53.2. In other words, whereas for Whites, membership in the D.R.C.'s and speaking Afrikaans as a mother tongue are nearly synonymous, this is very far from true for the Coloureds. It is not unreasonable to attribute much of the disaffection of Coloureds from the D.R.C.'s to the latter's racial policies. Cf. Horrell, *A Survey of Race Relation in South Africa*, 1959–1960, pp. 25, 27.

9. Anonymous, *The Racial Issue in South Africa*, p. 9.

of its former self. Large nations were broken up (as were the Zulu after the war of 1879) to destroy their military power; chiefs were divested of most important powers; the White government arrogated itself the power to install and dismiss chiefs; standing armies were dissolved, etc. In short, while the forms of traditional rule were retained, within well-defined limits, to facilitate administration, much of the substance of power and authority was removed from African political systems.

Thirdly, "Native Law and Custom" have been reinterpreted, consciously and unconsciously, in terms of Western values. Here we return to our earlier question, namely how European values have affected practical policy. Not only have these values influenced policy directly through the operation of ethnocentrism, but they have also been introduced indirectly, under the guise of preserving "Native institutions." "Native Law and Custom" were codified by Whites in the Province of Natal, and a special system of Native courts was instituted, wherein Africans are judged by low-ranking White commissioners; the latter often have neither a knowledge of African languages nor any formal legal training. Court proceedings are translated by White interpreters who themselves typically have only an imperfect and unnuanced command of Bantu languages.

It is easy to imagine what distortions and misunderstandings arise from the routine administration of "justice" in such courts, all the more so when cases are expedited at a rate of twenty to thirty an hour, the average for pass offences.[10] But even the codification and interpretation of African law are distorted. In the first place, "Native Law" was deliberately changed to make it congruent with the codifiers' conceptions of "civilization," "humaneness," and "justice," in such matters as penal sanctions, "sorcery," and the like. Furthermore, European biases and insufficient ethnographic knowledge led to unconscious misunder-

10. The record speed which I witnessed during a morning's observation in Durban was fifty seconds; the longest case took four and one-half minutes; the average was about two minutes and forty-five seconds.

standings and distortions of traditional law. Finally, the application in an urban and industrial society of a code of law which
evolved in a rural, non-literate society has paradoxically encouraged a complete transformation in the functions and significance of such institutions as the *lobola.*

The second broad source of value conflict in South African
society is perhaps even more important than the first. The crux
of the conflict is found in the internal contradictions within the
value system of the dominant White group. Not only is the
ascriptive and particularistic ideology of racialism in disharmony
with other elements of the social structure, notably with principles of economic rationality in an industrial system of production; racism also conflicts with basic political, ethical, and
religious values which are an integral part of the Western
tradition. While South African racialism constitutes a major
deviation from the dominant current of the modern Western
ethos, this deviation coexists, within the White group, with the
Christian ethic of love, brotherhood, and charity, and, to a
lesser extent, with the Western political ideology of democracy,
freedom, and equality. This deep conflict within the value system
of the dominant White group is becoming increasingly acute, and
can itself be decomposed into two primary aspects, namely its
effect on the non-Whites, and on the Whites. We shall successive-
ly examine the complex ramifications of this second type of value
conflict on the two sides of the colour-bar.

In spite of the anti-assimilationist policy of the successive
South African governments, acculturation of the non-Whites to
the Western way of life started in the seventeenth century, and
continues at a rapid pace. The process can be roughly divided
into two phases. The first phase of Westernization, which lasted
until the third or fourth decade of the nineteenth century, gave
rise, in combination with extensive miscegenation, to the Cape
Coloureds.

The Coloureds find themselves in a typically marginal position. On the one hand, they have assimilated Western values

(including, for the most part, the White outlook on colour), and have become culturally undistingishable from the Europeans. On the other hand, the Coloureds are the object of racial discrimination, and find themselves rejected by White society, solely on grounds of colour. Their steadily deteriorating position makes any hope of eventual assimilation to the Whites more unrealistic than ever.

The position of the Coloureds shows that acculturation does not lead to the elimination of value conflicts. In the presence of racial prejudice and discrimination, acculturation is likely to *accentuate* value conflicts. To the extent that the Coloureds share White values, they face, in a particularly acute form, all the contradictions inherent in the dominant value system of the Europeans. So far, the prevalent Coloured "solution" to these contradictions has been to use the egalitarian, Christian aspect of the White ideology to demand acceptance into European society, while, at the same time, adopting White colour attitudes to keep themselves separate from the Africans. Furthermore, the adoption of physical criteria of status among Coloureds has led to profoundly divisive tensions within the Coloured community, not to mention more latent attitudes of self-hatred and self-deprecation.[11] In recent years, however, the Coloured leadership and intelligentsia have become clearly aware that racial prejudice among Coloureds undermines any legitimacy to claims of equality with the White group, and that the obvious solution to the value conflict lies in the total rejection of prejudice.

The second phase of acculturation in South African history

11. Racialism among Coloureds goes back to the days of slavery, when women slaves were already trying to "improve the stock" by having affairs with White men. Cf. V. de Kock, *op. cit.*, p. 118. Sparrman gives evidence of self-deprecation among Westernized Hottentots in the eighteenth century. He writes: "Some Hottentots, who spoke the Dutch language readily, and with whom, both in company and separately, I conversed on this subject [i.e., the existence of God], always answered me to this effect; *We are poor stupid creatures, and have never heard, neither are we able to understand, any thing of the matter.*" Sparrman, *op. cit.*, p. 220 (author's italics).

affected the Africans and the Indians, and began with missionary penetration into the territory of the African nations in the third decade of the nineteenth century. Unlike at the Cape, this second phase of acculturation was not accompanied by any large-scale miscegenation. For both Indians and Africans, the major agents of Westernization have been formal education (which has been almost entirely along Western lines), the wage economy, and, more recently, the mass media of communication and entertainment.

In the case of African acculturation, the Christian missions have played a preponderant role, the revolutionary implications of which were recognized by the Boers quite early in the nineteenth century. Because the missionaries all but monopolized African education until the 1950's, and insofar as they have emphasized (in theory, if seldom in practice) the egalitarian and universalistic aspects of the Western ethic, they have been the first and most effective agents to spread the values with which Africans were later to challenge the legitimacy of White supremacy. In South Africa as in many other parts of the continent, Christianity, which preceded or accompanied European conquest, has spread the seeds of the destruction of colonialism. But whereas elsewhere this Hegelian dialectical process was recognized only quite late, in South Africa, the Afrikaners have, from the seventeenth until the nineteenth century, combated the spread of the Gospel as conducive to the "corruption of the Natives." The Boers opposed the baptism of slaves quite early in the history of the Cape settlement, and later they consistently and bitterly opposed the activities of the London Missionary Society.[12]

12. For evidence of opposition by the Cape Town burghers of the eighteenth and early nineteenth century to non-Whites being baptised or married, receiving religious instruction, or attending church, see Wright, *op. cit.*, pp. 4, 14–15; De la Caille, *Journal Historique du Voyage fait au Cap de Bonne-Espérance*, pp. 309–311; Andrew Sparrman, *op. cit.*, pp. 303–304, 306. Concerning the conflict between the Dutch colonists and the missionaries, see Marais, *op. cit.*, pp. 134–136.

When the Nationalist government took away the African schools from the Protestant and Catholic missions in 1954, and assumed direct control of "Bantu Education," it gave the logical final touch to a long tradition of Boer anti-missionary and anti-assimilation attitudes and policies. Of course, by the 1950's, the process of African acculturation was far too advanced to be reversed, and the government's aim to "keep the Bantu essentially Bantu" was doomed to failure. With the advent of the twentieth century, the participation of large numbers of Africans in the wage economy began to compete with the missions as a source of acquisition of Western values, or, rather, to reinforce mission influence in that respect. As literacy spread, so did the impact of the press which, combined with the radio and the cinema, has increasingly exposed Africans to outside influences, particularly in the field of political ideology.

Whether of religious or secular origin, the process of acculturation has been selective. As might be expected, educated Africans have most readily accepted the Western values with which they could challenge the legitimacy of the *status quo*. Paradoxically, then, the value system of Westernized Africans is closer to the mainstream of European culture than that of White South Africans. By selectively retaining the values of universalism, achievement, freedom, individualism, and equality, and rejecting the White syndrome of racialism, Africans have resolved the contradictions inherent in the values held by most Whites and Coloureds.

While, in some respects, White anti-assimilationist policies may have slowed down the process of acculturation by limiting social contact and educational opportunities, they have certainly not prevented Westernization, and they may even have accelerated it in devious ways. For example, the surest way to turn educated Africans strongly against traditional culture is for the government to adopt a "nativistic" policy. This situation leads to the amusing paradox that, in other parts of the continent, notably in West Africa, where the African elites have met with less resistance to their political aspirations and to acceptance into White society, they have, on the whole, reacted against Western culture to a greater extent than in South Africa.

I am not suggesting that White racism has not also contributed to anti-Western reactions among Africans. In the Transkei, for example, the population has been split for a century into the "school" (i.e., Christian and mission-influenced) people and the "red" (i.e., traditional) people; the former show great cultural conservatism and reject all that is connected with the Whites.[13] Discrimination, segregation, and White control within Protestant denominations have undoubtedly contributed to the proliferation of African Separatist Churches, many of which have a strong anti-White and revivalistic slant.[14] In the political sphere, the rise of militant Black racialism, as exhibited by the Pan-African Congress, is another reaction to White rejection. Among the African intelligentsia there is a growing disillusionment with Christianity, or, at least, with the conservative stand taken by many denominations in South Africa.[15] But this reaction indicates not so much a blanket rejection of Western culture, as a movement towards secularization and rationalization.

On the whole, the majority of urbanized Africans, and certainly of the politically influential intelligentsia, do not reject Western culture. On the contrary, most Westernized Africans exhibit an attitude of "cultural shame" towards the traditional way of life, which they consider "backward," and share an antagonistic or, at least, ambivalent outlook towards African political and legal institutions, and the use of Bantu languages as media of school instruction.[16] While they do not

13. Cf. Mayer, *op. cit.*

14. Cf. Sundkler, *op. cit.*

15. See, for example, Mphahlele, *Down Second Avenue*, pp. 177–179, 221–222. Even as staunch a Christian as Chief Luthuli is openly critical of the passivity and paternalism of church denominations in South Africa. Cf. *Let My People Go*, pp. 80, 131.

16. As an example of ambivalent attitudes towards African culture, see Noni Jabavu, *Drawn in Colour*.

desire to become assimilated to *White society* as most Coloureds still do, they accept Western values, insofar as they have found these values a congenial platform for attacking the *status quo*. This Western orientation is clearly illustrated by the formal organization, policies, and methods of most African voluntary associations. In the political field, increasing numbers of intellectuals are attracted by leftist radicalism, but, after all, Marxism is itself a cultural product of the West.

The attitudes of Westernized Africans towards indigenous traditions deserve closer examination because of their complexity. "Cultural shame" reflects, in part, an adoption of Western criteria and values inculcated largely in mission schools, and an implicit acceptance of European deprecation of everything "pagan," "tribal," and "primitive." This attitude is particularly prevalent among the first Western-educated generation which is now regarded by the "angry young men" as consisting of "Uncle Toms," "compromisers," and "tea-drinkers."[17] Professor D. D. T. Jabavu, the South African Booker T. Washington, strongly exhibits this deprecatory or, at least, ambivalent attitude towards African traditions. In the 1920's he wrote:

> From what we learn, the primitive Natives, though not religious in the modern sense of the word, were at least superstitious enough to have their moral life restrained by certain crude but nevertheless moral scruples . . . . The names of our earliest Native Missionaries will make us feel a flow of joy and pride in this excellent record of work in uplifting their people.[18]

Elsewhere he wrote:

> They [the Natives] live on the absolute minimum that mother earth can yield, and they invariably follow the path of least resistance. They are satisfied to live from hand to mouth.[19]

17. "Tea-drinker" is a term of sarcasm used by urban Africans to designate other Africans who are eager to associate (and drink tea) with Whites.
18. D. D. T. Jabavu, *The Black Problem*, p. 155.
19. *Ibid.*, p. 102. Such adoption of a Western outlook and deprecation

More recently, the African intelligentsia still rejects "tribalism," but for somewhat different reasons. They no longer exhibit a respectful and uncritical emulation of Western culture, though most urban Africans obviously agree on the desirability of attaining a European standard of living, in the material sense. Tribalism is now rejected for two related reasons. In the first place, it is considered unviable in a modern urban environment, and technologically retarded. Secondly, tribalism is opposed as a source of political reaction and divisiveness in the struggle for freedom. The Western-educated Africans of the younger generation strongly react against the Pretoria brand of compulsory nativism, and against traditional chiefs who have compromised themselves with the government.

The prostitution of African traditionalism by the Afrikaner Nationalist government is itself a complex phenomenon. Politically conscious Africans view what we might call "Pretoria nativism" as a deliberate weapon of obscurantism (e.g., in the use of mother-tongue instruction in "Bantu Education"), and of divisiveness between the various linguistic groups. Undoubtedly, Bantustan policy is motivated in part by a desire to combat the growing solidarity of all Africans. However, such an explanation oversimplifies Afrikaner motivation to some extent. In particular, the Afrikaners project their own feelings of cultural pride and identity onto Africans, and have difficulty in conceiving that African nationalism is not defined in cultural terms to any significant extent. The government feels that the "tribal" way of life, though supposedly "backward," is peculiarly suited to the "primitive" mentality of the Africans, and, hence, that the latter must be kept "essentially Bantu."

Whatever the government's motivations may be, the reactionary use of tribal revivalism makes it very difficult for Africans to seek identity and self-respect in their cultural heritage. In

---

of traditional African culture has also been documented in my study of Caneville.

addition, the educated elite which is at the vanguard of the political struggle has been largely weaned from traditionalism, has interests which are antithetical to those of chiefs, and understandably resents any suggestion by Whites, however well-meaning, that Africans should revert to their own traditions. Mphahlele, a prominent South African novelist and essayist, expresses these themes very cogently in his critique of *Négritude* and of what he regards as the myth of the African Personality:

> Traditional culture, much of which the missionary destroyed, has come to be associated by the Negro with an inferior political status and ethnic grouping which will destroy all the work that has been done by the educated Negro to unify all the tribes. A gramophone record company . . . tries to sell its wares by telling us that Duke Ellington, Louis Armstrong, Beethoven, Mozart and so on are foreign and so we should love and stick to our own music.[20]

It is not difficult to see a Hegelian dialectic of ideological conflict operating here. The cultural attitude of the African intelligentsia is, to a large degree, antithetical to that of the colonial regime. Although Western-educated Africans no longer accept uncritically Western culture and Christianity *in toto*, they have, for the main part, remained predominantly Western in outlook. The government has contributed to this state of affairs by endeavouring to impose its version of "tribal authorities," "mother-tongue instruction," "Bantustans," "Native law and custom," and all the rest of "Pretoria nativism." The negative case of *Négritude* lends further support to this interpretation. Indeed, *Négritude*, a nostalgic return to the mystical essence of "Negroness," arose paradoxically among the Gallicized Negro elite of the French West Indies and of Senegal, in antithesis to the French colonial policy of assimilation.

To summarize the argument, acculturation, while bringing about greater cultural homogeneity, has intensified value conflicts because of the internal contradictions in the *Weltanschauung*

20. Mphahlele, *The African Image*, pp. 33–34.

of the dominant Whites. Westernized Africans have largely resolved these contradictions by selectively adopting the egalitarian,
universalistic ethos of the broader Western, Christian tradition;
and by using that ethos to attack the local White variant of
Western culture with its racialist, ascriptive, and particularistic
values. The same applies, in large measure, to the Indian population, but the Coloureds are in a much more difficult position; they
have, on the whole, adopted the White South African value
system *in toto*. This led them to an ideological *impasse* from
which they are only beginning to extricate themselves.

Another facet of the effect of acculturation on Africans must
be briefly considered. To be sure, Westernization in South Africa
contributed to cultural homogeneity by creating an intelligentsia,
a white-collar class, and a proletariat among whom ethnic affiliation is of decreasing significance. Conversely, however, Western
influence, by *differentially permeating* various layers of African
society, introduced a new dimension of cultural heterogeneity,
and, hence, of value dissension, within populations that were
originally homogeneous. Although Westernization has been considerably more profound in South Africa than in almost every
other part of the continent, Western culture, except in the
Western Cape, did not displace indigenous culture anywhere
near completely. Consequently, different degrees of traditionalism
or Westernism between rural and urban Africans, between the
Western and the traditionally educated, between the old and the
young, lead to profound dissension and tension among people
who may, nevertheless, all claim membership in the same ethnic
group. The "school"-"red" dichotomy in the rural Transkei shows
that this divisive influence of acculturation is found even in the
most "untouched" districts. In cities, this form of value conflict
is often most acute between generations, and can lead to severe
strains in family life, much as among European or Asian immigrant groups in the United States. This difference of outlook
between generations often touches on such central attitudes as
the desirability of a large progeny, of respect towards chiefs and

elders, of the emancipation of women, of kinship obligations, of love marriages, etc. Not uncommonly, intergenerational dissension is now translated in political disagreement between the more conservative elders and the militant young men (e.g., Professor Z. K. Matthews and his son Joe).

Value conflict is also present within the White group. Since that conflict is largely a product of the White racialist syndrome, and since it has important ramifications in all the population groups, the value position of Whites is obviously crucial. The central thesis of Myrdal concerning the "American Dilemma" can be applied *mutatis mutandi* to South Africa.[21] Myrdal argues that one of the major sources of strain in Negro-White relations in the United States arises from the contradiction between the dominant American creed of democracy, freedom, and equality of opportunities, and the clearly discriminatory treatment of Negroes. Much the same contradiction exists in the White South African value system, although in a less acute and less political form, because the dominant White group has developed elaborate myths and rationalizations to "resolve" value conflicts.

Prominent aspects of both Afrikaner and English ideology and ethical outlook conflict logically with White colour attitudes. This statement applies, of course, to the Christian ethos in general, although we have seen that the exclusivistic and particularistic slant of Calvinism favoured a racial reinterpretation of the Bible, in much the same way as fundamentalistic sects have done in the American South. There is, however, a strong element of frontier individualism, egalitarianism, and love of freedom (or, at least, impatience with authority) in the Afrikaner political ideology and tradition. Similarly, the nineteenth-century British ideology of individualism, liberalism, democracy, and fair play has, together with Christian values, contributed to shaping the outlook of English South Africans. At the same time, both White groups hold deeply ingrained attitudes of racialism which

21. Myrdal, *op. cit.*·

directly clash with these other values. The question then becomes: How has the White group attempted to reconcile these opposites?

This is where the analogy with the "American Dilemma" stops. In the United States the dominant trend has been, certainly in the last three decades, towards the slow but gradual elimination of racial discrimination and segregation. In other words, the value conflict has tended to resolve itself by a slow yielding of the more specific, racialist syndrome to the more general, democratic values of the dominant political and moral creed. While South Africa also shows some evidence of a similar trend, that "liberalizing" tendency has distinctly been a secondary one, and the main trend has gone in the opposite direction. I.e., the general democratic and egalitarian norms have become redefined and reinterpreted in terms of the specific racial syndrome.

The basic mechanism for "resolving" the White South African value conflict has been a clear dichotomization of thinking along racial lines. Rather than abandoning either set of values, the Whites have clearly and rigidly delineated the spheres of applicability of each of these value sets: the egalitarian, universalistic norms apply to the Whites, whereas the discriminatory, particularistic norms apply to the non-Whites. The latter must, thus, be denied full human status. This statement may appear exaggerated, and when directly asked whether they consider non-Whites human, most Whites would answer in the affirmative. Yet they would immediately qualify their answer by saying that, although human, non-Whites are nevertheless fundamentally different from, and inferior to, the Whites.

The prevalence of this dichotomized outlook, even among people who are not rabid racists, is indicated more by inference than by open statements. Even the more "moderate" Europeans, who would not subscribe to overt statements of racialism, indirectly reveal their racially compartmentalized thinking. When, for example, a White speaks or writes about "people" and "South Africans" he almost invariably means "Whites." Conversely, if he refers to non-Whites he will almost always use a racial label. In the press or radio, Europeans are referred to by name and courtesy titles, whereas non-Whites often remain anonymous. (E.g.: "Mr. Jan Joubert, 41, was killed this morning when his car overturned near Bloemfontein. He had a wife and three children. Two Natives were also killed in the accident.") This same dual standard applies to every practical aspect of life. E.g., a house or salary that would be considered "very good" for an African would attract commiseration if occupied or earned by a White, the non-White being supposed to live comfortably on much less than a European. A non-White is expected to show "gratitude" for whatever he has, no matter how inferior, the implication being that a non-European has no *right* to anything. Working conditions that Whites would view as intolerable for themselves are considered perfectly normal for Africans, who are supposedly "used to it." The privileges of citizenship, such as the franchise and freedom of movement, are self-evident for the Whites, but disfranchisement and pass laws are "normal" for the "Natives." One should be charitable but "charity begins at home." One should love and respect one's neighbour, and we are all God's children, but that does not mean that you have to treat an African courteously and as an equal.

Most White South Africans are conditioned since early childhood to divide humanity into two radically different groups, and this dichotomous outlook is so basic to the integrity of White South Africans that it is almost impossible to shake off. As we shall see presently, the few Europeans who have truly emancipated themselves from their racialist heritage have to pay a heavy price for their tolerance. It is therefore naive to expect that the mass of White South Africans will spontaneously show a "change of heart" on the colour issue. The Whites have too much to lose in the way of material, political, and status privileges to be expected to change their outlook and behaviour. Furthermore, by doing so, they expose themselves to ostracism from fellow Whites, and even to severe sanctions by the government.

But these strong dissuading factors do not touch the crux of the matter, namely that racial prejudice for a White South African is *functionally necessary to his self-respect and ego-integrity.* The only alternative is an almost unbearable burden of guilt.

At this point, one important question must be answered. Why did White South Africa "choose" rigid, racial dichotomization as a "solution" to its value conflict, rather than follow the American alternative for solving an essential, similar dilemma? Several complementary answers suggest themselves. First, Calvinist exclusiveness and the notion of predestination appear to have favoured the early development of this colour dichotomization, as we have already suggested. Once the basic equation of Black with heathen and evil became established in the outlook of the Boers, one could argue that the racialist mold was cast, and that further extensions of that outlook to the secular fields of politics and economics followed the line of least resistance.

Even if this hypothesis accounts for the genesis of the phenomenon, it is not sufficient to explain its perpetuation in the face of mounting tensions. Both the numerical ratios and the forms of contact between Whites and non-Whites differ markedly in the United States and in South Africa. In North America, Whites have always been in a large majority; Negro slaves were introduced into an already settled society which, along the Atlantic seaboard, had survived the dangers of frontier warfare; and the Northern White population did not develop slavery nor a substantial vested interest in anti-Negro prejudice. Had the Cape Colony remained isolated from the rest of the African continent, one can cogently suppose that White-Coloured relations would have undergone an evolution similar to White-Negro relations in the United States.[22]

22. Actually, much the same racial dichotomization between "people" and "sub-people" took place in the United States throughout the slavery period and even until the first decades of the twentieth century. Myrdal's thesis of conscious ideological conflict and guilt over the treatment of Negroes does not apply to the nineteenth century. During that period, the

However, the frontier explosion which started with the Great Trek prolonged the hazards of continuous warfare for nearly half a century, and drew large numbers of Africans into what was to become the South African body politic. The Whites consequently remained a minority, and fear of being "swamped" became a permanent part of their *Weltanschauung*. Attitudes of exclusiveness, superiority, and domination, which originally may, indeed, have been functional for survival, or at least for the preservation of cultural identity, thus perpetuated themselves and gave rise to the modern system of White supremacy. Once the latter was firmly entrenched (i.e., around 1880 when the African nations ceased to be a military menace), the cumulative benefits accruing from the Whites' privileged position made any change in values increasingly costly and, hence, unlikely.

All factors combine to make a "spontaneous" change in the colour outlook of the mass of the Whites less probable than ever before. Beyond the White desire to preserve political, social, and economic privileges, the mounting demands of the non-Whites increase European fears and reinforce an extremist, back-to-the-wall stand. The Nationalist and United parties both resort to the "Black danger" bogey to attract political support, and the government has long passed the point of no return on the road to oppression. Only by becoming increasingly tyrannical can it maintain its power, and a policy of gradual "concessions" would open the floodgates of revolution, as the Nationalists clearly perceive.

This is not to say that a clean break from *Herrenvolk* mentality is impossible. A few thousand Whites have, in fact, dissociated themselves clearly from racialism, and identified, in varying degrees, with African aspirations. These defections from the

---

United States was as much of a "*Herrenvolk* democracy" as South Africa is today. Only recently did racism lose its respectability in the United States, leading to a significant change in values and to the birth of the "American Dilemma."

solid front of White opinion have, however, been confined almost exclusively to a small segment of the intellectual, religious, and managerial elite. A few leading industrialists like Harry Oppenheimer, and Progressive Party politicians like Jan Steytler and Helen Suzman reject colour discrimination in principle, and consider apartheid morally wrong; but they remain socially and economically conservative. In practice, they make so many reservations that they fall short of complete liberalism, and cannot win the confidence of the non-Whites, except for a few old-style "Uncle Toms." The same applies to the "Black Sash," a highly "respectable" league of English women for the defence of civil liberties, and to the majority of the White Protestant clergy in the English denominations.

A number of Afrikaner university professors (mostly at Stellenbosch) and a few leading clergymen in the Dutch Reformed Churches have taken more or less open stands against apartheid as practiced by the government. They have sought to dissociate the cultural aspects of Afrikaner Nationalism (i.e., the promotion of Afrikaner language and traditions) from the racial policies of the government. Some of them who constituted the "left wing" of the South African Bureau of Racial Affairs (SABRA) have gone no further than to advocate a more "equitable" apartheid for the Africans and considerable integration for the Coloureds. Many English-speaking wishful thinkers looked upon them as the nucleus of a split within the Nationalist Party, or at least as a potential source of pressure for more moderate government policies. However, since the 1961 SABRA purge, these "deviationists" have lost what little moral or intellectual influence they had in Afrikaner Nationalist circles.

On the whole, these SABRA and Dutch Reformed Church dissidents are politically to the right of the Progressive Party, and desperately attempt to retain an increasingly marginal and uncomfortable position on the fringe of Afrikanerdom. The most interesting aspect of their ideological position concerns their attitudes towards the Coloureds. Moderate Afrikaner intellectuals

advocate social assimilation of the Coloureds (short of miscegenation, of course) for a combination of practical and deeper psychological reasons. On practical grounds, they argue that the
Coloureds belong to Western and, for the most part, to Afrikaner
culture, and, hence, that their assimilation would strengthen
Afrikanerdom. At a more covert level, they exhibit considerable
guilt *vis-à-vis* the Coloureds, for whose existence they feel col-
lectively responsible, and whom they regard as related by blood
through male ancestors, and essentially identical to themselves
except for colour.

Even much less numerous than these various groups of
moderate, cautiously progressive Englishmen and Afrikaners are
the few hundred Whites who are openly and unreservedly liberal
in their outlook. They include some of the students and many
of the professors and lecturers at the English universities (particularly in Cape Town and the Witwatersrand), a few leading
trade-union organizers, some writers like Alan Paton, young
artists and professionals, and a few members of the high clergy,
notably the Catholic Archbishop Denis Hurley of Durban, and
the Anglican bishops Joost de Blank of Cape Town and Ambrose
Reeves of Johannesburg.[23] (Bishop Reeves, who exposed the facts
of the police massacre of Sharpeville, went into exile in Britain,
and had to abandon his diocese when he was refused permission
to return to South Africa.) Politically, many of these Whites
belong either to the Liberal Party or to the (largely Communist)

---

23. In a letter of April 22, 1964, to the London *Times*, Bishops de Blank
and Reeves spoke of the non-Whites "suffering grievously both from the
mass of repressive legislation under which they live, and also from the
poverty wages they receive." Arguing in favor of international sanctions
against South Africa, they stated that even if sanctions would adversely
affect the non-Whites, the latter "are prepared to suffer still more for a
short time, if by so doing there is some chance that their present intolerable
situation will be ended." They concluded: "Those who oppose sanctions
must put forward some alternative method for bringing home to the South
African Government the enormity of their policies." Cf. *The Times*, London,
April 24, 1964.

Congress of Democrats, although some have not joined any party.

The position of White liberals in South Africa is perhaps the most unbearable of all, a factor which accounts for their scarcity, and for the fact that many of them now emigrate permanently.[24] Not only are tolerance and non-discrimination punished by sanctions ranging from social ostracism to police intimidation, arrest, and stiff gaol sentences (for "immorality," for example), but, more importantly, the White liberal finds himself impotent to avert the impending tragedy, and guilty, through his actions, of condoning against his will a system which he abhors. Privileges which he considers unjust are forced upon him. He must use segregated transport facilities, and send his children to segregated schools. Unless he foregoes most forms of entertainment and cultural life, he must go to segregated cinemas, theatres, concerts, libraries, etc. If he wants to practice sports he must go to segregated beaches, swimming baths, tennis courts, etc. When travelling he is forced to eat in all-White restaurants and sleep in all-White hotels. If he courts arrest, he will be put in a prison which will be comfortable by comparison with that of his fellow non-White prisoners. If, in desperation, he should commit suicide, he will be buried in a cemetery "for Europeans only." In short, there is no escape from apartheid, unwanted privileges, and the resulting guilt feelings, except deliberate unconcern for ethical problems, or racial dichotomization.

Furthermore, social conditions make a totally unstrained, "natural" relationship across the colour-bar virtually impossible. The range of activities and places open to interracial groups is extremely limited. The White liberal also has to overcome the initial suspicion aroused among non-Whites by the unusual nature of his behaviour and attitudes. He must be careful lest a perfectly innocent remark be misinterpreted in a racialist sense. Above all, he must free himself of the presumption on the part

24. For a moving personal account of conversion from racialism see Patrick van Rensburg, *Guilty Land*.

of non-Whites that he is simply a paternalist and a "do-gooder." In short, almost whatever he does is likely to increase his sense of guilt, to be misinterpreted, or to expose his non-White friends to embarrassment. Under such conditions, it is remarkable, not that there are so few White liberals, but rather that there should be any at all (at least outside of psychiatric hospitals).

As this chapter has tried to show, the manifold ramifications and the various levels of value conflict in South Africa make the "American Dilemma" look extremely simple by comparison. South Africa shares with all culturally pluralistic societies a lack of value consensus. Acculturation is gradually reducing the heterogeneity of cultural values, insofar as there is a clear trend towards the increasing Westernization of an ever greater proportion of the population. As acculturation has been accompanied by social rejection, political oppression, and economic exploitation, however, that process has unleashed new sources of tension which threaten the *status quo.* The Africans have selected from the contradictory White values those with which they could challenge the legitimacy of the *status quo.* The Whites have "solved" the contradictions in their value system by dichotomizing the sphere of applicability of these respective values along colour lines. The Coloureds, by adopting White values *in toto,* find themselves in an untenable position.

At the very root of the "South African Dilemma" lies White racialism. Without having to decide the question of historical precedence, or having to commit oneself to a position of ideological determinism, it is clear that, if one took away the racialist syndrome, the entire structure of South African society would be deeply affected. The very obviousness of this proposition leads one easily to wish racialism away, and hope that, somehow, there will be a White "change of heart." We have seen how remote the prospect of such a development is, until *after* the collapse of the *status quo.* After the structure of South African society will have radically changed, White attitudes will most probably readjust themselves to the new situation. I would even expect that this readjustment will be faster and less difficult than many observers suppose.

Under present conditions, however, a "change of heart," except on the part of a small, White, intellectual elite, is practically excluded. The entire social structure of the country militates against it. If White racialism has powerfully contributed to the creation and the continuation of South African society in its present form, it will just as surely help to bring about the total collapse of White domination. Such is the basic dialectical process of change in South Africa.

## CHAPTER TEN

## External Pressures

N o analysis of South African society is complete without an account of the numerous external pressures to which it is subject.[1] Not only is South Africa ridden with tensions and conflicts originating from within, but it also faces a hostile world as a result of government policies. Condemnation of apartheid is one of the few international issues on which all countries (except Portugal) find themselves in agreement. In an ironic way, South Africa thus contributes to international understanding by being the skunk of the world.

The South African government itself has implicitly admitted that it has acquired this unenviable distinction. It now avoids the unsavory term "apartheid," which it used as a slogan for more than a decade, and coined a new euphemism for its racial policy: "separate development." When Chief Albert Luthuli received the Nobel Peace Prize in 1961, Afrikaner Nationalist newspapers, the radio, and the government vilified the recipient, and interpreted the award as a "deliberate slap for the South African Government."[2] However much the government pretends to ignore international censure, or attempts to escape it by coining new euphemisms and retreating into ever greater isolation, one can

1. A statement of South Africa's position in the world can be found in: Peter Calvocoressi, *South Africa and World Opinion*. See also Appendix C.

2. *Natal Mercury*, October 25, 27, 1961.

safely predict that external pressures will steadily increase, and eventually help in bringing about radical change in South Africa.

Of all foreign countries, Great Britain has probably had the longest and the most complex relationship with South Africa. As we have seen earlier, the two countries have a long history of close but uneasy contact. The clash between Boer expansionism and British imperialism dominated most of the nineteenth century, and was finally resolved in 1910. From 1820, the settlement of English colonists in South Africa, by putting in presence two settler stocks, complicated relations between the two countries. Starting in the 1860's, the development of mining, and, later, of secondary industry, made for close financial and commercial ties between the United Kingdom and South Africa. Even today, Britain remains the major source of foreign capital, and by far the most important trade partner for South Africa.

The settlement of Union in 1910 opened a new phase in British-South African relations. For nearly forty years, a relatively stable *modus vivendi* was reached on the basis of mutual cooperation. The only outstanding bone of contention between the two countries was the control over the three High Commission Territories of Swaziland, Basutoland, and Bechuanaland. While the South Africa Act provided for continued British sovereignty over these territories, it also contained a clause on the eventual transfer of power to South Africa at an unspecified date. As Britain consistently adopted the position that the transfer could only take place with the consent of the indigenous population, such a transfer is totally excluded. The three territories are now slowly moving towards independence, and Basutoland and Bechuanaland will most probably adopt a hostile policy towards White South Africa.

Starting with the independence of India and Pakistan in 1947, and the coming to power of the Nationalists in 1948, South Africa's position in relation to Britain and the Commonwealth began to change once more. Two separate and opposed developments led, in 1961, to the final break in the compromise of Union.

On the one hand, the Nationalist government steadily undermined South Africa's already mostly symbolic ties with the British Crown, while, on the other hand, the Commonwealth changed its character through the admission of independent Afro-Asian members. To these two factors must be added Britain's abandonment of her traditional policy of White supremacy in much of South, Central, and East Africa which became unequivocal in early 1960 with Macmillan's famous Cape Town speech. Since then, the Tory government is busily liquidating its imperial responsibilities, and turning its remaining African colonies and protectorates over to majority, i.e., Black governments. All these developments arrived at their logical end-result during the London Commonwealth Prime Ministers' Conference of 1961. The Nationalists fulfilled their Republican dream by winning the Referendum of October, 1960, and pressure from the non-White members of the Commonwealth forced South Africa's withdrawal from the "Club" in May, 1961.

Whether the government intended to provoke South Africa's withdrawal from the Commonwealth by declaring a Republic is an open question. The fact is that, from the government's point of view, the breaking of Commonwealth ties is a mixed blessing. To be sure, the Nationalists rallied the enthusiastic support of Afrikanerdom by exploiting the Republican issue; and increasing isolation from hostile forums of international affairs may give the government a spurious sense of security. At the same time, however, Britain becomes freer to adopt a stronger anti-apartheid position in the United Nations, and is saved the embarrassment of trying to restrain other Commonwealth members who want to take drastic sanctions against South Africa.

By far the greatest source of external pressure comes, of course, from the Afro-Asian countries. This pressure has steadily increased since the end of World War Two, as one country after another became independent. Since 1958 the meteoric collapse of European colonialism in Africa has isolated South Africa at the tip of a hostile continent. While South Africa is still protected from the "winds of change" by a *cordon sanitaire* of colonial or White-settler controlled territories to the north (Angola, Mozambique, and Southern Rhodesia), such a protection will certainly be short-lived. The disintegration of the Central African Federation is now an accomplished fact, leaving only Southern Rhodesia under precarious White control, and the breakdown of the Portuguese empire appears imminent. The liberation of Southern Rhodesia, Angola, Mozambique, and the High Commission Territories will leave South Africa with a wide-open, hostile frontier of over two thousand miles.

Afro-Asian pressure against South Africa is exerted on several fronts, foremost among which are the United Nations. Ironically, the country of General Smuts, one of the architects of the United Nations, is now the principal defendant in that organization. Two main issues open South Africa to attack in that international forum: racial discrimination and the status of South West Africa.

India and Pakistan were among the first nations to protest against South Africa's racial policies (one of the few issues on which the two Asian governments agree). Indeed, the treatment of Indian immigrants to South Africa has been a source of international tension long before Indian independence. Starting in the 1860's, the British-controlled government of India protested at the indignities to which indentured "coolies" were subjected in Natal, and temporarily stopped Indian emigration to South Africa. Since 1947 India and Pakistan have introduced in the U.N. General Assembly yearly motions of censure against South Africa's racial policies. In recent years, however, the African countries have taken the lead against South Africa at the U.N. The growing tide of world indignation is reflected in the increasingly condemnatory language of the anti-apartheid resolutions, and in the growing unanimity with which these resolutions have been passed.

In October, 1958, for example, the General Assembly adopted by 70 votes against 5, and 4 abstentions, a resolution expressing "regret and concern" over South Africa's governmental policies which "impair the right of all racial groups to enjoy the same rights and fundamental freedom."[3] Three years later, in November, 1961, a lengthy and vigorous onslaught against apartheid in the General Assembly led to a vote of 97 to 2, with 1 abstention, against South Africa.[4] The resolution called apartheid "reprehensible and repugnant to human dignity," and urged member nations to take "separate and collective action" to force its abandonment. African states are quickly intensifying their maneuvers to bring about South Africa's expulsion from the world body, and these pressures are likely to be successful in the near future. In November, 1962, a much stronger resolution requesting member states to break off diplomatic relations with South Africa, to boycott her goods, and to consider her expulsion from the U.N. finally received the necessary two-thirds majority (67 to 16, with 23 abstentions) after several unsuccessful tries in previous years. In August, 1963, the Security Council, by a vote of 9 in favour, none opposed, and 2 abstentions (Britain and France) called upon all states to "cease forthwith the sale and shipment of arms, ammunition of all types, and military vehicles to South Africa."[5] For the first time, the United States stated its willingness to impose sanctions against South Africa, and the American representative, Adlai Stevenson, called apartheid "an evil business," "abhorrent," and "calculated retrogression."[6]

The South African government's position on the issue of apartheid is, of course, that its racial policies are strictly an internal concern, and, hence, that U.N. interference or censure is a violation of the Charter. All other countries, except Portugal, take the position that racial discrimination against non-Whites constitutes a blatant disregard of Article 55 of the U.N. Charter, and, hence, is a matter of international concern.[7] The moral weakness of

3. *Africa Special Report,* Vol. III, No. 12, p. 6.
4. *Ibid.,* Vol. VII, No. 1, p. 12.
5. *The Times,* London, August 8, 1963.
6. *Ibid.,* August 3, 1963.
7. Article 55 reads: ". . . the United Nations shall promote . . . univer-

South Africa's stand is clearly revealed by the fact that the government's main line of defence lies in attacking other countries for alleged discrimination against their minority groups.

The South West Africa issue, while a more legalistic one, threatens perhaps more directly the Nationalist government. The administration of that territory, which was formerly a German colony, was granted to South Africa in 1919 under a Mandate of the League of Nations, and as a consequence of its participation in World War One operations against Germany. The United Nations consider themselves the successor of the defunct League of Nations, and all colonial powers, except South Africa, have accepted the transformation of their Mandates into U.N. Trusteeships. South Africa, on the other hand, denies the U.N. any jurisdiction over South West Africa, and has, for all practical purposes, annexed that territory as a fifth province of the Republic. In 1960 Liberia and Ethiopia brought the issue to the International Court of Justice in a bid to expel South Africa from her Mandate. At the time of writing, the matter is still *sub judice,* but the final judgment is unlikely to be favourable to South Africa.

Outside the forum of the United Nations, the independent African states have also spearheaded the international crusade against South Africa. The Republic is either excluded from all regional conferences of African states, or represented by leading exiles and opponents of the government. The latter is invariably the target of vehement attacks on the part of all participating countries. In 1958 the first All-Africa People's Conference of Accra urged all states to initiate economic sanctions against South Africa "as a protest against racial discrimination." The onslaught intensified at later Pan-African meetings, notably at the Tunis

---

sal respect for, and observance of, human rights and fundamental freedom for all without distinction as to race, sex, language, or religion." Article 56 adds: "All members pledge themselves to take joint and separate action in co-operation with the Organization for the achievement of the purposes set forth in Article 55."

All-Africa People's Conference of December, 1959; the June, 1960 Conference of Independent African States in Addis Ababa; the Casablanca Conference of 1961; the Freedom Fighters' Conference of Accra in 1962; and the 1962 Summit Meeting of Casablanca Powers in Cairo. In spite of the rift which, until 1963, separated the "moderate" Monrovia group from the more militant Casablanca powers, all African states are unanimous in their abhorrence of apartheid, and in their readiness to combat it by all available means. At the 1963 Addis Ababa Conference, all independent African states, in view of the failure to liquidate colonialism by other means of opposition, urged the use of force in South Africa and the Portuguese territories, established a freedom fund, and discussed methods of military co-operation and aid. Most African states have already taken action against South Africa. Between 1961 and 1963 twenty-one nations have declared a trade embargo against the Republic, namely: The Sudan, Ethiopia, Ghana, Nigeria, Sierra Leone, Liberia, Guinea, the U.A.R., Mali, Algeria, Upper Volta, Rwanda, Libya, Cameroon, Senegal, Uganda, Tanganyika, Kenya, Niger, Dahomey, and Mauritania.[8] Cairo Radio broadcasts a steady stream of anti-apartheid propaganda. Ghana has, for some time, made the entry of South Africans conditional on a declaration of opposition to apartheid. Other states have denied transit facilities to South African ships and aircrafts. No independent country in the Soviet or Afro-Asian bloc has diplomatic relations with South Africa, except Japan.[9] In 1960 the United Arab Republic, which had been the only independent African state to keep a diplomatic mission in South Africa, broke off all relations with that country.

8. *Africa Today*, 11, March, 1964, p. 11.

9. In the latter case, Japan and South Africa agreed in 1961 to establish relations for purposes of foreign trade; the Nationalist government (in a move reminiscent of Hitler's granting the Japanese the status of "honourary Aryans") promptly declared that the Japanese would be considered as "White." The Chinese, however, continue to share with the Indians the inferior status of "Asiatics."

Since its independence in 1962, Algeria is actively training saboteurs to fight against Portugal and the South African government.

A wide range of non-governmental bodies has also initiated protest actions against South Africa. An opposition in exile constituted itself as the South African United Front with offices in London, Accra, Cairo, Dar-es-Salaam, and New York, and attempts to mobilize world opinion against apartheid. Mass anti-Nationalist demonstrations in Trafalgar Square, and a call for a British boycott of South African goods followed the Sharpeville incident of 1960. The International Commission of Jurists declared apartheid to be "morally reprehensible and violating the rule of law." World sport organizations, such as the Olympic Games Committee and the International Federation of Football Associations, have either excluded South Africa from participation, or threatened to do so unless racial discrimination in sports is abolished.

International religious bodies, notably the World Council of Churches, have unanimously condemned apartheid as contrary to Christianity and the laws of God. Even the Netherlands Reformed Church declared its abhorrence of racial discrimination and broke off relations with its South African sister churches. Labour unions have also threatened action. In December, 1959, the I.C.F.T.U. passed a resolution in favour of boycotting South African goods. German, British, and Scandinavian trade-union councils followed suit. South Africa was excluded from the 1961 International Labour Conference, and dockworkers' unions in East Africa agreed on a boycott of South African goods. In short, an imposing number of private international organizations covering most fields of human activity have taken an indignant stand against the racial policies of the Nationalists.

What have been the practical effects of such overwhelming anti-apartheid sentiment throughout the world? So far, boycotts and other sanctions have had little, if any, perceptible influence on the South African economy. It is likewise doubtful that the

United Nations, or even individual African or Asian states, will initiate any direct military action against the Nationalist government. Nevertheless, it would be fallacious to conclude that international pressures have had no effect on the internal scene, or that they will be ineffectual in the future. Let us first examine more closely the internal influence of outside antagonism, then assess the implications of the present world balance of power for South Africa, and, finally, attempt to predict future developments.

The most obvious impact of world condemnation on South Africa has been to force the latter to retreat into increasing diplomatic and military isolation. Supporters of the government pretend to welcome that trend, and to disregard world opinion. The growing menace of isolation to the South African government is, however, realized by the more intelligent Nationalists. When the tide of African independence will have reached the borders of South Africa, the Republic will be highly vulnerable to foreign-based terrorist organizations, and to economic sanctions (such as stopping the supply of foreign labour). Except in the unlikely case of direct Soviet or Chinese intervention, South Africa cannot count on any foreign aid against internal or external hostility. Several African states, notably Egypt, Algeria, and Ghana, have already offered and given financial support and training in sabotage and subversion techniques to South African exiles.

The present loose alliance between Portugal, Southern Rhodesia, and South Africa will not greatly impede the progress of African Nationalism, as two of the partners are already in a shaky political, economic, and military position, and as South Africa is itself too weak to extend military aid to its northern neighbours. Furthermore, this alliance between racialist South Africa and the supposedly "non-racial" Portugal involves ideological strains and international embarrassment for Salazar, who is already hard-pressed at the helm of his sinking ship. The closer the alliance is, the more openly its true colonialist and racialist character has to be admitted.

External hostility also affects internal opinion. World condemnation consolidates and accentuates the existing polarization of South African opinion into two irreconcilable camps. Any hope that overseas pressure may lead to a "liberalizing" of apartheid policies is, I believe, unrealistic.[10] At most, world opinion acts as a deterrent to large-scale killings of the Sharpeville type. The government recognizes that further shootings of this type would probably entail strong international sanctions, and therefore tends to become less indiscriminate in its use of firearms. But, far from deviating from its policy of apartheid, it constantly perfects its machinery of repression, substituting more efficient means of intimidation for the old-style shooting down of unarmed crowds. At the same time, the non-White opposition is turning away from peaceful mass demonstrations, which have proven ineffective, and evolving more efficacious means of protest.

As repeatedly stated by Nationalist officials, no amount of overseas stigmatization or castigation will lead to a reappraisal of racial policies. On the contrary, outside pressure can only confirm the government in its views and rally behind it the majority of the Whites. Indeed, the United Party opposition rightly views world opinion as hostile to all brands of racialism, and consequently supports the Nationalists against what it views as unfair and intolerable foreign intervention in the internal affairs of South Africa.[11] The English variety of White supremacist con-

10. Some observers have interpreted the 1962 Transkei developments as resulting from overseas pressures, but I disagree with this view, largely because I do not regard the Transkeian Constitution as a "liberalizing" of apartheid.

11. See, for example, this editorial comment from the *Natal Mercury* of September 29, 1962: "Even those Whites who are vigorously antagonistic toward rigid apartheid find themselves morally compelled to stand behind Mr. Louw [the Foreign Minister] in his condemnation of the extravagant and demonstrably untrue accusations so glibly levelled against South Africa by countries whose internal affairs do not even begin to measure up to the principles they seek to persuade U.N. to impose on others." The *Natal Mercury* generally follows a political line to the *left* of the United Party, and represents more the Progressive Party position.

siders any foreign attack against apartheid as an onslaught against South Africa as a whole, and views any appeal to world public opinion as treasonable or, at least, unpatriotic.

To the tiny minority of liberal Whites and to the non-Whites, world condemnation of racism gives strong moral support. Many democratic South Africans are disappointed with the lack of effectiveness of outside pressure, and become even bitter and cynical about the Western nations' unwillingness to adopt a firmer stand against the government. Yet world opinion confirms the legitimacy of democratic demands, and outside moral support for these demands enhances the prestige of the non-White and liberal White leaders among the masses. The tonic effect of Luthuli's Nobel Prize Award, for example, can hardly be overestimated.

In short, external pressures have, so far, *accentuated* the existing polarization of internal opinion, rather than effected a change thereof. At most, these pressures act as a brake on mass murder of Africans by the police, and lead a few well-meaning, "middle-of-the-road" Whites to reconsider their position, and to make a clean break with racialism. The latter phenomenon is particularly apparent among some leading Dutch Reformed Church ministers. Clearly then, outside pressures have, like internal forces, intensified conflict in South Africa, and pushed the country towards revolution. At the same time, however, these pressures have not yet reached the level necessary to precipitate the internal outburst. We shall return presently to the policy implications of these findings.

Rapid changes on the international scene suggest that, however ineffective outside pressures have been so far, these pressures are going to intensify in the future, and will help in bringing about the downfall of White supremacy in South Africa. Indeed, independent African states now hold well over thirty seats at the United Nations and constitute the largest single continental bloc in that organization. Together with twenty-two Asian countries, the African nations exert a strong influence on the world body's policy concerning South Africa. The Afro-Asian group is unanimous in seeking to overthrow apartheid, and to prevent unilateral action by either the Soviet Union or the Western powers. The Soviet Union is unlikely to intervene directly, and to repeat thereby its Congo mistake of disregarding and antagonizing the neutralist nations for comparatively low stakes.

Afro-Asian solidarity on the South African issue, by neutralizing the threat of Soviet intervention, thus deprives the South African government of its last trump card *vis-à-vis* the West, namely that it is anti-Communist and strategically important in the Cold War.

Let us now analyse the position of the Western powers, and particularly of the United States. Until about 1960, the United States foreign policy towards Africa in general was characteristically wavering, although generally aligned with that of its colonial allies.[12] While verbally anti-colonialist and anti-racialist, the United States was caught in its great postwar dilemma of trying to antagonize neither its NATO allies, nor the emerging Afro-Asian nations. Due, however, to the existence of racial discrimination at home, and its indirect support of the French in Algeria (and now the Portuguese in Angola), the United States acquired a strongly pro-colonialist image throughout Africa.

More specifically, in relation to South Africa, the United States followed until 1960 the British policy of abstaining from censuring apartheid in the United Nations, while hoping for a gradual "change of heart" and liberalizing of the Nationalist regime. The United States government even condoned racial segregation in South Africa by not sending any Negro diplomats to that country, and by keeping a strict colour-bar in its embassy and consulates.[13] A crucial turn in United States, British, French,

12. The one notable exception was, of course, during the Suez crisis of 1956.

13. As late as 1961, the United States made the phenomenal blunder of sending a navy squadron to Durban on a "courtesy call," on the eve of an anti-apartheid general strike organized by the Congress Alliance. United States Marines went ashore and demonstrated their weapons (such as flame-throwers and machine guns) to the South African Army. Helicopters were

and Belgian policy towards Africa took place in the 1957–1960 period. When Great Britain granted independence to the Gold Coast in 1957, she triggered off the rapid liberation of some two-thirds of Black Africa within three years. De Gaulle's 1958 Referendum led, within two years, to the complete independence of Madagascar and all of French West and Equatorial Africa. Within a few days of the January, 1959 riots in Léopoldville, Belgium promised independence to the Congo, and granted it within eighteen months.

The "decolonization" of British East Africa is now completed, and the White-settlers' stand in Southern Rhodesia presents the last major stumbling block to British colonial disentanglement on the continent. The 1962 Algerian settlement and the independence of Ruanda and Burundi in the same year marked the final withdrawal of France and Belgium from Africa (except for the small enclave of French Somaliland, where Somali-Ethiopian antagonism keeps the *tricolore* flying). Spain still holds on to the Rio de Oro and other insignificant enclaves, but, as she is not a member of NATO, she does not directly implicate the other Western powers. As to Portugal, the days of her presence in Africa are definitely counted, and she is too weak to be of any importance to the Western alliance system.

On February 3, 1960, Macmillan's "winds-of-change" speech in the Cape Town Parliament, though mild and courteous, gave South Africa its first warning that Britain could no longer refrain from attacking Nationalist colour policies. The following month, after Sharpeville, an official U.S. statement condemned the Nationalists in moderate but unambiguous language.[14] Thereafter,

---

flown at low altitudes over African "locations," much as the South African police does to spot and disperse crowd concentrations. Obviously, almost all Africans interpreted the American visit as a show of force in favour of Verwoerd. The United States fleet then repeated its performance in Portuguese-held Lorenço Marques.

14. The text read: "The United States deplores violence in all its forms and hopes that the African people of South Africa will be able to obtain

the United States has consistently voted in favour of U.N. resolutions condemning apartheid. South Africa's membership in the Commonwealth restrained British condemnation until 1961. For the first time, in April, 1961 (i.e., less than a month after South Africa announced her withdrawal from the "Club"), Britain voted against apartheid in the U.N. General Assembly. Since then, the Nationalists can only count on the support of Salazar's regime.

To be sure, the Western nations are not yet prepared to adopt strong sanctions against South Africa, such as a trade embargo or a rupture of diplomatic relations. So far, the United States and Britain have made the mistake of hoping against all evidence that change in South Africa could be through gradual reforms within the existing framework of White supremacy. They have failed to realize that South Africa has engaged itself on the road of White oppression far beyond the point where racial policies can be peacefully and gradually reversed. If they now begin to realize it, they are still reluctant to draw the revolutionary implications of the present situation in South Africa. Only in August, 1963, did the United States belatedly approve an arms embargo, but, by then, its effectiveness was likely to be negligible, as France and other NATO countries did not follow suit, and as South Africa has considerably expanded her armaments industry in the last two years. By December, 1963, Great Britain seemingly followed the United States lead on the arms embargo, by barring the import of weapons which could be used to enforce apartheid. However, it reserved itself the right to supply arms to South Africa for defence against external aggression.

The stand of the United States and Great Britain on the South African issue is of decisive importance. Indeed, the two countries together account for about half of South Africa's foreign investments and trade.[15] Unless America and Britain join other coun-

---

redress for legitimate grievances by peaceful means . . . it cannot help but regret the tragic loss of life resulting from the measures taken against the demonstrators in South Africa."

15. In 1959, for example, South Africa bought 31 per cent of its total

tries in adopting sanctions against South Africa, these sanctions are unlikely to have anything but a moral effect. Of course, it is partly because of their sizeable trade and investments in South Africa that the United Kingdom and the United States are so reluctant to impose effective sanctions against that country. In December, 1961, for example, direct and indirect British assets in South Africa were estimated at £1,550,000,000, and United States investments at £290,000,000. American economic interests in South Africa have greatly increased over the years. In 1962 alone, United States investments have increased by £15,700,000. Profits from United States companies in South Africa have grown steadily from £15,400,000 to £25,700,000 between 1959 and 1962.[16] In 1960 nationals of NATO countries owned 93 per cent of the foreign investments in South Africa; the British share was 58 per cent, and that of the United States, 19 per cent; Western European countries accounted for another 16 per cent.[17]

In August, 1963, Sir Patrick Dean, the British U.N. representative, admitted that one of the reasons for Britain's abstention on the resolution calling for sanctions against South Africa was that "we have a considerable trade with and a considerable investment in South Africa. This is of great importance to the external economic position of the United Kingdom, and therefore has implications for world trade generally." Sir Patrick also mentioned three other reasons, namely South Africa's strategic position and her importance in Britain's special defence obligations, Britain's responsibility for the well-being of the High Commission Territories, and "long historical connection, ties of kith and kin forged in times of danger."[18]

---

imports from the United Kingdom and 17 per cent from the United States. Germany came third with 10 per cent; 28 per cent of South African exports went to Britain, 14 per cent to the United States and 9 per cent to Germany. Cf. Calvocoressi, *op. cit.*, p. 67.

16. *Africa Today*, 11, March, 1964, p. 5.
17. *Ibid.*, p. 2.
18. *The Times*, London, August 7, 1963.

My contention, however, is that the cautious Anglo-American position is contrary to Western interests, and will, in any case, prove untenable in the near future. Rather than be reluctantly forced to yield to Afro-Asian demands for stronger sanctions, the United States and Britain have a unique opportunity to take the lead, and stem the tide of anti-Western hostility among the "non-aligned" nations. The West has almost nothing to lose, and a great deal to gain, by taking an active stand against Verwoerd (and Salazar). This is true not only in the rest of Africa, but also in South Africa. Indeed, the longer the revolution is delayed, the more violent, long-drawn, and anti-Western it is likely to be. The Western allies have rarely had such a propitious occasion of leading the inevitable course of history, rather than reluctantly following it to the growing annoyance of two-thirds of mankind.

To conclude the empirical part of our inquiry, we may attempt to predict, or, perhaps better, to prophesy South Africa's future. Although the exact course of events is impossible to foresee in any detail, the likelihood of revolution seems high. Mounting internal strains and external pressures doom White supremacy and racial segregation within the near future; the entire evolution of race relations since Union, and even more since 1948, excludes the possibility of a peaceful and gradual reversal of the present situation. Far from making any concessions, the government moves faster than ever in the reactionary direction, and becomes more and more repressive. This course is, in fact, the only one left to the Nationalists in order to prolong their stay in power. Any retreat would precipitate the crisis, but every new repressive measure, while postponing the explosion, also increases its potential violence.

At present, repressive measures appear to have disorganized the African opposition, and the prospect of a successful revolt seems slender in the immediate future. Once the colonial territories to the north of South Africa will have become independent, however, the collapse of White supremacy will be imminent. With foreign bases' of operation along a two-thousand-mile frontier, and military assistance from outside, guerrilla operations in South Africa will be extremely difficult to counteract, as indeed any underground movement which has the passive or active support of the mass of the population. Furthermore, once the fight will have reached the stage of large-scale terrorism, Afro-Asian demands for international sanctions or U.N. intervention will undoubtedly be stepped up, and become much more effective.

Revolutionary change will thus probably result from a combination of several of the following actions: strong international sanctions, strikes and passive resistance in the urban centres, peasant revolts in the rural areas, and well-organized sabotage from a foreign-based underground receiving outside military assistance and training. Since late 1961, sabotage activities, while still sporadic, ineffectual, and amateurish, show signs of becoming regular features of the South African scene. The near-collapse of South Africa's colonial *cordon sanitaire* (Rhodesia, Angola, and Mozambique) suggests that conditions will become favourable for these developments within five years at most. As to the mounting international pressures, they have so far had little tangible impact on the internal situation, but they are likely to play a crucial role in the revolutionary changes to come.

The ideological course of the revolution is even more difficult to predict. Two major possibilities appear most likely: either a militant Black racialist movement along the lines of the Pan-African Congress, or a socialist, non-racist movement along African National Congress lines. An expedient, short-term alliance of African leaders with "progressive" White elements is possible, but unlikely to last long. Large separatist ethnic movements are unlikely in view of the advanced stage of Westernization, though local peasant *Jacqueries* are probable. Both the Coloureds and the Indians will probably remain on the sidelines of the struggle, except for a few individual leaders.

A South Africa divided against itself awaits the impending and inexorable catastrophe. The Whites claim a right to survival which hardly anybody denies them. But in claiming to assert that right, they have set themselves against the course of history, and have become an arrogant, oppressive albinocracy. Their pride and prejudice may well be their undoing. *Quos vult Jupiter perdere, dementat prius.*

## CHAPTER ELEVEN

## Some Theoretical Considerations

T HE previous chapters of this book, while largely analytical, in the sense of being rather far removed from sheer factual description, have deliberately not dealt with basic theoretical issues.[1] Obviously, South Africa is a very special type of society. Indeed, in many respects it is unique. So is every other society, or, for that matter, any entity whatever. The easiest intellectual escape from the problems of uniqueness is to adopt a historicist belief in the impossibility of arriving at valid generalizations about human behaviour. I believe, however, that general theory is the ultimate aim of any scientific investigation, and that the special nature of South African society calls not for despair concerning the feasibility of social theory, but rather for a critical reconsideration of basic assumptions and concepts. Because of its idiosyncracies, South Africa raises fundamental, but not unsurmountable, problems for sociological theory.

While much of my analysis of South African society has been in structural terms, I have already suggested at various points some inadequacies of conventional "structure-function" theory for the case at hand. At the same time, I have introduced on occasions a Hegelian dialectic in my arguments, and indicated

1. This chapter is a revised and expanded version of my paper "Toward a Sociology of Africa." I am mostly indebted to the theoretical formulations of Max Gluckman, Georges Balandier, and Ralf Dahrendorf in this chapter.

the usefulness of such an approach to analyse the conflicts and contradictions in South Africa. Yet it is equally clear that an orthodox dialectic, in either its Hegelian or its Marxian form of single-factor determinism, is inadequate. Elsewhere I have sketched what I considered the basic assumptions, the strengths, and the limitations of both functionalism and the Hegelian-Marxian dialectic, and I suggested that these two seemingly antithetical approaches were, in fact, complementary and reconcilable.[2] Here I do not intend to repeat myself, but rather to examine the main characteristics of South African society, and their implications for sociological theory.

The most salient idiosyncracy of South Africa is, of course, its racial syndrome. As we have repeatedly seen, whatever thread one picks up in the social fabric of the country, one ends up with "race." Race, in the social as opposed to the biological sense, is a special criterion of ascription based on human phenotypes. Physical characteristics have no intrinsic significance; they only become relevant as they are seized upon in a given society as criteria of group definition, and as pegs on which to hang prejudices and discrimination. South Africa is not the only racist country in the world. The closest parallels are the southern states of the United States at the height of the Jim Crow era (i.e., between 1890 and 1920), and Southern Rhodesia which, to a considerable extent, was settled by White South Africans. Other colonial or formerly colonial societies also have rigidly ascribed colour-castes. However, South Africa represents an extreme case in terms of the persistence and thoroughness with which the system of racial inequality is maintained, and a peculiarly complex case by virtue of the number of groups involved.

Two important consequences follow from the White ideology of racism. First, racism is one of the main factors which make for lack of value consensus in South Africa. In no meaningful

2. Van den Berghe, "Dialectic and Functionalism: Toward a Theoretical Synthesis." Rolf Dahrendorf has argued along somewhat similar lines. See his *Class and Class Conflict in Industrial Society*.

way can one say that the great majority of South Africans share a common system of beliefs concerning what they consider desirable. We have already shown that South Africa invalidates in this respect the postulate of value consensus advanced by some functionalists, notably by Talcott Parsons.[3] Consensus about basic values is undoubtedly an important source of social integration; its absence can produce serious strains; but it is not a prerequisite to the existence of a society, and other bases of integration can hold a society together.

Secondly, racist ideology, insofar as it is applied in practice, constitutes the major facet of what may be termed the *social* (as opposed to *cultural*) pluralism of South Africa. Society is compartmentalized into four main racial castes with a quadruplicated set of institutional structures. Not only do the four colour-castes show a low degree of integration and complementarity, and have highly segmentary relations with one another, but these relations are based mostly on conflict. Other factors, notably linguistic divisions and social class, also contribute to social pluralism, but the ubiquity and increasing rigidity of racial barriers relegate these other factors to a secondary position. Such is the case of the Afrikaner-English split among Europeans, which, although still important, is overshadowed by the racial conflict.

Of greater interest yet is the lack of salience of social class in South Africa. To be sure, there exist income and occupational strata within each of the four races, but, at the same time, there is a high correlation between socio-economic variables and race. Social classes in the Marxian sense of relationship to the means of production exist by definition, as they must in any capitalist country, but they are not meaningful social realities. Clearly, pigmentation, rather than ownership of land or capital, is the most significant criterion of status in South Africa. The attempt to salvage Marxian orthodoxy by identifying the Whites with the

3. See, for example, Parsons, *The Social System*, pp. 36–37, 326, 350–351.

capitalists and the Africans with the proletariat is inacceptable because it does violence to the facts and is, at best, a grossly distorted oversimplification. Conversely, to lump White and non-White wage earners in one supposedly unified, class-conscious proletariat with common interests against the bourgeoisie is obviously nonsensical. As to traditional African societies, they cannot be analysed in Marxian class terms at all, as African socialists rightly point out. Communal land tenure, for example, puts the African peasantry in a radically different "class" position than the peasantry of Europe dealt with by Marx.

Cultural heterogeneity is another characteristic of South Africa which that country shares, of course, with many others, but in an extreme form. The cultures of three continents meet in South Africa, each of these major strains being subdivided into several linguistic groups. Furthermore, the dominant culture, although it has deeply influenced the total structure of the country, encompasses only about one-third of the population. This cultural heterogeneity adds another dimension to the lack of consensus, as each culture has its own ethos, and as the respective values held are often conflicting, incompatible, or, at any rate, completely different. One may then speak of a *cultural* aspect of pluralism as distinct from social pluralism. The relationship between these two forms of pluralism is particularly interesting. Originally, cultural lines of cleavage coincided with racial lines. The latter became increasingly rigid as cultural and racial distinctions overlapped less and less, due to miscegenation and acculturation. Apartheid ideology persists in identifying and confusing the two (speaking, for example, of "White civilization"), in wishing away the lack of identity, or, where it has recognized the trend towards increasing dissociation of race and culture, in implementing measures to reestablish the identity which existed for a short period in the seventeenth century. As we have already seen, this constitutes one of the major sources of strain in South African society.

Two last facets of pluralism must be mentioned again briefly, namely the political and the economic dualisms which result partly from cultural, partly from social pluralism, but which may best be considered as special aspects of social pluralism. As a body politic, South Africa has the dual character of parliamentary government for Whites and an arbitrary colonial regime for Africans (and increasingly for Asians and Coloureds). To a limited extent this political dualism is being blurred, on the one hand, by the undermining of White parliamentary democracy and the extension of instruments of tyranny to the *Herrenvolk*, and, on the other hand, by creating the fiction of "independent" Bantustans. Basically, however, the dichotomy remains. Economically, South Africa consists partly of a booming and complex money or market sector, and a sub-subsistence sector.

Let us pause for a moment and examine more closely the concept of pluralism. The term "plural society," first coined by Furnivall who identifies it with tropical societies, is now being used so freely as to cover any group which is not culturally and socially homogeneous.[4] Smith reacts against this loose usage of pluralism, restricts the term to societies that contain incompatible institutions, and criticizes its application to societies which are simply stratified racially or socially, or which exhibit several variants of a common culture. Furthermore, he reserves the use of the term to countries where a cultural minority is dominant.[5] Braithwaite defines cultural pluralism in terms of diversity of values, but tends to regard racial or class heterogeneity as a form of pluralism.[6] Boeke applies the concept to economics in dealing with the Western and non-Western sectors of the Indonesian economy.[7] Kuper suggests three levels of analysis in dealing with pluralism: the units of cleavage (ethnic or racial), the cultural diversity in basic patterns of behaviour associated

4. J. S. Furnivall, *Colonial Policy and Practice,* and *Netherlands India, A Study of Plural Economy.*
5. M. G. Smith, "Social and Cultural Pluralism."
6. Lloyd Braithwaite, "Social Stratification and Cultural Pluralism."
7. Boeke, *op. cit.*

with these cleavages, and social pluralism or separation in social organization.[8] A similar distinction between social and cultural pluralism is made by Padilla.[9]

Little seems to be gained by restricting the concept as Smith does. Clearly, pluralism is best conceived as a dimension rather than as an all-or-none phenomenon. A society is pluralistic to the extent that it is structurally segmented and culturally diverse. In more operational terms, pluralism is characterized by the relative absence of value consensus; the relative rigidity and clarity of group definition; the relative presence of conflict or, at least, of lack of integration and complementarity between various parts of the social system; the segmentary and specific character of relationships, and the relative existence of sheer institutional duplication (as opposed to functional differentiation or specialization) between the various segments of the society. Institutions do not have to be incompatible for a society to be pluralistic, but a degree of structural and functional duplication has to be present. In other words, a society is pluralistic insofar as it is compartmentalized into quasi-independent subsystems, each of which has a set of homologous institutions, and only specific points of contact with the others (e.g., common participation in a money economy, and subjection to a common body politic). A pluralistic society is one in which one cannot, to use Marcel Mauss' phrase, take a "total social phenomenon" and trace its ramifications in the entire society.[10]

From the above treatment of pluralism it should be clear that I use the concept in a broader sense than have American political scientists in the de Tocquevillian tradition. Interestingly, this latter tradition, applying the concept to the analysis of competing political interest groups, has tended to associate pluralism with democracy and political integration. Possibly this difference in the analysis of the consequences of pluralism is due to the

8. L. Kuper, "Some Aspects of Urban Plural Societies in Africa."
9. Elena Padilla, "Peasants, Plantations and Pluralism."
10. Marcel Mauss, *Sociologie et Anthropologie.*

restricted application of the concept to the political sphere and to societies which, like the United States, exhibit a fairly low degree of pluralism. Indeed the pluralism that de Tocqueville talked about presupposed consensus about essential social values and aims, and acceptance of the legitimacy of the existing political system. Conflicts exist insofar as various contending groups have different interests; the latter are viewed as exerting more or less random pulls in various directions, so that they tend to cancel each other out, and to lead to a harmonious democracy. Clearly, this older conception of pluralism deals with a limiting case of minimal pluralism which must not be confused or identified with the much broader class of phenomena analysed here.[11]

What are the implications for functionalist theory of the multi-dimensional pluralism found in South Africa? Much of functionalist theory has been based on a monistic model of society. In its most extreme form, functionalism assumes an almost complete cultural homogeneity within a society, whereas more sophisticated functionalists, such as Parsons, and Clyde and Florence Kluckhohn, speak of "dominant" as opposed to "deviant" or "variant" subcultures.[12] This is not to say that functionalism advances an undifferentiated model of society. On the contrary, differentiation and specialization of function and structure between complementary and interdependent parts are cornerstones of functionalism. But neither the concept of differentiation, nor that of deviance (or variance) is adequate to deal with plural societies. South Africa is partly differentiated into complementary parts, but it is also split into non-complementary, non-functional, and often conflicting segments. The Whites are dominant in terms of power, wealth, religion, and language, but

11. I am indebted to my colleagues Ken Downey and Claude Welch for calling this basic terminological and conceptual confusion on the term "pluralism" to my attention.

12. Parsons, *The Social System;* Clyde Kluckhohn, *Culture and Behavior,* see bibliography, pp. 373–397; Florence Kluckhohn and Fred L. Strodtbeck, *Variation in Value Orientations.*

the other groups, with the possible exception of the Coloureds, cannot be called "variants" of the dominant group.

Pluralism raises the question of social integration. The two terms seem antithetical: the more a society is segmented into heterogeneous and non-complementary parts, the less integrated it is. In Durkheimian terms, a pluralistic society is low on both "mechanical" and "organic" solidarity, insofar as it is composed neither of similar units joined by a strong collective consciousness, nor of interdependent units.[13] Whereas most African countries, in the face of pluralism, endeavour to foster integration, the South African government wants to perpetuate racial, political, and cultural pluralism by deepening existing cleavages and counteracting the integrative forces of acculturation, urbanization, and industrialization. Nevertheless, South African society is integrated in some ways, otherwise one would not be able to speak of it as a society. This point is stressed by Gluckman in his analysis of African-White relations in Zululand, which he views as a system of counterbalancing conflict and co-operation, cleavage and integration.[14]

Again the functionalist model of integration is inadequate in several ways. Merton and other sophisicated functionalists have successfully repudiated the extreme Malinowskian views that a society is a perfectly integrated whole in which every part has a function and is indispensable.[15] But even the more cautious proposition that integration or equilibrium is a limit towards which societies tend is very questionable. South Africa has been moving towards increasing malintegration for half a century,

13. Emile Durkheim, *De la Division du Travail Social.*
14. Gluckman, *op. cit.,* pp. 26, 46, 68, 70.
15. Robert Merton, *Social Theory and Social Structure,* pp. 30–37; B. Malinowski, "Anthropology" *Encyclopedia Britannica,* pp. 132–136. Gluckman gives a devasfating critique of Malinowski's inability to deal with pluralistic societies and with problems of conflict. See his *Order and Rebellion in Tribal Africa,* pp. 207–234; and B. Malinowski, *The Dynamics of Culture Change, An Inquiry into Race Relations in Africa.*

and seems inevitably headed for disintegration. As we already suggested, South Africa offers the spectacle of a social system that "went amok." Economic forces have brought about much the same set of transformations as in many other "developing" countries, including a tendency to undermine the traditional, paternalistic system of race relations, and the quasi-colonial body politic. But, far from adjusting internally to economic transformations, and externally to the drastically changed postwar international scene, the White ruling albinocracy proved sternly uncompromising, and bitterly determined to maintain its monopoly of power and wealth, basing its claim on racial superiority. Every attempt was made to resist social (in contrast to strictly *technological*) change, or even to revert to a paternalistic, master-and-servant model of society. Lack of change (or reactionary change) can thus result in ever increasing malintegration, and one may describe the political deadlock as one of static disequilibrium.

Clearly, the Nationalist government is doomed to failure, and hardly any of its aims has come nearer realization. On the contrary, there developed a growing tension and disharmony between economic imperatives and political objectives, between the fluid class system created by urbanization and the rigidly ascriptive mold of colour-castes, between the protest ideology of the non-White masses and the *status quo* ideology of the Whites, between the benevolent despotism of "ideal" apartheid and the ruthless tyranny used in trying to implement that racialist utopia. The entire society is caught in a vicious circle which can no longer be reversed by gradual, adaptive change, as the functionalist model of dynamic equilibrium postulates. South Africa not only shows that the "tolerance limits" for disequilibrium and conflict are very much wider than functionalist theory would lead one to expect; it also impels one to predict that change must be revolutionary, i.e., abrupt, profound, qualitative, and probably violent. In short, the Hegelian-Marxian dialectic of change through conflict seems to impose itself to the analysis of South Africa, though more as a complement than as an alternative to a functionalist approach.

The functionalist notion of integration is inadequate on another count, namely in its answer to the question: *What* makes a society hang together? We have dealt with the inadequacy of the postulate of value consensus advanced by the main stream of functionalism from Comte to Parsons via Durkheim. What are, then, some of the alternative bases of social integration? Coercion, which plays an increasingly dominant role in South Africa, is obviously an alternative, though a notoriously unstable one, leading to the eternal vicious circle of tyranny. However, to reduce the problem of integration to a consent-coercion dichotomy, or to varying blends of these two elements, is still far from adequate. More important than coercion as an alternative to consensus is economic interdependence, or what Durkheim called "organic solidarity," which goes together with any complex division of labour.[16] Clearly, participation of disparate ethnic groups in a common system of production is a crucial integrative factor in all African countries, and is one of the major factors which has held such a conflict-ridden society as South Africa together for so long. The utter dependence (at a starvation or near-starvation level) of the African masses on the "White" economy in South Africa has been one of the main inhibiting factors to such mass protest actions as general strikes. There is, of course, a reverse side to economic integration in South Africa. The more economic interdependence there is, the less feasible apartheid becomes. Two major elements of the social structure, namely the polity and the economy, pull in opposite directions, thereby creating rapidly mounting strains.

Finally, there often exists *compliance* in the absence of consensus. One can "play the game" without accepting the rules. Such is the aim of coercion, but behavioural conformity to norms

16. Durkheim, *op. cit.*

of another group is also often the result of free choice, for the sake of status, convenience, monetary gain, etc. Punctilious adherence to arbitrary and often trivial norms, combined with conflict of basic interests and disagreement about basic aims, takes an extreme form in international diplomacy, for example. Similarly, Philip Mayer, Clyde Mitchell, and other anthropologists familiar with urban African conditions have observed how migrant workers can adjust to town life, so that, while in town, they appear quite Westernized, only to become very traditional again at home in the rural areas.[17] In my study of Caneville, I have shown how many Africans and Indians comply with the etiquette of race relations by behaving subserviently towards Whites, without in any way internalizing a sense of inferiority.[18]

To phrase the above remarks in more general form, plural societies are compartmentalized into autonomous subsystems. The notion of autonomy is, of course, not incompatible with a functionalist viewpoint. Indeed, interdependence of functionally differentiated parts of a system implies the mirror-image concept of relative autonomy. But the kind of autonomy dealt with here is different. We are concerned neither with "organic solidarity" of complementary parts, nor with "mechanical solidarity" of self-sufficient parts united by adherence to a common system of values and norms. Plural societies are characterized in part by the coexistence of autonomous but non-complementary subsocieties which do not share common values, but individual members of which interact in highly segmental, though crucial relationships. Rather than consensus and interdependence of parts, what holds such societies together is thus partially a network of segmental ties between individual members of ethnic or racial groups, some of whom may indeed "shuttle" or "commute" between cultural subsystems.

This last formulation introduces a new dimension in the

17. Mayer, *op. cit.*; Clyde Mitchell, *Tribalism and the Plural Society*.
18. Van den Berghe, *Caneville, The Social Structure of a South African Town*.

analysis of acculturation or cultural contact. Much of the work done in that field has suffered from at least two shortcomings. First, acculturation or "detribalization" (to use a word dear to Africanists) has generally been conceived as a continuum on which individuals could be placed, and where movement is overwhelmingly away from "traditionalism" and towards "Westernization." While such a conception provides a reasonably approximate description of the over-all tendency, it breaks down if one endeavours to apply it to individuals, because it grossly underrates the individual's adaptive flexibility, and his capacity to "shuttle" between two cultures. In practice, it is often difficult to determine how "detribalized" an individual is, because he may continually oscillate between two systems, rather than move steadily towards one and away from another. Indeed, the applicability of a unidimensional continuum to as complex a process as culture change through contact is highly problematical, but a discussion of this point would take us too far.

Second, studies of culture contact have overemphasized "borrowing" of cultural items as the major process of change through contact. Naturally, acculturation theory is not based on a simplistic and mechanistic model wherein traits are exchanged like bananas or groundnuts on a cultural market place. All anthropologists are aware of the complicating factors of selectivity and reinterpretation of items or traits, and, indeed, many avoid altogether such atomistic concepts as "item" or "trait." Nevertheless, the fact that cultures almost invariably *adjust to* and *react against* as well as *borrow from* one another has, I think, been underemphasized. White colonial society is different from White society in Europe, not so much because it borrowed from African culture, but because it adapted its values, its eating, drinking, and sleeping habits, its architecture, etc., to African and colonial conditions. African societies similarly adapted themselves to the conquerors in terms of their own internal dynamics. When, for example, an urban woman in South Africa earns her own *lobola* (or bride-wealth) in order to hasten her marriage, she is obviously not becoming Westernized; she finds a radically new solution to a new situation but in terms of a traditional institution. Or, to use another illustration, most messianistic religious sects do contain elements borrowed from Christianity, but, at the same time, they constitute a reaction against European domination, as Sundkler shows in the case of South Africa.[19] In short, societies in contact do not only undergo a process of cultural osmosis, however complex, but they also generate change from within, in terms of both adaptation to, and conflict against, other societies. We shall return to that point presently.

So far we have considered cultural pluralism in its most obvious form, i.e., the coexistence of different ethnic groups. This pluralism is gradually reduced by acculturation, which has created a Westernized (or, in the case of the Sudan belt, an Islamized) elite that often transcends ethnic particularism. Conversely, however, acculturation has introduced another form of pluralism, and increased cultural heterogeneity. Nowhere in Africa did European culture come close to eradicating indigenous traditions, except in the Western Cape Province of South Africa. Consequently, by differentially permeating various layers or segments of ethnic groups that were originally homogeneous, Westernization added a new dimension to cultural pluralism, as we have already suggested earlier. Philip Mayer, for example, documents in detail the profound and enduring rift between the "red" and the "school" people among the Xhosa of the Eastern Cape.[20] While, elsewhere, acculturation has typically not given rise to a sharp dichotomous cleavage in the indigenous population, it invariably introduced a new dimension of heterogeneity.

Related to pluralism are of course, the problems of conflicts and contradictions arising out of social and cultural heterogeneity, and the resulting dynamics of change. Here, too, the functionalist approach suffers from serious limitations. I do not

19. Sundkler, *op. cit.*
20. Mayer, *op. cit.*

wish to repeat the unfair criticism that functionalism is a static approach. Though Radcliffe-Brown and Malinowski have, each in his own way, introduced an a-historical bias in much African anthropology, functionalism as such allows for at least three sources of social change: individual invention and discovery; adaptation to external change; and a gradual, orderly process of growth in size and complexity through functional and structural differentiation. However, this approach to change is only a partial one, and must be complemented by an Hegelian-Marxian view of change as an internally generated process of conflict and contradiction between opposites. Much change is abrupt, qual- itative, and revolutionary; and pluralism often fosters acute conflict. Whether one adopts a positivist view of the Hegelian dialectic as inherent in the reality studied, or a nominalist one, considering it simply as a useful analytical tool, need not con- cern us here, though I personally lean towards the nominalist approach. Nor does one have to adopt Hegelian idealism, or Marxian materialism, or any other dogmatic application of the dialectic based on one-factor determinism. My argument is simply that the dialectic method complements the functionalist approach to change. This point has already been expended on elsewhere.[21] Here, I shall confine myself to illustrating very sketchily the usefulness of a dialectic approach in dealing with South Africa, by recapitulating some of the arguments made in previous chapters. Several of my remarks are applicable, *mutatis mutandi*, to the rest of the continent.

A society as ridden with tension as South Africa offers almost too facile an application of the Hegelian dialectic. Let us con- centrate on the major source of conflict, namely the syndrome of White domination, and show how it called forth its opposite and sowed the seeds of its own destruction. At the level of values and ideology, the European settlers developed an elaborate racial mythology to rationalize their rule, but at the same time they

21. Van den Berghe, "Dialectic and Functionalism: Toward a Theoreti- cal Synthesis."

brought with them a libertarian and egalitarian tradition which they applied to themselves, and which they wittingly or unwittingly spread among Africans through missionary education and other forms of culture contact. This ideological contradiction takes both a political and a religious aspect. While the fundamentalistic Calvinism of the Boers has been reinterpreted to defend racialism, the English missionaries generally taught a more universalistic gospel of brotherhood and human dignity.

Politically, the *"Herrenvolk* egalitarianism" of the Boer Republics, and later of the Union of South Africa, coexisted with arbitrary and despotic colonial government for the Africans. Western-educated Africans eventually adopted much of the universalistic, liberal, and Christian ethos, became aware of the contradictions in the value system of the local Whites, and used Christianity and liberalism to challenge the legitimacy of White domination. At the same time, White racialism called forth its antithesis, namely the Black racialism represented in the local brand of Pan-Africanism, and in some religious sects of the "Zionist" variety. Similarly, Afrikaner nationalism and African nationalism developed side by side with, but in opposition to, each other. To the cry of White unity against the "Black peril," there arose, in response, the call for non-White unity against "White oppression." Ever since Union, there has been a steady polarization of political opinion along colour lines.

White supremacy is busily digging its own grave in many ways other than ideological. Economically, the exploitation of South African resources became a large-scale venture only with the development of diamond and gold mining in the second half of the nineteenth century. This led to rapid urbanization and industrialization with their host of familiar consequences: the breakdown of geographical isolation; the spread of mass media of communication, elementary education, literacy, European languages, and industrial skills among Africans; the annual migration of hundreds of thousands of workers who are seasonally or permanently cut off from their rural environment and thrown in the great ethnic melting pot of workers' compounds; the decay of traditional authority; the undermining of family life; the rise of individualism, etc. Certainly, all these developments contributed, at least as much as ideology, to the breakdown of ethnic particularism among Africans, and to the rise of militant, politically conscious, urban masses.

In erecting a rigid colour-bar, the dominant Whites succeeded in maintaining a monopoly of leading positions in government, commerce, industry, finance, farming, education, and religion. By the same token, they prevented the rise of a substantial class of Africans with a stake in the *status quo*. For all practical purposes, there is no African landed peasantry or bourgeoisie (in the Marxian sense of owners of means of production). Conversely, the Whites created an exploited urban proletariat, a middle class of underpaid clerks and other petty white-collar workers, and a tiny elite of professionals and semiprofessionals who are strongly discriminated against. All these strata share a common interest in radical change. The African intelligentsia furnishes the leadership of the liberatory movements; the white-collar workers, many of the local organizers; and the proletariat, the mass support. As to the traditional African framework of authority, the government rightly viewed it as a conservative force, and tried to preserve it, if only for administrative economy and convenience; but at the same time the government undermined the traditional system by misunderstanding its nature, transforming it for its own ends, and subjecting it to the onslaughts of urbanization. In short, then, the ruling White group, as in much of the rest of the continent, inevitably undermined what it sought to preserve, and brought into being what it tried to prevent. It so completely monopolized wealth and power, and so rigidly identified itself with the *status quo* that any change in the distribution of social rewards must be against it.

All the above illustrations are rather obvious, and have been elaborated on earlier. South Africa and, more generally, pluralistic societies call for a model of change which gives conflict, contradiction, revolution, and malintegration a prominent place. If functionalism be called the thesis, and the Hegelian-Marxian dialectic the antithesis, then African societies, because of their pluralism and their extraodinary dynamism, offer us a unique opportunity to reach a new synthesis in sociological theory. Briefly, I suggest that both approaches be stripped of their needless postulates, be reformulated in minimal form, and be reconciled in a grand new general theory. What few more concrete suggestions I have already advanced towards this ambitious aim have been stated elsewhere.[22] A theoretical treatise would be out of place here. However, at the risk of sounding insufferably avuncular, I should like to make one last remark. Functionalist and structuralist anthropology and sociology have reached such pinnacles of conceptual and descriptive elegance in the works of such giants of the tradition as Lévi-Strauss and Evans-Pritchard that one might have feared premature fossilization of the behavioural sciences. Now that functionalism is coming under increasingly intense fire, that danger is effectively warded off. But there might now exist another danger, namely that the recognition of the limitations of the "structure-function" approach might herald a new wave of sterile historicism, and of despair about the feasibility of social theory. The perverse complexity of a society like South Africa should not only be an excuse for exploding the boundaries of existing theory, but also a challenge for the construction of more generally applicable theory.

22. Van den Berghe, "Dialectic and Functionalism: Toward a Theoretical Synthesis."

# Chronology of South African Events*

1488    Bartholomew Diaz discovered the Cape.

1602    Netherlands United East India Company (*Vereenigde Oost Indische Compagnie*) formed.

1652    On April 6, Jan van Riebeeck landed at the Cape and formed the first white settlement.

1657    First Free Burghers at Rondebosch.

1658    About 400 slaves imported from West Africa.

1688    Arrival of the first Huguenot settlers.

1699–1707    Governor Willem Adriaan van der Stel.

1713    First smallpox epidemic.

1760    Orange River crossed by Coetzee.

1774    First mission station in South Africa, at Genadendal, established by George Schmidt of the Moravian Mission Society.

1778    The Fish River made the eastern boundary of Cape settlement.

1779    Xhosas, who crossed the Fish River into the Cape Colony, repelled in the First "Kaffir War."

1780–1783    War between Holland and England. Decline of the Netherlands East India Company.

1792    Second "Kaffir War."

1795–1803    First British occupation of the Cape.

1799    Third "Kaffir War."

1803–1806    Cape returned to Batavian Republic. Janssens and De Mist joint governors.

1806    Second occupation of the Cape by Britain.

1812    Fourth "Kaffir War." "Black Circuit."

1814    Holland ceded the Cape to Britain.

1815    Slagter's Nek episode.

* Sources: *State of the Union Year-Book for South Africa,* 1959–1960, pp. 17–25; Lord Hailey, *An African Survey,* 1957.

1819　Cape boundary extended to Keiskama River. Fifth "Kaffir War."

1820　Arrival of 5,000 British settlers.

1828　Death of the Zulu King Shaka. English becomes the official language. Passes for Hottentots abolished and all free Coloureds in Cape placed on political level with Europeans through 50th Ordinance.

1829　University of Cape Town opened.

1834　Slavery abolished. Sixth "Kaffir War."

1835　Durban founded. Beginning of the Trigardt Trek.

1836　Great Trek from the Cape.

1837　Matabele crossed over to the north of the Limpopo. Retief treks to Natal.

1838　Retief's Treaty with Dingaan. Massacre of Boers under Retief by Dingaan. Andries Pretorius won battle of Blood River. Dingaan overthrown. Republic of Natal founded.

1843　Natal proclaimed a British colony.

1844　Majority of *Voortrekkers* left Natal. Natal incorporated in Cape Colony.

1845　Natal separated from Cape Colony.

1846　Bloemfontein founded. Seventh "Kaffir War."

1847　East London founded. British rule extended over Kaffraria.

1848　British sovereignty proclaimed between Orange and Vaal rivers. Skirmish between British and Boers at Boomplaats.

1850　Eighth "Kaffir War."

1851　First Basuto War.

1852　Britain recognised independence of Transvaal in Sand River Convention.

1853　"Representative Government" granted to Cape Colony with qualified franchise rights extended to non-Whites.

1854　Britain recognised independence of Orange Free State in Convention of Bloemfontein. First Cape Parliament in session.

1855　Pretoria founded.

1856　Natal made separate colony. Lydenburg seceded from South African Republic. Xhosa prophetic movement and cattle killing.

1858　Second Basuto War.

1860　First importation of labourers from India for sugar plantations in Natal.

1865　Kaffraria annexed to Cape. Third Basuto War.

1867　First diamond discovered near Hopetown.

1868   Basutoland annexed by Britain.
1869   British intervention in Basutoland. Diamonds discovered near Kimberley.
1870   Diamond fields annexed by Britain.
1872   "Responsible Government" granted to Cape Colony.
1877   Transvaal proclaimed British territory.
1879   Zulu rebellion under Cetewayo. Britain occupied Zululand.
1880   Formation of Afrikaner Bond. First Anglo-Boer War.
1881   Transvaal regained "independence," albeit under British suzerainty. Use of Afrikaans in Cape Parliament permitted.
1883   Paul Kruger President of South African Republic. Republics of Stellaland and Goshen founded.
1884   German protectorate over South West Africa. London Convention (February 27) granted Transvaal full independence with exception of treaties with foreign states. Basutoland Crown Colony.
1885   Bechuanaland British Protectorate. Railway Cape Town-Kimberley opened.
1886   Johannesburg founded. Opening of Witwatersrand gold fields.
1888   First Rhodesian mining concessions granted by Lobengula. Matabeleland and Mashonaland declared British spheres of influence.
1889   Alliance between Orange Free State and South African Republic. British South Africa Company established.
1890   Cecil Rhodes Prime Minister of the Cape. British troops occupied Mashonaland. Anglo-German Agreement in which the boundaries of South West Africa fixed.
1892   Railway Cape Town-Johannesburg completed.
1893   "Responsible Government" for Natal. Mahatma Gandhi arrived in South Africa.
1894   Pondoland annexed to Cape Colony. Natal Indian Congress founded.
1895   Annexation of Bechuanaland to Cape Colony. Jameson Raid.
1896   Rising of Matabele in Rhodesia. Surrender and trial of Jameson.
1899–1902   War between Great Britain and the two Boer Republics.
1902   Treaty of Vereeniging (May 31). Transvaal and Orange Free State British colonies. Death of Cecil Rhodes.
1904   Importation of Chinese labourers for gold mines of Transvaal.
1905   Beginning of second *Afrikaanse Taal* movement. Lord Milner left South Africa.

1906 Self-government granted to the Transvaal. Cabinet formed by Louis Botha. Zulu Poll-Tax Rebellion.

1907 Orange River Colony granted self-government. Importation of Chinese stopped.

1907–1913 Mahatma Gandhi's first *Satyagraha* campaign.

1908 National Convention in Durban; further meetings in 1909 in Cape Town and Bloemfontein.

1909 South Africa Act passed by Imperial Parliament.

1910 Constitution of the Union of South Africa, May 31. Louis Botha first Prime Minister.

1912 African National Congress founded. Resignation of Prime Minister Louis Botha, who formed new cabinet with Hertzog.

1913 Hertzog formed National Party. Miners' strike and riots on Witwatersrand. March of Natal Indians into Transvaal.

1914 Industrial disturbances on Witwatersrand. Union income tax introduced. Mahatma Gandhi left South Africa. Outbreak of First World War, August 4. Union Parliament, on September 10, decided, with 91 against 12 votes, in favour of participation in war. Outbreak of Afrikaner Rebellion. Martial Law proclaimed. Military expedition to South West Africa.

1915 Surrender of the German forces in South West Africa.

1916 Union Expeditionary Force to German East Africa under command of Jan Smuts.

1918 November 11, Armistice. Serious influenza epidemic.

1919 Union granted Mandate over South West Africa. Death of Louis Botha. Smuts Prime Minister.

1920 Strike of 40,000 African miners on Rand.

1921 South African Reserve Bank established. Amalgamation of South African Party and Unionist Party. Postwar depression.

1922 General Strike followed by widespread revolutionary movements in mining districts. Martial Law. Rebellion of Bondelzwart Hottentots in South West Africa.

1924 In parliamentary election, National Party won 63 seats and its ally, the Labour Party, 17 seats. Hertzog Prime Minister.

1925 Afrikaans recognized as second official language.

1926 Hertzog at Imperial Conference in London. Dominions granted equal legal status with Britain.

1929 June 12, at General Election National Party won 18 seats.

1930 Enfranchisement of European women. Quota Act introduced which restricted immigration from certain countries.

1931    Statute of Westminster passed by Imperial Parliament. Union given full freedom of legislation.

1932    On December 29, Union abandoned gold standard. Imperial Conference at Ottawa.

1933    Coalition government of National and South African parties, under Hertzog as Prime Minister.

1935    All-African Convention founded.

1936    Passing of Representation of Natives Act. *"Stem van Suid-Afrika"* National Anthem.

1937    First South African citizen, Sir Patrick Duncan, appointed Governor General.

1938    General election. Centenary celebrations of Great Trek. Foundation stone laid for Voortrekker Monument at Pretoria.

1939    Resignation of Hertzog Cabinet. Smuts Prime Minister. On September 6, Union Parliament, with 80 votes against 67, decided to enter war against Germany.

1942    Death of Hertzog.

1943    Death of Sir Patrick Duncan. Parliamentary election. Majority of 64 seats for United Party. Smuts Prime Minister.

1945    End of hostilities.

1946    Asiatic Land Tenure and Indian Representation Act passed. Strike of 60,000 African miners on Rand.

1948    General election on May 26: National Party 70 seats; its ally, Afrikaner Party, 9 seats; United Party (Opposition) 63 seats; Labour Party (Opposition) 6 seats. D. F. Malan Prime Minister.

1949    Serious rioting in Durban by Zulus against Indians: 142 killed, 1,087 injured. Voortrekker Monument unveiled. Devaluation of sterling. Programme of Action proclaimed by ANC.

1950    Appeal to Privy Council abolished. Death of Jan Smuts.

1951    Amalgamation of National and Afrikaner parties.

1952    Tercentenary celebrations of arrival of Jan van Riebeeck and establishment of first White settlement in Cape. Passive Resistance Movement. African unrest and riots.

1953    April 15, General Election. National Party 94 seats, United Party 57, Labour Party 5, Natives' Representatives 3. Liberal Party founded.

1954    D. F. Malan retired. J. G. Strijdom Prime Minister.

1955    Proclamation of Freedom Charter by Congress Alliance. Senate Act passed.

1956   Johannesburg bus boycott. Cape Coloured disfranchised after five-year constitutional struggle. December 19, preparatory examination began in Johannesburg against 150 persons for alleged treason.

1957   As from April 6, Union Flag hoisted as only flag on all government buildings. May 3, *Die Stem van Suid-Afrika* only National Anthem. November 27, Union withdraws from active participation in United Nations and leaves only token representation.

1958   Treason Trial begins. April 14, a non-White "stay-at-home" protest against the South African General Election fails and the African National Congress calls on supporters to return to work. April 16, White South Africa votes in general election for 12th Parliament. The result: National Party 103 seats, United Party 53 seats, Labour Party eliminated. Death of the Prime Minister J. G. Strijdom. September 2, H. F. Verwoerd chosen as leader by the National Party caucus, thereby becoming Prime Minister. African women protested against extension of "pass laws." Split in the African National Congress. December 18, Basutoland granted a new constitution by Britain, giving the Basutos greater control over their own affairs.

1959   Death of D. F. Malan. Progressive Party and Pan-African Congress (PAC) founded as splinter groups of United Party and African National Congress respectively.

1960   Police massacre at Sharpeville. Nation-wide African revolt. Pondoland uprising. State of Emergency. ANC and PAC banned. Assassination attempt against Verwoerd. Mass arrests.

1961   South Africa became a Republic and withdrew from Commonwealth under pressure from Afro-Asian members. Last vestige of African representation in Parliament abolished. New Nationalist victory in general election. Sabotage acts begin. Army greatly strengthened.

1962   Sabotage acts increased. Mass arrests and repressive measures intensified. Passage of "Sabotage Act."

1963   "No Trial" Act passed. Afro-Asian campaign to expel South Africa from United Nations. Independent African states establish a freedom fund at Addis Ababa conference, and urge use of force against South African government.

1964   "Rivonia" and other sabotage trials. Continued underground activity, and military build-up by government.

1966   Verwoerd assassinated. B. J. Vorster becomes Prime Minister.

## Statistics

TABLE I

Racial Composition of the South African Population
in Thousands (1904–1960)

| Year | Whites | Africans | Asians | Col-oureds | All non-Whites | Total all races |
|------|--------|----------|--------|------------|----------------|-----------------|
| 1904 | 1117 | 3491 | 123 | 445 | 4059 | 5176 |
| 1911 | 1276 | 4019 | 152 | 526 | 4697 | 5973 |
| 1921 | 1519 | 4698 | 166 | 546 | 5409 | 6929 |
| 1936 | 2004 | 6597 | 220 | 770 | 7586 | 9590 |
| 1946 | 2373 | 7832 | 285 | 928 | 9046 | 11,418 |
| 1951 | 2643 | 8535 | 367 | 1103 | 10,005 | 12,648 |
| 1960 | 3088 | 10,908 | 477 | 1509 | 12,894 | 15,982 |
| 1966(est.) | 3500 | 12,500 | 547 | 1800 | 14,847 | 18,347 |

(Sources: *Official Year Book of the Union,* No. 27, 1952–1953, p. 1089;
W. H. Hutt, *The Economics of the Colour Bar,* p. 181; *South African Scope,*
Nov. 1966.)

TABLE II

Racial Groups as Percentage of
Total South African Population (1904–1960)

| Year | Whites | Africans | Asians | Col-oureds | All non-Whites | Total all races |
|------|--------|----------|--------|------------|----------------|-----------------|
| 1904 | 21.6 | 67.4 | 2.4 | 8.6 | 78.4 | 100.0 |
| 1911 | 21.4 | 67.3 | 2.5 | 8.8 | 78.6 | 100.0 |
| 1921 | 21.9 | 67.8 | 2.4 | 7.9 | 78.1 | 100.0 |
| 1936 | 20.9 | 68.8 | 2.3 | 8.0 | 79.1 | 100.0 |
| 1946 | 20.8 | 68.6 | 2.5 | 8.1 | 79.2 | 100.0 |
| 1951 | 20.9 | 67.5 | 2.9 | 8.7 | 79.1 | 100.0 |
| 1960 | 19.4 | 68.2 | 3.0 | 9.4 | 80.6 | 100.0 |
| 1966(est.) | 19.1 | 68.1 | 3.0 | 9.8 | 80.9 | 100.0 |

(Sources: M. H. Alsop, *The Population of Natal,* p. 10; *Official Year Book
of the Union,* No. 27, 1952–1953, p. 1089; *South African Scope,* Nov. 1966.)

TABLE III
*Distribution of South African*
*Population by Province in Thousands* (1904–1960)

| Year | Cape | Natal | Transvaal | O.F.S. | Total |
|------|------|-------|-----------|--------|-------|
| 1904 | 2410 | 1009 | 1270 | 387 | 5176 |
| 1911 | 2565 | 1194 | 1686 | 528 | 5973 |
| 1921 | 2783 | 1429 | 2088 | 629 | 6929 |
| 1936 | 3530 | 1946 | 3341 | 772 | 9590 |
| 1946 | 4046 | 2198 | 4272 | 877 | 11,392 |
| 1951 | 4417 | 2408 | 4802 | 1018 | 12,646 |
| 1960 | 5357 | 2958 | 6281 | 1386 | 15,982 |

(Sources: A. Gordon-Brown, ed., *The Year Book and Guide to Southern Africa*, 1955, p. 69.)

TABLE IV
*Percentage of South African Population*
*Living in Urban Areas by Race* (1921–1951)

| Year | Africans | Europeans | Coloureds | Asians |
|------|----------|-----------|-----------|--------|
| 1921 | 12 | 56 | 46 | 31 |
| 1936 | 17 | 65 | 54 | 66 |
| 1946 | 22 | 73 | 58 | 70 |
| 1951 | 27 | 78 | 64 | 78 |
| 1960 | 32 | 84 | 68 | 83 |

(Sources: *Second Report of the United Nations Commission on the Racial Situation in the Union of South Africa*, 1954, p. 47; W. H. Hutt, *The Economics of the Colour Bar*, p. 181.)

TABLE V
*South African Birth and Death Rates*
*by Race\* (1946–1953)*

| Year | Whites Birth Rate | Whites Death Rate | Coloureds Birth Rate | Coloureds Death Rate | Asians Birth Rate | Asians Death Rate |
|---|---|---|---|---|---|---|
| 1946 | 26.9 | 8.7 | 44.9 | 20.6 | 37.2 | 13.4 |
| 1947 | 27.2 | 8.6 | 45.6 | 20.2 | 40.0 | 12.4 |
| 1948 | 26.5 | 8.9 | 47.1 | 21.2 | 39.0 | 13.0 |
| 1949 | 25.9 | 8.8 | 47.6 | 22.0 | 37.0 | 11.0 |
| 1950 | 25.1 | 8.7 | 46.9 | 20.3 | 38.1 | 11.5 |
| 1951 | 25.0 | 8.8 | 47.9 | 19.7 | 35.5 | 9.7 |
| 1952 | 25.2 | 8.2 | 47.6 | 18.5 | 34.8 | 9.2 |
| 1953 | 25.7 | 8.8 | 48.8 | 18.9 | 34.2 | 10.1 |

\* Accurate figures for Africans are not available.
(Source: *Official Year Book of the Union*, No. 27, 1952–1953, pp. 1124, 1128.)

TABLE VI
*Distribution of African Population*
(1911, 1951)

| | 1911 Number (000's) | 1911 % of Total | 1951 Number (000's) | 1951 % of Total |
|---|---|---|---|---|
| Urban Areas | 510 | 12.7 | 2312 | 27.1 |
| "Native Reserves" | 1768 | 43.9 | 3633 | 42.6 |
| White owned farms | 1750 | 43.4 | 2590 | 30.3 |
| Total | 4028 | 100.0 | 8535 | 100.0 |

(Sources: *Statistical Year Book of the Union of South Africa*, No. 1, 1913, p. 29; *Summary of the Report of the Commission for the Socio-Economic Development of the Bantu-Areas within the Union of South Africa*, p. 27.)

TABLE VII

*Linguistic Distribution of Bantu-Speaking South Africans* (1957 estimates in millions of persons)

| | |
|---|---|
| Xhosa | 2.77 |
| Zulu | 2.46 |
| Northern Sotho | 1.05 |
| Southern Sotho | 1.02 |
| Tswana | 0.78 |
| Tsonga | 0.45 |
| Swazi | 0.33 |
| Ndebele | 0.24 |
| Venda | 0.16 |
| Others | 0.28 |
| Total | 9.54 |

(Source: A. Gordon-Brown, ed., *The Year-Book and Guide to Southern Africa*, 1962, p. 115.)

TABLE VIII

*Countries of Origin of Foreign Africans Residing in South Africa in Percentage of Total* (1957)*

| | |
|---|---|
| Basutoland | 37% |
| Mozambique | 26% |
| Nyasaland | 11% |
| Southern and Northern Rhodesia | 9% |
| Bechuanaland | 8% |
| Swaziland | 6% |
| Other territories | 3% |
| | 100% |

* These percentages were based on a 1957 estimate that 767,370 "foreign Natives" lived in South Africa. More recent estimates have put these figures at over one million.

(Source: *Year-Book and Guide to Southern Africa*, 1962, p. 116.)

TABLE IX

## Number of White Immigrants and
## Emigrants to and from South Africa (1948–1958)

| Year | Immigrants | Emigrants | Gain or Loss |
|------|-----------|-----------|--------------|
| 1948 | 35,631 | 7,534 | +28,097 |
| 1949 | 14,780 | 9,206 | + 5,574 |
| 1950 | 12,803 | 14,644 | − 1,841 |
| 1951 | 15,243 | 15,382 | −   139 |
| 1952 | 18,473 | 9,775 | + 8,698 |
| 1953 | 16,257 | 10,220 | + 6,037 |
| 1954 | 16,416 | 11,336 | + 5,080 |
| 1955 | 16,199 | 12,515 | + 3,684 |
| 1956 | 14,917 | 12,879 | + 2,038 |
| 1957 | 14,615 | 10,943 | + 3,672 |
| 1958 | 14,673 | 8,807 | + 5,866 |

(Source: *State of the Union Year-Book for South Africa*, 1959–1960, p. 81.)

TABLE X
*South African Election Results:*
*Number of Seats Won by Party* (1910–1961)

| Year of Election | 1910 | 1915 | 1920 | 1921 | 1924 | 1929 |
|---|---|---|---|---|---|---|
| Total No. of Seats | 121 | 130 | 134 | 134 | 135 | 148 |
| No. of Seats Won by: | | | | | | |
| South African Party | 66 | 54 | 41 | 77 | 54 | 61 |
| Unionist Party | 38 | 40 | 25 | — | — | — |
| National Party | — | 27 | 43 | 44 | 63 | 77 |
| Labour Party | 4 | 3 | 21 | 10 | 17 | 8 |
| Independent | 13 | 6 | 3 | 1 | 1 | 1 |
| (Vacant Seats) | — | — | 1 | 2 | — | 1 |

| Year of Election | 1933 | 1938 | 1943 | 1948 | 1953 | 1958 | 1961 |
|---|---|---|---|---|---|---|---|
| Total No. of Seats | 150 | 153 | 153 | 153 | 159 | 163 | 156 |
| No. of Seats Won by: | | | | | | | |
| National Party | 75 | 27 | 43 | 70 | 94 | 103 | 105 |
| South African Party | 61 | — | — | — | — | — | — |
| United Party | — | 111 | 89 | 65 | 57 | 53 | 49 |
| Labour Party | 4 | 3 | 9 | 6 | 5 | — | — |
| Roos Party | 2 | — | — | — | — | — | — |
| Dominion Party | — | 8 | 7 | — | — | — | — |
| Home Rule Party | 2 | — | — | — | — | — | — |
| Socialist Party | — | 1 | — | — | — | — | — |
| Natives' Representatives | — | 3 | 3 | 3 | 3 | 3 | — |
| Coloureds' Representatives | — | — | — | — | — | 4 | — |
| Independent | 6 | — | 2 | — | — | — | — |
| Afrikaner Party | — | — | — | 9 | — | — | — |
| National Union | — | — | — | — | — | — | 1 |
| Progressive Party | — | — | — | — | — | — | 1 |

(Sources: *State of the Union Year-Book for South Africa*, 1959–1960, pp. 38–39; *The Natal Mercury*, Oct. 20, 1961.)

TABLE XI
*South African Election Results:*
*Number of Votes Cast by Party* (1910–1961)

| Year of Election | 1910 | 1915 | 1920 | 1921 | 1924 | 1929 |
|---|---|---|---|---|---|---|
| Number of Registered Voters | — | 365,307 | 421,790 | 499,531 | 413,136 | 461,820 |
| Total No. of Votes Polled | — | 261,433 | 282,361 | 277,742 | 319,047 | 347,924 |
| Total Vote Polled by: South African Party | — | 94,285 | 90,512 | 137,389 | 148,769 | 159,896 |
| Unionist Party | — | 49,917 | 38,946 | — | — | — |
| National Party | — | 75,623 | 101,227 | 105,039 | 111,483 | 141,579 |
| Labour Party | — | 24,755 | 40,639 | 29,406 | 45,380 | 33,919 |
| Socialist Party | — | 140 | 202 | — | — | — |
| Independent | — | 12,383 | 5,986 | 3,385 | 10,610 | 8,503 |
| (Spoilt Papers) | — | 4,330 | 4,876 | — | — | — |

(Sources: *State of the Union Year-Book for South Africa,* 1959–1960, pp. 38–39; *The Natal Mercury,* Oct. 20, 1961.)

TABLE XI (cont.)

| Year of Election | 1933 | 1938 | 1943 | 1948 |
|---|---|---|---|---|
| Number of Registered Voters | 957,636 | 1,052,652 | 1,114,110 | 1,337,534 |
| Total No. of Votes Polled | 323,417 | 835,378 | 885,623 | 1,073,364 |
| Total Votes Polled by: | | | | |
| National Party | 101,159 | 259,543 | 321,601 | 401,834 |
| South African Party | 71,486 | — | — | — |
| United Party | — | 446,032 | 435,297 | 524,230 |
| Labour Party | 20,276 | 48,641 | 38,206 | 27,360 |
| Afrikaner Party | — | — | 15,601 | 41,885 |
| Dominion Party | — | 52,356 | 29,023 | — |
| Roos Party | 27,441 | — | — | — |
| Home Rule Party | 12,328 | — | — | — |
| Socialist Party | — | 4,963 | 6,350 | — |
| Independent | 87,321 | 17,362 | 30,185 | — |
| Others | — | — | — | 70,662 |
| (Spoilt Papers) | 3,406 | 6,481 | 9,360 | 7,393 |

| Year of Election | 1953 | 1958 | 1961 |
|---|---|---|---|
| Number of Registered Voters | 1,385,591 | 1,530,000 | 1,823,883 |
| Total No. of Votes Polled | 1,218,631 | 1,156,069 | 797,645 |
| Total Votes Polled by: | | | |
| National Party | 598,718 | 642,069 | 370,431 |
| United Party | 576,474 | 503,639 | 286,124 |
| Labour Party | 34,730 | 2,670 | — |
| Liberal Party | — | 2,934 | 2,461 |
| Independent | — | — | 10,085 |
| Others | — | 4,757 | 9,173 |
| National Union | — | — | 50,329 |
| Progressive Party | — | — | 69,042 |
| (Spoilt Papers) | 8,709 | — | — |

TABLE XII
*Number of Convictions (in Thousands)*
*by Race and Seriousness of Offence (1952)*

|  | All races | Whites | Africans | Asians | Coloureds |
|---|---|---|---|---|---|
| Non-serious crime | 1,095 | 146 | 823 | 24 | 103 |
| Serious crime | 69 | 11 | 45 | 1 | 11 |
| Total | 1,154 | 157 | 868 | 25 | 114 |

(Source: *Official Year-Book of the Union,* No. 27, 1952–1953, p. 445.)

TABLE XIII
*Sentences Imposed for Serious Crimes, South Africa (1952)*

| Sentence | Europeans | Africans | Asians & Coloureds |
|---|---|---|---|
| Fined only | 4,058 | 2,164 | 801 |
| Prison without option | 976 | 20,112 | 4,977 |
| Prison with option | 3,815 | 12,147 | 2,751 |
| Suspended sentence | 879 | 1,465 | 637 |
| Corporal punishment | 422 | 7,893 | 2,992 |
| Death | 2 | 67 | 14 |
| Other | 421 | 1,410 | 443 |
| Total convictions | 10,573 | 45,258 | 12,615 |

(Source: *Official Year-Book of the Union,* No. 27, 1952–1953, pp. 447–448.)

**TABLE XIV**
*Religious Affiliation of South African*
*Population by Race* (1951)

| Religion | Total No. of adherents | White | Col- oured | Asian | African |
|---|---|---|---|---|---|
| CHRISTIAN- | | | | | |
| DUTCH REFORMED | | | | | |
| N. G. Kerk | 1,696,127 | 42.0 | 26.4 | — | 3.5 |
| Hervormde | 213,845 | 7.0 | 0.9 | — | 0.3 |
| Gereformeerde | 144,384 | 4.2 | 2.2 | — | 0.1 |
| CHRISTIAN- | | | | | |
| ENGLISH-SPEAKING | | | | | |
| SWISS, FRENCH, | | | | | |
| GERMAN, ETC. | | | | | |
| Methodist | 1,363,958 | 8.3 | 9.2 | 0.5 | 12.2 |
| Anglican | 1,230,509 | 15.8 | 20.8 | 1.3 | 6.8 |
| Roman Catholic | 784,414 | 5.3 | 6.6 | 2.1 | 5.4 |
| Lutheran | 499,336 | 1.0 | 5.2 | — | 4.9 |
| Presbyterian | 276,997 | 3.8 | 0.3 | — | 2.0 |
| Apostolic | 268,715 | 2.9 | 3.5 | 0.2 | 1.8 |
| Congregational | 247,452 | 0.5 | 10.2 | — | 1.4 |
| Baptist | 113,360 | 1.0 | 0.7 | 0.5 | 0.9 |
| Other | 282,671 | 3.0 | 5.5 | 1.6 | 1.6 |
| CHRISTIAN- | | | | | |
| Native Separatist | 1,594,740 | — | 0.1 | — | 18.6 |
| JEWISH | 108,743 | 4.1 | — | — | — |
| ASIAN RELIGIONS | | | | | |
| Hindu | 246,820 | — | — | 67.2 | — |
| Islamic | 146,829 | — | 5.7 | 21.5 | 0.1 |
| Other | 2,501 | — | — | 0.6 | — |
| OTHER BELIEFS | 46,755 | 0.2 | 0.3 | 2.0 | 0.4 |
| NO RELIGION OR | | | | | |
| "HEATHEN" | 3,405,348 | 0.5 | 1.4 | 1.2 | 39.4 |
| UNSPECIFIED | 98,358 | 0.4 | 0.9 | 1.3 | 0.6 |

(Source: Muriel Horrell, *A Survey of Race Relations in South Africa,*
1959–1960, p. 27.)

TABLE XV
*Summary of South African Educational
Statistics by Race* (1910–1950)

|  | Year | Population (in thousands) | Total No. in school (in thousands) | % getting post-primary education | Total State Expend. (in £ millions) |
|---|---|---|---|---|---|
| Whites | 1910 | 1256 | 165 | 10.8 | 1.6 |
|  | 1920 | 1500 | 314 | 13.4 | 6.3 |
|  | 1930 | 1798 | 371 | 16.0 | 8.4 |
|  | 1940 | 2153 | 416 | 21.2 | 10.7 |
|  | 1950 | 2620 | 507 | 22.0 | 25.4 |
| Africans | 1910 | 3953 | 186 | — | 0.1 |
|  | 1920 | 4630 | 185 | 1.5 | 0.3 |
|  | 1930 | 5858 | 287 | 1.5 | 0.6 |
|  | 1940 | 7116 | 471 | 2.6 | 1.0 |
|  | 1950 | 8347 | 767 | 4.2 | 5.8 |
| Coloureds & Asians | 1920 | 707 | 56 | — | — |
|  | 1930 | 880 | 100 | 1.44 | 0.5 |
|  | 1940 | 1069 | 175 | 3.05 | 1.0 |
|  | 1950 | 1353 | 266 | 3.66 | 4.7 |

(Source: A. Gordon-Brown, ed., *The Year-Book and Guide to Southern Africa*, 1955, p. 120.)

**TABLE XVI**
*Annual State Expenditures for Education
in Pounds per Pupil* (1940, 1950, 1962)

| Race of Pupil | 1940 | 1950 | 1962 |
|---|---|---|---|
| Whites | 26.4 | 50.1 | 65.0 |
| Asians & Coloureds | 5.7 | 17.4 | — |
| Africans | 2.2 | 7.6 | 6.4 |

(Sources: A. Gordon-Brown, ed., *The Year-Book and Guide to Southern Africa,* 1955, p. 109; *Africa Today,* 11, March, 1964, p. 1.)

**TABLE XVII**
*Number of Students Enrolled at South African
Universities by Race* (1957)

| | Whites | Africans | Coloureds | Asians |
|---|---|---|---|---|
| Cape Town | 4,326 | 29 | 306 | 121 |
| Natal | 2,309 | 181 | 24 | 350 |
| Orange Free State | 1,651 | — | — | — |
| Potchefstroom | 1,374 | — | — | — |
| Pretoria | 5,858 | — | — | — |
| Rhodes | 921 | — | — | — |
| Stellenbosch | 3,335 | — | — | — |
| Witwatersrand | 4,463 | 59 | 20 | 135 |
| University of South Africa | 5,538 | 1,085 | 209 | 565 |
| Fort Hare | — | 283 | 48 | 47 |
| Total | 29,775 | 1,637 | 607 | 1,218 |

(Source: *State of the Union Year-Book for South Africa,* 1959–1960, p. 121.)

TABLE XVIII
*Distribution of Geographic National
Income in South Africa* (1912–1958)

| Item | 1912 | 1918 | 1928 | 1938 | 1946 | 1949 | 1958 |
|---|---|---|---|---|---|---|---|
| **Per cent of total in:** | | | | | | | |
| Farming & Fishing | 16.1 | 21.6 | 18.2 | 12.0 | 12.0 | 14.2 | 12.3 |
| Mining | 27.5 | 20.3 | 18.6 | 19.5 | 13.6 | 10.7 | 12.9 |
| Manufacturing | 6.8 | 9.6 | 13.2 | 17.6 | 20.1 | 22.4 | 24.5 |
| Trade | 13.8 | 15.6 | 15.7 | 13.8 | 15.0 | 14.5 | 12.5 |
| Finance | — | — | 2.1 | 3.0 | 2.4 | 2.4 | 3.6 |
| Transportation | 7.6 | 5.7 | 6.4 | 6.7 | 5.4 | 8.6 | 8.1 |
| Other | 28.3 | 27.2 | 25.7 | 27.3 | 31.4 | 27.1 | 26.1 |
| Total (£ Millions) | 130.9 | 170.9 | 270.3 | 373.6 | 703.8 | 898.2 | 1988.1 |
| National Income at 1938 prices (£ Mil.) | 163.6 | 165.9 | 252.6 | 382.4 | 523.5 | 577.9 | n.a. |
| Per capita Income at 1938 prices (£) | 27.2 | 25.2 | 31.5 | 38.9 | 46.2 | 48.5 | n.a. |

(Sources: J. C. Du Plessis, *Economic Fluctuations in South Africa,* p. 21;
and *State of the Union Year-Book for South Africa,* 1959–1960, p. 306.)

TABLE XIX
### The Flow of Private Capital into (+)
### and out of (—) South Africa (1950–1960)

| | Private capital (net) in £ million |
|---|---|
| 1950 | +67 |
| 1951 | +78 |
| 1952 | +60 |
| 1953 | +50 |
| 1954 | +76 |
| 1955 | +11 |
| 1956 | + 9 |
| 1957 | —30 |
| 1958 | +21 |
| 1959 | —24 |
| 1960 | —97 |

(Source: Heinz Hartmann, *Enterprise and Politics in South Africa,* p. 20.)

TABLE XX
### South African Imports and Exports in
### £ Millions (1938–1958)*

| Year | Imports | Exports (excluding gold) | Trade Balance (excluding gold) | Gold | Trade Balance (including gold) |
|---|---|---|---|---|---|
| 1938 | 95.8 | 33.7 | — 62.1 | 73.4 | + 11.3 |
| 1948 | 352.8 | 137.9 | —214.9 | 242.1 | + 27.2 |
| 1950 | 304.1 | 218.2 | — 85.9 | 121.9 | + 36.0 |
| 1951 | 466.8 | 288.4 | —178.4 | 152.4 | — 26.0 |
| 1952 | 416.9 | 285.6 | —131.3 | 158.9 | + 27.6 |
| 1953 | 424.3 | 296.3 | —128.0 | 150.5 | + 22.5 |
| 1954 | 439.0 | 331.5 | —107.5 | 156.4 | + 49.0 |
| 1955 | 482.2 | 369.1 | —113.1 | 178.1 | + 65.0 |
| 1956 | 494.9 | 412.2 | — 82.7 | 193.2 | +110.6 |
| 1957 | 549.8 | 451.7 | — 98.1 | 216.9 | +118.8 |
| 1958 | 556.8 | 390.5 | —166.3 | 221.9 | + 55.6 |

* Figures include South West Africa and the High Commission Territories.

(Source: *State of the Union Year-Book for South Africa,* 1959–1960, p. 284.)

TABLE XXI
*Percentage of Total South African Imports
and Exports by Country* (1957, 1958)*

|  | Imports | | Exports | |
|---|---|---|---|---|
|  | 1957 % | 1958 % | 1957 % | 1958 % |
| United Kingdom | 32.6 | 33.7 | 27.7 | 30.3 |
| United States | 19.6 | 17.5 | 6.4 | 7.2 |
| Germany | 8.1 | 10.6 | 5.1 | 4.0 |
| Italy | 1.9 | 2.1 | 4.3 | 4.2 |
| France | 1.8 | 1.8 | 3.8 | 3.0 |
| Netherlands | 2.0 | 2.0 | 2.9 | 2.2 |
| Belgium | 2.2 | 1.7 | 4.6 | 3.8 |
| Japan | 3.2 | 2.5 | 2.3 | 1.4 |
| Sweden | 1.9 | 1.8 | 0.6 | 0.6 |
| Commonwealth and Ireland | 45.0 | 45.4 | 47.8 | 50.6 |
| Other Foreign Countries | 54.9 | 54.5 | 52.1 | 49.4 |

* Gold is excluded from export figures.

(Source: *State of the Union Year-Book for South Africa,* 1959–1960, p. 287.)

TABLE XXII

Distribution of South African National Income, Composition of Population, and Ratio in Per Capita Earnings (Africans = 1.0) by Race (1936, 1954, 1960)

| | Whites | | | Africans | | | Asians & Coloureds | | | Total | | |
|---|---|---|---|---|---|---|---|---|---|---|---|---|
| | 1936 | 1954 | 1960 | 1936 | 1954 | 1960 | 1936 | 1954 | 1960 | 1936 | 1954 | 1960 |
| % of Nat. Income received by | 74.5 | 74.5 | 67.0 | 19.6 | 19.2 | 26.5 | 5.8 | 6.3 | 6.5 | 99.9* | 100.0 | 100.0 |
| % of Total Population constituted by | 20.9 | 20.4 | 19.3 | 68.8 | 67.7 | 68.4 | 10.3 | 11.9 | 12.4 | 100.0 | 100.0 | 100.1* |
| Ratio in Per Capita Earnings (Africans =1.0) | 12.5 | 12.7 | 9.0 | 1.0 | 1.0 | 1.0 | 2.0 | 1.9 | 1.4 | — | — | — |

* Percentages do not add up to 100 because of rounding errors.
(Sources: Investment in Union of South Africa, p. 8; F. P. Spooner, South African Predicament, p. 173; Report of the Special Committee on the Policies of Apartheid of the Government of the Republic of South Africa, p. 101.)

TABLE XXIII

*Comparison of Living Conditions of the Different Population Groups in South Africa* (1938–1939, 1953–1954)

|  | Whites | Asians & Coloureds | Africans |
|---|---|---|---|
| Average family income 1938/9 | £ 530 | £ 134 | £ 50.1 |
| Average family income 1953/4 | £ 1,616 | £ 308 | £ 119.2 |
| Rise in living costs over 15 years 1938/9 to 1953/4 | 108% | 108% | 152%* |
| Average family income 1953/4 in 1938/9 pounds | £ 777 | £ 148 | £ 47.3 |
| Changes in purchasing power of family income over 15 years | + £ 247 | + £ 14 | − £ 2.8 |
| Percentage increase (+) or decrease (−) in living standard | + 46% | + 11% | − 6.5% |

* The increase in the cost of living is relatively higher for Africans than for other racial groups, largely because of the disproportionate rise in the price of staple African foods.

(Source: F. P. Spooner, *South African Predicament*, pp. 284–285.)

TABLE XXIV

### Ratio of White to Non-White Wages in Secondary Industry, South Africa (1915–1953)

| Year | Ratio | Year | Ratio | Year | Ratio |
|------|-------|------|-------|------|-------|
| 1915–16 | 4.84 | 1927–28 | 4.16 | 1939–45 | n.a. |
| 1916–17 | 4.90 | 1928–29 | 4.08 | 1946–47 | 3.54 |
| 1917–18 | 4.76 | 1929–30 | 4.10 | 1947–48 | 3.63 |
| 1918–19 | 4.76 | 1930–31 | n.a. | 1948–49 | 3.71 |
| 1919–20 | 4.84 | 1931–32 | n.a. | 1949–50 | 3.87 |
| 1920–21 | 5.13 | 1932–33 | 4.02 | 1950–51 | 3.94 |
| 1921–22 | 5.11 | 1933–34 | 4.14 | 1951–52 | n.a. |
| 1922–23 | 4.75 | 1934–35 | 4.29 | 1952–53 | 4.15 |
| 1923–24 | 4.72 | 1935–36 | 4.38 | 1958–59 | 4.80 |
| 1924–25 | 4.55 | 1936–37 | 4.30 | 1959–60 | 4.74 |
| 1925–26 | 4.37 | 1937–38 | n.a. | 1960–61 | 4.71 |
| 1926–27 | 4.29 | 1938–39 | 4.36 | | |

(Sources: *Investment in Union of South Africa*, p. 105; J. M. Tinley, *The Native Labour Problem of South Africa*, pp. 123, 128.)

TABLE XXV

### Percentage Constituted by Each Racial Group in Total Labour Force of Major South African Industries (1946)

| | Whites | Coloureds | Asians | Africans | Total |
|------|--------|-----------|--------|----------|-------|
| Agriculture | 6.9 | 3.9 | 0.5 | 88.6 | 99.9%° |
| Mining | 4.2 | 0.4 | 0.1 | 95.3 | 100.0% |
| Sec. Industry | 28.0 | 14.8 | 3.1 | 54.0 | 99.9%° |
| Commerce | 84.6 | 2.6 | 7.6 | 5.2 | 100.0% |
| Pers. Service | 4.0 | 10.7 | 1.0 | 84.3 | 100.0% |
| Transport | 37.6 | 9.1 | 1.8 | 51.5 | 100.0% |
| Professions | 69.6 | 5.9 | 1.2 | 23.4 | 100.1%° |
| All above | 16.9 | 6.4 | 1.4 | 75.3 | 100.0% |

° Percentages do not add up to 100 because of rounding errors.

(Source: M. H. Alsop, *The Population of Natal*, p. 128.)

TABLE XXVI

*Occupational Distribution of South
Africans over 15 Years of Age by Race
in Percentages* (1946)

|  | Whites | Coloureds | Asians | Africans |
|---|---|---|---|---|
| Agriculture | 10.2 | 17.8 | 8.6 | 37.2 |
| Mining | 1.2 | 0.4 | 0.2 | 7.4 |
| Sec. Industry | 12.1 | 19.7 | 14.6 | 6.7 |
| Commerce | 12.7 | 1.2 | 12.4 | 0.2 |
| Personal Service | 1.7 | 14.4 | 4.9 | 10.5 |
| Transport | 5.2 | 3.9 | 2.7 | 2.0 |
| Professions | 7.9 | 2.0 | 1.5 | 0.8 |
| Other | 2.6 | 5.5 | 6.9 | 2.0 |
| Dependent and Independent | 46.4 | 35.0 | 48.1 | 33.1 |
| Total | 100.0% | 99.9%° | 99.9%° | 99.9%° |

° Percentages do not add up to 100 because of rounding errors.
(Source: M. H. Alsop, *The Population of Natal,* p. 120.)

TABLE XXVII

*Percentage of South African Industrial
Workers of Each Race in Various Skill
Levels* (1951)

|  | Skilled | Semi-Skilled | Unskilled |
|---|---|---|---|
| Whites | 85 | 30 | 1 |
| Africans | 5 | 40 | 85 |
| Coloureds & Asians | 10 | 30 | 14 |
| Total | 100% | 100% | 100% |

(Source: *Summary of the Report of the Commission for the Socio-
Economic Development of the Bantu-Areas within the Union of South
Africa,* p. 36.)

TABLE XXVIII
*Percentage of South African Manual Workers of Each Racial Group in Various Skill Levels*

| | Whites | | | |
|---|---|---|---|---|
| | 1947 | 1950 | 1955 | 1956 |
| Skilled | 81.4 | 82.5 | 86.1 | 86.4 |
| Semi-skilled | 16.5 | 15.5 | 12.7 | 12.5 |
| Unskilled | 2.1 | 2.0 | 1.2 | 1.1 |
| Total | 100.0 | 100.0 | 100.0 | 100.0 |

| | Africans | | | |
|---|---|---|---|---|
| | 1947 | 1950 | 1955 | 1956 |
| Skilled | 4.1 | 4.2 | 4.6 | 5.2 |
| Semi-skilled | 12.7 | 12.2 | 15.4 | 15.0 |
| Unskilled | 83.2 | 83.6 | 80.0 | 79.8 |
| Total | 100.0 | 100.0 | 100.0 | 100.0 |

| | Coloureds | | | |
|---|---|---|---|---|
| | 1947 | 1950 | 1955 | 1956 |
| Skilled | 14.5 | 15.2 | 18.1 | 19.2 |
| Semi-skilled | 30.7 | 29.8 | 30.9 | 30.1 |
| Unskilled | 54.8 | 55.0 | 51.0 | 50.7 |
| Total | 100.0 | 100.0 | 100.0 | 100.0 |

| | Asians | | | |
|---|---|---|---|---|
| | 1947 | 1950 | 1955 | 1956 |
| Skilled | 31.9 | 33.0 | 37.4 | 38.6 |
| Semi-skilled | 32.2 | 31.4 | 30.9 | 30.2 |
| Unskilled | 35.9 | 35.6 | 31.7 | 31.2 |
| Total | 100.0 | 100.0 | 100.0 | 100.0 |

(Sources: *Report of the Department of Labour;* Muriel Horrell, *A Survey of Race Relations in South Africa,* 1953, p. 76, and 1957, pp. 176–177.)

TABLE XXIX
*Distribution of African Pupils by School Grade, 1958*

|  | No. of pupils (in thousands) | Percentage of Total |
|---|---|---|
| Sub-Standards |  |  |
| A & B | 609.3 | 45.2 |
| Standard I | 218.2 | 16.2 |
| Standard II | 163.8 | 12.2 |
| Standard III | 128.4 | 9.5 |
| Standard IV | 80.0 | 5.9 |
| Standard V | 59.0 | 4.4 |
| Standard VI | 46.3 | 3.4 |
| Standard VII | 30.0 | 2.2 |
| Standard VIII | 8.8 | 0.7 |
| Standard IX | 1.8 | 0.1 |
| Standard X | 0.9 | 0.1 |
|  | 1346.5 | 99.9* |

* Percentage does not add up to 100.0 because of rounding errors.
(Source: *Report of the Special Committee on the Policies of Apartheid of the Government of the Republic of South Africa,* p. 95.)

TABLE XXX
*Estimates of Expenditure for Defence and Police*
( £ Million )

|  | 1960–61 | 1961–62 | 1962–63 | 1963–64 |
|---|---|---|---|---|
| Defence | 21.8 | 35.8 | 59.9 | 78.5 |
| Police | 18.1 | 19.2 | 20.4 | 25.4 |
| Total | 39.9 | 55.0 | 80.3 | 103.9 |

(Source: *Report of the Special Committee on the Policies of Apartheid of the Government of the Republic of South Africa,* p. 120.)

## International Resolutions Concerning Human Rights in South Africa*

DOCUMENT No. 1: *Resolution on Racialism Adopted by the First Conference of Independent African States, Accra, April 1958*

The Conference of Independent African States,

Considering that the practice of racial discrimination and segregation is evil and inhuman,

Deeply convinced that racialism is a negation of the basic principles of human rights and dignity to the extent where it is becoming an element of such explosiveness which is spreading its poisonous influence more and more widely in some parts of Africa that it may well engulf our Continent in violence and bloodshed,

Noting with abhorrence the recent statement made by the head of the South African Government on his re-election to the effect that he will pursue a more relentless policy of discrimination and persecution of the coloured people in South Africa,

1. Condemns the practice of racial discrimination and segregation in all its aspects all over the world, especially in the Union of South Africa, in the Central African Federation, Kenya, and in other parts of Africa;

2. Appeals to the religious bodies and spiritual leaders of the world to support all efforts directed towards the eradication of racialism and segregation;

3. Calls upon all members of the United Nations and all peoples of the world to associate themselves with the Resolutions passed by the United Nations and the Bandung Conference condemning this inhuman practice;

4. Calls upon all members of the United Nations to intensify their efforts to combat and eradicate this degrading form of injustice;

* Source: Colin Legum, *Pan-Africanism*, pp. 142–254.

5. Recommends that all Participating Governments should take vigorous measures to eradicate where they arise vestiges of racial discrimination in their respective countries.

DOCUMENT NO. 2: *Resolution on Racial Discrimination Adopted by the Monrovia Conference of Foreign Ministers of Independent African States, August 1959.*

The Conference of Independent African States,

Deeply convinced that the practice of racial discrimination and segregation is evil and inhuman and diametrically opposed to the provisions of the Universal Declaration of Human Rights,

Considering that racialism is a threat to international peace and security wherever it is practiced,

Noting with concern the relentless manner in which the Government of South Africa is putting into practice its apartheid policy,

1. Condemns the practice of racial discrimination and segregation in all of its aspects all over the world, especially in the Union of South Africa, in the Central African Federation, in Kenya, and in other parts of Africa.

2. Calls upon all members of the United Nations and all peoples of the world to associate themselves with the resolutions passed by the United Nations and the Bandung and Accra Conferences condemning this inhuman practice.

3. Recommends that the different Governments take such measures as to contribute effectively to persuade the Union of South Africa to implement the resolutions of the United Nations on racial questions.

DOCUMENT NO. 3: *Resolution on South Africa Adopted by the Second All-African Peoples Conference, Tunis, Jan. 1960.*

The Second All-African Peoples Conference, having examined the situation in South Africa which has only worsened, urges the African peoples and Trade Unions as well as the Governments of the Independent African States to organize a boycott of goods from South Africa and South-West Africa

Instructs the Secretariat of the Conference to take all effective measures for the practical application of this decision.

DOCUMENT NO. 4: *Resolution on the Policy of Apartheid and Racial Discrimination in Africa Adopted by the Second Conference of Independent African States, Addis Ababa, June 1960.*

The Conference of Independent African States meeting in Addis Ababa,

Having learned with indignation of the death of many African political leaders in the prisons of the Union of South Africa, thus adding to the already long list of victims of the shameful policy of racial discrimination;

Recalling resolution No. 1375 (XIV) adopted by the United Nations General Assembly, condemning the policy of apartheid and racial discrimination practised by the Government of the Union of South Africa;

Recalling further the Security Council's Resolution of April 1, 1960, recognising the existence of a situation in South Africa which, if continued, might endanger international peace and security;

Reaffirming the declaration of Bandung and the resolutions adopted at Accra and Monrovia regarding this shameful policy;

Noting that, despite world opinion and the resolutions adopted by the United Nations, the Government of the Union of South Africa still persists in its evil policy of apartheid and racial discrimination;

1. Desires to pay homage to all victims of the shameful policy of apartheid and racial discrimination;

2. Decides to assist the victims of racial discrimination and furnish them with all the means necessary to attain their political objectives of liberty and democracy;

3. Calls upon Member States to sever diplomatic relations or refrain from establishing diplomatic relations as the case may be, to close African ports to all vessels flying the South African flag, to enact legislation prohibiting their ships from entering South African ports, to boycott all South African goods, to refuse landing and passage facilities to all aircraft belonging to the Government and companies registered under the laws of the Union of South Africa and to prohibit all South African aircraft from flying over the air-space of the Independent African States;

4. Invites the Arab States to approach all petroleum companies with a view to preventing Arab oil from being sold to the Union of South Africa and recommends that the African States refuse any concession to any company which continues to sell petroleum to the Union of South Africa;

5. Invites the Independent African States which are members of the British Commonwealth to take all possible steps to secure the exclusion of the Union of South Africa from the British Commonwealth;

6. Recommends that appropriate measures be taken by the United Nations in accordance with Article 41 of the Charter;

7. Appeals to world public opinion to persevere in the effort to put an end to the terrible situation caused by apartheid and racial discrimination;

8. Decides to instruct the Informal Permanent Machinery to take all steps necessary to secure that effect shall be given to the above recommendations and to furnish full information on cases of racial discrimination in the Union of South Africa, so that the outside world may be correctly informed about such practices.

DOCUMENT No. 5: *Resolution on Apartheid and Racial Discrimination Adopted by the Casablanca Conference, January 1961.*

The Casablanca Conference,

Recalling the resolutions of the United Nations Organisation which denounced the Apartheid policy and the racial discrimination practised by the Government of the Union of South Africa, and

Recalling in particular the resolution of the Security Council of the 1st of April, 1960, which considers the policy of racial discrimination pursued by the Government of the Union of South Africa as a threat to world peace and security,

1. Denounces the Government of the Union of South Africa for its contempt of the decisions taken by the United Nations Organisation and by the African and Asian Conferences and condemns its obstinacy in pursuing a policy which affects human dignity and constitutes a flagrant violation of human rights;

2. Denounces the imperialist Powers who continue to lend moral, political and military support to the racialist Government of the Union of South Africa;

3. Reaffirms and undertakes to implement and decisions taken at the Bandung, Accra, Monrovia and Addis Ababa conferences on this subject and urges all African States to implement these decisions;

4. Calls upon the United Nations Organisation to invoke the sanctions provided for in Articles 40 and 41 of the United Nations Charter should the Government of the Union of South Africa not put an end to its policy of racial discrimination.

DOCUMENT No. 6: *Resolution on South-West Africa Adopted by the Third All-African Peoples Conference, Cairo, March 1961*

The Third All-African Peoples Conference emphatically condemns the Government of the Union of South Africa and its policies in South-West Africa,

Demands that the South African Administration quits the territory of South-West Africa forthwith,

Energetically calls on the United Nations to act against South Africa with uncompromising firmness and utmost immediacy,

Calls on the African Independent States to take the initiative in S.-W. Africa by actively backing the entrance of the Committee on S.W.A. into S.W.A.,

Calls on the African States to press for and impose sanctions on South Africa, economic, diplomatic and otherwise,

Calls on all freedom-loving countries of the world to condemn British UN policy towards the South-West Africa issue.

DOCUMENT NO. 7: *Resolution on South Africa Adopted by the Third All-African Peoples Conference, Cairo, March 1961.*

1. The Third All-African Peoples Conference,

Noting with concern that the vicious economic exploitation, brutal political oppression and savage social degradation of the oppressed majority of the people of South Africa by the colonial Government of South Africa and by colonial imperialist interests continues unabated;

Noting, also, with dismay the sinister determination of the colonial Government of South Africa and imperialist interests to prevent at all cost the takeover by governments of the majority;

Noting further, with jubilation the virtual expulsion of the colonial government of South Africa from membership of the Commonwealth,

The Conference resolves as follows:

(a) Condemns all foreign and colonial investors who continue to allow the investors and landed industrial and commercial interests to be used for the exploitation, oppression and degradation of the indigenous people and other oppressed minorities, and for the prevention of a peaceful takeover by the people of South Africa;

(b) Deplores and deprecates investment and landed industrial and commercial interests by outsiders, because by so doing they become parties in the exploitation, oppression and degradation of the people of South Africa;

(c) Urges that no members of the Commonwealth Prime Ministers' Conference should have any practical relations with South Africa as formerly exercised before the withdrawal of South Africa from the Commonwealth;

(d) Calls on the Afro-Asian Group in the United Nations to press for the earliest expulsion of South Africa from that organisation.

2. The Conference further resolves as follows:

Appeals to all Independent African States and other freedom-loving countries of the world to:

(i) Sever diplomatic relations with South Africa;

(ii) Close all their ports to South African vessels and any other vessels registered in terms of the laws of that country;

(iii) Prevent their own ships from entering South African ports;

(iv) Boycott South African goods;

(v) Refuse landing and passage facilities to all aircraft belonging to the South African Government and companies registered under the laws of that country;

(vi) Appeals to PAFMECA and other African territories to endeavour to prevent and halt labour supply from reaching the mines and factories of the Union;

(vii) Urges the Trade Union Movement and workers in Africa and throughout the world to refuse to handle cargo to and from South Africa;

(viii) Welcomes the move for barring South Africa from the Federation of International Football Associations, and urges the formation of the All-African Sports Federation.

# Selected Bibliography

For a more complete bibliography of journal articles and unpublished M.A. and Ph.D. theses dealing with South Africa, see Monica Wilson, "Recent Research on Race Relations," and Pierre L. van den Berghe, "Some Trends in Unpublished Social Science Research in South Africa."

## PERIODICAL PUBLICATIONS

*Africa.* London (quarterly).
*Africa Institute, International Bulletin.* Pretoria (monthly).
*Africa Report.* Washington (monthly).
*Africa South.* Johannesburg (quarterly).
*Africa Today.* New York, American Committee on Africa (bi-monthly).
*African Digest.* London, The Africa Bureau (bi-monthly).
*African Studies* (formerly *Bantu Studies*). Johannesburg (quarterly).
*African World.* London (monthly).
*Africana Nova, A Quarterly Bibliography of Books Currently Published in and about the Union of South Africa.* Cape Town, South African Public Library (quarterly).
*Bantu.* Pretoria (monthly).
*Bantu Education Journal.* Pretoria (monthly).
*Bantu Studies.* See *African Studies.*
*Cahiers d'Etudes Africaines.* Paris (quarterly).
*Civilisations.* Brussels (quarterly).
*The Forum.* Johannesburg (monthly).
*Government Gazette.* Pretoria (weekly).

*Journal of Racial Affairs.* Stellenbosch, South African Bureau of Racial Affairs (quarterly).

*The New African.* Cape Town (monthly).

*Optima.* Johannesburg (quarterly).

*Quarterly Bulletin of the South African Library.* Cape Town (quarterly).

*Race Relations Journal.* Johannesburg (quarterly).

*The South African Financial Year Book.* Cape Town, Beerman (annual).

*South African Scope.* Pretoria (bi-monthly).

Muriel Horrell, *A Survey of Race Relations in South Africa.* Johannesburg, South African Institute of Race Relations (annual).

*Thought.* Johannesburg, South African Institute of Race Relations (quarterly).

*The Year Book and Guide to Southern Africa.* London, Hale (annual).

INDIVIDUAL PUBLICATIONS (*articles, books, official reports, pamphlets, theses, etc.*)

Peter Abrahams, *The Path of Thunder.* New York, Harper, 1948.

———, *Tell Freedom.* New York, Knopf, 1954.

———, *Wild Conquest.* London, Faber and Faber, 1951.

Adamastor, *White Man Boss.* London, Gollancz, 1950.

*The African Factory Worker.* Cape Town, London, and New York, Oxford University Press, 1950.

*African Farm Labour.* Johannesburg, South African Institute of Race Relations, 1959.*

*L'Afrique du Sud et la Primauté du Droit.* Geneva, Commission Internationale de Juristes, 1961.

J. A. I. Agar-Hamilton, *The Native Policy of the Voortrekkers, 1836–1858.* Cape Town, Maskew Miller, 1928.

R. Ainslie and D. Robinson, *The Collaborators.* London, Anti-Apartheid Movement, 1964.

Ray Alexander and H. J. Simons, *Job Reservation and the Trade Unions.* Cape Town, Enterprise Publishing, 1959.

Garry Allighan, *Curtain-Up on South Africa.* London, Boardman, 1960.

———, *Verwoerd — The End: A Look-Back from the Future.* Cape Town, Purnell, 1961.

G. W. Allport, *The Nature of Prejudice.* Cambridge, Addison-Wesley, 1954.

* This organization is hereafter referred to as "S. A. Institute."

————, *Personality and Social Encounter.* Boston, Beacon, 1960.

————, *Prejudice in Modern Perspective.* Durban, S. A. Institute, 1956. ,

———— and T. F. Pettigrew, "Cultural Influence on the Perception of Movement: The Trapezoidal Illusion among Zulus." *Journal of Abnormal and Social Psychology,* 55, 1957, pp. 104–113.

M. H. Alsop, *The Population of Natal.* Cape Town, London, and New York, Oxford University Press, 1952.

Phyllis Altman, *The Law of the Vultures.* London, Cape, 1952.

A. P. Altmeyer, *Südafrika, Europas Letzte Grenze.* Zürich, Stauffacher, 1956.

H. T. Andrews *et al.,* eds., *South Africa in the Sixties: A Socio-Economic Survey.* Cape Town, South African Foundation, 1962.

*Apartheid in South Africa.* New York, United Nations, 1963.

Hugh Ashton, *The Basuto.* London, Oxford University Press, 1952.

*Die Asiaat en Afrika.* Stellenbosch, The South African Bureau of Racial Affairs, 1956.[*]

Dennis Austin, *Britain and South Africa.* New York, Oxford University Press, 1966.

James Backhouse, *A Narrative of a Visit to the Mauritius and South Africa.* London, Hamilton, Adams and Co., 1844.

Jean Badertscher, *La Ségrégation Raciale en Afrique du Sud.* Lausanne, Horizons, 1962.

C. D. C. Bain, "Non-European Affairs." *The Manufacturer,* May 1956.

Georges Balandier, *Sociologie Actuelle de l'Afrique Noire.* Paris, Presses Universitaires de France, 1955.

Ronald B. Ballinger, *South-West Africa: The Case against the Union.* Johannesburg, S. A. Institute, 1961.

*Bantu Authorities and Tribal Administration.* Pretoria, Department of Native Affairs, 1958.

*Bantu Education, Oppression or Opportunity?* Stellenbosch, SABRA, 1955.

Anthony Barker, *Giving and Receiving: An Adventure in African Medical Service.* London, Faith Press, 1959.

Anthony Barker, *The Man Next to Me.* New York, Harper, 1960.

Dudley Barker, *Swaziland.* London, Her Majesty's Stationery Office, 1966.

John A. Barnes, "Race Relations in the Development of Southern Africa." In Andrew W. Lind, ed., *Race Relations in World Perspective.* Honolulu, University of Hawaii Press, 1955.

Leonard Barnes, *Caliban in Africa. An Impression of Colour-Madness.* London, Gollancz, 1930.

[*] This organization is hereafter referred to as "SABRA."

John Barrow, *An Account of Travels into the Interior of Southern Africa in the Years 1797 and 1798*. New York, 1802.

Roger Bastide, "Dusky Venus, Black Apollo." *Race*, 3, no. 1, 1961, pp. 10–18.

———, *Sociologie et Psychanalyse*. Paris, Presses Universitaires de France, 1950.

H. M. Bate, *South Africa Without Prejudice*. London, Laurie, 1956.

Edward Batson, "A Contribution to the Study of Urban Coloured Poverty." *Race Relations Journal*, 9, 1942, pp. 1–11.

*Baumannville: A Study of an Urban African Community*. London, Oxford University Press, 1959.

Fred W. Bell, *The South African Native Problem, A Suggested Solution*. The Central News Agency, 1909.

Mary Benson, *The African Patriots*. London, Faber and Faber, 1963.

———, *Chief Albert Lutuli of South Africa*. London, Oxford University Press, 1963.

———, *Tshekedi Khama*. London, Faber and Faber, 1960.

Arthur D. Bensusan, *South Africa, The Land and the People*. Cape Town, Timmins, 1960.

*A Bibliography of African Bibliographies Covering Territories South of the Sahara*. Cape Town, South African Library, 1955.

S. Biesheuvel, "Further Studies on the Measurement of Attitudes Towards Western Ethical Concepts." *Journal of the National Institute of Personnel Research*, 7, 1959, pp. 141–155.

———, "Methodology in the Study of Attitudes of Africans." *Journal of Social Psychology*, 47, 1958, pp. 169–184.

———, "The Nation's Intelligence and its Measurement." *South African Journal of Science*, 49, 1952, pp. 120–138.

———, "The Study of African Ability." *African Studies*, 11, 1952, pp. 45–58, 105–117.

Leslie Blackwell, *Are Judges Human?* London, Bailey and Swinfen, 1963.

E. Blenck and H. Blenck, *South West Africa*. Zürich, Atlantis, 1958.

Harry Bloom, *Episode*. Garden City, Doubleday, 1955.

Leonard Bloom, "Self Concepts and Social Status in South Africa: A Preliminary Cross-Cultural Analysis." *Journal of Social Psychology*, 51, 1960, pp. 103–112.

———, A. C. De Crespigny, and J. E. Spence, "An Interdisciplinary Study of Social, Moral and Political Attitudes of White and Non-White South African University Students." *Journal of Social Psychology*, 54, 1961, pp. 3–12.

*Blueprint for Bondage*. Pietermaritzburg, Liberal Party of South Africa, n.d.

Myrna Blumberg, *White Madam.* London, Gollancz, 1962.

C. Board, *The Border Region: Natural Environment and Land Use of the Eastern Cape.* Cape Town, Oxford University Press, 1962.

J. H. Boeke, *Economics and Economic Policy in Dual Societies.* New York, Institute of Pacific Relations, 1953.

Paul Bohannan and George Dalton, eds., *Markets in Africa.* Evanston, Northwestern University Press, 1962.

John Fairfield Bok, "The Doctrine of Apartheid: A Study of Racial Policies in South Africa." Unpublished thesis, Harvard University, 1952.

J. Borde, "Le Problème Ethnique dans l'Union Sud-Africaine." *Cahiers d'Outre-Mer, 12,* 1950.

C. G. Botha, *Collectanea.* Cape Town, The Van Riebeeck Society, 1924.

——, *Social Life in the Cape Colony in the 18th Century.* Cape Town and Johannesburg, Juta, 1926.

J. H. Botha, *Die Arbeidsvraagstuk van Suid-Afrika.* Amsterdam, Paris, 1928.

Sean Boud, "Apartheid and the Church." *Commonweal, 72,* 1960, pp. 250–253.

Jacques Boulenger, *Voyages de F. Vaillant dans l'Intérieur de l'Afrique, 1781–1785.* Paris, Plon, 1932.

Alexander Brady, *Democracy in the Dominions: A Comparative Study in Institutions.* Toronto, University of Toronto Press, 1958.

Lloyd Braithwaite, "Social Stratification and Cultural Pluralism." *Annals of the New York Academy of Sciences, 83,* 1959–1960, pp. 816–831.

R. H. Brand, *The Union of South Africa.* Oxford, Clarendon Press, 1909.

M. Brandell, "Urban Lobolo Attitudes." *African Studies, 17,* 1958, pp. 34–50.

E. Russell Brayshaw *et al., Racial Problems in South Africa.* London, Society of Friends, 1938.

E. A. Brett, *African Attitudes: A Study of the Social, Racial and Political Attitudes of Some Middle-Class Africans.* Johannesburg, S. A. Institute, 1963.

William W. Brickman, "Racial Segregation in Education in South Africa." *School and Society, 88,* 1960, pp. 258–269.

Cornelis B. Brink, *Die Kerk en die Rassevraagstuk.* Cape Town, N.G. Kerkuitgewers, 1957.

Edgar H. Brookes, *The City of God and the Politics of Crisis*. London, Oxford University Press, 1960.

———, *The Colour Problems of South Africa*. London, Lovedale, 1934.

———, *The History of Native Policy in South Africa*. Cape Town, Nasionale Pers, 1924.

———, *South Africa in a Changing World*. Cape Town, Oxford University Press, 1953.

——— and N. Hurwitz, *The Native Reserves of Natal*. Cape Town, London, and New York, Oxford University Press, 1957.

——— and J. B. Macaulay, *Civil Liberties in South Africa*. Cape Town, Oxford University Press, 1958.

——— and Amry Vandenbosch, *The City of God and the City of Man in Africa*. Lexington, University of Kentucky Press, 1964.

M. Broughton, *Press and Politics of South Africa*. Cape Town, Purnell, 1961.

Douglas Brown, *Against the World: A Study of White South African Attitudes*. London, William Collins Sons, 1966.

William E. Brown, *The Catholic Church in South Africa*. New York, Kennedy, 1960.

William O. Brown, "Race Consciousness Among South African Natives." *American Journal of Sociology*, 40, 1935, pp. 569–581.

———, *Race Relations in the American South and in South Africa*. Boston, Boston University Press, 1959.

Edmund Brunner, "Problems and Tensions in South Africa." *Political Science Quarterly*, 70, 1955, pp. 368–387.

J. P. Bruwer, *Die Bantoe van Suid-Afrika*. Johannesburg, Afrikaanse Pers, 1957.

Alfred T. Bryant, *Bantu Origins: The People and Their Language*. Cape Town, Struik, 1963.

———, *Olden Times in Zululand and Natal*. London, Longmans, 1929.

———, *The Zulu People*. Pietermaritzburg, Shuter and Shooter, 1949.

Raymond L. Buell, "The Race Problem in South Africa." *Foreign Affairs*, 4, 1928, pp. 265–276.

T. V. Bulpin, *The Golden Republic*. Cape Town, Timmins, n.d.

———, *Shaka's Country, A Book of Zululand*. Cape Town, Timmins, 1956.

———, *Storm over the Transvaal*. Cape Town, Timmins, 1955.

———, *To the Shores of Natal*. Cape Town, Timmins, n.d.

Brian Bunting, *The Rise of the South African Reich*. Baltimore, Penguin, 1964.

Sonia Bunting, "The Prisons of Apartheid." *Africa South,* 4, 1960, pp. 42–48.

William J. Burchell, *Travels in the Interior of Southern Africa.* London, Oxford University Press, 1935.

Jan Burger, *The Gulf Between.* Cape Town, Timmins, 1960.

John Burger, *The Black Man's Burden.* London, Gollancz, 1943.

John R. Burrows, *The Population and Labour Resources of Natal.* Pietermaritzburg, University of Natal, 1959.

——, *et al., Indian Life and Labour in Natal.* Johannesburg, S. A. Institute, 1952.

Johannes J. Buskes, *South Africa's Apartheid Policy—Unacceptable.* Heidelberg, Transvaal, 1956.

Jeffrey E. Butler, "The Liberal Party and South Africa, 1895–1902." Unpublished Ph.D. thesis, Wellesley, 1963.

——, ed., *Boston University Papers in African History.* Boston, Boston University Press, 1964.

C. Cadoux, *L'Afrique du Sud.* Paris, Librairie Générale de Droit et de Jurisprudence, 1966.

Edward Callan, *Albert John Luthuli and the South African Race Conflict.* Kalamazoo, Western Michigan University Press, 1962.

G. H. Calpin, *Indians in South Africa.* Pietermaritzburg, Shuter and Shooter, 1949.

——, *There Are No South Africans.* London, Nelson, 1946.

——, *The South African Way of Life.* Melbourne, London, and Toronto, Heinemann, 1953.

Peter Calvocoressi, *South Africa and World Opinion.* London, Oxford University Press, 1961.

Alexander Campbell, *The Heart of Africa.* London, Longmans, 1954.

——, *South Africa, What Next?* Cape Town, Stewart, 1947.

John Campbell, *Travels in South Africa.* London, Black and Parry, 1815.

Waldemar B. Campbell, *The South African Frontier, 1865–1885: A Study in Expansion.* Pretoria, Office of the Chief Archivist, 1960.

Frank R. Cana, *South Africa from the Great Trek to the Union.* London, Chapman and Hall, 1909.

*Carnegie Commission on the Poor White Problem in South Africa.* Pro Ecclesia Drukkery, 1932.

Albert Carter, *South-West Africa (1884–1915).* London, T. Werner Laurie, 1915.

Gwendolen M. Carter, "Can Apartheid Succeed in South Africa?" *Foreign Affairs,* 32, 1954, pp. 296–309.

——, *Independence for Africa.* New York, Praeger, 1960.

——, *The Politics of Inequality, South Africa Since 1948.* New York, Praeger, 1958.

——, *South Africa.* New York, Foreign Policy Association (Headline Series, no. 109), 1955.

——, "South Africa's Rubicon." *The Nation, 109,* 1960, pp. 327–330.

——, "The Consequences of Apartheid." *Annals of the American Academy of Political and Social Science, 306,* 1956, pp. 37–42.

——, "Union of South Africa: Politics of White Supremacy." *Annals of the American Academy of Political and Social Science, 298,* 1955, pp. 142–150.

——, ed., *Five African States, Responses to Diversity.* Ithaca, Cornell University Press, 1963.

James Chapman, *Travels in the Interior of South Africa.* London, Bell and Daldy, 1868.

*Christian Literature for the Bantu of Southern Africa.* Johannesburg, Committee of South African Churches, 1957.

*Christian Principles in Multi-Racial South Africa.* Pretoria, Dutch Reformed Church, 1953.

*Christian Responsibility Toward Areas of Rapid Social Change.* Johannesburg, Report of the Multi-Racial Conference, 1959.

Rhona Churchill, *White Man's God.* London, Hodder and Stoughton, 1962.

John D. Clark, *The Prehistory of South Africa.* Harmondsworth, Penguin, 1959.

*Classification of Publications Issued by the South African Institute of Race Relations.* Johannesburg, S. A. Institute, 1962.

George Clay, "The Pass System, How It Operates." *Africa Report, 5,* 1960, p. 7.

H. Cloete, *The History of the Great Boer Trek and the Origin of the South African Republics.* London, Murray, 1900.

Austin Coates, *Basutoland.* New York, British Information Service, 1966.

Abel Coetzee, *Ons Volkslewe, Volkskundige Opstelle.* Pretoria, van Schaik, 1949.

J. A. Coetzee, *Politieke Groopering in die Wording van die Afrikaner-nasie.* Johannesburg, 1941.

Rachel M. Coke, *South Africa as Seen by the French, 1610–1850, A Bibliography.* University of Cape Town, 1957.

Monica M. Cole, *South Africa.* London, Methuen, 1961.

Colin B. Collins, *Catholic Bantu Education.* Pretoria, 1957.

"The Communist Party in South Africa." *Africa Report, 6,* March 1961, pp. 5–6, 15.

P. A. W. Cook, *The Education of a South African Tribe*. Cape Town, Juta, 1934.

Jack Cope, *The Golden Oriole*. London, Heinemann, 1958.

John Cope, *South Africa*. New York, Frederick A. Praeger, 1965.

G. E. Cory, *The Rise of South Africa*. London, Longmans, 1910.

Walter A. Cotton, *Racial Segregation in South Africa*. London, Sheldon, 1931.

C. W. Coulter, *Empire Unity*. Cape Town, Stewart, 1944.

D. V. Cowen, *Constitution-making for a Democracy*. Johannesburg, supplement to *Optima*, 1960.

———, *The Foundations of Freedom*. Cape Town, Oxford University Press, 1961.

———, *Liberty, Equality, Fraternity—Today*. Johannesburg, S. A. Institute, 1961.

———, *Parliamentary Sovereignty and the Entrenched Sections of the South Africa Act*. Cape Town, Juta, 1951.

Oliver C. Cox, *Caste, Class and Race*. Garden City, Doubleday, 1948.

F. S. Crafford, *Jan Smuts*. London, Allen and Unwin, 1946.

Edward Crankshaw, *The Forsaken Idea, A Study of Viscount Milner*. London, Longmans, 1952.

G. Cronjé, *Afrika Sonder die Asiaat*. Johannesburg, Boek-en Kunssentrum, 1946.

——— and E. P. Groenewald, *Regverdige Rasse-Apartheid*. Stellenbosch, C. V. S. Boekhandel, 1947.

H. P. Cruse, *Die Opheffing van die Kleurling-Bevolking*. Cape Town, Citadel Pers, 1947.

Arthur G. J. Cryns, *Race Relations and Race Attitudes in South Africa*. Nymegen, Janssen, 1959.

L. Curtis, *With Milner in South Africa*. Oxford, Blackwell, 1951.

Y. M. Dadoo, *Facts About the Ghetto Act*. Johannesburg, Communist Party, 1946.

Ralf Dahrendorf, *Class and Class Conflict in Industrial Society*. Stanford, Stanford University Press, 1959.

Christian F. Damberger, *Travels in the Interior of Africa from the Years 1781 to 1797*. London, Longmans and Rees, 1801.

K. Danziger, "Ideology and Utopia in South Africa: A Methodological Contribution to the Sociology of Knowledge." *British Journal of Sociology*, 14, 1963, pp. 59–76.

———, "The Psychological Future of an Oppressed Group." *Social Forces*, 42, October 1963, pp. 31–40.

———, "Self-Interpretations of Group Differences in Values." *Journal of Social Psychology*, 47, 1958, pp. 317–325.

————, "Value Differences Among South African Students." *Journal of Abnormal and Social Psychology,* 57, 1958, pp. 339–346.

Raymond A. Dart, "*Australopithecus Africanus,* the Man-Ape of South Africa." *Nature, 115,* 1925, pp. 195–199.

————, "Cultural Status of the South African Man-Apes." In *Annual Report of the Smithsonian Institution,* Washington, 1955.

Basil Davidson, *Report on Southern Africa.* London, Cape, 1952.

T. B. Davie, *Education and Race Relations in South Africa.* Johannesburg, S. A. Institute, 1955.

Ioan Davies, *African Trade Unions.* Baltimore, Penguin, 1966.

Allison W. Davis, B. B. Gardner, and M. R. Gardner, *Deep South.* Chicago, University of Chicago Press, 1941.

G. M. Davis and F. B. du Randt, *Urban Native Law.* Port Elizabeth, Grotius, 1959.

John A. Davis and James K. Baker, eds., *Southern Africa in Transition.* New York, Praeger, 1966.

Z. J. DeBeer, *Multi-Racial South Africa.* London, Oxford University Press, 1961.

Harm J. de Bly, *Africa South.* Evanston, Northwestern University Press, 1962.

P. de Briey, "The Productivity of African Labour." In Peter R. Gould, ed., *Africa, Continent of Change.* Belmont, Wadsworth, 1961.

H. F. Dickie-Clark, *The Marginal Situation: A Sociological Study of a Coloured Group.* London, Routledge and Kegan Paul, 1966.

Joy de Gruchy, *The Cost of Living for Africans.* Johannesburg, S. A. Institute, 1959.

Henri Dehérain, *Le Cap de Bonne-Espérance au XVII<sup>e</sup> Siècle.* Paris, Hachette, 1909.

————, *L'Expansion des Boers au XIX<sup>e</sup> Siècle.* Paris, Hachette, 1905.

Cornelis W. De Kiewiet, *America's Role in Africa.* Durban, University of Natal, 1960.

————, *The Anatomy of South African Misery.* London, New York, and Toronto, Oxford University Press, 1956.

————, *British Colonial Policy and the South African Republics.* London, Longmans, 1929.

————, "Fears and Pressures in the Union of South Africa." In C. Grove Haines, ed., *Africa Today.* Baltimore, Johns Hopkins University Press, 1955.

————, *A History of South Africa, Social and Economic.* Oxford, Clarendon Press, 1941.

————, *The Imperial Factor in South Africa.* Cambridge, Cambridge University Press, 1937.

M. H. De Kock, *The Economic Development of South Africa.* London, King, 1936.

Victor de Kock, *Those in Bondage*. London, Allen and Unwin, 1950.

Nicolas de la Caille, *Journal Historique du Voyage Fait au Cap de Bonne-Espérance*. Paris, Guillyn, 1763.

Anthony Delius, "At the Cape of Desperate Hope." *The Reporter*, 23, 1960, pp. 19–23.

———, *The Day Natal Took Off*. Cape Town, Insight Publications, 1963.

———, *The Last Division*. Cape Town, Human and Rousseau, 1959.

J. A. De Mist, *Memorandum on the Cape, 1802*. Cape Town, The Van Riebeeck Society, 1920.

J. C. de Ridder, *The Personality of the Urban African in South Africa*. London, Routledge and Kegan Paul, 1961.

Ram Desai, ed., *Christianity in Africa as Seen by the Africans*. Denver, Swallow, 1962.

H. H. W. De Villiers, *Rivonia, Operation Mayibuye*. Johannesburg, Afrikaanse Pers, 1964.

M. D. C. De Wet Nel, "Bantu Policy in South Africa." In James Duffy and Robert A. Manners, eds., *Africa Speaks*. Princeton, Van Nostrand, 1961.

H. I. E. Dhlomo, *Valley of a Thousand Hills*. Durban, Knox, 1941.

L. R. Dison and I. Mohamed, *Group Areas and Their Development*. Durban, Butterworth, 1960.

C. M. Doke, *Bantu: Modern Grammatical, Phonetical and Lexicographical Studies Since 1860*. International African Institute, 1945.

John Dollard, *Caste and Class in a Southern Town*. New Haven, Yale University Press, 1937.

G. V. Doxey, *The High Commission Territories and the Republic of South Africa*. London, Oxford University Press, 1963.

———, *The Industrial Colour Bar in South Africa*. Cape Town, Oxford University Press, 1961.

M. Draper, *Sport and Race in South Africa*. Johannesburg, S. A. Institute, 1963.

Charles Dundas, *South-West Africa, the Factual Background*. Cape Town, South African Institute of International Affairs, 1946.

——— and Hugh Ashton, *Problem Territories of Southern Africa*. Cape Town, South African Institute of International Affairs, 1952.

C. N. J. Du Plessis, *The Transvaal Boer Speaking for Himself*. London, Jarrold and Sons, 1898.

J. Du Plessis, *A History of Christian Missions in South Africa*. London, Longmans, 1911.

J. C. Du Plessis, *Economic Fluctuations in South Africa, 1910–1949.* Stellenbosch, 1950.

Andries B. Du Preez, *Inside the South African Crucible.* Cape Town, H.A.U.M., 1959.

*The Durban Housing Survey.* Pietermaritzburg, University of Natal Press, 1952.

Emile Durkheim, *De la Division du Travail Social.* Paris, Alcan, 1893.

*The Dutch Reformed Churches in South Africa and the Problem of Race Relations.* Gereformeerde Kerk van Suid Afrika, n.d.

Anthonie E. du Toit, *The Cape Frontier: A Study of Native Policy with Special Reference to the Years 1847–1866.* Pretoria, The Government Printer, 1954.

Eugene P. Dvorin, *Racial Separation in South Africa.* Chicago, University of Chicago Press, 1952.

Jacqueline Eberhardt, "Messianisme en Afrique du Sud." *Archives de Sociologie Religieuse,* 4, 1957, pp. 31–56.

*Economic and Social Consequences of Racial Discriminatory Practices.* New York, United Nations, 1963.

*The Economic Development of the Reserves.* Johannesburg, S. A. Institute, 1959.

*Education for Isolation.* The Black Sash, 1960.

Isobel E. Edwards, *The 1820 Settlers in South Africa.* London, New York, and Toronto, Longmans, 1934.

———, *Protectorates or Native Reserves?* London, Africa Bureau, n.d.

———, *Towards Emancipation: A Study in South African Slavery.* Cardiff, Gomerian Press, 1942.

S. P. Engelbrecht, *History of the Nederduits Hervormde Kerk.* Pretoria, 1925.

Maurice S. Evans, *Black and White in South East Africa.* New York, Longmans, 1911.

*Experiment at Edendale.* Department of Economics, University of Natal, 1951.

H. A. Fagan, *Co-existence in South Africa.* Cape Town, Juta, 1963.

———, *Our Responsibility.* Cape Town, Juta, 1959.

T. J. D. Fair, *The Distribution of Population in Natal.* Cape Town, London, and New York, Oxford University Press, 1955.

Edward Feit, *South Africa, The Dynamics of the African National Congress.* London, Oxford University Press, 1962.

C. J. Ferguson-Davie, *The Early History of Indians in Natal.* Johannesburg, S. A. Institute, 1952.

M. L. Fick, *The Educability of the South African Native.* South African Council for Educational and Social Research, 1939.

G. Findlay, *Miscegenation.* Pretoria, Pretoria News and Printing Works, 1936.

Ruth First, *117 Days.* New York, Stein and Day, 1965.

——, *South West Africa.* Baltimore, Penguin, 1963.

Lionel Forman and E. S. Sachs, *The South African Treason Trial.* New York, Monthly Review Press, 1958.

M. Fortes and E. E. Evans-Pritchard, eds., *African Political Systems.* London, Oxford University Press, 1950.

A. Francos, *L'Afrique des Afrikaners.* Paris, Julliard, 1966.

S. H. Frankel, *Africa in the Re-making.* Johannesburg, Witwatersrand University Press, 1932.

——, *The Tyranny of Economic Paternalism in South Africa.* Johannesburg, supplement to *Optima,* December 1960.

N. N. Franklin, *Economics in South Africa.* Cape Town, London, and New York, Oxford University Press, 1954.

——, *Natives and the Administration of Justice.* Johannesburg, S. A. Institute, 1936.

E. Franklin Frazier, *Race and Culture Contacts in the Modern World.* New York, Knopf, 1957.

Louis F. Freed, *The Problem of European Prostitution in Johannesburg.* Cape Town, Juta, 1949.

J. J. Freeman, *A Tour of South Africa.* London, Snow, 1851.

Henry E. S. Freemantle, *The New Nation.* London, Ousely, 1909.

Gilberto Freyre, *The Masters and the Slaves.* New York, Knopf, 1956.

Bernard Friedman *et al., Looking Outwards: Three South African Viewpoints.* Johannesburg, S. A. Institute, 1961.

Marion Friedmann, ed., *I Will Still Be Moved: Reports from South Africa.* Chicago, Quadrangle, 1963.

Margaret L. Friend, *Without Fear or Favour.* Cape Town, 1958.

Basil Fuller, *South Africa—Not Guilty?* London, Jarrolds, 1957.

J. S. Furnivall, *Colonial Policy and Practice.* Cambridge, Cambridge University Press, 1948.

——, *Netherlands India, A Study of Plural Economy.* Cambridge, Cambridge University Press, 1939.

John S. Galbraith, *Reluctant Empire: British Policy on the South African Frontier, 1834–1854.* Berkeley, University of California Press, 1963.

G. H. Galpin, *La Nation Sud-Africaine.* Monaco, Editions du Rocher, 1954.

Mohandas K. Gandhi, *Autobiography or The Story of My Experiences with Truth.* Ahmedabad, Navagivan, 1927.

————, *Satyagraha in South Africa*. Madras, Ganesan, 1928.

Lewis H. Gann, "Liberal Interpretations of South African History," *Rhodes Livingstone Journal*, 25, 1959.

————and Peter Duignan, *White Settlers in Tropical Africa*. Baltimore, Penguin, 1962.

Gerald Gardiner, *The South African Treason Trial*. London, Christian Action, 1957.

M. S. Geen, *The Making of South Africa*. Cape Town, Miller, 1958.

G. Geertsema, *Guide to Statistical Sources in the Republic of South Africa*. Pretoria, University of South Africa, 1962.

C. W. M. Gell, "Hard Choices in South Africa." *Foreign Affairs, 31*, 1953, pp. 287–300.

————, "Sport in South Africa." *Africa Today, 5*, 1958.

G. B. A. Gerdener, *Recent Developments in the South African Mission Field*. Pretoria, N. G. Kerk-Uitgewers, 1959.

A. S. Geyer *et al., Delayed Action*. Pretoria, privately published, 1961.

Henry Gibbs, *Background to Bitterness, The Story of South Africa, 1652–1954*. London, Muller, 1954.

————, *Twilight in South Africa*. London, Jarrolds, 1949.

J. Y. Gibson, *The Evolution of South African Native Policy*. Pietermaritzburg, Davis, 1919.

————, *The Story of the Zulus*. London, Longmans, 1911.

Olive Gibson, *The Cost of Living for Africans*. Johannesburg, S. A. Institute, 1954.

S. F. N. Gie, *Geskiedenis van Suid Afrika*. Stellenbosch, Universiteits Uitgewers, 1955.

J. M. Gillespie and G. W. Allport, *Youth's Outlook on the Future*. New York, Doubleday, 1955.

Paul Giniewski, *Une Autre Afrique du Sud*. Paris, Berger-Levrault, 1962.

————, *Bantustans, A Trek Towards the Future*. Cape Town, Herman and Rousseau, 1961.

————, *The Two Faces of Apartheid*. Chicago, Henry Regnery, 1965.

Max Gluckman, *Analysis of a Social Situation in Modern Zululand*. Manchester, Manchester University Press, 1958.

————, *Custom and Conflict in Africa*. Oxford, Blackwell, 1955.

————, *Malinowski's Sociological Theories*. Rhodes-Livingstone Paper no. 16, 1949.

————, *Order and Rebellion in Tribal Africa*. New York, The Free Press, 1963.

————, *Rituals of Rebellion in South-East Africa*. Manchester, Manchester University Press, 1954.

———, "The Rise of the Zulu Empire." *Scientific American, 202,* April 1960, pp. 157–168.

———, "Zulu Women in Hoe Culture Ritual." *Bantu Studies, 9,* 1950.

*Go Forward in Faith.* Johannesburg, S. A. Institute, 1952.

*God's Kingdom in Multi-Racial South Africa.* Johannesburg, Report on the Inter-Racial Conference of Church Leaders, 1954.

I. Goldblatt, *The Mandated Territory in South West Africa in Relation to the United Nations.* Cape Town, Struik, 1961.

Collin Gonze *et al., South African Crisis and United States Policy.* New York, American Committee on Africa, 1962.

D. M. Goodfellow, *A Modern Economic History of South Africa.* London, Routledge, 1931.

D. P. Goosen, ed., *Triomf van Nasionalisme.* Johannesburg, 1953.

Nadine Gordimer, *A World of Strangers.* New York, Simon and Schuster, 1958.

Peter Gould, ed., *Africa, Continent of Change.* Belmont, Wadsworth, 1961.

J. A. Gray, ed.; *South Africa To-day.* London, St. Bride Foundation Institute, 1960.

Rodney Gray, "South Africa under the Nationalist Party." *International Journal, 4,* 1948-1949, pp. 52–59.

L. P. Green, *History of Local Government in South Africa.* Cape Town, Juta, 1957.

——— and T. J. D. Fair, *Development in Africa.* Johannesburg, Witwatersrand University Press, 1962.

Erwin N. Griswold, "Observations on Treason Trial." *Africa Today, 5,* 1958.

J. H. Grobler, *Africa's Destiny.* Johannesburg, Book of the Month Club, 1958.

Johannes F. W. Grosskopf, "The Position of the Native Population in the Economic System of South Africa." *Weltwirtschaftliches Archiv, 38,* 1933, pp. 414–441.

*Group Areas and Residential Segregation.* Stellenbosch, SABRA, 1952.

T. J. Haarhoff, *Stranger at the Gates.* London, Blackwell, 1948.

———, *Why Not Be Friends? Natural Apartheid and Natural Friendliness in South Africa.* Central News Agency, n.d.

——— and C. M. van den Heever, *Afrikaans, Its Origin and Development.* London, Oxford University Press, 1936.

H. R. Hahlo and Ellison Kahn, *The Union of South Africa: The Development of its Laws and Constitution.* London, Stevens, 1960.

Lord Hailey, *An African Survey.* London, New York, and Toronto, Oxford University Press, 1957.

———, *The Republic of South Africa and the High Commission Territories.* London, Oxford University Press, 1963.

Ellen S. Haines, "The Transkei Trader." *South African Journal of Economics, 1,* 1933, pp. 201–216.

Samuel James Halford, *The Griquas of Griqualand.* Cape Town, Juta, n.d.

W. Hallenbeck, ed., *The Baumannville Community: A Study of the Family Life of Urban Africans.* Institute for Social Research, University of Natal, 1955.

I. G. Halliday, "Natal and Indentured Indian Immigration." *South African Journal of Economics,* 8, 1940, pp. 51–59.

Jack Halpern, *South Africa's Hostages: Basutoland, Bechuanaland and Swaziland.* Baltimore, Penguin, 1965.

W. D. Hammond-Tooke, *Bhaca Society: A People in the Transkeian Uplands, South Africa.* Cape Town, Oxford University Press, 1962.

———, *Tribes of the Willowvale District.* Department of Native Affairs, Ethnological Publications no. 36, 1957.

William K. Hancock, *Smuts, The Sanguine Years.* New York, Cambridge University Press, 1962.

———, *Survey of British Commonwealth Affairs.* London, Oxford University Press, 1942.

——— and Jean van der Poel, *Selections from the Smuts Papers.* Cambridge, Cambridge University Press, 1966.

Rex Hardinge, *South African Cinderella.* London, Jenkins, 1937.

E. E. Harris, *White Civilization.* Johannesburg, S. A. Institute, 1953.

Heinz Hartmann, *Enterprise and Politics in South Africa.* Princeton, Princeton University Press, 1962.

John Charles Hatch, *The Dilemma of South Africa.* London, Dobson, 1952.

Alan F. Hattersley, *The British Settlement of Natal.* Cambridge, Cambridge University Press, 1950.

———, *South Africa, 1652–1933.* London, Butterworth, 1933.

Cecil Headlam, ed., *The Milner Papers.* London, Cassell, 1931.

Kenneth A. Heard, *Political Systems in Multi-Racial Societies.* Johannesburg, S. A. Institute, 1961.

G. M. Heaton-Nicholls, *The Native Problem in South Africa.* Pretoria, Native Affairs Department, n.d.

———, *The Problem of the Native in South Africa.* Pretoria, The Government Printer, 1937.

———, *South Africa in My Time.* London, Allen and Unwin, 1961.

Ellen Hellmann, *In Defence of a Shared Society.* Johannesburg, S. A. Institute, 1956.

———, "Native Life in a Johannesburg Slum Yard." *Africa,* 8, 1935, pp. 34–62.

———, *Problems of Urban Bantu Youth.* Johannesburg, S. A. Institute, 1940.

———, *Racial Laws Versus Economic and Social Forces.* Johannesburg, S. A. Institute, 1955.

———, *Rooiyard, A Sociological Survey of an Urban Slum Yard.* Cape Town, Rhodes-Livingstone Paper no. 13, 1948.

———, *Sellgoods, A Sociological Survey of an African Labour Force.* Johannesburg, S. A. Institute, 1953.

———, ed., *Handbook of Race Relations in South Africa.* Cape Town, London, and New York, Oxford University Press, 1949.

Brunhilde Helm, *Social Work in a South African City.* Cape Town, University of Cape Town Board of Sociological Research, 1962.

Alex Hepple, *The African Worker in South Africa: A Study in Trade Unionism.* London, African Bureau, 1956.

———, *Censorship and Press Control in South Africa.* Johannesburg, 1960.

———, *Poverty Wages.* Johannesburg, Wages Committee, 1959.

———, *South Africa: A Political and Economic History.* New York, Frederick A. Praeger, 1966.

———, *Trade Unions in Travail.* Johannesburg, Unity Publications, 1954.

Louis Herrman, *A History of the Jews in South Africa.* London, Gollancz, 1930.

Kurt Hesse, *Wirtschaftswunder Südafrika.* Düsseldorf, Droste-Verlag, 1954.

P. D. Hey, *The Rise of the Natal Indian Elite.* Pietermaritzburg, Natal Witness, 1961.

P. Hinchliff, *The Anglican Church in South Africa.* Darton, 1963.

H. E. Hockly, *The Story of the British Settlers of 1820 in South Africa.* Cape Town and Johannesburg, Juta, 1948.

A. W. Hoernlé and G. Hellman, *The Analysis of Social Change and its Bearing on Education.* Johannesburg, S. A. Institute, 1952.

R. F. Alfred Hoernlé, "Anatomy of Segregation." *Race Relations Journal, 3,* 1936, pp. 14–21.

———, *South African Native Policy and the Liberal Spirit.* Johannesburg, Witwatersrand University Press, 1945.

J. H. Hofmeyr, *Christian Principles and Race Problems.* Johannesburg, S. A. Institute, 1945.

———, *Native Welfare in the Union of South Africa.* New York, Union of South Africa Government Information Office, 1946.

———, *South Africa.* London, Benn, 1932.

J. F. Holleman, *African Interlude.* Cape Town, Nasionale Boekhandel, 1959.

———, "Die Bantoehuwelik op die Kruispad." *Journal of Racial Affairs, 11,* 1960, pp. 82–117.

————, "Bantu Marriage at the Crossroads." *Race Relations Journal*, *28*, 1961.

————, *Sabra 1961: The Great Purge.* Institute for Social Research, University of Natal, 1961.

————, *The Tightrope Dancers.* Durban, Institute for Social Research, n.d.

————, ed., *Experiment in Swaziland.* London, Oxford University Press, 1964.

John E. Holloway, *Apartheid, Un Problème, Une Solution.* Paris, Génin, 1965.

————, *The Problems of Race Relations in South Africa.* New York, Union of South Africa Government Information Office, n.d.

Charles Hooper, *Brief Authority.* London, Collins, 1960.

Tom Hopkinson, *Drum: In the Fiery Continent.* London, Gollancz, 1962.

Muriel Horrell, *Action, Reaction and Counteraction.* Johannesburg, S. A. Institute, 1963.

————, *African Education.* Johannesburg, S. A. Institute, 1963.

————, *Days of Crisis in South Africa, A Fact Paper.* Johannesburg, S. A. Institute, 1960.

————, *A Decade of Bantu Education.* Johannesburg, S. A. Institute, 1964.

————, *Economic Development of the "Reserves."* Johannesburg, S. A. Institute, 1960.

————, "Evolution de la Conception du 'Bantoustan' en Afrique du Sud." *Civilisations, 13*, 1963, pp. 203–211.

————, *The Group Areas Act: Its Effect on Human Beings.* Johannesburg, S. A. Institute, 1956.

————, *Legislation and Race Relations.* Johannesburg, S. A. Institute, 1963.

————, "La Législation Sud-Africaine en 1962." *Civilisations, 12*, 1962, p. 422.

————, *The Liquor Laws.* Johannesburg, S. A. Institute, 1959.

————, *Non-European Policies in the Union and the Measure of Their Success.* Johannesburg, S. A. Institute, 1954.

————, "Pass Laws." Johannesburg, S. A. Institute, 1953.

————, *The People of South Africa and Their Hopes for the Future.* Johannesburg, S. A. Institute, 1964.

————, *Population of the Union of South Africa.* Johannesburg, S. A. Institute, 1953.

————, *Race Classification in South Africa, Its Effects on Human Beings.* Johannesburg, S. A. Institute, 1959.

————, *Racialism and the Trade Unions*. Johannesburg, S. A. Institute, 1959.

————, *South African Trade Unionism*. Johannesburg, S. A. Institute, 1961.

————, *South Africa's Non-White Workers*. Johannesburg, S. A. Institute, 1956.

Ralph Horwitz, *Expand or Explode: Apartheid's Threat to South African Industry*. Cape Town, Business Bookman, 1957.

————, *South Africa's Business*. Cape Town, The African Bookman, 1946.

D. Hobart Houghton, *Economic Development in a Plural Society*. Cape Town, Oxford University Press, 1960.

————, *Life in the Ciskei*. Johannesburg, S. A. Institute, 1955.

————, *Some Economic Problems of the Bantu*. Johannesburg, S. A. Institute, 1938.

————, *The South African Economy*. Cape Town, Oxford University Press, 1963.

————, *The Tomlinson Report*. Johannesburg, S. A. Institute, 1956.

———— and Edith Walter, *The Economy of a Native Reserve*. Pietermaritzburg, Shuter and Shooter, 1953.

George M. Houser, "Mr. Louw and the Declaration." *Africa Today*, 5, 1958.

Thomas Hovet, *Africa in the United Nations*. Evanston, Northwestern University Press, 1963.

Trevor Huddleston, *Naught for Your Comfort*. New York, Doubleday, 1956.

————, "The Racial Conflict in South Africa." *Journal of Human Relations*, 8, 1960, pp. 473–478.

Archibald P. Hunter, "The Reorientation of Educational Policy in South Africa Since 1948." Unpublished Ed. D. thesis, University of California at Los Angeles, 1963.

Monica Hunter, *Reaction to Conquest*. London, Oxford University Press, 1936.

Denis E. Hurley, *Apartheid, A Crisis of the Christian Conscience*. Johannesburg, S. A. Institute, 1964.

Nathan Hurwitz, *Agriculture in Natal, 1860–1950*. Cape Town, London, and New York, Oxford University Press, 1957.

————, *The Economics of Bantu Education in South Africa*. Johannesburg, S. A. Institute, 1964.

W. H. Hutt, *The Economics of the Colour Bar*. London, Deutsch, 1964.

Elspeth Huxley, *Red Strangers*. London, Chatto and Windus, 1955.

————, *A Thing to Love*. London, Chatto and Windus, 1954.

J. Huxley, A. C. Haddon, and A. M. Carr-Saunders, *We Europeans.* Harmondsworth, Penguin, 1935.

R. W. Imishue, *South West Africa.* London, Pall Mall Press, 1966.

*The Indian in South Africa.* New York, Union of South Africa Government Information Office, n.d.

*Industrial Development in South Africa.* Pretoria, The Government Printing and Stationery Office, 1924.

*Industrial Profile: Republic of South Africa.* Johannesburg, Da Gama, 1962.

*Integration or Separate Development?* Stellenbosch, SABRA, 1952.

*Investment in Union of South Africa.* Washington, United States Department of Commerce, 1954.

James Irving, *Macleantown, A Study of a Small South African Community.* Grahamstown, Rhodes University, 1959.

———, *Report on Rent and Income Structure in a Grahamstown African Housing Scheme.* Grahamstown, Rhodes University Institute of Social and Economic Research, 1958.

D. D. T. Jabavu, *The Black Problem.* Lovedale, The Book Department, 1921.

———, *Native Disabilities in South Africa.* Cape Province, Lovedale, 1932.

———, *The Segregation Fallacy.* Cape Province, Lovedale, 1928.

Noni Jabavu, *Drawn in Colour.* London, Murray, 1960.

———, *The Ochre People, Scenes from a South African Life.* London, Murray, 1963.

M. Janish, "Some Administrative Aspects of Native Marriage Problems in an Urban Area." *Bantu Studies, 15,* 1941.

E. J. Jansen, *Native Policy in the Union of South Africa.* Pretoria, State Information Office, 1950.

M. A. Jaspan, "South Africa 1960–1961: The Transition from Passive Resistance to Rebellion." *Science and Society, 25,* 2, 1961, pp. 97–106.

M. D. W. Jeffreys, "Lobolo Is Child Price." *African Studies, 10,* 1951.

Edith B. Jones, "South African Native Land Policy." *Bantu Studies, 14,* 1940, pp. 175–197.

J. D. R. Jones, *At the Crossroads.* Johannesburg, S. A. Institute, 1953.

L. Joos, *Histoire de l'Afrique du Sud.* Paris, Le Centurion, 1966.

C. J. Jooste, "Die Maatskaplike en Ekonomiese Positie van die Kleurlinge en Indiërs." *Journal of Racial Affairs, 13,* 1962, pp. 112–118.

Helen Joseph, *If This Be Treason.* London, Deutsch, 1963.

P. S. Joshi, *The Struggle for Equality.* Bombay, Hind Kitabs, 1951.

———, *The Tyranny of Colour.* Durban, E.P. and Commercial Printing, 1942.

Henri A. Junod, *The Life of a South African Tribe.* London, Natt, 1912.

Henri P. Junod, *Bantu Heritage.* Johannesburg, Hortors, 1938.

———, *Revenge or Reformation?* Pretoria, Christian Council for South Africa, 1944.

Violaine Junod, "South Africa: Reality and Unreality." *Journal of Human Relations,* 8, 1960, pp. 551–567.

Isobel Jurgens, *Why Cry Beloved Country?* Stockwell, 1958.

Thomas G. Karis, "South Africa." In Gwendolen M. Carter, ed., *Five African States, Responses to Diversity.* Ithaca, Cornell University Press, 1963.

———, "The South African Treason Trial." *Political Science Quarterly,* 56, 1961, pp. 217–241.

Sidney L. Kark and Guy W. Stewart, eds., *A Practice of Social Medicine.* Edinburgh and London, Livingstone, 1962.

B. B. Keet, *The Ethics of Apartheid.* Johannesburg, S. A. Institute, 1957.

———, *Whither South Africa?* Stellenbosch and Grahamstown, University Publishers, 1956.

W. P. M. Kennedy and H. J. Schlosberg, *The Law and Custom of the South African Constitution.* London, Oxford University Press, 1935.

Arthur Keppel-Jones, *Friends or Foes.* Pietermaritzburg, Shuter and Shooter, n.d.

———, *South Africa.* London, Longmans, 1951.

———, "South Africa: Racialism and Republicanism." In Millar Maclure *et al.,* eds., *Africa: The Political Pattern.* Toronto, University of Toronto Press, 1961.

———, *When Smuts Goes: A History of South Africa from 1952 to 2010.* Cape Town, African Bookman, 1947.

Carl Keyter, *Feeding Customs and Food Habits of Urban Africans.* Johannesburg, S. A. Institute, 1962.

———, *Industrial Feeding of African Workers.* Johannesburg, S. A. Institute, 1962.

Tschekedi Khama, *Bechuanaland and South Africa.* London, Africa Bureau, 1955.

Sir Shafa'at Ahmad Khan, *The Indian in South Africa.* Allahabad, Kitabistan, 1946.

John Kirk, *Economic Aspects of Native Segregation in South Africa.* London, King, 1929.

Kenneth Kirkwood, *The Group Areas Act.* Johannesburg, S. A. Institute, n.d.

*Die Kleurling in die Suid Afrikaanse Samelewing.* Stellenbosch, SABRA, 1955.

Clyde Kluckhohn, *Culture and Behavior.* Glencoe, The Free Press, 1962.

Florence Kluckhohn and Fred L. Strodtbeck, *Variations in Value Orientations.* Evanston, Row, Peterson, 1961.

D. F. Kokot, "Desert Encroachment in South Africa." In Peter R. Gould, ed., *Africa, Continent of Change.* Belmont, Wadsworth, 1961.

Peter Kolben, *The Present State of the Cape of Good Hope.* London, Innys, 1731.

Katiti Komambo, "Le Développement du Nationalisme Africain en Afrique du Sud-Ouest." *Présence Africaine, 49,* 1964, pp. 89–103.

Heinrich Krieger, *Das Rassenrecht in Südafrika.* Berlin, Junker und Dunnhaupt, 1944.

Eileen J. Krige, *The Social System of the Zulus.* Pietermaritzburg, Shuter and Shooter, 1950.

———— and Jacob D. Krige, *The Realm of a Rain Queen.* London, Oxford University Press, 1943.

Jacob D. Krige and Eileen J. Krige, "The Lovedu of the Transvaal." In D. Forde, ed., *African Worlds.* London, Oxford University Press, 1954.

Uys Krige, *The Dream and the Desert.* London, Collins, 1953.

Daniel Wilhelmus Krüger, *The Age of the Generals.* Johannesburg, Dagbreek, 1961.

————, ed., *South African Parties and Politics, 1910–1960: A Select Source Book.* London, Bowes and Bowes, 1960.

B. Kuper, *A Bibliography of Native Law in South Africa, 1941–1961.* Johannesburg, Witwatersrand University Press, 1962.

Hilda Kuper, *An African Aristocracy.* London, Oxford University Press, 1947.

————, *Bite of Hunger.* New York, Harcourt Brace and World, 1965.

————, "Changes in Caste of the South African Indians." *Race Relations Journal, 22,* 1955, pp. 18–26.

————, "An Ethnographic Description of Kavady, A Hindu Ceremony of South Africa." *African Studies, 18,* 1959, pp. 118–132.

————, *Indian People in Natal.* Natal, University of Natal Press, 1960.

————, *The Swazi, A South African Kingdom*. New York, Holt, Rinehart and Winston, 1963.

————, *The Uniform of Colour*. Johannesburg, Witwatersrand University Press, 1947.

———— and S. Kaplan, "Voluntary Associations in an Urban Township." *African Studies*, 3, 1944.

———— and Fatima Meer, *Indian Elites in Natal*. Durban, Institute for Social Research, 1956.

Leo Kuper, *An African Bourgeoisie*. New Haven, Yale University Press, 1965.

————, "The Background to Passive Resistance (South Africa, 1952)." *British Journal of Sociology*, 4, 1953, pp. 243–256.

————, *The College Brew*. Durban, privately published, 1960.

————, "The Control of Social Change. A South African Experiment." *Social Forces*, 33, 1954, pp. 19–29.

————, "The Heightening of Racial Tension." *Race*, 2, 1960, pp. 24–32.

————, *Passive Resistance in South Africa*. New Haven, Yale University Press, 1960.

————, "The Problem of Violence in South Africa." *Inquiry*, 7, 1964, pp. 295–303.

————, "Racialism and Integration in South African Society." *Race* 4, 1963.

————, "Sociology: Some Aspects of Urban Plural Societies," in Robert A. Lystad, ed., *The African World: A Survey of Social Research*. New York, Frederick A. Praeger, 1965.

————, "Some Aspects of Urban Plural Societies in Africa." Unpublished paper.

————, "Some Demographic Aspects of White Supremacy in South Africa." *British Journal of Sociology*, 1, 1950, pp. 144–153.

————, Hilstan Watts, and Ronald Davies, *Durban, A Study in Racial Ecology*. London, Cape, 1958.

G. S. T. Kushke, *Industrial Development in South Africa*. Johannesburg, Industrial Development Corporation, 1962.

Elizabeth S. Landis, "South African Apartheid Legislation." *Yale Law Journal*, 71, November 1961, January 1962.

————, "South West Africa in the International Court of Justice." *Africa Today*, 11, April 1964, pp. 10–12.

————, "UN Stepchildren." *Africa Today*, 5, 1958.

Peter Lanham and A. S. Mopeli-Paulus, *Blanket Boy*. New York, Crowell, 1953.

C. I. Latrobe, *A Journal of a Visit to South Africa*. London, Seeley, 1821.

G. C. Lawrie, "South Africa's World Position." *Journal of Modern African Studies*, 2, 1964, pp. 41–54.

A. D. Lazarus, "The Aspirations of the Indian People in South Africa." *Optima*, 12, 1962, pp. 53–58.

Colin Legum, *Pan-Africanism*. New York, Praeger, 1962.

——, "South Africa, The Doomed Republic." *Africa Today*, 10, November 1963, pp. 4–7.

—— and Margaret Legum, *South Africa, Crisis of the West*. New York, Praeger, 1964.

H. C. V. Leibbrandt, *Précis of the Archives of the Cape of Good Hope*. Cape Town, Richards, 1896.

G. H. L. Le May, *British Supremacy in South Africa*. Oxford, Clarendon Press, 1965.

Jean-Alain Lesourd, *L'Union Sud-Africaine*. Paris, Presses Universitaires de France, 1951.

Charlotte Leubuscher, *Der Südafrikanische Eingeborene als Industriearbeiter und als Stadtbewohner*. Jena, Fisher, 1931.

Ruth Levin, *Marriage in Langa Native Location*. Cape Town, School of African Studies, 1947.

Olga Levinson, *The Ageless Land, The Story of South West Africa*. Cape Town, Tafelberg, 1961.

Julius Lewin, *An Outline of Native Law*. Johannesburg, S. A. Institute, 1959.

——, *Politics and Law in South Africa*. New York, Monthly Review Press, 1963.

——, "Power, Law and Race Relations in South Africa." *Political Quarterly*, 30, 1959, pp. 389–399.

——, "The Rise of Congress in South Africa." *Political Quarterly*, 24, 1953, pp. 292–307.

——, "Sex, Colour and the Law." *Africa Today*, June 1963, pp. 9–12.

——, "Some Lobolo Cases in Native Law." *African Studies*, 3, 1944.

——, "South African Native Policy Never Changes." *Political Quarterly*, 28, 1957.

——, *Studies in South African Native Law*. Cape Town, The African Bookman, 1947.

——, "The Struggle for Law in South Africa." *Political Quarterly*, 27, 1956, pp. 176–182.

Henry Lichtenstein, *Travels in Southern Africa in the Years 1803, 1804, 1805, and 1806*. Cape Town, The Van Riebeeck Society, 1928.

David Livingstone, *Missionary Travels and Researches in South Africa*. New York, Harper, 1858.

B. K. Long, *In Smuts' Camp*. London, Oxford University Press, 1945.

Laura Longmore, *The Dispossessed: A Study of the Sex-Life of Bantu Women in Urban Areas in and Around Johannesburg*. London, Cape, 1959.

————, "The Teenage Vote in South Africa." *Political Quarterly, 30,* 1959, pp. 131–141.

H. Lothe, *Die Christliche Mission in Südwestafrika*. Berlin, Akademie-Verlag, 1963.

Eric H. Louw, *Whither the United Nations?* New York, Information Service, 1962.

Reginald I. Lovell, *The Struggle for South Africa, 1885–1899*. New York, Macmillan, 1934.

Allard Lowenstein, *Brutal Mandate*. New York, Random, 1962.

Albert Luthuli, *Let My People Go*. New York, McGraw-Hill, 1962.

I. D. MacCrone, *Group Conflicts and Race Prejudice*. Johannesburg, S. A. Institute, 1947.

————, "The Great Trek and its Centenary Celebration in the Light of Group Psychology." *Race Relations, 5,* 1938, pp. 81–84.

————, *Race Attitudes in South Africa*. London, New York, and Toronto, Oxford University Press, 1937.

Austin F. Macdonald, "Politics in the Union of South Africa." *Annals of the American Academy of Political and Social Science, 228,* 1953, pp. 140–152.

Allister Macmillan, *The Golden City*. London, Collingridge, n.d.

William M. Macmillan, *Bantu, Boer and Briton: The Making of the South African Native Problem*. London, Faber and Gwyer, 1928.

————, *The Cape Colour Question, A Historical Survey*. London, Faber and Gwyer, 1927.

————, *Complex South Africa: An Economic Foot-note to History*. London, Faber and Faber, 1930.

J. W. Macquarrie, "Race and Education in South Africa." *Phi Delta Kappan, 41,* 1960, pp. 169–173.

Nosipho Majeke, *The Role of the Missionaries in Conquest*. Johannesburg, 1952.

Paul Makatini, "The Pinko Problem." *The New African, 1,* May 1962, pp. 6–7, 10.

Daniel F. Malan, *Afrikaner-Volkseenheid en my Ervarings op die Pad Daarheen*. Cape Town, Nasionale Boekhandel, 1961.

————, *Apartheid—South Africa's Answer to a Major Problem.* Pretoria, State Information Office, n.d.

————, *Foreign Policy of the Union of South Africa.* Pretoria, State Information Office, 1948.

E. G. Malherbe, *The Autonomy of our University and Apartheid.* Privately published, 1957.

————, *Education in South Africa, 1652–1922.* Cape Town, Juta, 1925.

————, *Race Attitudes and Education.* Johannesburg, S. A. Institute, 1946.

B. Malinowski, "Anthropology." In *Encyclopaedia Britannica,* first supplementary volume. London, 1926, pp. 132–136.

————, *The Dynamics of Cultural Change, An Inquiry into Race Relations in Africa.* New Haven, Yale University Press, 1946.

Nelson Mandela, *L'Apartheid.* Paris, Editions de Minuit, 1965.

J. W. Mann, "Group Relations and the Marginal Personality." *Human Relations, 11,* 1958, pp. 77–92.

————, "Race-linked Values in South Africa." *Journal of Social Psychology, 58,* 1962, pp. 31–41.

————, "Rivals in Different Ranks." *Journal of Social Psychology, 61,* 1963, pp. 11–27.

O. Mannoni, *Prospero and Caliban.* New York, Praeger, 1956.

Nicholas Mansergh, *South Africa, 1906–1961, The Price of Magnanimity.* New York, Praeger, 1962.

J. Ben Marais, *The Colour Crisis and the West.* Pretoria, van Schaik, 1953.

————, *Die Kleur-Krisis in die Weste.* Johannesburg, Goeie Hoop Uitgewers, 1952.

Johannes Stephanus Marais, *The Fall of Kruger's Republic.* Oxford, Clarendon Press, 1961.

————, *The Cape Coloured People, 1652–1937.* London, New York, and Toronto, Longmans, 1939.

W. S. Mare, *African Trade Unions.* Cape Town, Longmans, 1949.

Leo Marquard, *The Native in South Africa.* Johannesburg, Witwatersrand University Press, 1944.

————, *The Peoples and Policies of South Africa.* London, New York, and Cape Town, Oxford University Press, 1962.

————, *South Africa's Colonial Policy.* Johannesburg, S. A. Institute, 1957.

————, *South Africa's International Boundaries.* Johannesburg, S. A. Institute, 1958.

————, *The Story of South Africa.* London, Faber and Faber, 1960.

Brian Allan Marwick, *The Swazi.* Cambridge, Cambridge University Press, 1940.

M. G. Marwick, "The Modern Family in Social Anthropological Perspective." *African Studies, 17,* 1958.

Philip Mason, *An Essay on Racial Tension.* London and New York, Royal Institute of International Affairs, 1954.

J. E. Mathewson, *The Establishment of an Urban Bantu Township.* Pretoria, van Schaik, 1957.

———, "Impact of Urbanization on Lobolo." *Journal of Racial Affairs, 10,* 1959, pp. 72–76.

Z. K. Matthews, "Another View." *Journal of International Affairs, 7,* 1953, pp. 145-150.

———, "Ethnic Universities." *Africa South, 4,* 1960, pp. 42–47.

E. L. Maurice, *The Colour Bar in Education.* Cape Town, Teachers' League of South Africa, 1957.

Marcel Mauss, *Sociologie et Anthropologie.* Paris, Presses Universitaires de France, 1950.

Henry J. May, *The South African Constitution.* Cape Town, Juta, 1955.

Philip Mayer, "Migrancy and the Study of Africans in Towns." *American Anthropologist, 64,* 1962, pp. 576–592.

———, *Townsmen or Tribesmen.* Cape Town, Oxford University Press, 1961.

Govan Mbeki, *South Africa: The Peasants' Revolt.* Baltimore, Penguin, 1964.

J. M'Carter, *The Dutch Reformed Church in South Africa.* Edinburgh, Inglis, 1869.

Grant S. McClellan, *South Africa.* New York, Wilson, 1962.

Fatima Meer, "African and Indian in Durban." *Africa South, 4,* 1960, pp. 30–41.

K. N. Menon, *Passive Resistance in South Africa.* New Delhi, 1962.

O. F. Mentzel, *A Description of the African Cape of Good Hope, 1787.* Cape Town, The Van Riebeeck Society, 1944.

Robert Merton, *Social Theory and Social Structure.* Glencoe, The Free Press, 1957.

P. J. Meyer, *Trek Verder: Die Afrikaner in Afrika.* Cape Town, H.A.U.M., 1959.

A. G. Mezerik, ed., *Apartheid in the Republic of South Africa.* New York, International Review Service, *10,* 1964.

Josephine F. Milburn and Taylor Cole, "Bibliographical Material on Political Parties and Pressure Groups in Australia, New Zealand, and South Africa." *American Political Science Review, 51,* 1957, pp. 199–220.

Sarah Gertrude Millin, *General Smuts*. Boston, Little, Brown, 1926.
————, *God's Stepchildren*. New York, Boni and Liveright, 1924.
————, *The Herr Witchdoctor*. London, Heinemann, 1941.
————, *King of the Bastards*. New York, Harper, 1949.
————, *The People of South Africa*. London, Constable, 1951.
————, *The South Africans*. London, Constable, 1926.
E. M. E. Mills and Monica Wilson, *Land Tenure*. Pietermaritzburg, Keiskammahoek Rural Survey, 4, 1952.
Clyde Mitchell, *Tribalism and the Plural Society*. London, Oxford University Press, 1960.
Julian Mockford, *The Golden Land*. London, Black, 1951.
Bloke Modisane, *Blame Me on History*. New York, Dutton, 1963.
Robert Moffat, *Missionary Labours and Scenes in Southern Africa*. New York, Carter, 1843.
Thomas Mofolo, *Chaka*. London, Oxford University Press, 1951.
T. Molnar, *L'Afrique du Sud*. Paris, Nouvelles Editions Latines, 1966.
D. B. Molteno, *Betrayal of "Natives" Representation*. Johannesburg, S. A. Institute, 1959.
————, *Towards a Democratic South Africa*. Johannesburg, S. A. Institute, 1959.
A. Moorees, *Die Nederduits Gereformeerde Kerk in Suid Afrika*. Cape Town, 1937.
James Morris, *South African Winter*. New York, Pantheon, 1958.
Ezekiel Mphahlele, *The African Image*. New York, Praeger, 1962.
————, "African Writing in English." Unpublished paper read at International Symposium on African Culture, Ibadan, 1960.
————, *Down Second Avenue*. London, Faber and Faber, 1959.
C. F. J. Muller, *Die Britse Owerheid en die Groot Trek*. Cape Town, 1947.
Edwin S. Munger, *Bechuanaland: Pan African Outpost or Bantu Homeland*. London, Oxford University Press, 1965.
————, *Problems of the Transkei*. New York, American University Field Staff, 1962.
————, "Race and National Identification: The Republic of South Africa." In K. H. Silvert, ed., *Expectant Peoples, Nationalism and Development*. New York, Random, 1963.
A. H. Murray, "The Trek and its Legacy." *Race Relations*, 5, 1938, pp. 76–79.
D. N. Murray and M. L. Edelstein, *Social Work in South Africa*. Privately published, 1959.
Reuben Musiker, *Guide to South African Reference Books*. Grahamstown, Rhodes University Library, 1963.
Gunnar Myrdal, *An American Dilemma*. New York, Harper, 1944.

N. T. Naicker, "The Indians in South Africa." *Journal of Human Relations*, 8, 1960, pp. 479–486.

Manfred Nathan, *The South African Commonwealth.* Johannesburg, Specialty Press, 1919.

———, *The Voortrekkers of South Africa.* London, Gordon and Gotch, 1937.

*The Native Policy of the United Party.* Bloemfontein, Union Congress of the Party, 1954.

*The Natives of South Africa.* London, Murray, 1901.

*Die Naturel in die Suid Afrikaanse Landbou.* Stellenbosch, SABRA, 1954.

*Die Naturelle-vraagstuk.* Stellenbosch, SABRA, 1950.

Marian Neal, "The United Nations and the Union of South Africa." *Journal of International Affairs*, 7, 1953, pp. 151–162.

Lawrence E. Neame, *General Hertzog.* London, 1930.

———, *The History of Apartheid.* London, Pall Mall, 1962.

———, *Today's News Today, The Story of the Argus Company.* Johannesburg, Argus, 1956.

———, *White Man's Africa.* Cape Town, General Publishing, 1953.

C. C. Nepgen, *Die Sociale Gewete van die Afrikaanssprekende.* Johannesburg, Christen-Studente Vereniging, 1938.

S. Daniel Neumark, *Economic Influences on the South African Frontier, 1652–1836.* Stanford, Stanford University Press, 1957.

"New Industrial Census Questionnaire." *The Manufacturer*, May 1956.

Arthur P. Newton, *Select Documents Relating to the Unification of South Africa.* London, Longmans, 1924.

——— and Ernest Benians, eds., *The Cambridge History of the British Empire*, 8. Cambridge, Cambridge University Press, 1963.

S. Bangeni Ngcobo, "African Elite in South Africa." *International Social Science Bulletin*, 8, 1956, pp. 431–440.

———, "The Response of Africans to Industrial Employment." *Race Relations Journal*, 21, 1954, pp. 10–17.

Jordan K. Ngubane, *An African Explains Apartheid.* New York, Praeger, 1963.

Charles R. Nixon, "The Conflict of Nationalisms in South Africa." *World Politics*, October 1958.

C. L. S. Nyembezi, *A Review of Zulu Literature.* Pietermaritzburg, University of Natal Press, 1961.

*Official Year Book of the Union, no. 2, 1918.* Pretoria, The Government Printing and Stationery Office, 1919.

*Official Year Book of the Union of South Africa, no. 27, 1952–53.* Pretoria, The Government Printer, 1953–1954.

*Official Year Book of the Union of South Africa, no. 28, 1954–55.* Pretoria, The Government Printer, 1955.

*Official Year Book of the Union of South Africa, no. 29, 1956–57.* Pretoria, The Government Printer, 1957.

James Oglethorpe, "Crisis in the Dutch Reformed Churches." *Africa South,* 5, 1961, pp. 44–48.

Lord Olivier, *The Anatomy of African Misery.* London, Hogarth, 1927.

N. J. J. Olivier, "Apartheid or Integration?" In P. Smith, ed., *Africa in Transition.* London, Reinhardt, 1958.

———, "Apartheid—A Slogan or a Solution?" *Journal of International Affairs,* 7, 1953, pp. 136–144.

J. D. Omer-Cooper, *The Zulu Aftermath: A Nineteenth Century Revolution in Bantu Africa.* Evanston, Ill., Northwestern University Press, 1966.

*Open Minds in Open Universities.* The Education League, 1956.

*Our First Half-Century, 1910–1960.* Johannesburg, Da Gama, 1960.

Elena Padilla, "Peasants, Plantations and Pluralism." *Annals of the New York Academy of Sciences,* 83, 1959–1960, pp. 837–842.

Mabel Palmer, *The History of the Indians in Natal.* Cape Town, Oxford University Press, 1957.

——— et al., *The Indian as a South African.* Johannesburg, S. A. Institute, 1956.

Talcott Parsons, *The Social System.* Glencoe, The Free Press, 1951.

———, *Structure and Process in Modern Societies.* Glencoe, The Free Press, 1960.

William Paterson, *A Narrative of Four Journeys into the Country of the Hottentots and Caffraria in the Years 1777, 1778, 1779.* London, Johnson, 1790.

Alan Paton, *The Charlestown Story.* Liberal Party of South Africa, 1960.

———, *Cry, the Beloved Country.* New York, Scribner, 1948.

———, *Hope for South Africa.* London, Pall Mall, 1958.

———, *The People Wept.* Privately published, 1958.

———, *South Africa in Transition.* New York, Scribner, 1956.

———, "South African Treason Trial." *Atlantic Monthly,* 205, 1960, pp. 78–81.

———, *Too Late the Phalarope.* New York, Scribner, 1953.

D. M. Paton, ed., *Church and Race in South Africa.* London, Student Christian Movement, 1958.

*The Pattern of Race Policy in South Africa.* Pretoria, State Information Office, 1956.

Sheila Patterson, *Colour and Culture in South Africa*. London, Routledge and Kegan Paul, 1953.

——, *The Economic Implications of Political Democracy*. Johannesburg, 1960.

——, *The Last Trek*. London, Routledge and Kegan Paul, 1957.

B. A. Pauw, *Religion in a Tswana Chiefdom*. London, Oxford University Press, 1960.

——, *The Second Generation, A Study of the Family among Urbanized Bantu in East London*. Cape Town, Oxford University Press, 1963.

S. Pauw, *Die Beroepsarbeid van die Afrikaner in die Stad*. Stellenbosch, 1946.

Roderick Peattie, *Struggle on the Veld*. New York, The Vanguard Press, 1947.

A. N. Pelzer, *Die Geskiedenis van die Suid-Afrikaanse Republiek*. Cape Town, 1950.

Robert Percival, *An Account of the Cape of Good Hope*. London, C. and R. Baldwin, 1804.

Margery F. Perham and Lionel Curtis, *The Protectorates of South Africa: The Question of Their Transfer to the Union*. London, Oxford University Press, 1935.

Thomas F. Pettigrew, "Personality and Sociocultural Factors in Intergroup Attitudes." *Journal of Conflict Resolution*, 2, 1958, pp. 29–42.

——, "Social Distance Attitudes of South African Students." *Social Forces*, 38, 1960, pp. 246–253.

S. Pienaar and Anthony Sampson, *South Africa, Two Views of Separate Development*. London, Oxford University Press, 1960.

Philippus V. Pistorius, *No Further Trek*. Johannesburg, Central News Agency, 1957.

John Philip, *Researches in South Africa*. London, Duncan, 1828.

Norman Phillips, *The Tragedy of Apartheid*. New York, McKay, 1960.

Ray E. Phillips, *The Bantu in the City*. Cape Province, Lovedale, 1938.

Sol T. Plaatje, *Mhudi*. Cape Province, Lovedale, 1930.

——, *Native Life in South Africa*. London, King, 1916.

F. T. P. Plimpton, *Statement on the Question of Apartheid*. New York, United States Delegation to the United Nations, 1961.

*The Political Rights of the Coloured People*. Johannesburg, S. A. Institute, 1954.

Hansi Pollak, *Social Development Since Union*. Johannesburg, S. A. Institute, 1959.

*The Poor White Problem in South Africa.* Stellenbosch, Carnegie Commission, 1932.

Ambrose Pratt, *The Real South Africa.* London, Holden and Harding-ham, 1913.

*A Précis of the Reports of the Commissions Appointed to Enquire into the Events Occurring March 21, 1960 at Sharpeville and Langa.* Johannesburg, S. A. Institute, Fact Paper no. 10, 1961.

*The Progress of the Bantu Peoples Towards Nationhood.* Johannes-burg, Hayne and Gibson, 1960.

G. B. Pyrah, *Imperial Policy and South Africa, 1902–10.* Oxford, Clarendon Press, 1955.

*The Racial Issue in South Africa.* Bloemfontein, Dutch Reformed Mis-sion Press, 1953.

*Racialism in South Africa.* London, South African Church Institute, 1953.

A. R. Radcliffe-Brown and D. Forde, eds., *African Systems of Kinship and Marriage.* London, Oxford University Press, 1950.

B. Rambiritch and Pierre L. van den Berghe, "Caste in a Natal Hindu Community." *African Studies, 20,* 1961, pp. 217–225.

Grantley D. Read, *No Time for Fear.* New York, Harper, 1955.

D. H. Reader, *The Black Man's Portion.* Cape Town, Oxford Univer-sity Press, 1961.

Wilson Record and Jane Cassels Record, eds., *Little Rock, U.S.A.* San Francisco, Chandler, 1960.

Ambrose Reeves, *Justice in South Africa.* London, The Africa Bureau, 1955.

———, *Shooting at Sharpeville.* London, Gollancz, 1960.

———, *South Africa — Yesterday and Tomorrow.* London, Gollancz, 1962.

D. Reitz, *Commando.* London, Faber and Gwyer, 1929.

———, *No Outspan.* London, Faber and Faber, 1943.

———, *Trekking On.* London, Faber and Faber, 1933.

*Report of the Cape Coloured Commission.* Pretoria, The Government Printer, 1937.

*Report of the Commission of Enquiry on Separate Training Facilities for Non-Europeans at Universities.* Pretoria, The Government Printer, 1954.

*Report of the Department of Labour, 1956.* Pretoria, The Government Printer, 1956.

*Report of the Economic and Wage Commission.* Pretoria, The Govern-ment Printer, 1926.

*Report of the Native Economic Commission, 1930–1932.* Pretoria, The Government Printer, 1932.

*Report of the Special Committee on the Policies of Apartheid.* New York, United Nations General Assembly, 1963.

*Report of the United Nations Commission on the Racial Situation in the Union of South Africa.* New York, United Nations General Assembly, Eighth Session, Supplement no. 16, 1953.

Lawrence Reyburn, *African Traders.* Johannesburg, S. A. Institute, 1960.

N. J. Rhoodie and H. J. Venter, *Apartheid: A Socio-Historical Exposition of the Origin and Development of the Apartheid Idea.* Amsterdam, De Bussy, 1960.

Margaret Roberts, "High Commission Territories: In Pawn to Apartheid?" *Africa Today, 10,* November 1963, pp. 12–15.

———, *Labour in the Farm Economy.* Johannesburg, S. A. Institute, 1958.

Michael Roberts and A. E. G. Trollip, *The South African Opposition, 1939–1945.* London, Longmans, 1947.

Hector M. Robertson, *South Africa, Economic and Political Aspects.* London, Cambridge University Press, 1957.

Eric Robbins, *This Man Malan.* Cape Town, South African Scientific Publishing, 1953.

Howard Rogers, *Native Administration in the Union of South Africa.* Pretoria, The Government Printer, 1949.

Mirabel Rogers, *The Black Sash.* Johannesburg, Rotonews, 1956.

Cowper Rose, *Four Years in Southern Africa.* London, Colburn and Bentley, 1829.

K. L. Roskam, *Apartheid and Discrimination.* Leyden, Sythoff, 1960.

Guy Routh, *Industrial Relations and Race Relations.* Johannesburg, S. A. Institute, n.d.

Edward Roux, *Time Longer than Rope.* London, Gollancz, 1948.

L. Rubin, *This Is Apartheid.* London, Gollancz, 1959.

Margo Russell and I. K. Allen, *Unemployment Among Indians in Durban 1962.* Durban, Institute for Social Research, 1962.

Bernard Sachs, *The Road to Sharpeville.* Johannesburg, Dial Press, 1961.

E. S. Sachs, *The Choice Before South Africa.* London, Turnstile Press, 1952.

———, *Rebel Daughters.* London, Macgibbon and Kee, 1957.

J. L. Sadie, *Die Afrikaner in die Landsekonomie.* Johannesburg, Swan, n.d.

Anthony Sampson, *Drum, A Venture into the New Africa*. London, Collins, 1956.

———, *The Treason Cage*. London, Heinemann, 1958.

L. H. Samuels, H. Houghton, and F. C. Fourie, *South Africa's Changing Economy*. Johannesburg, S. A. Institute, 1955.

Sandor, *The Coming Struggle for South Africa*. London, Fabian Society, 1963.

Gustav Saren and Louis Hotz, eds., *The Jews in South Africa: A History*. London, Oxford University Press, 1955.

Isaac Schapera, *Government and Politics in Tribal Societies*. London, Watts, 1956.

———, *The Khoisan Peoples of South Africa*. London, Routledge, 1930.

———, *Married Life in an African Tribe*. London, Faber and Faber, 1940.

———, *Migrant Labour and Tribal Life*. London, Oxford University Press, 1947.

———, *Western Civilization and the Natives of South Africa*. London, Routledge, 1934.

———, ed., *The Bantu-Speaking Tribes of South Africa*. London, Routledge, 1937.

———, ed., *The Early Cape Hottentots*. Cape Town, The Van Riebeeck Society, 1933.

K. Schlosser, *Eingeborenenkirchen in Süd-und Südwestafrika, ihre Geschichte und Sozialstruktur*. Kiel, Mülau, 1959.

Franck L. Schoell, *Les Tensions Raciales dans l'Union Sud-Africaine et leurs Incidences Internationales*. Paris, Minard, 1956.

G. D. Scholtz, *Het die Afrikanervolk 'n Toekoms?* Johannesburg, Voortrekkerpers, 1954.

———, *Die Oorsake van die Tweede Vryheidsoorlog*. Johannesburg, 1948.

J. P. Scholtz, *Die Afrikaner en sy Tal*. Cape Town, 1939.

Olive D. Schreiner, *Political Power in South Africa*. Johannesburg, S. A. Institute, 1963.

———, *South Africa — United or Divided?* Johannesburg, S. A. Institute, 1964.

———, *Thoughts on South Africa*. London, T. Fisher Unwin, 1923.

Wolfgang Schüler, *"Apartheid" Regiert Südafrika*. Berlin, Dietz, 1961.

C. G. W. Schumann, *Die Ekonomiese Positie van die Afrikaner*. Nasionale Pers, 1940.

———, *Die Reddingsdaadbond as Volksophou*. Johannesburg, F. A. K., 1941.

Michael Scott, *Civilisation Indivisible*. London, Africa Bureau, 1953.

——, *The Orphan's Heritage*. London, Africa Bureau, 1958.

——, *A Time to Speak*. London, Faber and Faber, 1958.

*Second Report of the United Nations Commission on the Racial Situation in the Union of South Africa*. New York, United Nations General Assembly, Ninth Session, Supplement no. 16, 1954.

R. Segal, *Into Exile*. London, Cape, 1963.

——, *The Tokolosh*. London, Sheed and Ward, 1960.

——, ed., *Sanctions against South Africa*. Baltimore, Penguin, 1964.

Charles G. Seligman, *Races of Africa*. London, Oxford University Press, 1957.

P. K. Isaka Seme, *The Regeneration of Africa*. New York, Columbia University Press, 1906.

Jean Sépulchre, *Gens et Choses de l'Afrique du Sud*. Elisabethville, Essor du Congo, 1945.

P. Serton, *Zuid-Afrika*. Meppel, Boom en Zoom, 1963.

S. M. Seymour, *Natal Law in South Africa*. Cape Town, Juta, 1953.

Barnabas Shaw, *Memorials of South Africa*. New York, G. Lane and P. P. Sandford, 1841.

Robert H. W. Shepherd, *Lovedale, South Africa*. Lovedale, 1940.

Rae Sherwood, "The Bantu Clerk: A Study of Role Expectations." *Journal of Social Psychology*, 47, 1958, pp. 285–316.

David Shrand, *The Financial and Statistical Digest of South Africa*. Cape Town and Johannesburg, Juta, 1955.

A. Siegfried, *Afrique du Sud*, Paris, Colin, 1949.

P. A. Silburn, *South Africa, White and Black — or Brown?* London, Allen and Unwin, 1927.

Ndabaningi Sithole, *African Nationalism*. Cape Town, Oxford University Press, 1959.

*Sixth Census of the Population of the Union of South Africa, 1936*. Vol. II, *Ages*. Pretoria, The Government Printer, 1938.

*Small Towns of Natal*. University of Natal Press, 1953.

H. Lindsay Smith, *Behind the Press in South Africa*. Cape Town, Stewart, n.d.

M. G. Smith, "Social and Cultural Pluralism." *Annals of the New York Academy of Sciences*, 83, 1959–1960, pp. 763–777.

Prudence Smith, ed., *Africa in Transition*. London, Reinhardt, 1958.

R. H. Smith, *Labour Resources of Natal*. London, Oxford University Press, 1950.

Jan C. Smuts, *The Basis of Trusteeship in African Native Policy*. Cape Town, S. A. Institute, 1942.

————, *Jan Christian Smuts*. London, Cassell, 1952.

————, *Plans for a Better World*. London, Hodder and Stoughton, 1942.

*Social Science Conference*. Durban, University of Natal, 1956.

John H. Soga, *The Ama-Xosa: Life and Customs*. London, Kegan Paul, 1932.

————, *The South-Eastern Bantu*. Johannesburg, Witwatersrand University Press, 1930.

H. Sonnabend and Cyril Sofer, *South Africa's Stepchildren*. Johannesburg, South African Affairs, n.d.

J. Soubeyrol, *L'Action Internationale Contre l'Apartheid*. Paris, Pedone, 1965.

*South Africa and the Rule of Law*. Geneva, International Commission of Jurists, 1960.

*South Africa in the African Continent*. Stellenbosch, SABRA, 1961.

*South Africa in the Sixties: A Socio-Economic Survey*. The South Africa Foundation, 1962.

*The South African Natives, Their Progress and Present Condition*. London, Murray, 1909.

"South Africa's Crime." *Journal of Racial Affairs*, 14, October 1963.

*South Africa's Heritage*. Cape Town, 1960.

Lewis Sowden, *The Union of South Africa*. Garden City, Doubleday, 1943.

Andrew Sparrman, *A Voyage to the Cape of Good Hope*. Dublin, White, Cash and Byrne, 1785.

Betty Spence, "How Our Urban Natives Live." *South African Architectural Record*, 35, 1950.

J. E. Spence, "The Political Implications of the South African Bantustan Policy." *Race*, 3, May 1962, pp. 20–30.

————, *Republic Under Pressure*. London, Oxford University Press, 1965.

————, "Tradition and Change in South African Foreign Policy." *Journal of Commonwealth Political Studies*, May 1962.

B. Spoelstra, *Ons Volkslewe*. Pretoria, 1924.

F. P. Spooner, *South African Predicament*. London, Cape, 1960.

*Spotlight on South Africa*. N.d.

Hilda Spottiswoode, ed., *South Africa, the Road Ahead*. London, Bailey and Swinfen, 1960.

Hannah Stanton, *Go Well, Stay Well: South Africa, August 1956 to May 1960*. London, Hodder and Stoughton, 1961.

*State of the Cape of Good Hope in 1822*. London, Murray, 1823.

*State of South Africa: Economic, Financial and Statistical Yearbook for the Republic of South Africa*. Johannesburg, 1962.

*State of the Union Year-Book for South Africa, 1959–60*. Johannesburg, Da Gama, 1960.

*Statement on the Native Question.* Bloemfontein, Dutch Reformed Churches Congress, 1950.

"Statistical Supplement." *International Labour Review,* 75, 1957.

*Statistical Year-Book of the Union of South Africa, no. 1, 1913.* Pretoria, The Government Printing and Stationery Office, 1913.

Sylvester Stein, *2nd-Class Taxi.* London, Faber and Faber, 1958.

E. J. C. Stevens, *White and Black, An Inquiry into South Africa's Greatest Problem.* London, Simpkin Marshall, n.d.

Alexander Steward, *The Sacred Trust.* Johannesburg, Da Gama, 1963.

——, *You Are Wrong, Father Huddleston.* London, Bodley Head, 1956.

Robert St. John, *Through Malan's Africa.* Garden City, Doubleday, 1954.

Eric Stockenstrom, *Vrystelling van die Slawe.* Stellenbosch, Pro Ecclesia Drukkery, 1934.

*Studies of Indian Employment in Natal.* Cape Town, Oxford University Press, 1961.

Newell M. Stultz, " 'Creative Self-Withdrawal' in the Transkei." *Africa Report,* 9, April 1964, pp. 18–23.

—— and Jeffrey Butler, "The South African General Election of 1961." *Political Science Quarterly,* 78, March 1963, pp. 86–110.

*Summary of the Report of the Commission on the Socio-Economic Development of the Bantu Areas Within the Union of South Africa.* Pretoria, The Government Printer, 1955.

Bengt G. M. Sundkler, *Bantu Prophets in South Africa.* London, Lutterworth, 1948.

——, *The Christian Ministry in Africa.* Uppsala, Studia Missionalia Upsaliensa, 1960.

——, *The Concept of Christianity in the African Independent Churches.* Durban, Institute for Social Research, 1958.

Helen Suzman, *A Digest of the Native Laws (Fagan) Commission.* Johannesburg, S. A. Institute, 1948.

—— and Ellison Kahn, *New Lines in Native Policy.* Johannesburg, S. A. Institute, 1947.

I. B. Tabata, *The All African Convention: The Awakening of a People.* Johannesburg, People's Press, 1950.

——, *The Boycott as a Weapon of Struggle.* Cape Town, All African Convention Committee, 1952.

——, *Education for Barbarism, Bantu Education in South Africa.* Durban, Prometheus, n.d.

W. J. Talbot, *Swartland and Sandveld*. Cape Town, Oxford University Press, 1947.

Raphael Tardon, *Noirs et Blancs*. Paris, Denvel, 1961.

C. M. Tatz, *Shadow and Substance in Africa, A Study in Land and Franchise Policies Affecting Africans 1910–1960*. Pietermaritzburg, University of Natal Press, 1962.

George McCall Theal, *History of the Boers in South Africa*. London, Sonnenschein, Lowrey, 1887.

———, *The Portuguese in South Africa*. London, T. Fisher Unwin, 1896.

———, *South Africa*. London, T. Fisher Unwin, 1917.

Erika Theron, *Fabriekswerksters in Kaapstad*. Cape Town, Nasionale Pers, 1944.

*Third Report of the United Nations Commission on the Racial Situation in the Union of South Africa*. New York, United Nations General Assembly, Tenth Session, Supplement no. 14, 1955.

Elizabeth M. Thomas, *The Harmless People*. London, Secker, 1959.

George Thompson, *Travels and Adventures in Southern Africa*. London, Colburn, 1827.

Leonard M. Thompson, *The Cape Coloured Franchise*. Johannesburg, S. A. Institute, 1949.

———, *Politics in the Republic of South Africa*. Boston, Little, Brown, 1966.

———, *The Unification of South Africa, 1902–1910*. Oxford, Clarendon Press, 1960.

Charles P. Thunberg, *Travels in Europe, Africa and Asia Made Between the Years 1770 and 1779*. London, Richardson, n.d.

H. Tingsten, *The Problem of South Africa*. London, Gollancz, 1955.

J. M. Tinley, *The Native Labor Problem of South Africa*. Chapel Hill, University of North Carolina Press, 1942.

Edward A. Tiryakian, "Apartheid and Education in the Union of South Africa." *Harvard Educational Review*, 25, 1955, pp. 242–259.

———, "Apartheid and Politics in South Africa." *Journal of Politics*, 22, 1960, pp. 682-697.

———, "Apartheid and Religion." *Theology Today*, 14, 1957.

Jan Toekoms, *South Africa's Eleventh Hour*. Central News Agency, 1958.

F. R. Tomlinson *et al.*, *Report Submitted by the Commission on the Socio-Economic Development of the Bantu Areas*. Pretoria, 1956.

A. M. F. Towert, *Constitutional Development in South Africa, 1949–1959*. Cape Town, University of Cape Town, 1959.

*The Transkei*. Pretoria, Department of Information, 1962.

Stanley Trapido, "Natal's Non-Racial Franchise, 1856." *African Studies*, 22, 1963, pp. 22–32.

————, "The Origins of the Cape Franchise Qualifications of 1853." *Journal of African History*, 5, 1964, pp. 37–54.

————, "Political Institutions and Afrikaner Social Structures in the Republic of South Africa." *American Political Science Review*, 57, 1963, pp. 75–87.

*Treatment of Indians in South Africa*. Washington, Government of India Information Services, n.d.

*Treatment of Indians in the Union of South Africa*. New York, Union of South Africa Government Information Office, 1947.

Freda Troup, *In Face of Fear, Michael Scott's Challenge to South Africa*. London, Faber and Faber, 1950.

*The Truth that Hurts*. New York, South African Information Office, 1961.

*Union of South Africa, An Economic Survey*. London, Barclays Bank, 1956.

S. Uys, "Dr. H. F. Verwoerd, Prime Minister of South Africa." *Africa South*, 3, n.d.

P. van Biljon, *Grensbakens tussen Blänk en Swart in Suid-Afrika*. Cape Town, Juta, 1949.

Pierre L. van den Berghe, "Albinocracy in South Africa," *Journal of Asian and African Studies*, 1:1, 1966, pp. 41–47.

————, "Apartheid, Fascism and the Golden Age." *Cahiers d'Etudes Africaines*, 8, 1962, pp. 598–608.

————, "Apartheid: une Interprétation Sociologique de la Ségrégation Raciale." *Cahiers Internationaux de Sociologie*, 28, 1960, pp. 47–56.

————, *Caneville: The Social Structure of a South African Town*. Middletown, Wesleyan University Press, 1964.

————, "Dialectic and Functionalism: Toward a Theoretical Synthesis." *American Sociological Review*, 28, 1963, pp. 695–705.

————, "Distance Mechanisms of Stratification." *Sociology and Social Research*, 44, 1960, pp. 155–164.

————, "The Dynamics of Race Relations: An Ideal Type Case-Study of South Africa." Ph.D. dissertation, Harvard, 1959.

————, "The Dynamics of Racial Prejudice: An Ideal-Type Dichotomy." *Social Forces*, 37, 1958, pp. 138–141.

————, "Indians in Natal and Fiji." *Civilisations*, 12, 1962, pp. 75–87.

————, "Institutional Licence and Normative Stability." *Cahiers d'Etudes Africaines*, 11, 1963, pp. 413–423.

————, "Miscegenation in South Africa." *Cahiers d'Etudes Africaines*, 4, 1960, pp. 68–84.

————, *Race and Racism*. New York, John Wiley, 1967.

————, "Race Attitudes in Durban, South Africa." *Journal of Social Psychology*, 57, 1962, pp. 55–72.

————, "Racialism and Assimilation in Africa and the Americas." *Southwestern Journal of Anthropology*, 19, 1963, pp. 424–432.

————, "Racial Segregation in South Africa: Degrees and Kinds," *Cahiers d'Etudes Africaines*, 6:23, 1966, pp. 408–418.

————, "Some Trends in Unpublished Social Science Research in South Africa." *International Social Science Journal*, 14, 1962, pp. 723–732.

————, "Toward a Sociology of Africa." *Social Forces*, 43, 1964, pp. 11–18.

———— and Edna Miller, "Some Factors Affecting Social Relations in a Natal North Coast Community." *Race Relations Journal*, 28, 1961, pp. 24–31.

C. M. van den Heever and P. de P. Pienaar, eds., *Kultuurgeskiedenis van die Afrikaner*. Cape Town, Nasionale Pers, 1947.

Sheila T. van der Horst, *The Economic Implications of Political Democracy*. Supplement to *Optima*, June 1960.

————, *Native Labour in South Africa*. London, Oxford University Press, 1942.

————, "Native Urban Employment." *South African Journal of Economics*, 16, 1948, pp. 251–259.

————, "The Union of South Africa: Economic Problems in a Multiracial Situation." *Annals of the American Academy of Political and Social Science*, 298, March 1955, pp. 71–83.

H. J. J. van der Merwe, *Segregeer of Sterf*. Johannesburg, Afrikaanse Pers, 1961.

P. J. van der Merwe, *Die Noordwaartse Beweging van die Boere voor die Groot Trek*. The Hague, Van Stockum, 1937.

————, *Trek*. Cape Town, Nasionale Pers, 1945.

————, *Die Trekboer in die Geskiedenis van die Kaapkolonie*. Cape Town, 1938.

W. van der Merwe, "Stratification in a Cape Colored Community." *Sociology and Social Research*, 46, 1962, pp. 302–311.

Willem Jacobus van der Merwe, *The Development of Missionary Attitudes in the Dutch Reformed Church in South Africa*. Cape Town, Nasionale Pers, 1936.

Jean van der Poel, *The Jameson Raid*. London, Oxford University Press, 1951.

A. J. H. van der Walt *et al.*, *Die Geskiedenis van Suid-Afrika*. Cape Town, Nasionale Boekhandel, 1955.

H. J. van Eck, *Some Aspects of the South African Industrial Revolution*. Johannesburg, S. A. Institute, 1951.

F. A. van Jaarsveld, *Die Afrikaner en sy Geskiedenis*. Cape Town, Nasionale Boekhandel, 1959.

———, *The Awakening of Afrikaner Nationalism, 1868–1881*. Cape Town, Herman and Rousseau, 1961.

———, *Die Eenheidstrewe van die Republikeinse Afrikaners*. Johannesburg, 1951.

Hans van Rensburg, *Their Paths Crossed Mine*. Central News Agency, 1956.

Patrick van Rensburg, *Guilty Land, The History of Apartheid*. New York, Praeger, 1962.

Jan van Riebeeck, *Journal*. Cape Town, The Van Riebeeck Society, 1952–1958.

T. S. van Rooyen, *Die Verhoudinge tussen die Boere, Engelse en Naturelle in die Geskiedenis van die Oos-Transvaal tot 1882*. Pretoria, The Government Printer, 1951.

J. van Tromp, *Xhosa Law of Persons*. Cape Town, 1948.

William Henry Vatcher Jr., *White Laager, The Rise of Afrikaner Nationalism*. New York, Praeger, 1965.

Heinrich Vedder, *South West Africa in Early Times*. New York, Barnes and Noble, 1966.

Petrus Johannes Venter, *Landdros en Heemrade 1682–1827*. Pretoria, The Government Printer, 1940.

H. F. Verwoerd, *Bantu Education: Policy for the Immediate Future*. Pretoria, Department of Native Affairs, 1954.

———, *Separate Development*. Pretoria, Information Service, 1958.

Absolom Vilakazi, "Race Relations in South Africa." In Andrew W. Lind, ed., *Race Relations in World Perspective*. Honolulu, University of Hawaii Press, 1955.

———, *Zulu Transformations: A Study of the Dynamics of Social Change*. Pietermaritzburg, University of Natal Press, 1962.

Vindex, *Cecil Rhodes: Political Life and Speeches, 1881–1899*. London, Chapman and Hall, 1900.

W. A. Visser't Hooft, *Christianity, Race and South African People: Report on an Ecumenical Visit*. New York, World Council of Churches, 1952.

*Volkskongres oor die Toekoms van die Bantoe*. Bloemfontein, 1956.

Eric A. Walker, *The Frontier Tradition in South Africa*. London, Oxford University Press, 1930.

———, *The Great Trek*. London, Black, 1938.

———, *A History of Southern Africa*. London, New York, and Toronto, Longmans, 1957.

Oliver Walker, *Kaffirs Are Lively*. London, Gollancz, 1948.

P. C. Gordon Walker, "The Industrial Revolution in Southern Africa." *African World*, October 1958.

James Walton, *African Village*. Pretoria, van Schaik, 1956.

R. G. T. Watson, *Tongaati, an African Experiment*. London, Hutchinson, 1960.

Maurice Webb, *Digest of the 1948 Broome Commission Report*. Johannesburg, S. A. Institute, 1948.

―――― and Kenneth Kirkwood, *The Durban Riots and After*. Johannesburg, S. A. Institute, 1949.

―――― and V. Sirkari Naidoo, *The Indian — Citizen or Subject?* Johannesburg, S. A. Institute, 1947.

Max Weber, *The Protestant Ethic and the Spirit of Capitalism*. London, Allen and Unwin, 1930.

John H. Wellington, *Southern Africa, A Geographical Study*. Cambridge, Cambridge University Press, 1955.

A. W. Wells, *Southern Africa Today and Yesterday*. London, Dent, 1956.

*We South Africans*. Cape Town, Communist Party, 1946.

G. M. B. Whitfield, *South African Native Law*. Cape Town, Juta, 1948.

"Who Are the Saboteurs?" *Africa Today*, 10, 4 (April 1963), p. 3.

*Who's Who of Southern Africa*. Johannesburg, Wootton and Gibson, 1961.

Quentin Whyte, *Go Forward in Faith*. Johannesburg, S. A. Institute, 1952.

R. W. Wilcocks, "The Poor White Problem in South Africa." In *Report of the Carnegie Commission*. Stellenbosch, 1932.

A. Wilkov, *Some English Writings by Non-Europeans in South Africa, 1944–1960: A Bibliography*. Johannesburg, Witwatersrand University Press, 1962.

A. F. B. Williams, *Botha, Smuts and South Africa*. New York, Macmillan, 1948.

Basil Williams, *Cecil John Rhodes*. London, Constable, 1926.

Eric Frédéric Wilson, "Les Partis et les Groupements Socio-politiques dans l'Union Sud-Africaine." Ll.D. thesis, University of Bordeaux, 1953.

Godfrey Wilson and Monica Wilson, *The Analysis of Social Change*. Cambridge, Cambridge University Press, 1954.

Monica Wilson, "Coherence of Groups in Towns." Paper read at the 1963 annual meeting of the African Studies Association, San Francisco.

————, "The Early History of the Transkei and Ciskei." *African Studies, 18*, 1959, pp. 167–179.

————, "The Principle of Maintaining the Reserves for the African." *Race Relations Journal, 29*, 1962, pp. 3–9.

————, "Recent Research in Race Relations." *International Social Science Journal, 13*, 1961, pp. 225–244.

———— *et al., Social Structure.* Keiskammahoek Rural Survey, 3, 1952.

———— and Archie Mafeje, *Langa, A Study of Social Groups in an African Township.* Cape Town, Oxford University Press, 1963.

Ethel Wix, *The Cost of Living, An Enquiry into the Cost of Essential Requirements for African Families Living in Johannesburg, Pretoria and the Reef Towns, August-December 1950.* Johannesburg, S. A. Institute, 1951.

Alwin W. Wolfe, "The African Mineral Industry: Evolution of a Supranational Level of Integration." *Social Problems, 11*, 1963, pp. 153–164.

O. D. Wollheim, "The Coloured People of South Africa." *Race, 5*, October 1963, pp. 25–41.

C. A. Woods, *The Indian Community of Natal.* Cape Town, London, and New York, Oxford University Press, 1954.

William Wright, *Slavery at the Cape of Good Hope.* London, Longmans, 1831.

A. B. Xuma, *Reconstituting the Union of South Africa.* Johannesburg, 1932.

B. A. Young, *Bechuanaland.* London, Her Majesty's Stationery Office, 1966.

C. Ziervogel, *Brown South Africa.* Cape Town, Maskew Miller, n.d.

# Index

(Figures in italics refer to major discussion of the indicated topic.)

## PUBLISHER'S NOTE

Pierre L. van den Berghe was born in Lubumbashi, the Congo, and has lived, studied and done field work in Europe, South Africa, the Congo, the United States, Mexico, and Guatemala.

He received his B.A. in Political Science from Stanford, and his Ph.D. in Sociology from Harvard. He has taught at the University of Natal, Durban, South Africa; at the Sorbonne, Paris; at Wesleyan University, Connecticut; and at the State University of New York at Buffalo. At present he is Professor of Sociology at the University of Washington, Seattle.

His other published books include *Caneville, The Social Structure of a South African Town; Africa, Social Problems of Change and Conflict;* and *Race and Racism, A Comparative Perspective.*